RIGHT BACK TO THE BEGINNING

RIGHT BACK TO THE BEGINNING

THE AUTOBIOGRAPHY

Jimmy Armfield

with Andrew Collomosse

headline

First published in 2004
by HEADLINE BOOK PUBLISHING

10 9 8 7 6 5 4 3 2 1

Cataloguing in Publication Data is available
from the British Library

ISBN 0 7553 1276 7

Typeset in Ehrhardt by
Letterpart Limited, Reigate, Surrey

Career statistics supplied
by Jack Rollin

Printed and bound in Great Britain by
Mackays of Chatham plc, Chatham, Kent

HEADLINE BOOK PUBLISHING
A division of Hodder Headline
338 Euston Road
LONDON NW1 3BH

www.headline.co.uk
www.hodderheadline.com

CONTENTS

Prologue: A football man   1
1   The house in Tyldesley Road   7
2   An incredible journey   25
3   The Army game   39
4   Local boy makes good   59
5   The incomparable Matthews   75
6   'Stand back, here come Blackpool!'   91
7   England my England   105
8   The Ramsey era dawns   129
9   England's finest hour   141
10   Farewell to the tangerine shirt   159
11   Welcome to the big-time   181
12   All change at Elland Road   199
13   The Black Lubianka   223
14   From the commentary box   239
15   Talking with legends   257
16   'There's a Mr Kelly on the line . . .'   273
17   Return of the headhunter   287
18   The way we are   303
19   Always something there to remind me   321
Career statistics   332
Index   335

ACKNOWLEDGEMENTS

Many people have given me their time and assistance and I thank them all. I would like to mention especially Roger Harrison at Blackpool FC; the journalists on the sports desk of the *Blackpool Evening Gazette*; Barry Foster, former football correspondent of the *Yorkshire Post*; Gosnays Sports Agency of Leeds; John Helm; and David Barber, the Football Association librarian. I would also like to say a special thank you to Andrew Collomosse, a former colleague at the *Daily Express*, who has given me such tremendous assistance in the production of this book.

A FOOTBALL MAN

I was born on a Saturday afternoon so it's little wonder that football has been a large part of my life. It still is. My body clock operates around football. I never take a holiday during the football season and I don't switch off until the final ball has been kicked in May. Then, unless there's a World Cup or a European Championship, I can lay the season to rest and allow my thoughts to wander in the direction of who might be selected for the England cricket team. But as soon as August comes round and the papers start carrying features about the build-up to the new season, the clock starts to tick again. By the time the first match kicks off at 3 o'clock on that first Saturday, I'm ready to go.

Football grabbed hold of me when I was a young lad running through the streets of Blackpool during the war years and just afterwards. The Blackpool team boasted some of the greatest players of the day – Stanley Matthews, Stan Mortensen and Harry Johnston. Like me, Johnston was born in Manchester and, ironically, the first time my mother and father ever came to Blackpool for a day trip, Harry's father, Harry senior, drove them over from Manchester. In 1953, Johnston lifted the FA Cup at Wembley after what has gone into folklore as the Matthews final. It was Coronation year, Everest had been conquered and Stanley Matthews finally got his hands on a winner's medal. In the same game, Mortensen became the only man to score a hat-trick in a

1

Wembley FA Cup final. Matthews was the talisman, 'Morty' the local hero, and the town went delirious.

When the team came home, they paraded the Cup along the promenade and into Talbot Square. The crowds were massive and I was there to greet the conquering heroes. I was 17 years old and still at school, although I had already attracted Blackpool's attention and had played for the club as a junior and in the reserves. I vowed there and then that I was going to be a professional footballer. It was a conscious decision, even though it was unlike me to do anything so spontaneous. I have always preferred to weigh up the pros and cons before making up my mind and, to be honest, it was a long shot. The only thing I had going for me in football terms was my pace. I could always run. I had never played in junior football as a youngster. We did have a side at Sunday school that played in the local youth league but often we were struggling to get a team together and eventually it just fizzled out. Even so, that night in Talbot Square, I was certain of my destiny.

Since then, I have been involved across the entire football spectrum – as a player for Blackpool and England and a manager at Bolton Wanderers and Leeds United; as a newspaper reporter with the *Daily Express* and a broadcaster with the BBC. I've been on the staff of the Football Association and worked behind the scenes in the appointment of two England managers, and I've also been the head coach of the Professional Footballers Association. I doubt if anyone else has undertaken such a journey. In many respects, I have been fortunate. I have never been anywhere near the big money but I have genuinely enjoyed a life in football and everything it has given me. I suppose that's why I'm still so involved. My passion for football burns as brightly as ever and I can talk about the game day and night, sometimes, I fear, to the point of boring people to death.

Now, 50 years on, I watch matches whenever and wherever I can. I'm sometimes asked if I ever grow tired of football and my answer is always the same – never! Most matches provide something different and something new to think about. When I have been with the BBC at World Cups, my broadcasting colleagues have struggled to come to terms with the way I go rushing off to all the training grounds to watch the world's best coaches in action and see how the different countries prepare. Any match I cannot see live, I watch on television. I haven't missed a World Cup game in 25 years. I have seen them all, either live or on the television or a video. It sounds incredible, doesn't it? I was unable to go to the 2002 World Cup in Korea and Japan so I tuned in to every live game I could and recorded the rest. I watched them all.

On a Sunday, I pick up the paper and look at every result, every goalscorer and every attendance – and not just in the Premiership and the Football League. I study the Conference, too, and even some of the lower leagues. I keep an eye on such clubs as Barrow, Workington and Gateshead, who have all dropped out of the League, and see how they are faring. I would hate to see them disappear altogether. Then there's Accrington Stanley. I'd love to see them back in the League one day – with a name like that, they deserve to be at the top, don't they? Over the last few years, I've kept a close eye on European leagues, too.

Football has given me excitement and heartache. It has enabled me to travel the world, meet people and make friends. It has been thought provoking and character building and provided a comfortable lifestyle. Above all, it has been a passion that has gripped me for over 50 years. Football isn't like any other game. It is the only one that has captivated the world. When football stages its World Cup, the whole world is interested, from Fiji to the Faroes, Liechtenstein to Liberia. It has conquered South America and Europe and now it is growing in Asia and Africa. I believe it will develop in the United States, too. Nothing can stop it and it must really rile people from other sports to see that football is the only truly global game. One of the reasons for that is that football is also the most democratic game, another of its beauties. On any given day, David can and does beat Goliath and every fan and every player goes to the match thinking it could just be their moment. That's what made the FA Cup great and why so many smaller nations have taken to football in such a big way. They know they can get through to the World Cup finals and play against the great football nations – and, every now and then, beat them.

I've witnessed many ups and downs over the last half century yet here I am, in my sixties, still heavily involved in football. I am also a director of an NHS Hospital Trust in Blackpool and I've been a school governor for 20-odd years. I'm president of the local branch of Age Concern and vice-president of Lancashire Outward Bound. I'm a member of the Cathedral Council at Blackburn, a church organist and treasurer, father of two and grandfather of four. So you might say I'm well occupied. I certainly haven't retired. Furthermore, I intend to carry on as long as my health holds up.

Like many former players, I do suffer from joint problems, particularly with my knees, and I suspect that before long the surgeon is going to have another go at me. I've reached the age where everything I've got hurts and the things that don't hurt probably aren't working anyway. Thank God for paracetamol! But I shouldn't be too concerned because although my legs hurt me now they have been faithful servants over the last six decades. They may have suffered quite a hammering but they have enabled me to outrun some of the best footballers in the world. I'm not complaining. Nevertheless, after so many years of high fitness, I find ageing a trying experience. I still exercise but I am now having to accept that I will have to walk more than I run, and that's not easy because from being a small boy I have always wanted to run.

I remember seeing a film when I was a lad in my teens about the great American athlete Jim Thorpe, who won the decathlon and pentathlon at the 1912 Olympics in Stockholm and later became a professional footballer. Even so, he finished up in a travelling circus – roll up, roll up, come and see the great Jim Thorpe, that kind of thing. Burt Lancaster took the part in the film and it has stayed with me all this time. As a kid, Thorpe used to run everywhere and there was a scene in the film in which he described how running had always been an uplifting experience. When he felt down, he simply went for a run. I was exactly the same. If I felt a bit low, I would go for a run and feel myself being spiritually lifted. People may think that's a load of nonsense but it's perfectly true. Running to me was like a drug and the problem with growing older is that you lose the prescription. I've come to terms with it now but it wasn't easy at first. Other things have taken its place. Music is one and watching sport another. But watching others play will always be second best. I've always preferred to do it for myself.

One way or another, now seems to be a good time to reflect on my life, but even though I'm in my third year as a pensioner, looking back is a novel experience. Until now, I have always looked forward. I've never collected souvenirs or kept scrapbooks and I have always believed that what's gone has gone. Tomorrow is the important thing. But the past has its place, too. Where we stand is important, as long as we know where we are going. These days, people look at Jim Armfield OBE and see an elder states-man and a pillar of society, but I wasn't always a church organist. I have had to graduate through the University of Life. I was a streetwise kid and I grew up on the back of a few battles. Don't get me wrong, I wasn't a bad lad or a hard case but I wasn't perfect either and I've always known how to look after myself. There have been one or two scrapes along the way but, as William Wordsworth wrote in his poem 'The Rainbow', 'The child is father of the man'. Perhaps it's only when you reach my age that you can look back and see how true that is.

THE HOUSE IN TYLDESLEY ROAD

In my playing days, people used to call me Gentleman Jim. I never really understood that. It probably came about because I was never sent off in 626 games for Blackpool, 43 appearances for England and nine Under-23 internationals, and I was booked just once, for two successive fouls in an FA Cup tie against Norwich. I'd played over 500 league games by then and the referee was almost apologetic about becoming the first man to enter the name of Jimmy Armfield in his little black book.

I wasn't the first 'gentleman' of the family, though. That distinction belonged to John Allen, my mother's father. Gentleman John Allen they used to call him, and an unforgettable character he was, too. I've never forgotten the day he arrived from Manchester to watch his grandson in action against Newcastle United at Bloomfield Road. It was during the 1955–56 season and I was just beginning to hold down a regular place in a Blackpool side that featured the one and only Stanley Matthews and other big names such as Ernie Taylor, Bill Perry, Jackie Mudie and George Farm. It was only a couple of years after the legendary Matthews final of 1953 and Blackpool were among the country's best teams and a very fashionable club. A lot of home games were 35,000 sell-outs and the lure of a Newcastle team including Jackie Milburn, Bobby Mitchell, Vic Keeble, Jimmy Scoular and a few more big names ensured that this was a game not to be missed.

Gentleman John Allen certainly agreed with that sentiment, as I was to discover a few minutes before the kick-off. It was a baking hot day and in the home dressing room, the players were going through their final warm-up routines when Joe Smith, the manager, called out, 'Come here Jim, I want a word.' I assumed he was going to talk tactics or give me a few quiet tips about the Newcastle attack but he took me to the open window from where you could see the crowd milling around outside, and asked, 'Who's that?' There, in a shiny blue suit, with his bowler hat on the back of his head, collar askew and a bottle of Guinness with a screw top in one hand was my grandfather, Gentleman John Allen. He looked as though he'd had a few more bottles of Guinness on the way to the ground as well.

'That's my granddad,' I replied.

He spotted me at the window and started shouting, 'There's my grandson, our Jim. I've come to see him play.'

'Right,' said Joe. 'Don't you worry. We'll sort it out.'

When we went out on to the pitch, I soon picked him out, standing up and waving his bowler hat at me. His waistcoat and shirt front were open and he was still carrying a bottle of Guinness. It wasn't easy as I tried to motion him to sit down and keep quiet but there was no chance of that. Once the action started, I forgot all about him. We won 5–1. After the game, I walked back home with my pals – not many players had cars in those days. When I arrived, my father was standing at the door with a long face.

'Hey, do you know who was at the match?' I asked.

'Oh yes,' he replied. 'We know all about that. You'd better go and see your mother.'

So I ran upstairs – we lived in the flat above my father's grocer's shop.

'My granddad's been to the match. Where is he?' I called, full of enthusiasm.

'By now, probably somewhere between Chorley and Bolton,' Mother answered.

'No, you've got it wrong,' I insisted. 'He was at the game. I saw him before the kick-off.'

'Well he isn't in Blackpool now.'

It turned out that Granddad had been invited into the directors' box in an attempt to calm him down, although he still kept a
firm hand on his bottle of Guinness with the screw top. We
scored a couple of goals and he'd been shouting his head off.
Eventually, the combination of the heat and the Guinness took its
toll and he passed out. So they carried him out, boots, bowler hat,
blue suit, flying collar, Guinness and all, and piled him into a taxi,
which took him back to our house. He wasn't there for long.
Before he could even think about getting out of the cab, my
mother hopped on board and instructed the driver to turn
straight round and head for the bus station. There they loaded
him on to the first bus back to Manchester, never to be seen again
– not at Bloomfield Road, anyway. He always was intimidated by
my mother, was Gentleman John.

He really was a rum devil. He was small, thin and bald, and
apart from the incident in the Bloomfield Road directors' box, he
could usually hold his drink forever. He came from Ireland
originally and was born out of wedlock on a lord's estate. His
mother was one of the servants. I don't think he ever knew who
his father was. It might have been an upstairs–downstairs affair –
who knows, I might have aristocratic blood in me somewhere
down the line. I could certainly have played for Ireland.

Grandfather was wounded at the Somme during the First
World War but recovered – it would have taken more than a few
German bullets to finish off Gentleman John Allen. He was a
bricklayer, first in the pits and then on building sites, and never
out of work because he was good at his job. Overall, he's the
hardest man I've ever known.

When I was a lad, I sometimes used to take him his lunch on a
building site at Belle Vue, a theme park in Manchester that no
longer exists. My grandmother, who suffered terribly from leg
ulcers, prepared it in a basin with a red and white handkerchief
tied across the top. It was usually some kind of stew or thick soup.
She was an expert at cooking those kinds of things and she was
also the first person I saw baking potatoes on the fire. If my
granddad's dinner was hot, I had to run to make sure it hadn't

gone cold by the time he ate it. One day, I carried the basin carefully on to the site and there was my granddad walking along the top of a wall that was just one brick wide, about 20 feet up and carrying a hod with nine bricks in it. He was over 60 years old at the time.

Joseph Armfield, my other grandfather, was more the typical Victorian, with a splendid white moustache. A lifelong Methodist and a kind and gentle man, he didn't have much money but he was always spotlessly turned out. He didn't like going into the pub so he used to send me in with a white jug and sixpence. The pub was called The Angel and was just at the top of the street. The landlord would fill the jug up with ale and I'd take it back to my granddad. He smoked a pipe – Erinmore Flake tobacco. He worked at the iron foundry and one day he was the victim of what we would now call an industrial accident when molten metal poured over his leg. It was horrendous. The heat of the metal curled up his foot. He was in hospital for six months and had to walk on a raised boot for the rest of his life. He walked on his heel. There was no compensation in those days so he just had to get on with it. To make it worse, his wife, my grandmother, had died before I was born.

His house, where my father, Christopher Armfield, was brought up, was in George Street, Denton, near Manchester. It was a two-up and two-down with gas but no electricity and it was always clean and tidy. Father was the middle one of three kids and left school at 14. He went to work at the Co-op in the grocer's store. On his first day, the manager lifted a trapdoor in the floor and told my dad to go down into the cellar. There were two big sacks. One contained sugar, the other paper bags. The manager showed him how to load sugar into 2lb bags and how to seal them up – no process packing like today. Then he went back upstairs and shut the trapdoor.

My father spent the first two weeks of his working life loading sugar into bags by candlelight – all day Monday to Friday and again on Saturday mornings. They used to open the trapdoor to let him out at lunchtime and then again at teatime when it was time to go home. He never forgot how to seal bags. If my father sealed a bag of sugar, it stayed sealed. After a while, he was promoted to pushing the handcart and eventually progressed to managing a store and then owning his own business. He was a grocer all his life and always totally organised.

My mother, Doris, was born in Gorton, Manchester, which was a very poor area at the time. We sometimes talk about poverty these days but you won't find anything like the Gorton in which my mother grew up. The family lived in Bank Street until the houses were pulled down in the 1950s. It was a true working-class area, for those who had a job anyway, where people never locked the front door and neighbours walked in and out freely. Frankly, there was nothing of value to steal. There was no electricity or running hot water and the tin bath was hung up on the wall in the yard. The houses all had hold-your-breath outside lavatories with just half a door. You could sit there and have a chat over the wall with the chap next door. People didn't buy toilet paper but used torn-up newspaper hung on a string.

My grandma had a neighbour called Mrs Bocking, and me and my cousin Alan Houlkar used to laugh about her, calling out, 'Things are shocking, Mrs Bocking!' behind her back until the time she heard us and gave us a clattering. One day, she walked in and said to my grandma, 'Sally, I've borrowed some sugar.' My grandma just said OK. She was poor and couldn't afford to give away her sugar but she knew Mrs Bocking would replace it later. That was the way people lived. They were good to each other. If you were ill, you couldn't afford a doctor but a neighbour would always come in and look after you. There was no television or radio and very few newspapers. I think they used to buy one a week to make sure there was a supply of toilet paper. People would go into one another's houses at night and talk – except Gentleman John Allen, of course, who would be in The Plough at the bottom of Wellington Street. They didn't have time to worry about the rest of the world because they had enough problems of their own.

Mother was the eldest of six, a machinist at the local clothes factory. She was a machinist until she was 74. She never retired. Before she started work, they used to let her out of school half an hour early so she could go home and make the tea for the rest of the family because my grandma worked at the weavers' shed nearby. When she was 13 she used to go out cleaning on a Saturday morning for a shilling. It was a tough upbringing but she was a tough woman. She was a very good swimmer and people used to say I looked like her rather than my father. She was what you might call a doer. She had little formal education but worked hard, preferring to go out to work to being a housewife, and she was very resilient. Once, she fell in the street and was taken round to the nearby ambulance station where her arm was put in a sling. They were going to take her home. Home? No chance! She went to work, only discovering later that she had a fracture.

She didn't believe in doctors and dentists. She never went anywhere near a doctor all her life and she cleaned her teeth with salt. One day, when she was in her seventies, she and my father came to our house in Blackpool for Sunday lunch. I opened the door to let them in and my father walked straight past me, muttering, 'Perhaps you can do something with her because I can't.' Mother was standing outside. Her face was so swollen on one side that she looked as if she had an apple in her mouth. I said, 'What have you done?' I looked in her mouth and she had this huge hole in her gum and one of her teeth was all twisted and broken. Even though it was Sunday, I rang a pal of mine, Ken Morrison, who also happened to be our local dentist. After saying how sorry I was for troubling him on a Sunday, I told him about mother's tooth, adding, 'Look, she hates dentists so try and take it easy.' Ken was a good-natured man and he came round.

'Oh dear,' he said, peering in her mouth. 'I'll do something for that, Mrs Armfield.' Ken took a hypodermic syringe out of his bag and squirted it in the air to make sure it was working properly.

'What are you going to do with that?' she said. She hadn't said a word till then.

'I'm going to inject something into your gum and it will kill the pain for you.'

'I don't want that.'

Ken started to point out that it would make life a lot easier if she had something to ease the pain but she interrupted him.

'I didn't send for you. He did [pointing at me]. I don't have anything to do with dentists. You can put your things together, pick up your bag and go home.'

I rushed Ken out of the house with profuse apologies. Incredibly, for a week my mother gritted her teeth until the nerve died in her gum and the pain disappeared. When she died, that tooth was still in her head.

In many ways, she and my father were total opposites. The only thing they really had in common was that both were workaholics. Mother had Irish blood, thanks to Gentleman John Allen, and was from a Roman Catholic background; Father was a staunch Methodist. They married when she was 18, mainly, I suspect, because she wanted to get out of the family house in Gorton. I don't really know how they got on so well but they do say unlike poles attract, don't they?

Their first home was two rooms at 10 shillings (50p) a week. By the time I was born on 21 September 1935, they had put down a deposit on a house in Marina Avenue, Denton, and moved in. I was the only child and I was always independent. I can remember going into Manchester by myself on the number eight bus that ran from Denton to Piccadilly, or on the number 19 tram – we used to call it the old boneshaker. I used to go to the cinema with my grandmother and cousin Alan – the Cosmo in Wellington Street, Gorton. The three of us could go in there and have a bag of chips afterwards for a shilling, five pence in today's money. They are still the best chips I've ever tasted. We used to sit right in the front row, my grandmother in the middle and me and Alan on either side. If the film was a bit scary, we'd all huddle together until the baddies went away. I think the first film I ever saw was *South of the Border*, a cowboy film with Gene Autry. There was another picture house nearby called the Rivoli, and the Olympia was just down the road. In Denton, we had the Barcliffe and the People's Hall, where there were wooden benches to sit on.

I grew up with a love of the cinema. The beauty of digital television these days is that I can watch all the old films over and over again, the older the better. I may have seen them all before but that doesn't stop me enjoying them again – right back to the thirties with such stars as James Cagney, George Raft, George Formby and Laurel and Hardy, the funniest duo of all time in my opinion. They were unique and I still laugh at them today. I used to like cowboy films, too, with Hopalong Cassidy, John Wayne and Roy Rogers. I still go to the cinema but these multi-screen complexes are a million miles away from the Cosmo. Anne and I sometimes take the grandchildren for a bit of a treat but it's popcorn and Pepsi instead of a bag of chips.

In the Denton of my early childhood, working barges plied their trade on the canals, there was a cotton mill, a Co-op and a coal mine, and the sound of brass band music. Then, in 1939, when I was nearly four, war broke out. I can remember the bombs. Not many fell on Denton, probably only two or three, but I can recall what was later described as the Manchester blitz night when the whole sky seemed to be on fire. My father went to enlist in the forces but was turned down because his eyesight wasn't up to it. So what did they do? Made him an air-raid warden to look out for German aircraft. It was real life 'Dad's Army' stuff. He was posted in Manchester and I don't know whether he was the only look-out with faulty eyesight, but over the years it has given us a few laughs. There was always a good sense of humour in the family.

Back home in Denton we had to prepare ourselves just in case there was a raid. We used to push the couch against the window and sleep behind it on the floor. Then if the window smashed, the glass would fall on the couch and not on us. I was on the receiving end once when I was staying with an aunt who lived nearer to Manchester than we did. A bomb went off close by and the blast was powerful enough to blow the door off. Frightening. During those days we often used to eat in what was called the British Restaurant. It was a makeshift café in a school hall and a place where people could sit and talk and have a cup of soup or something like that. It cost sixpence (2½p). There was never anything special to eat because of the food shortages.

My schooldays started at Denton Council School but I don't

recall too much about it. I didn't stay long because when I was about seven, my life turned completely upside down. It happened totally out of the blue. One day we were living in Denton, the only home I had known; the next day, I found myself in a boarding house in Blackpool. Why? I'll never really know. It did occur to me later that a short time before, we had all been issued with gas masks at school. Perhaps this brought it home to my mother that if we stayed in Denton, her little boy might be evacuated and moved away like many other children. Whatever the reason was, she decided to move out and head for Blackpool. She never told me why she chose Blackpool. It wasn't as if we had relatives there or anything like that. In fact, I'd only ever been there once and that was for a week's holiday that I was too young to remember.

All I knew was that, one day, my father went to work as usual, my mother packed a suitcase, we caught a bus to Victoria Station in Manchester and climbed aboard a train for Blackpool. My father used to come to visit us at weekends and I don't think he was totally thrilled with the situation but my mother could be very determined. I suppose that came from being the eldest of six. If she set her mind on something, it wasn't easy to shift her. So Blackpool it was. I remember arriving at Blackpool Station, wearing a cap and carrying a little leather suitcase. Because of the war, there were no day-trippers or holidaymakers. It was a different world. At first, I thought it would be only a matter of time before we returned to Denton where everything would be familiar again, but we stayed in Blackpool – and I've been there ever since. We shared a little room on the top floor of a boarding house where my mother worked to pay our keep. Eventually, she ran the boarding house on her own but she never owned it. We did everything in that room for the next three years and it was our only bit of privacy.

The house, owned by a family called Booth, was in Tyldesley Road, just behind the promenade, and on the ground floor was a butcher's shop. It's still there, and every time I go past I have a look up at the little window of the room that was once home, with its three-quarter size bed. There was one lavatory for all three floors and one bathroom, but you were only allowed one bath a week anyway to save water and heating, so we used to go to the swimming baths instead, or we went for a swim in the sea. A tramp used to come to the back door of the boarding house a couple of times each week and my mother would give him his dinner. He'd sit on the step and eat it. I remember someone asking her why she encouraged him. 'When you've been poor, you'll understand,' she replied.

Some servicemen were billeted in the boarding house. Most of them were Polish airmen stationed in Blackpool and more often than not we ate our meals downstairs with them. One of them, Frank Jaglinski, stayed with us after the war, working in my father's grocery shop until he died. He became virtually a member of the family.

There were uniforms everywhere, which was fascinating to a young boy. When I think back, the troops are my first real memory of Blackpool. They used to assemble in Tyldesley Square every morning at seven o'clock and march off in their platoons. In winter, one airman would walk ahead holding a white lamp while another would walk behind the main group with a red lamp. They would march past the house whistling 'Colonel Bogey'. It was straight out of *Bridge on the River Kwai*. That marching and whistling woke me up every morning as they headed for the sands to do their physical training. They'd strip down to the waist in all weathers and go through their exercises.

Blackpool beach was dotted with huge metal poles – otherwise the seven miles of golden sands they talk about in the holiday brochures would have been perfect for enemy aircraft to land. I have often wondered how they managed to drive those poles into the sand and keep them there. Twice a day the tide would roll in and out and when the sea went back, the poles were as solid as ever. I took them for granted. I assumed they'd always been there and it was a memorable experience when they were taken away at the end of the war.

The war dominated everything. For example, the local bank was taken over by the airforce for use as a navigation training centre, and I can remember people coming along and taking away the railings at the front of the house. There was no warning. One day, the railings were there, the next they had gone to be used in the war effort. Even today, you can still see places all around the town where the railings were sawn off all those years ago. They would come and collect pots and pans, too. If people had four or five pans, they were asked to give one up. We were OK in the boarding house because they were needed to feed the troops. A chap who lived two doors away dug up his yard. He took up all the concrete, bought some soil and dug for victory, planting cabbages and carrots.

My first school in my new home town was Revoe Primary. My mother took a couple of hours off work to go with me on my first morning but it wasn't the start of a new school year or term so I was just thrown in at the deep end. It must have been winter because I remember the cold. I had to walk about three-quarters of a mile there and back. There was no traffic around because there was no petrol. Some of the corporation buses were even fuelled by gas from a trailer that they towed at the back. At first, I used to walk home at lunchtime as well because I didn't have school dinners, so I was making that trip four times a day.

I soon started to play truant. Whether it was because I was fed up with all the walking or just unhappy in my new surroundings, I don't really know. I suppose I was just uncomfortable with the whole situation. My father was in Manchester and we were in Blackpool. Back in Marina Avenue, I had a friend, Tony, who lived up the road but I didn't have any friends here. I suppose I'd lost my roots. It was strange, even though Blackpool was quite a place compared with Denton. Anyway, one day when the weather was improving, I decided I would be better off not going to school. I went down to the beach instead to see the man who ran the donkeys on the sands. He lived in Ibbison Street and I knew him as the Donkey Man. His real name was Jack Smith and he was very kind to me, letting me help with the donkeys for a while – and never asking why I wasn't at school.

On other occasions, I would wander around the streets, just watching what was going on. I always found ways to occupy myself. I had a worn-out tennis ball with all the textured covering missing. It was just the rubber shell and I used to put it in my pocket and carry it everywhere. I can still visualise it now. There was a disused water tank nearby and I used to kick my ball up against that, or up against a garage door or the wall. Sometimes I'd throw the ball up on to a roof and when it came down, I'd jump up and head it. That tennis ball was my first step into football.

I didn't miss school every day. I tried to be crafty. I would make a token appearance every now and then, just to let them know I was still alive. If anyone asked where I'd been the previous two days, I'd say my mother was ill or I'd been unwell, or something like that. I didn't think I was doing anything wrong. I just preferred life on the street to being cooped up in a new school that I didn't really like. Inevitably, I was found out. One day I returned from one of my walks around town to see a man in a suit knocking at the door. I knew straightaway why he was there. I was on the other side of the road so I hid in a doorway and waited until he came out before strolling into the house as if nothing had happened. But clearly the game was up. Mother took me straight down to the school and truancy ended there and then. I was caned – and that slowed me down a bit, too.

Gradually, I settled in and Revoe was good for me. The lads round there were all pretty tough but I got to be one of the boys and, in the end, I became firm friends with quite a few of them. It was a hardening process. My image was bolstered one day when the ball we used to play with, my tennis ball, got stuck on the roof. That ball was like gold. There weren't any more because all the available rubber was needed for the war. So it had to be recovered and I was the one who shinned up the drainpipe to rescue our precious possession. I clambered on to the roof, threw down the ball to cheers of delight from my mates – and looked straight into the eyes of the headmaster, Mr Williams. He was less than impressed.

'Now Jim,' he said, 'come on down. Steady. Take it easy.' He was a kind man and he was genuinely worried. He took me by the hand, hauled me off to his study and gave me the cane, three on each hand. It didn't half hurt but nevertheless, in time, I came to respect him.

He was Welsh and always immaculately dressed with a stiff collar and highly polished shoes. He preached patriotism and the four school houses were named after colonies of the British Empire because of their involvement in the war effort. I was in South Africa and the others were Australia, Canada and New Zealand. He had a wonderful singing voice and, looking back, I can imagine him singing in a chapel down in the Valleys. He was the first person to spark my interest in hymns and church music. He knew all the great Welsh tunes off by heart – 'Cwm Rhondda' which we know in the Church of England as 'Guide Me Oh Thou Great Redeemer', and 'Blaenwern', 'Love Divine All Loves Excelling'. It was the start of my musical education.

Even though the truancy had stopped, I was still an adventurer. One day during the school holidays, I decided to go to see my dad back in Denton on my recently acquired second-hand bike. I can't have been more than nine or 10 years old at the time and it was 60 miles there and 60 miles back. I wasn't totally sure of the route and there were no road signs in wartime. I just kept going straight through all the towns along the way. It took me around five hours to get there and my father couldn't believe it when he saw me. I stayed for an hour or so and then rode back – another five hours. Astonishing, really. My mother couldn't believe it when she discovered what I'd done.

Revoe also introduced me to the world of Polish dancing. I don't know how I came to be involved because it didn't quite square up with my streetwise persona. Perhaps we were selected in alphabetical order. Anyway, it did wonders for my footwork in later years! We had to learn a dance called the Cracowiak with the girls from the girls' school. An officer from the Polish army, Mr Tadek, taught us. He was stationed in Blackpool and I can remember him vividly. He was about 45 with very straight black hair and if he was alive today, I'm sure I would recognise him immediately. Once we had perfected the dance, we were sent round to perform for all the Polish servicemen in the area. We went all over the place, quite often in an army lorry, including a hospital in Ormskirk where injured airmen were being treated. There was a Polish club in Blackpool and I can see all the airmen now, watching us with tears rolling down their cheeks. It must have brought back so many memories of home. They were stunned. We danced in couples and, believe it or not, three couples behind me in the same troupe was Anne Ashurst, a year older than me and the girl who would one day become my wife. Small world.

But dancing was an aside, really. Football was starting to get into my blood and as I grew up, I spent more and more time kicking a ball. My best pal was Kenny Booth. He wasn't from the Booth family who ran the boarding house but he lived down the other end of the street. Like me, he was fanatical about football. His dad had played for Blackpool and Birmingham and I used to listen to his stories for hours. We invented our own game called flick soccer. We'd cut pictures of players out of the paper, stick them on to cigarette cards and flick the cards around the table. The ball was a dried pea and the goals were made of balsa wood.

When we weren't playing flick soccer, we'd play out in the streets under the gas lamps or on the sands or even on Stanley Park, usually commentating on the action as we played. One of our favourite playing areas was the Coliseum Bus Station, where the excursion buses used to roll in and out. There were no buses during the war, so it became a great football pitch. Once, during the school holidays just after the war, we were on a bus going towards Fleetwood when we spotted a proper football pitch with nets in the goals. It was the ICI ground at Thornton. We'd never seen goals with nets before except at Bloomfield Road, so the next day we set off on our bikes, this time with a ball, and we spent hours kicking the ball into the empty nets.

The Polish airmen who were staying at the boarding house often used to go along to Bloomfield Road, and sometimes they'd take me, too, so I started to watch Blackpool on a fairly regular basis. It wasn't the same Blackpool side as before the war because most of those players were serving overseas, but during hostilities, clubs could enlist anyone who happened to be stationed in or around the town. Blackpool had Stanley Matthews and Jock

Dodds playing for them, two of the biggest names in the game at the time, and one year they won the Wartime Cup. They reached the final on another occasion.

Football and Bloomfield Road grabbed me. I loved the occasion and the crowd. I soaked up the atmosphere. Blackpool seemed to beat everybody and if you didn't go early, you didn't get in. For an hour or more before the kick-off, the RAF band used to play in front of the South Stand where the players came out. They used to play all the great Sousa marches and I know those tunes backwards – and I can still remember the wartime team. Savage was in goal with Pope and Kinsell at full-back. The half-backs were Farrow, Hayward and Ivor Powell, who later became Carlisle's manager and earned legendary status among the press corps with after-match quotes such as, 'There's complete harmonium in the dressing room.' Matthews, Dix, Dodds, Finan and Burbanks were the forwards. They were the team of All Stars and nobody could really live with them. They once beat Manchester City 6–1. My father was a bit of a City fan, not a fanatic, though, and when he heard the result, he asked if Peter Doherty, the Irish international inside-forward, had been playing for City. I said I couldn't remember. 'He can't have been,' he said. 'They would never have lost 6–1 if Doherty had been playing.'

As well as Blackpool, there was a Blackpool Services team. They were virtually the same players except they played in blue instead of tangerine. The Polish lads had a team, too, and I remember once going with them for a game against the local RAF at Kirkham. It was snowing. They put a greatcoat down on the ground for me to sit on and wrapped all the other players' greatcoats around me to keep me warm.

Blackpool FC were an integral part of wartime Blackpool, the world I was growing up in. The town never suffered from bombing as so many bigger cities did, although there was a time when an aircraft crashed into Central Station. That caused a bit of a mess. American airmen were stationed at Burtonwood near Warrington and they would come into town for a day off or a weekend. One of them got more than he bargained for when he was hit over the head with a vinegar bottle. It happened in

Howson's Fish Shop in Foxhall Square and I was in the queue waiting for my chips. There were two Americans at the front with an English couple behind. One of the Americans must have passed some remark about the woman because the next thing I knew, her husband had picked up the vinegar bottle and hurled it at the American's head. It caught him full on the forehead and there was blood everywhere. Fortunately, not on my chips, though. Both the Americans started on the Englishman but other people who had seen the incident piled in and sorted it out. When I got home I had some explaining to do about the vinegar stains on my clothes.

On another occasion, when I was about nine, I had to make a hasty escape from a couple of men who were up to no good in a dark alley. I was walking past the end of the alley, heard voices and went to investigate. They weren't happy about me being there and told me in no uncertain terms where to go. I replied in similar vein and one of them grabbed hold of me. He lifted me off the floor and held me in front of him while the other one advanced.

I kicked out at the man in front of me, crashed my head back into the face of the one holding me and ran. I was absolutely petrified. They chased after me but it was difficult to see me in the gloom and I was quicker than they were anyway. I had a good engine, even in those days. I remember running straight past our front door so that they wouldn't know where I lived and when I had lost them, I crept quietly back home. It was a nasty incident and I never went down that back alley again.

Blackpool during the war and immediately afterwards attracted a lot of people of all types and it was tough at times. I once saw two blokes having a bit of an altercation in the street and it ended with one of the guys being thrown bodily through a shop window. There was glass all over the place but at first he stood up and looked all right. Then all of a sudden it was as if his head had opened up and blood started streaming down his face.

A Christmas party organised by the Poles in Tyldesley Road was a less traumatic experience. They were in charge of the catering and the drink and I joined in with a vengeance – not a good idea for a nine-year-old. Apparently, I ended up the worse for wear but, needless to say, I can't remember much about it. I can recall smoking my first cigar at around that time and mother going into hospital for a major operation. I had to more or less fend for myself, with the airmen and the Booth family keeping an eye on me just in case – independent, you see. Over the next couple of years, I developed whooping cough and then impetigo, which meant staying in a darkened room for what seemed like an age. My face was covered in sores and I had a large scab on the top of my head.

In wartime Britain, people didn't have very much and had to make their own entertainment, particularly at night time in winter when the streets were dark and all the windows had to be blacked out, but I don't recall having any problem with boredom. I used to read a lot and listen to the radio – Tommy Handley and the ITMA Show were favourites – and I've enjoyed the radio ever since. I used to play Ludo and Snakes and Ladders with my mother, or sometimes a friend came round. We played cards, too, and there was always flick soccer with Kenny Booth. Generally speaking, we were as well read as the children of today and we were certainly physically fitter because, as you can imagine, child obesity wasn't a problem in wartime, and we went to bed early and got plenty of sleep.

Fortunately, we did have the cinema and it was a godsend. In Blackpool there were 20-odd picture houses and my locals were the Alexandra – the building is still there – and the Ritz on the Prom, which has now gone. The newsreels kept us up to date with the war and we never realised how much propaganda was involved. Britain was seemingly impregnable, Churchill and Montgomery were our heroes and there was massive national pride. Everything and everybody supported the war effort and Britain was more united then than at any time I have since known. No one ever really questioned authority or the importance to the community of the local doctor, teacher, vicar and policeman. They were the people we looked to for leadership and we took notice of them.

Eventually, the war ended. First we had VE Day and then VJ

Day. The celebrations were enormous. Blackpool went absolutely berserk. There were street parties during the day and at night they lit bonfires all along the beach. People were ripping up the benches on the promenade and throwing them on the fires. To me, the flames seemed to be leaping right up to the sky. I'd never seen a bonfire before. There was no 5 November during wartime and it wasn't until the late forties that I saw my first fireworks. There were so many things I never knew that youngsters growing up today take for granted. I grew up with ration books, food coupons and identity cards. I never had sweets and these days I rarely eat them. My mother used to give our sweet coupons away in exchange for butter coupons or some other more sensible food. I've never missed them. Even now, I hate to see waste. I wasn't allowed to leave the table until I had cleared my plate and, quite honestly, during the war you had to eat what you were given because there wasn't anything else available. It's a habit that has never gone away. I never leave anything on a plate.

Looking back, the war was an incredible experience for a little boy. Seven or eight is a very impressionable age and a perfect time to teach kids good habits. I was observant and intelligent and I absorbed everything I saw. Even though we didn't have things like television, spacecraft and, fortunately, mobile phones, we had people. I've always loved watching people – nothing else on the planet is anywhere near as interesting. As I've grown older, I hope I've become wiser. I've learned that people and human relationships are the most important thing of all, and people never really change. There's less poverty these days but back in wartime Blackpool people had their dreams and nightmares. They were laughing and crying, loving and hating, and watching football – just like today.

C H A P T E R 2

AN INCREDIBLE
J O U R N E Y

I was 10 years old when hostilities ended, a child of the war. It never actually touched me, apart from the odd bomb here and there, but it affected my whole life. Nothing concentrates the mind like war. People assumed that once the war was over, life would improve but of course it didn't, or not for a long time, anyway. However, I was about to embark on an incredible journey, an experience that even now, when I look back, seems unbelievable. For just six years later, I was playing football for Blackpool, even though I had never had any formal coaching and my only experience was a handful of games for my Sunday school team. I played rugby union at school and in my early days as a Blackpool player, I had the problem of juggling the two sports – first-team rugby at Arnold School and soccer in the juniors, the A team and the reserves at Blackpool.

It simply could not happen today and there can't be many people who have taken such an unorthodox route into professional sport, if anybody. I had virtually no sporting background at all. My father was a football fan and I think my Uncle Bill played football for a team in Denton, but there were no other connections with football or any other sport. And yet I did all right. I was the school athletics champion two years running and won the 220 yards in the inter-schools sports. As well as playing rugby for Arnold School at all age levels, I was also captain of the cricket team, an all-rounder, a good bowler and fielder and a reasonable batsman. As a competitive team sport, football didn't exist although, like so many boys before and since, I had a burning desire to play the game every minute of every day.

However, a career in professional football was way over the horizon when my father joined us in Blackpool as soon as the war was over. He left Manchester and his air-raid patrol and rented a little shop at the corner of Tyldesley Road and Princess Street. It isn't there any more. It was a grocer's shop but in 1945 it had been closed for some time and I remember going along for the first time with my parents after they had collected the keys. We opened the door to find the place thick with dust and cobwebs everywhere. It was like something out of a Dickens novel. An old-fashioned wooden counter had a cash drawer underneath with little sections for all the different types of coins, and when we opened that drawer it was absolutely full of mice – hundreds of them. They had been using it as a nesting place. So we closed the drawer, went home and came back later with our cat Tiddles. That did the trick. But cleaning up the shop was a hell of a job.

My mother and I were still living in the same room in Tyldesley Road. At first, my father had another room in the boarding house but that arrangement didn't last long, no more than three or four months. Fifty yards away, on the corner of Bairstow Street and Dale Street, there was another empty grocer's shop, this time with living accommodation upstairs. So Father gave up the first shop and we moved in – together again as a family after almost three years. I had my own bedroom in the attic. Next door, and actually attached to our building, was a pub, the Princess. It was about 50 yards from the promenade and it certainly wasn't uptown. The area was nicknamed 'The Bowery', after a tough part of New York, and I saw plenty of brawls. During the war, people had existed on so little for so long that afterwards they wanted a good time. That usually meant a few pints and of course some people only have to smell the barman's apron to get into trouble.

One night, I saw a man stabbed. I was looking out of my attic window and noticed someone lurking in the shadows across the road. He definitely wasn't drunk. He was waiting. He was wearing a dark blue suit, red shirt and white tie, and his hair, parted down the middle, was thick with Brylcreem. If he stood in front of me in an identity parade today, I'd pick him out straightaway. When his quarry left the Princess, he moved quickly across the road, stabbed the other man and then disappeared into thin air. I quietly lowered my attic window and never said a word to anybody, not even my mother and father.

My father ran that shop until he was 65, although he never actually owned it. My mother went back to work as a machinist and to earn extra money, she took an evening job in the snack bar on Central Pier, where she worked for many years. The stars who were performing in the theatre at the end of the pier would pop in for a cup of tea before, during or after the show, some of the biggest names in showbusiness among them. One was an up-and-coming young comedian called Ken Dodd. Years later, I was introduced to Doddy and asked him if he remembered the snack bar on Blackpool Central Pier. I told him my mother used to work there and he replied, 'Doris was your mother? A lovely lady. Tell her that one of these days I'll pay her for all those cups of tea!'

Between them, my mother and father earned enough to keep things going but they couldn't afford to buy anywhere to live. In the end, I bought them a bungalow for their retirement. The shop depended on the boarding-house trade and the post-war years from 1945 to 1950 were a boom time for Blackpool's boarding houses although the illuminations had still not been switched on. The season would start around Whitsuntide and go right the way through until early September, when the kids went back to school. It was non-stop. I rode the delivery rounds on the shop bike, a bit like the David Jason character Granville from the television show, 'Open All Hours'. I shuttled bread round to all the boarding houses and sometimes there would be an order of 20 loaves for one house alone. That meant two trips. I delivered the groceries as well and believe me, there was a knack to riding that bike, especially when there was a bit of weight in the basket. You turned the wheel but the basket didn't turn with you; it followed later and it was a very tricky business. I spilled it once or twice and had loaves rolling all round the street before I finally came to terms with the problem – and David Jason never seemed to perfect it!

My father's reappearance on the scene marked a significant change in our lifestyle. Discipline tightened up overnight, as I found to my cost when I started messing about at Sunday school. The Sunday schools were the feed into the youth clubs where we would play table tennis and badminton and take part in small discussion groups – nothing like today's groups, though, where they seem to discuss everything on the planet. Initially, I went to the Sunday school at Chapel Street Methodist Church, which is no longer there. But there was still a bit of impishness in me and I was asked to leave for singing the wrong words to a hymn or something like that. When my father discovered what had been going on, he was not a happy man and straightaway he frog-marched me down the road to the next nearest Sunday school, which was at St Peter's Church. I'm still involved at St Peter's to this day. In fact, that's how I became an Anglican. I don't know what John Wesley would have made of it all but the die was cast.

Father's approach to my education was equally unequivocal. Despite the early days of truancy, I was a relatively bright lad and when I passed the eleven-plus, it was time to move on and take my place at Arnold School. I wasn't too keen on it at first. It was a typical old-style grammar school and completely different from the Arnold School of the twenty-first century. I'm vice-chairman of the governors these days and Arnold is very much the modern independent school with wonderful up-to-date facilities for over 1,000 pupils. They even take girls – I wish they had in my day. In the after-war years, it was a different world. The desks had been around since before the war and they were old and pitted. Frank Holdgate, the headmaster, ran the school with a firm hand, to put it mildly, and it all came as a bit of a shock. I was in a class of boys who were academically very bright. I was a steady Eddie and they dragged me along with them, which probably explains why I collected some good O levels and A levels. Six of my classmates won state scholarships and went on to Oxford or Cambridge. The eleven-plus system is out of favour these days but it did a lot for me and for many other boys whose families could never have afforded to send them to a school like Arnold.

In my early years, though, I was still a bit of a Jack the lad and never too far away from trouble. There were plenty of prefects' detentions for fighting or for kicking a ball against the wall or around the fives court, which was strictly out of order at a rugby school. However, I managed to avoid too many bad reports from the classroom until the day Dr Joe Brice struck. Each boy had a little green book that the teachers would write up every month, saying how the pupil was performing in and out of class. We had to take the book home to be inspected and signed by a parent, and bring it back to school the next day.

Dr Brice, who was a Methodist minister, used to take Religious Education, or Divinity as we called it in those days, and in the last month or so, I hadn't been doing too well. Dr Brice didn't mince words, writing, 'James must improve in both work and behaviour.' I didn't like the look of that at all, so when I handed the book to my father I retired to what I hoped would be a safe distance. Seconds later, he appeared round the door and, without speaking, clouted me. Then he laid into me verbally, telling me I was a disgrace and I should be ashamed of myself. He telephoned the headmaster and they had an ominously long conversation.

I suspected that would not be the end of the matter and I was right. At assembly each morning, the head used to read out the names of all the boys he wanted to see in his study, usually for disciplinary reasons. My name was first on the list, a bit like the final line in the poem 'Abou Ben Adhem' by Leigh Hunt – 'And lo, Ben Adhem's name led all the rest.' Sure enough, the name of Armfield led all the rest as the head read out his roll call of malefactors. He really tore into me and finished by saying, 'You can either have the stick or a Saturday afternoon detention.' I thought quickly and remembered Blackpool were at home to Fulham in the FA Cup on the Saturday so I opted for the stick.

'I thought you'd say that,' he replied, 'but you can't. I've changed my mind. There's no choice and I'll see you at two o'clock on Saturday afternoon.'

So that was it – no Blackpool v. Fulham for me. Instead, a lad

called Stephen Thomas and I spent Saturday afternoon writing
an essay, watched over by Frank Holdgate. Afterwards he warned
me that if I didn't improve in and out of the class, detention
would be doubled. In a fortnight, I went from 23rd in the class to
12th, and once again, my name led all the rest on the headmaster's list in assembly. 'I want to see the following in my study
afterwards: Armfield . . .' I thought what have I done now?

He used to leave the door slightly ajar and when he was ready,
he would just shout 'Come!' He would be writing as you walked
in and wouldn't even look up. You had to stand at the end of the
desk, waiting for him to speak. He said, 'James [not Armfield this
time], you've improved. Something has happened in your life,
hasn't it?'

'Yes, sir.' No matter what he said, you said, 'Yes, sir.'

'Good. Now I shall watch you every single day of your life and
I never want to see you in trouble again. Goodbye.'

And I never have been in serious trouble since that day. What's
more, Frank Holdgate really did continue to keep an eye on me as
I discovered when I bumped into him at Bloomfield Road before
a game early in my career. He was at the match with Bill
Haythornthwaite, the deputy head and a season-ticket holder. I
said, 'Hello, sir.' Old habits died hard.

'Hello, James. I have come to see how you're doing. Have you
got an insurance policy in case you get injured?' This was outside
the ground before a First Division match – can you imagine
David Beckham having a conversation like that with his old
headmaster? I admitted that I hadn't but I was planning to do so
soon. 'When you get one, I would like to have a look at it,' said
Frank. So a few days later I rang him up at school and told him I
had taken out a policy. He was pleased. 'Well done, James. I am
glad to see you are doing all right.'

There were two sports fields at Arnold and it didn't take me
long to work out that's where I wanted to be. I had never played
rugby union before and, to be honest, I didn't really know much
about it, but I was athletic and the staff had obviously seen me
running around the playground so they gave me a run-out in the
Feathers, the junior team. The Feathers were the youngest, then

came the Bantams, the Colts, the Second XV and the First XV. I think they name the sides by age groups these days. I played on the right wing because I was quick. Our first game was against Blackpool Grammar School and while I can't remember the exact score, I know that we lost – heavily. In fact, we lost track of the score and in the end we could have done with log tables to work out the exact total. Obviously, there was big local rivalry and in the first couple of seasons they hammered us every time, but as the years went by, we started to improve, to catch up and finally we were much better than they were.

The teacher in charge of rugby was Bill Howarth, who played for Fylde and Lancashire. He took me for geography right through the school and always used to go on at me about being 'one of these soccer types'. George Eastham, another Arnold pupil who went on to play football for England, was in the year below me and he came in for the same treatment. It was as if Bill was looking down his nose at football but I discovered in later years that he had actually won a Blue at Cambridge for football. For most of us, it's a case of 'if you can't play football, try rugby'. It was the other way round for Bill Howarth and he must have believed he had settled for second best at Cambridge. He was never thrilled with us playing football. I bumped into him a few years after I left school – I was an England player by then but he never mentioned it or said he was glad to see how well I had done. I didn't lose any sleep over that.

All the way through the school one of my team-mates was Malcolm Phillips who went to Oxford University, won a rugby Blue and later captained England. I played on the wing, Malcolm was in the centre and, in my later years, George Eastham was fly-half. Malcolm and I were in the same form right through school and there can't have been many school classes that have produced two England captains at different sports; nor, for that matter, a school team with three future England internationals. There's an old school photograph of the three of us in that rugby team.

Rugby was all right, nothing more – but I like all team games and I'll watch rugby on the television today. I carried on playing right through school and made it into the First XV, still on the right wing. I used to take all the kicks and was leading points scorer for two or three years, but somehow I never really felt involved. My heart was elsewhere and I felt as if I was killing time until I could play football. One thing rugby did do, though, was teach me about winning and losing. That's an important discipline. We all love winners, of course we do, but there can be only one winner. One of the ideals of my life in sport has been losing with at least a bit of dignity. You can gain from losing, as our young rugby team did. We were thrashed by Blackpool Grammar School the first time we played but we didn't throw in the towel. We worked and we improved, all the time getting closer to Blackpool – and they knew we were coming. By the time we reached the Colts we were just as good as they were, and in the First XV, they couldn't hold us.

The same applies to football. A player can learn from losing and become a better player and a better person through the experience. Some of the very finest players have never done so. A few years ago, I was speaking to a leading coach at Clairefontaine, the French Football Academy, about Eric Cantona, who was then at the height of his powers at Leeds United. I asked why such a gifted player was not included in the national side. The answer was that while Cantona was a great footballer, he had never learned how to lose. I knew exactly what he meant.

So how did my life move from this rugby environment to football? I learned my football by running that old tennis ball down the street on my own. When I bought my first second-hand bike for 15 shillings (75p), it had to have a saddle bag for my tennis ball. The streets were my training ground and the only games I had been involved with were a few matches for my Sunday school team. One of them was against a Tyldesley Youth Club side that included a gentleman by the name of Brian Harper, who, as Brian London, would one day become British and European Heavyweight champion and fight Muhammad Ali for the world title. We had seven men and they beat us by more than 20 goals. To this day, Brian tells the tale of how he once played for a side that scored over 20 goals against Jimmy Armfield's team.

Perhaps it's not surprising that the team just faded away after a thrashing like that.

It was Arnold School that provided the unlikely catalyst in the shape of our PT master, George Neal, a retired sergeant major from the Army School of Physical Training. He was a real character. We used to call him 'Buddha' because of his build. He had a little hut that we christened Buddha's Temple, where he kept all the army rifles for the School Cadet Force. He was renowned among the boys for his sayings that we called Buddha-isms. On a cold day, we'd be out in the yard doing PT just wearing shorts and Buddha would call out, 'Close the gate, son, there's a bit of a draught.' Another one was 'pair off in threes . . .' and then there was, 'When I say go, I want to see the last one out of sight.'

George Neal was a football fan and one spring day, totally out of the blue, he came up to me in the schoolyard and said, 'Would you like to play football at Bloomfield Road?' I was 15 years old. It was the equivalent today of asking a child running around a park in Stretford if he would like to play at Old Trafford. Blackpool were just about the most famous club in the land. They had played in the FA Cup final in 1948 and 1951 and it was every schoolboy fan's dream to play at Bloomfield Road. I thought Buddha was joking. But no, he asked me again. 'They are having a trial match on Friday teatime. They're looking for one or two players and I've told them about you. They say you can go on Friday. Have you got any boots?' If I hadn't, I would have got hold of a pair somehow.

Friday was a day of intermittent sun and rain and at Bloomfield Road there was an air of organised chaos. A man was pulling the teams together, asking each boy what position he played and telling him to put on either a tangerine or a white shirt. His name was Vince McKenna and, like Buddha, he was to play a crucial role in shaping my future. I was wearing my Arnold School blazer and Vince took one look at me and said, 'What are you doing here? You're from Arnold.' I gave him my name and said George Neal had suggested I should come down for a trial. 'Right,' said Vince. 'What position do you play?' Now that was a tricky one. I didn't have a position because I'd never really played in a team before. So

I said I was a winger and was told to find a white shirt and play on the wing. We won 4–1 and I scored all four goals!

Vince had two more coaches with him that evening, Alex Roxburgh, the former Blackpool goalkeeper, and Danny Blair, the former Blackpool and Aston Villa player. More significantly, Joe Smith, the Blackpool manager, was watching from the stand. After the game, Alex and Danny took me to one side and asked if I would like to play for Blackpool Colts. I nearly jumped out of my skin.

'Oh yes!' I replied. I couldn't believe it.

'Can you play on Saturday afternoon?' That was another tricky one.

'Well no. I'm playing rugby for Arnold School.'

So came the first hurdle I had to cross on my journey into the professional game. I had no choice. School and rugby had to come first. So they asked me to report for pre-season training later that summer. It would be 1951. To be honest, I think they had forgotten all about me by the time I turned up. I trained with the lads but once the school holidays were over, I was back in the school rugby team every Saturday. However, we didn't play rugby after Christmas – hockey took over as the main school sport. I didn't play hockey, on purpose. Instead, I was finally able to turn out for Blackpool Colts in the Fylde League, a 16-year-old playing against men. That was the start. Our home pitch was Bispham Education ground and Vince McKenna was in charge of the team. It included four or five young pros with the rest made up of local lads. I didn't always make the starting line-up but there was one match when I scored twice and my name appeared in the local paper. At school the following Monday, Bill Howarth asked me, 'Is that you?' I said it was. He wasn't impressed and his attitude never changed, which didn't make life easy for me.

I progressed quickly, moving into the A team to play against Preston, Blackburn, Burnley and Bolton in the Lancashire League. I was doing well – nothing spectacular but steady progress – and then came the match that was to change my life. It was 21 March 1953. Down at Villa Park, Blackpool were playing Spurs in the semi-final of the FA Cup and at Bloomfield Road I was playing for the A team. Someone on the touchline had a radio. There was a feeling in the town that Blackpool's time had come, that they were finally going to win the Cup in Coronation year, and all the spectators were listening to the semi-final instead of watching us, which was fair enough.

We were winning 1–0 – I had scored the goal – when our right-back was injured. There were no substitutes allowed in those days and Vince was wondering what to do, so I volunteered to play right-back and right-wing combined. I said I would be a wing-back. It was the first time I had played at the back and I remember thinking how much easier it was than being up there in the front line. It seemed so natural for me to be there and from that point, I never really played anywhere else. I had a few more matches on the wing but I knew that I had discovered my true position. After the game, we were all thrilled to bits because we had won with 10 men and Blackpool had beaten Tottenham in the semi-final and would be meeting Bolton Wanderers in the Coronation Cup final. Vince approached me and said, 'You looked all right there, Jim. Do you want to play full-back again?' Of course I said yes, but I would have played in any position.

I made my debut for the reserves against Bury soon afterwards, playing on the wing, and it was my second game of the day. In the morning, I had played right-back against a Leeds youth team and afterwards Sam Jones, the reserve-team manager, said to me, 'Do you think you'd be able to play for the reserves this afternoon?'

'Of course.'

'On the wing?'

'Yes, no problem.'

So I ran all the way home to tell my dad I was going to play for the reserves in the afternoon. It was a good three-quarters of a mile from the ground to Bairstow Street. I had a sandwich for lunch and then ran all the way back to the ground and played 90 minutes for the reserves. We won 1–0 and I missed an absolute sitter in the last few minutes, probably a case of over-excitement. It was an incredible time to be involved with Blackpool Football Club. A young lad, still at school, here I was playing for the reserve team of one of the greatest sides in the country, a club that was about to take part in an FA Cup final that would go down in football folklore. I went to Wembley as a Blackpool player, even though I had not yet signed professional forms.

It was my third sight of the Twin Towers. In 1948, my father had somehow managed to get hold of two tickets for the final against Manchester United. We left Blackpool at around six in the morning and my father carried a biscuit tin that contained our sandwiches and a cake. It was to serve a dual purpose – I stood on it during the match. It was the only way I could see the action. We were in the ground by one o'clock and I still remember walking up the steps to the back of the Kop and looking out across Wembley Stadium for the first time. It was more or less empty and I can still see the sea of blue seats in the two stands on either side of the ground. Blackpool were beaten 4–2 that day and they lost again on my second trip three years later, this time 2–0 against Newcastle. But in 1953, we knew it would be different.

The club took the whole staff down to Wembley for the day. We travelled on the morning train from Blackpool Central Station, had lunch on the train – unheard of for me – and then walked up Wembley Way. The young players stood on the Spion Kop behind the goal, at the opposite end to where the Blackpool fans had been when the team lost in 1948 and 1951. We knew Blackpool would win – it was fate, destiny, call it what you like – even when we were 3–1 down. With Stanley Matthews around, anything could happen. We were standing at the end where the Blackpool goals went in on the way to that 4–3 victory in what will always be remembered as the Matthews final. Amazing that, when you think that Stan Mortensen became the only player to score a hat-trick in a Wembley FA Cup final. Morty had been suffering from cartilage trouble and he had an operation a few weeks before the game. He had hardly trained, yet he came out and scored a hat-trick.

When the game was over, we rushed back to the station, climbed aboard the train and went home. When we arrived back at around midnight, we discovered that Blackpool had gone crazy. Central Station was awash with tangerine and for the next 48 hours until the players arrived home, the whole town was ecstatic.

There was tangerine and white everywhere. In one way, it was the Matthews final because Stanley finally collected a winner's medal at the age of 38, but it was more than that – it was Blackpool's final, making up for the bitter disappointment of those two defeats. When the team arrived home on Monday evening in one of Sam Wood's Seagull Coaches, they drove along the promenade and pulled up in front of the town hall. I was packed in with the rest of the supporters calling for Matthews the talisman, Morty the local hero and Harry Johnston the leader, and I will always remember what Stanley said when it was his turn to speak to the fans – 'People are calling this the Stanley Matthews final. That's not true. This is a team game and it has been a team effort.' Even though I was still an amateur, I attended the celebration dinner at the Spanish Hall Winter Gardens and every player had his photograph taken with the Cup. Yes, even the youngsters, including me.

The following season, I continued to play for Blackpool whenever I wasn't involved with the school rugby team. I was doing my A levels as well but I've always been able to cram a pint into a gill. I had applied to Liverpool University and Loughborough College and there was a vague plan that I would one day become a teacher. But deep down, I knew where I was going. My only real apprehension was how my father would react when decision day came along after I had passed my A levels in history, geography and economics and been accepted at Liverpool and Loughborough. I shouldn't have worried. I could not have had a better father. He was kind and gentle but firm. I suppose he under-achieved in his own life, which was probably why he derived so much satisfaction from my success later on. When I told him I was going to give football a go, I expected him to go crackers. I should have known better. He said, 'It's your life and you have to lead it. You have to make decisions and stand by them. It's up to you.'

Much later, when I was a manager at Leeds, people used to talk about my so-called indecisiveness. 'The manager's indecision is final,' was the standing joke. Indecisive? That's the last thing I have ever been. I don't believe in rash judgements and I always like to consider both sides of the story. I ponder issues before making up my mind or passing judgement, but when I have to make a decision, I do so. Back in 1954, after weighing up all the pros and cons between football, Liverpool University and Loughborough College, I knew there was only one decision to be made – I would sign for Blackpool. Before that dream could become reality, however, I had to move on to another world altogether – the Army.

CHAPTER 3

THE ARMY GAME

'You may think you're a footballer, Armfield, but you'll never make a soldier!' My welcome from corporals Cathcart and Hargreaves of the King's Own Royal Regiment, based at Bowerham Barracks, Lancaster, was not warm. They were not the kind of men who specialised in helping raw recruits feel at home, and in my early days in the Army, I had to learn to put up with their jibes. What's more, they were wrong. I came through two years of National Service with flying colours, advancing from Private James Christopher Armfield, number 23072334, to Corporal Armfield, Physical Training Instructor. I was even offered the chance to become an officer but football was still my all-consuming passion and I politely declined the opportunity.

During my final year at Arnold School, I became a regular in the reserves at right-back and after leaving school in July 1954, I went into pre-season training with the full squad, still an amateur. I knew Blackpool were keen to sign me and in the first four or five reserve games of the new season, I played really well. Then, one morning, a brown envelope dropped through the letterbox containing an offer I could not refuse in the shape of my call-up papers. National Service was still compulsory so I knew it was coming. So did Blackpool. They agreed to sign me on a retainer of £1 a week with £3 extra if I played in the reserves and £6 extra in the first team.

So I became a Blackpool player at £1 a week. I thought it was pretty miserly and even £7 a week if I made the first team wouldn't look too good after tax. But they assured me I would be taken on to the full staff when I was demobbed in two years' time and basically I just wanted to play football. I don't know whether other clubs operated the same kind of system because I never asked. All I knew was that £1 was twice as much as my first week's pay in the Army so I wasn't complaining. There was no chance of affording any of life's luxuries, though, and it wasn't until the end of my time in the Army that I had saved enough to buy a little Ford 8 for £70. It blew up on me after about four miles.

Throughout my time at Arnold I had been a member of the school's Combined Cadet Force. It was compulsory but I enjoyed it and reached the dizzy height of sergeant. So I was vaguely under the impression that I knew what was coming when, along with one of my Arnold classmates, Frank Roberts, I boarded the train for Lancaster and life in the King's Own Royal Regiment. It just shows how wrong you can be, and any prospect of an early return home to play for Blackpool was knocked on the head straightaway because we were confined to barracks for a month – no weekends at home, no trips into town. You're in the Army now!

I was dumped into a long room at Bowerham – today it's St Martin's College – with the other 89 members of the intake, and what a place that was, a throwback to another era. I could imagine the same buildings being used in the build-up to the Boer War. Although I had not enjoyed an easy existence as I grew up, I had never experienced anything like this and it was a real shock to the system.

At the start, it was a serious case of bullshit baffles brains. We soon had a saying – if it moves, salute it; if it doesn't, whitewash it. On the first day we were each handed a metal plate covered in gunge that had to be removed before we could put any food on it. Needless to say, we weren't given anything to remove it with. It was the same with our black leather boots. They were covered in protective pimples, which had to be removed before the boots could be polished to the required sheen. But how to get rid of the pimples? In the end, we discovered they could be melted away with a red-hot iron. Then we had to work on the boots with spit and polish until they had buffed up into a real shine. I can still do it. Your number – and no old soldier ever forgets his number, it's indelibly imprinted on the brain – had to go on every item of clothing and equipment.

Then there was the rifle. Each recruit was issued with a rifle and anyone foolish enough to lose his rifle really was in trouble big-time. So the rifles were usually kept under lock and key. The first time they were given an airing was at Crag Bank firing ranges on Morecambe Bay. It was a cold, wet October day, the wind was whistling in from the Irish Sea and we were all feeling under the weather after receiving our jabs for yellow fever. We felt a lot worse after a day in the rain at Crag Bank.

I didn't have to wait long for my Army haircut. I was marched into a bare room where the local barber was waiting, electric clippers in hand. I sat down and he gave me the full treatment. In a matter of seconds, all my hair had gone, apart from one little tuft at the front. My hair has never been the same to this day. I was courting Anne at the time and after six weeks, we were allowed a visit from relatives. Anne came with my father and they couldn't believe what they saw. I had lost half a stone and didn't have a hair on my head, apart from that one little tuft. I had asked them to bring me some cakes and sandwiches and they watched in amazement as I gobbled them all down at one sitting.

However, despite the shouting and bawling from Cathcart and Hargreaves, we survived and eventually found plenty to laugh about. I've always been able to see the funny side of most situations and the Army was no different. What's more, I collected the medal for the best recruit in the intake, awarded for drill, shooting, sport, cleanliness and, I suppose, general attitude. We also had our first game of football and it must have been pretty obvious to the full-time staff that I could play a bit better than the other lads. Within two weeks I was in the regimental team. They hadn't won anything for years but during my time there we won the North West District League two years in a row. The first season, we never lost a match.

I was soon promoted to lance corporal and that's when my officer potential must have surfaced because I was offered a commission, probably because of my three A levels and my years in the Combined Cadet Force at Arnold. I was asked if I would like to go on a course for officers but I said no. The major in charge couldn't get over it. He asked me again later and once more I told him no, I had decided to be a footballer. So instead of joining the officers, I was given the chance to become a Physical Training Instructor. While the rest of the boys went off to the Far East to be based in Kowloon, Hong Kong, I was one of the three or four who were kept back on the permanent staff. I had no complaints about that. I went to Hong Kong later in life and I suspect it looked a lot better from a hotel room than from Kowloon barracks.

I quickly settled into Army life as a trainee PTI and as well as playing for the King's Own, I was chosen for the Western Command team and then the British Army. I also managed enough weekends off to play fairly regularly for Blackpool's reserve team and I was starting to make an impression. The reserves were a good side, I was playing well and the press began to take notice of a local boy making good. But the first team were going downhill. After winning the Cup in 1953, it became clear that some of the great players, including Mortensen and Johnston, were past their peak. It was a difficult time for the club and as Christmas approached, Blackpool were down in the bottom six of the First Division, an unheard of situation.

Christmas Day was on a Saturday in 1954 and I came home on leave expecting to turn out for the reserves on the Monday. We didn't play on Sundays in those days and, in fact, some clubs wouldn't play on Christmas Day or Good Friday for religious reasons. Blackpool wasn't one of them, although later on we had a player called David Durie, a staunch Methodist, who refused to turn out on either day. Blackpool were due to play Portsmouth at Bloomfield Road on Christmas Day morning with the return game at Fratton Park on the Monday. I went to the Christmas match, which finished 2–2, and I was still in bed the next morning when the phone rang downstairs. My father took the call in the shop and hurried upstairs, saying, 'You're wanted on the phone. It's the manager, Joe Smith.'

I ran down the stairs and picked up the phone. Joe said, 'We've got an injury or two. We want you down at Portsmouth. Will you be all right?' Under normal circumstances, the answer would have been an unequivocal yes, but these weren't normal circumstances. This was the Army. I was due back in Lancaster on the Tuesday and I had to work out whether I could make it. Joe said the club would make sure I was back in barracks on time, and so my first team career began. On the Sunday, we travelled from Blackpool to Preston by bus and caught the train to London. We were booked overnight at the Grand Hotel, which despite its name turned out to be an ordinary little place in Holborn. But London was out of reach for people like me and it might just as easily have been Buckingham Palace. When we arrived we had a meal. There were no television sets in the rooms or any of the mod cons people take for granted today and in the evening we just sat around and chatted. I remember feeling very awkward and keeping myself to myself. Stanley Matthews and Morty were injured and didn't travel but the team still included Johnston, Jackie Mudie, Ernie Taylor, Hughie Kelly, George Farm and Bill Perry – great players who were household names throughout the land. They had always been my idols and here I was about to play alongside them, even though they hardly knew me. I was only a retained pro and didn't train regularly with the team because I was away at Army camp. They must have wondered who I was and what the hell was happening to Blackpool when a young lad they had scarcely seen before was suddenly thrust into their midst.

I didn't sleep well that night. In fact, I've never slept well in hotels even though I seem to have spent half my life in them. The next morning we got up, ate breakfast, caught a bus to Waterloo Station and then a train to Portsmouth. We had lunch on the train and when we reached Portsmouth station another bus collected us and took us to the ground. It was on that journey between the station and Fratton Park that I really realised what was happening to me. There seemed to be thousands of people milling around and when we arrived at the ground, the gates had already been closed on the club's biggest gate of the season, 43,896. It was a big match. Blackpool had won the Cup in 1953 and a lot of people went to all their games in the hope of seeing Matthews. The Portsmouth fans were to be disappointed on this occasion, although their team soon helped them get over it. For the record, the teams lined up, in the old 2–3-5 formation:

Portsmouth – Norman Uprichard, Tom McGhee, Jack Mansell, Len Phillips, Doug Reid, Reg Pickett, Peter Harris, John Gordon, Jackie Henderson, Michael Barnard, Gordon Dale.
Blackpool – George Farm, Jimmy Armfield, Roy Gratrix, Jim Kelly, Harry Johnston, Hughie Kelly, Johnny McKenna, Ernie Taylor, Len Stephenson, Jackie Mudie, Bill Perry.

Pompey were a good side, second or third in the table at the time and going for the championship. When we reached the dressing room, I was told I would be playing at right-back. I sat down, started to change and I don't think I said a word before it was time to go into the tunnel. When we ran out on to the field, the noise was incredible, something I had never experienced before. Portsmouth scored after 90 seconds and before I had even touched the ball. Incredibly, the same thing happened when I made my England debut against Brazil at the Maracana Stadium in Rio five years later. I can't believe anyone else has suffered that particular fate – surely not! Things quickly went from bad to worse and we were 3–0 down after about 25 minutes. Portsmouth were strong and very quick with some class players in their line-up and the world seemed to be passing me by. I was marking Dale, a good player, who had joined Portsmouth from Chesterfield. He was a tall, rangy winger, a neat footballer, clever, and almost completely bald. For the first 45 minutes, I couldn't get near him.

Harry Johnston came over to me at half-time and said, 'Look Jim, Dale's been around, he knows what it's all about. Just stick with him, that's all.' That's exactly what I did in the second half. I never left his side. He didn't get a kick and neither did I, but we stemmed the flow and lost 3–0. In fact, we might easily have finished up getting something out of it because we had a couple of chances late on and should have had a penalty as well. I started to get the feel of things as the match went on. I was picking up the pace and learning all the time and I was just starting to enjoy myself when the final whistle sounded and it was time to go home. We piled back on to the bus at around five o'clock, caught the train to Waterloo and went back to the Grand Hotel. Some of the players went out for a drink but I stayed in the hotel. The next morning we caught an early train to Preston and finally the coach to Blackpool. We had left home first thing on the Sunday morning and staggered back on Tuesday afternoon. I felt as if I had been travelling forever. Thank goodness for motorways! The rest of the players had a chance to put their feet up for a couple of days before starting preparations for the next match on Saturday but I was straight on to another train, this time to Lancaster, arriving back in barracks on the evening of Tuesday, 28 December.

The following Saturday, New Year's Day, Blackpool were playing Manchester United at Old Trafford and on the Friday, I received a call from Joe Smith. 'Can you play at Manchester United tomorrow?' Fortunately, we had the day off so I replied 'Yes, no problem,' and off I went again. This time, I caught the train from Lancaster to Preston on Saturday morning, walked to nearby Penwortham Bridge where the team bus collected me en route to Old Trafford. I was wearing my uniform and carrying my boots in an Army bag.

I was more confident this time and I did all right, even though I took a knock early on. We lost 4–1 but in the dressing room afterwards, Joe said, 'You've done well today, very well for a young lad.' Now that really was praise because Joe didn't hand out the plaudits lightly, especially when the team lost. The next day, I went out and bought a couple of national newspapers. I have never been one to look for my name in the papers but this was only my second game after all and I had played well, so why not? I was only 19 and entitled to have a few stars in my eyes. I particularly remember the report in the *News Chronicle*, which read: 'A name to note is Jimmy Armfield, a Manchester-born full-back playing for Blackpool, who made light of a painful injury to be one of his side's best players.' Wow, I thought. That's it, I've arrived. Joe brought me straight back down to earth – I played in the reserves the following week and didn't appear in the first team again all season.

During the early months of 1955 I became fully entrenched in Army life, complete with guard duties at night. I took PT classes for new recruits every day, went down to the NAAFI, and had the occasional trip to the local cinema. We were up at 6.15 every morning, washed and shaved and in the cookhouse for breakfast by seven and on parade in the square at 7.55. That was to be my life for two years. It was impossible to plan for anything outside the Army because you never knew what might happen in some distant corner of the world. The Far East was still a problem area after the Korean War and trouble was brewing in the Middle East so there was constant talk of being sent there or to one of the other trouble spots. It was as uncertain as that.

My immediate priority was to become a fully qualified PTI and I was sent on a course to Oswestry in Shropshire, from where the people who passed moved on to the Army School of Physical Training at Aldershot for another six weeks. Would-be PTIs arrived from regiments all over the country. One of them was Stan Boardman, the Merseyside comedian, and Micky Lill, the Wolves winger of the fifties and sixties, was another. By the end of the summer, I had qualified and was promoted to corporal. When Brian Williams and Sid Halliwell, the two senior corporals at the King's Own, were demobbed, I became the senior corporal, which involved taking soldiers for the PE tests. Gradually, the Army became a way of life.

Unfortunately, there was a rail strike during most of my time at Oswestry, which made life difficult to say the least. Getting there from Blackpool without a car wasn't easy at the best of times, let alone when there was a rail strike. There was only the odd train here and there and, one Sunday night, I caught the 10 o'clock from Blackpool to Crewe, where I was due to change. I climbed aboard the Oswestry train, due to leave at midnight, and promptly fell asleep. When I woke up again at two in the morning, the train hadn't moved. We eventually made it to Oswestry at five o'clock and I was on parade for a full day's PE an hour later. I slept well that night.

Obviously, it was worth exploring alternative methods of transport. Dave Bowers had an old motorbike a bit down on its luck, a BSA 350 with a green tank. Dave was also in the King's Own Regiment and was on the course with me so he said he would take me home, riding pillion, for the weekend. Saturday lunchtime, we set off up the A483 to Chester and then on through the Wirral to Birkenhead, through the Mersey tunnel and up the A6 to Preston, where I caught the train home – so far, so good. On the Sunday night, Dave picked me up in Preston and we started to retrace our steps on the return journey. Halfway through the Mersey tunnel, the chain came off. Because of the rail strike, the tunnel was busier than usual and, as our two heroes battled to replace the chain, a massive traffic jam built up. We were on the inside lane and it took us a quarter of an hour to get the chain back on. All the time, cars were trying to manoeuvre around us, horns were blaring, curses were flowing and not a soul came to help us. We couldn't work out what had happened to the police. Wasn't it their job to help motorists in distress and keep the traffic flowing?

Sure enough, as we emerged from the tunnel covered in oil, the long arm of the law was waiting for us. A burly Merseyside police officer imperiously waved us to the side of the road and announced to the world at large, 'Well, who have we here? General Montgomery and Field Marshal Harding? What the 'ell have you been doing in there?' We shamefacedly told him about the chain and how we were due back in camp at Oswestry that night. He was super. He gave us a police escort all the way through Birkenhead where he came to a halt and waved us back on to the main road to Chester and our ultimate destination. We made it back in time.

Fortunately, the train strike was over by the time I started at Aldershot because that was quite a journey in those days. It didn't help that I was loaded down with my full kit. Wherever a soldier went, his kit went with him. There was no question of leaving anything in a locker until you returned, so on the journey to Aldershot, I had full service marching order of small and large pack, pouches and kitbag plus my sports gear and a bag containing my personal belongings. I had to cart this lot all the way there and then cart it all the way back at the end of the course, which just happened to be a hot day at the height of summer. The prospect of a train from Aldershot to Waterloo, tube across London to Euston, another train to Preston and finally the connection to Blackpool, complete with all my gear, didn't exactly appeal.

The tube was absolutely packed, standing room only, and I was boiling over. My kit bag felt as if it weighed a ton so I lifted it off my shoulder – and dropped it on to my neighbour's foot. He was a big man, who looked angry, and I was just about to say sorry when he started sounding off about 'you toy soldiers today' and all that kind of stuff. The situation might easily have turned nasty if a US Army sergeant hadn't decided to advance the cause of Anglo-American relations by springing to my aid. He fixed my antagonist with a no-nonsense stare and said, 'This guy is protecting you, pal, and if you want to make something of it, take it out on me.' Peace was restored forthwith. When we emerged from the tube at Euston, the sergeant and I, discovering we both had time to spare before our trains north were due to leave, had a drink in the bar. His name was Marriott and I often wonder if he founded the famous hotel chain.

After leaving Aldershot, I took a week's leave for pre-season training with Blackpool, and I had played the first few games of the season for the reserves when, in September 1955, my football career took a significant step forward. Eddie Shimwell, Blackpool's regular right-back and one of the few players to have appeared in all three Wembley finals, broke his shoulder. Joe Smith sent for me once more, this time for the game against Manchester City, another massive match played in front of a crowd of more than 60,000.

I'd been to Maine Road many times as a spectator, standing on the Kippax with my cousin Alan, who was a lifelong City fan. There were only 10 months between us and we were as close as cousins could be. He was a fantastic artist and should have been a cartoonist on a newspaper but instead he became a draughtsman. He missed his way, really. He died from Hodgkin's disease in Christie's Hospital, Manchester, at the age of 41. I was manager of Leeds at the time and in the weeks before his death, I was dashing across to see him as often as I could.

People sometimes say that one way to ensure a big funeral is to die young but it didn't happen with our Alan. There were only four of us there, his mother, his auntie, his best friend and me. He married in his twenties and had a little girl. After he was taken ill, his father-in-law won the pools and his wife left, taking their daughter with her. I haven't seen either of them to this day. It's very sad.

I've often wondered whom Alan was rooting for whenever I played against City – he would always have wanted to cheer on his cousin but I suspect that his beloved City would have won the day.

When I made that first appearance at Maine Road, they were one of the top teams and went on to win the FA Cup, having lost to Newcastle in the 1955 final. They had developed the Revie Plan, a system that involved the use of a deep-lying centre-forward, Don Revie. Don was to play a significant part in my career nearly 20 years down the line. City beat us 2–0 and at the end of the match, Revie made a point of coming over, shaking me by the hand and saying well played, young man. He said it in a very sincere way, not just a quick word at the end of an easy victory. I was impressed and I remember telling my dad afterwards.

Joe Smith must have agreed with Revie because from then on, I became a first-team regular even though I was still in the Army. I travelled home and back at weekends and the club would call on Thursday or Friday to make sure I was available. It was a wonderful time. Players today talk about having to take part in too many matches – they should try my schedule in the Army. I thought nothing of playing for Blackpool on Saturday, for the

Regiment or Western Command on Tuesday and the Army on Thursday. In between, I would be running all over the place, refereeing matches at the camp. Too much football? I couldn't get enough – and I didn't need to train.

All the time I was driving myself on. I had no choice because there was no one else to push me. I met up with the team on a Saturday, played the match and went back to camp the next day. Everyone assumed I would be able to take time off each weekend but it was never easy. Once I was on guard duty all Friday night and still played on the Saturday. I was on duty until eight in the morning, went back to the barracks, collected my boots and caught the bus to Blackpool at the bottom of the road. I arrived at 11.30, walked home and had a lie-down for an hour. Then I had a bite to eat, walked down to the ground and played for 90 minutes. Needless to say, I never told a soul.

When it came to evening matches, I had to enlist the help of my Quartermaster Staff Instructor, Sergeant Major Jimmy Lockwood, a Scouser, football fan and a great chap. He'd been awarded the MBE as well as a military decoration for his work on troopships during the war, helping injured servicemen with their rehabilitation programmes. He was on the North Atlantic convoys, one of the toughest theatres of war. It was a subject he rarely talked about but he used to have a laugh with us about his MBE. He was a little fellow, completely bald, and he would stand face to face and say, 'Now lad, you may think I'm an ugly little bugger, but just remember, the King has looked at me!'

Jimmy helped me a lot and always followed my career. He came to watch me once or twice with our Company Sergeant Major, Joe Heath. Obviously, it paid to stay on the right side of those two because they signed the passes out. Three of the officers, Majors Evans and Roberts and Captain Hill, took an interest in my football, too, because it was a feather in the regiment's cap to have a player in the British Army team. I think I was the first. If I left camp at around 3.45 in the afternoon, I could be in Blackpool for an evening kick-off. In the days before floodlights, those games were played at the beginning or the end of the season, usually with a 6.30 p.m. start. If it was an away game at somewhere such as Arsenal or Newcastle, I had to plan in advance and try to get a couple of days' leave.

Once or twice I had to thumb a lift home from Lancaster because I didn't have enough for my bus fare. Imagine that! Hitching a lift home while playing for one of the best teams in the land. My travel expenses were £1, which I used to collect from Joe Smith after the game. Once, I couldn't find Joe anywhere so I approached Johnny Lynas, who was Joe's right-hand man, our trainer, physio and kit man. 'What does he give you?' asked Johnny. I told him it was a pound, so he gave me a £1 note. As luck would have it, I emerged from the players' entrance to find Joe standing outside the ground with some of his pals. He spotted me and said to his mates, 'Here he is, our right-back,' and he dug into his back pocket, producing a huge wad of notes rolled up in an elastic band. He licked his thumb and peeled off a pound note, which he handed over. 'Thanks very much,' I said and went on my way.

The following week, we were playing away from home and I met the bus as usual on Penwortham Bridge in Preston. Joe had not seen me for a week but his greeting was brief and to the point.

'You owe me a quid.'

'Why?'

'I gave you a pound last week and so did Johnny Lynas.'

'I thought you might be doubling up because you know I'm struggling a bit.'

'Well, you won't need one this week, I'm telling you.'

That caused a bit of a problem as I was banking on that pound to get me back to Lancaster. So after the match, I went over and said to him, 'Look, I can't get back to camp without that pound. The bus fare is four shillings and I haven't got it.'

With a smile on his face, he replied, 'Well, you keep telling me how much running you do in the week. You can bloody well run back to camp.'

'But I need the money to get back to camp,' I insisted. So he delved into his pocket, brought out that wad and reluctantly gave me a ten bob note.

'You tight beggar,' I thought but I didn't say it.

People were starting to take notice of me. Henry Rose of the *Daily Express*, who was the doyen of the press corps, used to compile a Top 20 of young English players destined for stardom and I appeared on his list. That meant a lot even though I'd played for Young England, the Football League and, of course, I'd represented the Army. What a side that was! Alan Hodgkinson of Sheffield United, a future England international, was in goal and the squad featured six more players who went on to win England caps – Alan's Sheffield United colleague Graham Shaw, Trevor Smith of Birmingham, Stan Anderson of Sunderland, me and two members of Manchester United's legendary Busby Babes, Bill Foulkes and Duncan Edwards. Eddie Colman, another of the Babes, was there, too, along with Maurice Setters of West Brom and Dave Dunmore of Spurs. We could compete with the best and we all became good mates. We played against all sorts of sides including Northern Ireland – yes, the full team – at Preston, beating them 4–3. We also played the Scottish League XI and top professional sides, including Rangers and Everton. We took part in the Kentish Cup, an annual competition between the army teams from the UK, France and Belgium, and earned the dubious distinction of failing to record a single win – despite having so many talented players in the side. In fairness, France had a few decent players, too, fielding six B internationals and three men who would go on to win full caps, including Rene Bliard and the great Just Fontaine, one of the stars of the 1958 World Cup in Sweden. So perhaps our 2–1 defeat by the French at Dulwich Hamlet's ground wasn't such a bad result. During the competition we were billeted at Woolwich Barracks and there was no preferential treatment for the footballers. If you wanted breakfast, you had to be in the canteen by 8 a.m. – because that's when the chef pulled down the shutters.

There was also a tour to Germany where we entertained the troops with games against Werder Bremen, Munster and Hanover, and we played Eintracht Frankfurt on the night they switched on their floodlights. Just before a game at East Fife, Alan, Duncan, Graham and I learned we had been selected for Young England.

They were marvellous times and friendships were forged that were destined to last for years.

Tragically, when the plane carrying the Manchester United squad home from a European Cup quarter-final in Belgrade crashed on the runway at Munich on 6 February 1958, eight players, three officials and eight newspapermen were killed, including my one-time Army team-mates Eddie Colman and Duncan Edwards. Twenty-three people died in all. Eddie was a typical Salford lad, a real barrel of laughs. He came from near Cross Lane, just behind the old Hippodrome. I knew it well. He was always the life and soul of the party, the one who stood up at the front of the team bus and belted out one of the big hits of the day to a chorus of boos and jeers from his team-mates. You couldn't help but like Eddie and enjoy his company. He was a great wing-half, too, and would surely have gone on to play for England many times. He was a push and run player, quick, nimble and skilful and the perfect foil for Edwards in what we would now call the midfield. He was just 21 when he died. So was Duncan, yet he had already been capped 18 times by England and appeared in over 150 matches for United at home and in Europe.

As a 19-year-old, Duncan played for England against West Germany in Berlin and destroyed the 1954 world champions. England won 3–1 and afterwards the German players said they had never encountered a player like Edwards. I know exactly what they meant. I have never seen his like before or since. Over the last 50 years, I have been privileged to watch or play against most of the world's great footballers but I have never seen another player quite like Big Dunc, as we called him. It's hard to imagine the impact such a young player could have on a game. He was big, mobile and powerful and he never tired. Despite his size, he was skilful, he could use either foot, he could pass the ball short or long, he was good in the air, had a tremendous shot and he was a fearsome tackler. Above all, he was a tremendous competitor. He had the lot – and I would go so far as to say that if Duncan, Eddie, Roger Byrne and Tommy Taylor had not died at Munich in 1958, England would have won the World Cup in Sweden later that year. I honestly believe that. Duncan would have been the inspiration and the mainstay of the England team right through to the World Cup in 1966.

We didn't have a great deal in common from our backgrounds but we got on well from the first time we met, playing for the Army. We became firm friends and usually sat together on Army away trips and also with Young England. He never liked flying. I occasionally sat with him and he would be nervous and tense until we got back on terra firma. One of my most vivid memories of Big Dunc is from our Army days. He was in the Royal Army Ordnance Corps, stationed at Nesscliffe near Shrewsbury, where the Western Command team were to assemble for a match. I travelled down by train and when I arrived, Dunc was the only other player there. He said, 'I've got a ball here, let's go out and have a kick-around.' It was a dry day and we decided to wear our pumps rather than boots but as I was fastening mine, the lace broke. Duncan said he would go out on his own until I found another lace, which wasn't easy in the Army. In fact, in the end, I had to improvise with a piece of string.

Halfway through my search for a substitute lace, I happened to look out of the army hut where we were based and saw Duncan out on the pitch. He was playing with the ball on his own and until that moment I never realised how skilful he was. He could do all the tricks – bouncing it on the floor with the sole of his foot, catching it on the back of his neck, backheeling it over his head, running across the field with the ball balanced on his head, flicking it from shoulder to shoulder. I stood and watched him, transfixed.

I saw the other side of Duncan in a game between Young England and Czechoslovakia in Bratislava. Czech football was pretty strong at the time and on paper, it was going to be a tough game – then they encountered Big Dunc. We won 2–0 and he scored both goals. The Czechs wouldn't tackle him. They just kept backing off. He intimidated them. He was never a dirty player, just massively powerful, and throughout his brief career, there were seasoned professionals and internationals who were afraid to stand up to him. Yet he was only a teenager. When I used to play against United, I always used to have a laugh and tell him, 'You'll not frighten me, Edwards!' But I still knew when he was coming!

Manchester United tried to buy me in 1957, although the first I knew about a possible transfer was when Joe Smith called me into his office and, in his usual put-down style, said, 'I always thought Matt Busby was a good judge of a player.'

I had no idea what he meant so I replied, 'Well, he isn't doing too badly at United, is he?'

'Maybe not. But he must be losing his marbles because he wants to buy you.'

I was stunned. The Busby Babes were league champions and seemingly destined to become one of the greatest club sides in history. This was a chance to become part of the legend. I mumbled something like, 'Oh, does he?'

'But I know all about you and Edwards,' was Joe's riposte. I didn't understand what he meant because as well as Duncan, there was another influential Edwards at Old Trafford in the shape of Louis, later to become club chairman. He and Matt Busby were big pals. I must have looked suitably puzzled because Joe went on, 'So you can tell that pal of yours, Duncan Edwards, that if wants to tap anybody about playing for United, he can come and tap me. Now bugger off!' End of story.

Had I joined United, of course, there's a chance I would have been on the plane home from Munich, sitting next to Duncan. Instead, I heard about the disaster after training on a cold, wet day in Blackpool. The local café had an old Rediffusion radio and we gathered round to hear the lunchtime news. I couldn't take it in. I remember trudging home, feeling numb as I thought about the tragedy and the friends I had lost. It took me a while to get over it.

I was due to be demobbed on 16 September 1956, five days before my 21st birthday. I don't know if my impending departure had anything to do with it, but that was the time Colonel Nasser of Egypt decided to close the Suez Canal, sparking an international crisis. I feared the worst. Just five days from freedom, it looked as if I would have to stay on and, who knows, be shipped out to the Middle East. It was not an attractive proposition. Thankfully, the authorities decided the Suez crisis could be resolved without me and I was allowed to leave. It was the best possible news. There was just one proviso. I was told that if the crisis escalated, I would be called up and would have to report to Garstang bus station. For anyone unfamiliar with the little town of Garstang, near Preston, I should explain that if war had been declared and all the reservists from the King's Own Infantry Regiment had descended on its bus station, absolute bedlam would have ensued. Even now, I can't help smiling at that 'Dad's Army' scenario whenever I drive through Garstang.

So I handed in all my gear and walked away from Army life. I was pleased to be out, of course, but as I walked down the hill to catch the train home from Lancaster, I had one last look back at the old place. On balance, I decided the Army had been good for me. It taught me discipline and self-sufficiency, humility and respect, and I emerged from the experience a better person. It was the first time I had been away from home and I learned to stand on my own two feet. It introduced me to another world and to people I would almost certainly never have met without National Service. In fact, the Army had turned around my life. I went in as a potential university student and left as a member of a Blackpool team with realistic championship ambitions, and with an England Under-23 call-up to my name. But I still had to make the final decision about my future.

I told my father that as I had come this far, I wanted to continue for another couple of years to see what I could make of it. He must have been disappointed in some ways. For someone from our background to gain a place at Liverpool University or Loughborough College of Physical Education would have been a really big thing. There were far fewer universities in those days and it was more difficult to be offered a place, but he continued to insist it was my decision and my life. He was never the kind of parent to go around boasting that 'Our Jim plays for Blackpool'. He reminded me about all the pitfalls of being a footballer, the risk of serious injury and the number of top-class players around who might prevent me from holding down a regular place, but all the while he must have known what my decision was going to be. I signed a professional contract and moved on once again.

LOCAL BOY MAKES GOOD

I seem to have become a better player as I've grown older. When I retired in 1970, I was described in the *Blackpool Evening Gazette* as Jimmy Armfield, the Seasiders' former England full-back and captain. Ten years later, I had become Armfield, the ex-England World Cup star, and in the nineties I achieved Soccer Legend status. There's not a lot left now, I suppose, except the late, great Jim Armfield! Back in 1956, however, I was Armfield, the promising full-back, the local boy trying to make good.

I left Army life behind, forsook the opportunity of a university degree and entered the world of professional sport – and a lifestyle that shared only a passing similarity to the superstar status enjoyed by Premiership footballers today. There was virtually no football on the television so newspapers, magazines and radio were the only source of information for the fans. There was a mystique surrounding the players because while many of them were household names, they were not instantly recognisable to supporters outside their home towns. The television cameras and newspaper photographers were not around to put their lives, on and off the field, under the most intense scrutiny. When Blackpool went to play in another town, it was their fans' once-a-year day and we would be judged on what those people saw with their own eyes – not by pundits in a television studio with the aid of slow-motion replays. That applied as much to Matthews, Mudie and Perry as it did to a young player such as myself.

Footballers were still in touch with the people, very much part of the community. After matches, Joe Smith sometimes used to say to us, 'Right, go outside and face the herd.' He wasn't being uncomplimentary to the world outside football; he was bringing us down to earth by telling us we were no different from anybody else, that each of us was one of the herd, too. We couldn't avoid the general public, nor did we seek to. Today, it's virtually impossible for kids to get Premiership autographs at training or after games. The players' entrance is closed off, the cars sweep up and the stars are ushered inside. Afterwards, they are driven away, often with their agents in close attendance. We were part of the real world.

The maximum wage was £16 a week, although the reserves and younger players received less, with a £4 bonus for a win and £2 for a draw. It doesn't sound a lot – but to put it into perspective, a gallon of petrol cost the equivalent of 22½p, a pint of beer less than 5p and the average house price was £2,280. Our wages were paid into the National Provincial Bank in Talbot Square every Friday and, after training, we would get on to the tram at Bloomfield Road and set off for the town centre. There would always be a few punters around when we arrived in Talbot Square, waiting to see the Blackpool players collect their money. It was quite an event in the town. Inside the bank we were each handed a little pay slip, about six inches long and two inches wide, which told us our earnings after tax. Rock 'n' roll had arrived from the USA and taken the world of popular music by storm. Elvis Presley had his first UK hits in 1956 but there was still room at the top of the charts for those who were perceived to be more mainstream performers – Doris Day, Guy Mitchell, Anne Shelton, Johnnie Ray and Frankie Laine. My own preference was for the big band sound of Ted Heath and his contemporaries.

The teamsheet was pinned up on a cupboard in the dressing room. We didn't have a noticeboard. Each week, a member of staff would walk into the dressing room, pin up the team and beat a retreat as we gathered around to see who would be playing.

There was no such thing as a squad. You were either in the starting 11 or not. There were no subs, just a 12th man in case anyone dropped out on the morning of the match. There were no floodlights so Cup replays had to be played on a Wednesday afternoon and evening games could be played in August, early September or April only. There was no perimeter advertising around the pitch or on the players' shirts and replica shirts were unheard of, as were away strips. If our tangerine shirts clashed with the opposition's at an away match, we wore white instead. If there was no clash, there was no change. We had numbers on our shirts but no names, and the referee and his linesmen always wore black. There were no red and yellow cards; the referee carried a little notebook in which he wrote the names of any offenders – hence the term 'booked'.

In my early days we played with a heavy leather ball, complete with a bladder inside, which was inflated with a bicycle pump. The hole into which the pump fitted was laced up afterwards and you could feel it if you headed the lace. Our standing joke was that Matthews, ever the perfectionist, always crossed the ball with the lace pointing towards goal to make sure his team-mates didn't hurt their foreheads. We didn't have undersoil heating and three-quarters of the accommodation at just about every stadium we played in was standing room only, usually uncovered. When I first started, admission to the Kop was two shillings, that's 10p in today's money, and seats in the stand were the equivalent of 25p.

Very few players had cars. Our skipper, Hughie Kelly, had one. Goalkeeper George Farm had a van because he combined his duties as Blackpool and Scotland goalkeeper with running a greengrocer's business. Of course, Stan Matthews had a car. They were the only ones at first but gradually other players acquired a car as their savings permitted. I used to go to the ground on my bike. I bought it second hand from a shop in King Street for thirty bob (£1.50). I parked it under the main stand and rode home again after training.

On matchdays, I generally walked to the ground along with the rest of the crowd. A friend used to meet me at the shop and we would walk to the match together. The fans would chat to me along the way and wish me well. When we reached Bloomfield Road, I would go through the players' entrance and my friend would go into the paddock. We would meet outside the main entrance afterwards for the walk back home. A few of the locals would be waiting in the shop and if we had lost, my mother would call out as soon as I walked through the door to tell me my tea was ready. There were no motorways so we often travelled to away games on the train, mingling with other travellers and the eager autograph hunters.

I had a strict pre-match ritual. Throughout my career I followed the club rulebook which stated: 'A player should not go into the saloon after Wednesday.' I used to rest on a Friday afternoon, although I didn't go to bed too early because I wouldn't sleep. I always had a lie-in on Saturday morning and when we were playing at home I would eat something like steak and egg with toast at around 11 o'clock. Then I would sit down for an hour or so and read the paper before walking to the ground. We had to be in the dressing room by 2.15. When we played away from home, we all had a pre-match meal together, either in the team hotel if we had stayed overnight or at a hotel on the way to the ground if we were playing locally. Sometimes we had a pre-match meal together before a home cup tie, too, and I once asked, if it was such a good idea for cup matches, why didn't we have a meal before every home game? I suspected cash came into it because the Blackpool directors certainly knew how to count the pennies. I never received a satisfactory answer and was accused of trying to complicate matters.

I was always inquisitive and I could see the folly of some of the things others took for granted, such as training in pumps, or gym shoes as some people called them. I pointed out that as we played in boots on matchdays, we should be training in them as well. The reply was that boots were too expensive. I persisted, saying that pumps wore out far quicker than boots did, so it was false economy. But no, we trained in pumps.

In fact, in my first six years as a professional, we didn't have our own training kit. The first in was the best dressed. We would arrive to find a pile of old shirts, shorts and socks on the dressing room table and it was every man for himself. We each found a strip that more or less fitted and out we went to train. If you look at old pictures of teams training in the fifties, you'll see the players will be wearing shorts, shirts, an ordinary pullover and pumps on their feet. That was the standard gear; tracksuits became commonplace only gradually.

We didn't have a training ground. We would train either at the club or on the beach. If we had played on the Saturday, Monday was a fairly light day but they really used to run the socks off us on Tuesday, either on the track around the pitch or in the sand dunes alongside the road to St Annes. Hard work! And for good measure, they would throw in a bit of weight training or agility work. We usually had a practice match on a Wednesday unless it was FA Cup week when we would go for a long walk on the promenade instead. Occasionally, we had a game of golf although not many of us were golfers because few could afford the membership fees or a set of clubs. On Thursday we would train specifically for the forthcoming match and on Friday there was just a brief work-out – a few exercises followed by sprints in running spikes.

As you will have gathered, there wasn't a lot of ball practice and sometimes on a Friday we would ask Johnny Lynas, our trainer, for a ball to kick around but Joe Smith didn't approve. 'You'll have plenty of chances for that tomorrow afternoon,' he would say. I used to go back at least one afternoon a week and do some ballwork, either in the mini gym under the south stand or on the car park. Alternatively, a few of us would get together for a game of head tennis. After one of my solo stints, running up and down the terracing on the Kop, I was on my way back to the dressing room when I noticed that an electric wire had caught fire at the back of the old wooden main stand and the flames were beginning to take hold. There didn't seem to be anyone around so I dashed under the stand to where Harry Cummings, the groundsman, kept a pile of sand that was used to soak up water in the goalmouths after heavy rain. I grabbed a shovel and threw a load of sand on to the flames, without too much success at first. So I hastily collected another shovelful and this time succeeded in putting out the embryo blaze that I suppose might eventually have engulfed the stand. I finally found Harry and explained what had happened, expecting fulsome praise for my fire-fighting heroics, but his only response was, 'Don't tell the chairman.'

Our boots cost around £5 a pair. We bought our own but were given an allowance of £3 by the club. Stan Mortensen had a sports shop in the town so we used to go there with our £3 chit and Morty always knocked a bit off the price of a new pair. I cleaned my own boots even though that was usually the apprentices' job – I liked to be in charge of my own kit. Boots were made of leather with a hard toe cap and I checked mine rigorously every Friday to make sure there were no cracks in the leather and, more important, none of the nails that held the studs in place were about to penetrate through the sole. If the ground was a bit firm, there was always a danger that a nail might come through and I always wore an inner sole as extra protection. The studs could twist as well, so I made sure they were nailed in securely. Some players used dubbin to keep their boots soft but I preferred polish. Eddie Shimwell had a novel way of breaking in his new boots – sitting in the bath. As boots tended to stretch a bit with wear, Eddie would buy some that were slightly tight and give them a good soaking to stretch the leather.

Our centre-half, Roy Gratrix, caused something of a sensation on a tour to Germany when he bought a pair of adidas football 'shoes', the forerunner of the boot we know today. They were as light as a feather, with rubber studs, and looked like a pair of carpet slippers compared with the old leather clodhoppers. Roy was very quick and reckoned he would be even faster with his lightweight boots. I couldn't wait for Joe Smith's reaction. Sure enough, our manager was not impressed.

'What the hell are those?' he asked. 'Where's your ankle protection?'

'I won't need any. No one will be able to catch me in these.'

'They're slippers. You won't be able to kick the ball. You're not playing in them.'

But Roy did – and before long, so did everyone else. Stan Matthews was one step ahead of the game, as usual, fixing up a sponsorship deal with the Co-op for his boots, which were the lightest of the lot. He didn't bother to break them in. He would just arrive with a pair of new boots, put them on, lace them up and go out and play. And no one ever suggested Stan had trouble kicking the ball properly.

Just like the old leather boots, our shinpads were museum pieces, too. They were huge and really cumbersome. I always felt awkward wearing them and in the end, I gave up.

Our dressing room was quite small and there was a massage table in the middle of the room if any of the players wanted a rubdown. I did my exercises and pre-match warm-up in there – there was no suggestion of half an hour's work-out on the pitch in those days – and I fell foul of the authorities again when I asked for a proper warm-up area. This time the answer was that Matthews had done OK with just a dressing room to warm up in, so why couldn't I?

There was a little hut at the side of the ground owned by a lady called Margaret and every day after training we would all pile in there for a cup of tea. There was nothing on offer at the club. On matchdays, there was a crate of lemonade under the benches and we could help ourselves to a bottle after the game. They provided a cup of tea as well but nothing for the wives and families, and there was nowhere for them to go, no players' lounge. If your wife wanted to wait for you, she had to stand outside the players' entrance with the autograph hunters. We didn't have a proper tea room for families until the late sixties.

Seating at the stadium was limited and invariably the five or six thousand seats sold out well in advance. Each married player was allowed two complimentary seats and the single lads had two complimentary tickets to stand in the paddock. I remember a game when one or two members of my family were coming to watch and I went to Joe Smith and asked for an extra seat.

'No,' he replied. 'If your own family won't pay to see you, who will?'

As soon as players got married they were expected to live in a club house at a rent of £1 a week. The club owned various properties around the town, many of them on the South Shore, which became known as the Barracks. Anne and I were married in June 1958, and I was given a house at the end of a terrace of four in Rosedale Avenue. The front door opened on to the lounge, with a staircase straight ahead. Through the back of the lounge were the kitchen and bathroom. Upstairs there was one decent-sized bedroom and one little one. That was it. When I went for a reconnaissance, the grass on the small lawn at the front of the house was about a foot high. The neighbours came out to greet me and one of them asked in a disapproving tone, 'Are you a footballer, then?'

'Yes.'

'Well I hope you're not going to be like all the rest and throw your empty beer bottles on to the grass.'

Sure enough, when we moved in, I inspected the grass and by the time my search was complete, I had collected two boxes full of beer bottles.

By this time, I was the proud owner of a black Morris Minor saloon, registration KFR 619, and I decided my first car deserved a comfortable home. There was a small area to one side of the house that belonged to the property and Anne's Uncle Teddy and I erected a garage there. We laid down the rough cast, constructed a drive and gate posts and Teddy made the gates himself. I set off to Manchester and paid £50 for a Kencast pre-fabricated garage.

The next time I went for my pay chit, there was a deduction of one pound ten shillings for rent. I went straight back to the club and asked Fred Jones, the secretary, why my rent had gone up by ten shillings.

'Well, you've got a garage now, that's ten bob extra,' he replied.

'But I built that garage myself.'

'Nobody asked you to.'

'Maybe not, but the garage has increased the value of your property.'

'So what are young going to do then? Knock it down or pay the extra rent?'

I paid up because in those days we were expected to know our place and keep our mouths shut. I can't see the Beckhams putting up with that kind of thing today!

My eldest son Duncan was born on 24 November 1961, a Friday afternoon, and John on Saturday 23 March 1963. I wasn't present on either occasion. When John was born, Anne went into hospital on a Friday morning at around the time the Blackpool coach was setting off for a game at West Brom the following day. These days, a player would expect to be allowed to stay behind to attend the birth and then rejoin the squad but that simply wasn't an option in my playing days. As far as the club was concerned, football came first. I learned that John had been born before the kick-off. We won 2–1 and it was champagne all the way when we broke the journey home for a meal at the Crown Hotel in Stone. But it was left to me to fork out for the bubbly, even though the directors were on the coach, too.

I was a Blackpool and England footballer at the time but the boys grew up in an ordinary family environment. There was no superstar status for footballers in those days. Anne worked full-time as a nurse and, fortunately, her mother was able to look after the boys sometimes. Later on, my father would pick them up from school if Anne or I couldn't be there. They used to come and watch me play when they were young, although Duncan was sometimes a bit reluctant because he was apprehensive about us losing.

Between 1959 and 1966, apart from the year of my groin injury, I was on tour with England for at least part of each summer but we always managed a family holiday. One of our first holidays abroad came courtesy of Fred Pontin, who began his business career by setting up holiday camps around the UK. He was a friend of Stan Mortensen through their work with the Variety Club of Great Britain, and Morty's appointment as manager of Blackpool in 1967 coincided with the opening of Fred's first hotel abroad, in Cala Mesquida on the north-east coast of Majorca. Fred asked Stan if the Blackpool players could fly out for a week's holiday. The idea was we would play a friendly match against an island side and then have a few days' relaxation. The following year he opened another new hotel, the Pontinental near Torremolinos on the Costa del Sol and arranged for a few of the players to go out with their families. We did what would now be called a bit of PR work but basically it was an opportunity to join the growing foreign holiday bonanza.

This went on for a few years and as time went by, players from other clubs came along, too, including Lawrie McMenemy and John Bond, who became good friends. Fred was a very generous man and his offer of a family holiday abroad was a terrific opportunity because we weren't flush with money. Ironically, Fred, who later became Sir Fred, moved to Blackpool for the last few years of his life. We were always grateful to him.

There was plenty of spare time in the afternoons and many of the players had sidelines, either as a way of boosting their income or as preparation for retirement. In 1959, when I was 24, I decided the time had come for me to start looking at an alternative as well. I had always been interested in journalism so I contacted Cliff Greenwood, the sports editor of the *Blackpool Evening Gazette*. He invited me into the office for a look around and the outcome was a regular three afternoons a week on the sports desk from 1959 to 1971. I wrote a column, learned about reporting and sub-editing, watched local games and so on. It was a bit of extra income but, more important, it was an insurance against the day when I would no longer be able to play football. I bought myself a second-hand typewriter for £2 from a shop in Caunce Street and started to learn shorthand. My teacher was a lady who lived locally but the lessons had to be halted abruptly when she became pregnant – although I hasten to add I had nothing to do with that! I never took it up again, which was a mistake.

Blackpool's tangerine shirts were famous everywhere and we had some great needle matches with our Lancashire rivals – Preston, Blackburn, Bolton, Burnley, Manchester United, Manchester City and Everton. Liverpool were still in the old Second Division. One of those games, against Preston at Bloomfield Road, provided one of the low points of my career. It was pouring with rain and we found ourselves two down after about 10 minutes. Then George Farm chipped a bone in his arm and obviously couldn't continue. Nobody volunteered to replace him in goal and after a while I was aware that all the rest of the players were looking at me. I thought, 'Hang on a minute', but I was nominated to 'don the green jersey', as the reporters used to say in those days.

Unlike some stand-in keepers, my first touch of the ball did not involve collecting it from the back of the net. Far from it – I pulled off a pretty good save and I was just starting to think there was nothing to this goalkeeping lark when I found myself in a one-to-one with Tom Finney. If any keeper, let alone a stand-in, had to choose one player to avoid in that situation, it would have been Tom. I went out to meet him in an effort to reduce his options, assuming he would try to go round me before slipping the ball home. No chance! He just lashed it and the ball flew past me like a bullet. I turned round to survey the wreckage and I have an abiding memory of the ball hitting the net and sending a huge shower of raindrops down on to the pitch. My spirits fell with those raindrops and I finished up letting in four. That game signalled the end of my goalkeeping career. Tom and I still have a laugh about it. To round off a bizarre afternoon, Farm returned to the fray late on with his arm in a sling and headed one of Blackpool's two goals.

A similar thing happened to me once when I suffered a nasty gash on the top of my head, had six stitches inserted into the wound at half-time and then went out and played a full second-half. I still carry the scar. On another occasion, we had to hold Farm down while the doctor put half a dozen stitches into the palm of his hand at half time.

George was one of the established players in a Blackpool team that had lost senior players from the 1953 side. Johnston, Shimwell and Mortensen had gone. Centre-half Roy Gratrix, wing-half Jimmy Kelly, inside-forward David Durie and I were the new boys, freshening up a team that also featured full-back Tommy Garrett, wing-half Hughie Kelly, who took over from Johnston as captain, Ernie Taylor at inside-right, Jackie Mudie at centre-forward and Bill Perry on the left-wing. And, of course, we still had Matthews. The side included seven full internationals – Farm, Garrett, Hughie Kelly, Matthews, Taylor, Mudie and

Perry. Gratrix was an England B international and I had played for the Under-23 side. Not a bad line-up! We had two full internationals in the reserves as well – Johnny McKenna and George McKnight. Joe Smith's reshaped team had finished runners-up to Manchester United at the end of the 1955–56 season, while I was still in the Army. We were going really well right up to Easter but then picked up two or three injuries at the wrong time – I was one of them. We lost 2–1 at Old Trafford in what looked like a title decider and had to settle for second place, the highest finish in Blackpool's history.

Our reward, called talent money, was the princely sum of £880 between us. If you played in every single match, you were entitled to one eleventh of the kitty, £80. If you'd missed two or three it went down proportionately. I had played in 30 matches out of the 42, so I collected about £60. That was the only bonus for finishing runners-up. European football was in its infancy. The champions qualified for the European Cup and there was no Cup-Winners' Cup or Fairs Cup – not like today when a side can finish halfway in the Premiership and still qualify for Europe through the InterToto Cup.

After finishing second, many people believed we would go one better in the near future. It was claimed that this was the best team ever to represent the club, although I'm not convinced about that. But it was a good side and I always felt we were in with a chance against any other team in the land. I also felt that as a regular member of the side, I was entitled to a bit more money. Sandy Harris, a young right-winger who understudied Matthews and Northern Ireland international Johnny McKenna, felt the same, and after playing our part in a comfortable home win over Newcastle, we decided to do something about it. Matthews and McKenna were away on international duty, so Sandy had come into the side and scored a couple of goals. I played pretty well, too, and we decided to go to see the manager.

It took us a couple of days to pluck up courage and, after a bit of haggling, Sandy agreed to go in first. There were two doors to Joe's office – an outer one that opened on to a little waiting room and a second door leading to the inner sanctum, where the Great

Man sat behind his desk. With me listening in from the waiting area, Sandy told Joe that he thought he'd played well and deserved a bit more money. Joe responded, 'Where was Matthews on Saturday?'

'Playing for England, Boss.'

'And where was McKenna?'

'Playing for Northern Ireland, Boss.'

'And where would you have been if they had both been available?'

'In the third team, Boss.'

'Right. Well, Matthews and McKenna will be back on Saturday and you'll be back in the third team. And I reckon the money you earn is good enough for a third-team player, don't you? Now bugger off!' Then he spotted me lurking in the outer office and said to Sandy, 'If he's after the same you know what to tell him!' And that was it. The whole episode was over in 90 seconds and I was never even granted an audience. We left with our tails between our legs.

Apart from injuries or international calls, Joe rarely changed the team, so once I was established as a regular, I could confidently expect to play week in and week out. The same applied to all the other players. For me, though, there was one exception. We played West Ham down at Upton Park on an absolute mud heap, and early on, I tried to head the ball back to George Farm – only to see it stick in the mud and leave him stranded. Vic Keeble nipped in and scored. George gave me an old-fashioned look and I could only hold up my hands and lamely apologise.

Afterwards, I was taking off my boots when Joe came over.

'Sorry, Joe,' I said. 'It was my fault.'

'Yes it was. But don't worry too much – you can have two or three games in the reserves to think about it.'

As it happened, I'd been carrying a knee injury for a while and when he recalled me a couple of weeks later, I was still feeling it a bit but I decided to play anyway. I didn't do much, to be honest, but Joe must have been satisfied with my performance because he told me later that he'd discovered what made me tick. I was never dropped again.

Mind you, I might not have been a million miles away from another adverse reaction when I stunned Joe, Stanley Matthews, my team-mates and around 30,000 Bloomfield Road fans by becoming the first overlapping full-back. These days, wing-backs are part of the furniture but early in my career, full-backs were there to defend, pure and simple. Eddie Shimwell, my predecessor in the Blackpool side, was a superb kicker of the ball but accepted that his role was to hoof the thing forward for the attackers to deal with. His principal job was to stop the opposition's left-winger and, to that end, Eddie perfected the art of kicking ball and man at exactly the same time, a more than useful deterrent down the years. He was a gentle giant off the field and a man who never resented my taking his place after he had made over 300 appearances for the club. Instead, he used to give me tips and encouragement and I really liked him.

I had been pondering a possible venture across the halfway line for some time before it actually happened. In just about every game, the opposition double-marked Stanley, with their left-winger dropping back to make the first tackle and the left-back waiting behind him should Matthews get past. This left me in acres of open space. So one day, I had a quiet word with Stan and told him my plan. I would sprint around his two markers on the outside and when I was in the clear, Stan could slip the ball into the open space ahead of me. He declined to comment and the idea went on to the back burner.

However, a couple of weeks later we were playing Wolves at Bloomfield Road and sure enough, Jimmy Mullen, their outside-left and an England colleague of Stan's, was dropping back to double-mark the Maestro, leaving me unmarked in loads of space. So I went for it. I skipped past Mullen and the left-back, called for the ball and Stanley provided the perfect pass. I was in the clear with only Bert Williams in the Wolves goal ahead of me. The crowd were on their feet, immortality beckoned, but I fluffed my lines! Stanley gave me a sidelong glance as I trotted past him on my way back to the halfway line and that was the end of the experiment for that particular afternoon.

We won the game and afterwards I awaited the arrival of the

manager with some trepidation. I wasn't disappointed. Joe came over to my corner of the dressing room and demanded, 'What was all that about?'

'How do you mean?'

'I mean all that running up and down. Now listen, if I wanted you to be a right-winger you would have a number seven on your back, not a number two. And in case you hadn't noticed, the number seven we've got is plenty good enough.'

But the overlapping full-back had arrived and, in fairness to Joe, he soon came round to the idea. So did the crowd, who had been equally unreceptive at first. What's more, Joe Smith was right about another thing – our number seven certainly was plenty good enough. His name was Stanley Matthews.

C H A P T E R 5
THE INCOMPARABLE MATTHEWS

Stanley Matthews celebrated his 42nd birthday on 1 February 1957. The following day, Blackpool played Charlton Athletic at The Valley. There were over 30,000 people in the ground and, long before the kick-off, the atmosphere was electric. Shortly before three o'clock, Stan emerged from the players' tunnel and to a man, those 30,000 supporters burst into song – 'Happy birthday to you, happy birthday to you, happy birthday dear Stanley, happy birthday to you!' I have never heard anything like it before or since and it summed up the depth of feeling for Stanley among his own people, the ordinary football fans – Matthews was truly the people's champion.

Other players have received a similar ovation from their own supporters at their own ground, but this was 250 miles away from Bloomfield Road on a cold, wet February day in south London and there can't have been more than a few hundred Blackpool fans in the ground. It was a memorable moment. I was an impressionable 21-year-old, just half his age, and had played in around 50 first-team games compared with Stanley's record of more than 600 appearances. The Valley choir brought a lump to my throat and I am sure the rest of the Blackpool players felt the same – all except Stanley Matthews. He never showed a flicker of emotion and just got on with the job of ruining Charlton's day. He produced all his party pieces and we strolled home 4–0.

Stanley was, and I believe still is, the greatest footballer of all time. He crossed the generation gap, making his name before the Second World War and continuing into the 1960s. He made the first of his 54 peacetime appearances for England as a 19-year-old against Wales at Cardiff on 29 September 1934; his final international was a World Cup qualifier against Denmark in Copenhagen on 15 May 1957, incredibly three months after his 42nd birthday. He also played in 29 wartime internationals and made almost 800 league and cup appearances for Stoke and Blackpool. Stan retired at the age of 50 shortly after becoming the first footballer to receive a knighthood. He always claimed he went too soon.

He lifted his sport into the modern era and he made professional football a real career. He was a talisman for the professional game. In all, he was to football what Donald Bradman was to cricket, Fred Perry to tennis, Joe Louis to boxing and Jesse Owens to athletics – men who took their sport into a new era and gave it a new dimension. To this day, people know exactly who they were, what they achieved and what they stood for. Stan did it for football and that's what made him different.

Stan was a man of the Potteries, where he was born and bred and where he died. But while he made his name in the early 1930s as a Stoke player and brought down the curtain on his career at Stoke in 1965, his real success as a footballer came in the tangerine shirt of Blackpool. He played more games for Blackpool than he did for Stoke.

When I started playing for the first team, I simply couldn't believe I was in the same dressing room as Stan. It was a small room and I used to sit and stare at him with a sense of awe. Nothing changed in the ensuing years. Towards the end of his Blackpool career, I sometimes used to wonder how he made it out on to the pitch at that age, but once he crossed the touchline, he was a different man. Blackpool Football Club was never quite the same after he rejoined Stoke in 1961.

Off the field, he was a gentle man, but on it, he was totally ruthless. That's the side of him not many people knew. I'm not talking about his physical approach because Stanley was never booked in all those games for club and country and rarely committed a foul. But his psychological approach was unforgiving and he used to urge me to impose myself on my opponent, not to show him any mercy. He demonstrated this in a game at Chelsea in the late fifties when their defenders, especially a young left-back called Ian McFarlane, made life tough for Stan in every sense of the word. It went on for over an hour. Matthews never complained to the referee and each time he was flattened, he picked himself up and got on with the game. Eventually, even he had to yield and left the field after taking one knock too many on his thigh. I thought we had seen the last of him for the day and as he hobbled across the old greyhound track that ran around Stamford Bridge, some Chelsea fans taunted him with cries of, 'Have you finished, Stanley?' Seven or eight minutes later, Stan reappeared on the greyhound track, his thigh heavily bandaged. I asked him if he was OK. In reply, he pointed to his feet and barked, 'Just get the ball over here.' I did exactly that and what happened next was truly remarkable from a man in his fifth decade. Looking back, I would love to have a film of that last 20 minutes as he tormented Chelsea's defenders to the point of humiliation. We won 4–1 and Stan scored the last goal. I have never seen him so riled – by the treatment meted out by the Chelsea players and possibly by the mockery of a few fans. He responded in the way he knew best, by ruthlessly destroying his opponents. Once, he beat McFarlane, stopped and allowed him to get back just so that he could beat him all over again. He was determined to humiliate Chelsea and he succeeded. In that mood, he was lethal.

At the end of the game, the crowd applauded him from the field but Stanley quietly made his way back to the dressing room without a hint of an acknowledgement. In fact, he never had any communication with the crowd. It just wasn't his style. Nor did he approve of other players displaying their emotions. I remember a game against Bolton at Bloomfield Road when Stanley was injured and watching from the stand. We won 2–1 and I played well. As I came off he field at the end, the crowd cheered me and shouted well played and I raised my hand in acknowledgement. I bumped into Stan at the ground on the Monday morning and he said,

'Why did you lift your arm up as you came off the field on Saturday?'

'Well, the crowd were cheering me . . .'

'Yes, because they knew you'd played well. But you don't need to respond like that.' I took the point, never even considering a reply.

People have described him as a loner but that is not strictly true. He did his own thing as far as training was concerned and out on the pitch, too. It was no use trying to dictate to Stanley how he should play and, in the immortal words of Joe Smith, it was a case of 'if in doubt, give it to Stan'. But while he was never really one of the lads, he enjoyed the jokes and the dressing-room banter and nothing made him happier than sitting down alongside Joe on the way home from away trips, recounting tales of old times and old players, sometimes fairly heavily embellished, I'm sure. One of his favourites concerned his first away trip to London as a Stoke player. He used to laugh about how his mother packed his best pyjamas and made sure he had everything he needed for the trip. He roomed with Freddie Steele, another Stoke player who went on to represent England, and at about quarter to ten on the Friday night, the senior players said to the two youngsters, 'Right lads, time for bed.' Stan and Freddie duly retired for the night and turned out the light in their room. Needless to say, they couldn't sleep and about half an hour later were disturbed by a knock on the door. Stan went to see who was there and in marched the rest of the team bearing bottles of beer, which they opened and poured into the china jerry under the bed.

Then they produced cups and started swilling down the ale. Stanley simply couldn't believe what he was seeing. He was horrified, and 20 years later, when I first heard him tell that story, he still had an expression of disbelief on his face. He vowed never to become involved in anything like that and true to his word, he never smoked or drank alcohol. He was fanatical about his fitness and was prepared to deprive himself of the good things in life to achieve his goal of becoming a great footballer. He never changed as the years rolled by. Sometimes on a Monday, he would not appear for training, preferring to stay at home and starve himself, resting his body completely. He just drank water or carrot juice to sustain himself, a way of cleansing the system and preparing for the battles ahead. Nobody else even dreamed of doing anything similar.

If I urgently needed to find Stanley, the first port of call was South Shore beach at 8.00 a.m. He would be there almost without fail, wearing a pair of slacks, a windcheater and flat cap, going through his deep breathing routine, his morning exercises and some gentle jogging. Then he would report for training at 10 o'clock – all this in his late thirties and early forties. I followed his example, taking an early morning run on the beach until I was 60. He was supremely fit, with excellent legs. He had a thin body but strong thighs and good calves. In fact, I used to wonder if he did extra work on his thighs away from the ground. I don't think I ever saw him out of breath during a match, he never tired and you couldn't give him the ball often enough. Throughout his career, he worked ceaselessly at his sprinting. England team-mates Tom Finney, Alf Ramsey, Billy Wright and Nat Lofthouse spoke with awe about Stanley's pace over the first five yards. He was like lightning from a standing start. Stan used to say that was all that mattered. 'Once you get the ball past your opponent, you must have the pace to leave him behind for good.' That was his forte and he could bring a defender to a halt like a matador confronting a bull and then suddenly take off. Once he was away, there was no catching him.

I once asked him what was the secret of his success and he replied, 'Work and practice. Practice, practice, practice. Players don't practise enough.' He was a perfectionist. As a boy, he used to persuade the local butcher to give him a pig's bladder. He would blow it up and run down the street, flicking it on and off the walls; or he would roll paper into a ball and practise with that. That explains why he was the greatest dribbler the game has ever seen and why, for example, I never saw him put a corner behind the dead-ball line. Think about that – in 34 years as a league professional, nobody could recall him putting the ball behind from a corner. That's incredible. It was the result of him working for hours at perfecting the art of taking a corner kick. He used to stroke that heavy ball into the goalmouth effortlessly, always swinging away from the goalkeeper. The fashion nowadays is for inswinging corners. Not Stanley! He wanted the keeper to be coming out for the ball as it drifted out of reach. He could take corners long or short, he could drive them in low, but he never, ever wasted a corner by putting the ball behind.

I never saw him lose his composure, either – doing that he would see as a sign of weakness. He gave his father credit for that. Matthews senior was a barber in Stoke and an amateur boxer. Stanley inherited his speed, agility and the mental toughness that kept him in control at all times. It was almost a fetish with him. He would urge us not to lose control at any time. In one derby match against Preston at Deepdale, things became a bit heated and, near the end, there was a fracas around our penalty area, which developed into a free-for-all. Stanley didn't get involved, of course; nor did Tom Finney. The match ended 3–3 and afterwards in the dressing room, Stanley wasn't happy. I could see it in his face. He rarely spoke much after a match but this time he let go.

'We lost our control. You have to keep control of yourselves. Control yourselves and you control the game. Lose control and you show your opponent a sign of weakness.'

No one was kicked more than Matthews and his self-discipline must have been tested to the absolute limit. Yet I never once saw him feign injury, complain to the referee, question a decision, remonstrate with an opponent or retaliate. He would have regarded any of those as signs of weakness. Diving? Beneath his dignity.

He was a hard taskmaster, though. Once, soon after I had started playing regularly, we went down to play Leicester at Filbert Street. The tactic was always to give the ball to Stan quickly and that's what I tried to do with a ball that came to me at an awkward angle on my left foot. Unfortunately, I got underneath it a bit and the ball ballooned into the air. Stan had to take it on his chest, giving their left-back, who had been run ragged up to that point, the perfect opportunity to clatter Stan when he finally brought the ball down. Stan displayed his usual lack of emotion towards the defender, quietly picking himself up, but he fixed me with an icy stare. If looks could kill, I would have died at Filbert Street that night. He said, 'Shocking, absolutely shocking.' It was like a dagger between the shoulder blades.

We went on to win 3–0 and I was bubbling when we reached the dressing room. Stanley wasn't. As he was taking off his boots, he called over to the manager, 'Joe, will you teach him how to pass. He'll get me killed.' On the coach home, he kept going on about it and he never let it go. In later years, it became a standing joke between us. At his 80th birthday celebration dinner, Stan stood up and said, 'I'm glad Jimmy Armfield's here tonight because I want to tell a story about him. In fact, playing all those years in front of him, I'm lucky to be alive!' And he recounted the Leicester incident. Oddly, as everybody laughed, I was touched with emotion as I finally realised how lucky I was to have played alongside the Great Man.

Solely because of Stanley Matthews, Blackpool had the best away gates in Division One for seven years in a row and it was not unusual for the gates to be closed when we arrived an hour before the kick-off. His presence alone was worth 10,000 on the gate and when we had an overnight stay away from home we always made sure Stanley saw the local evening paper. There was usually a story on the back page about how the opposition had made plans to bottle up Matthews and how their full-back was going to make a name for himself. That was all the incentive he needed to turn it on the next day.

Fathers would take their sons along to see Matthews to show them how football should be played, and while opposing supporters wanted to see their own team win, they also went along wanting Matthews to play well. It must seem a strange scenario now but that's exactly how it was. Matthews was revered wherever the game was played, like no one before or since. Eric Hayward, Blackpool's reserve-team coach and a former colleague of Stan at Bloomfield Road, always called him Maestro in the dressing room or on the training ground. The only other players to have come anywhere near achieving the same status in the English game were Tom Finney, Bobby Moore and Bobby Charlton, and I would guess that all three, in their modest way, would insist that Stan led the way.

I first sampled his global drawing power in 1958 on the Stanley Matthews Round the World Tour, financed by a millionaire Australian entrepreneur who asked Stanley to put a team together for a six-week series of exhibition games in the USA, Australia and Hong Kong. Stanley's side was Blackpool. We left after the final game of the season at Tottenham. I was injured and didn't play at White Hart Lane but nothing was going to stop me climbing aboard the Boeing Stratocruiser that shortly afterwards left what was then known simply as London Airport, bound for New York via Iceland. None of us had ever experienced anything like it. The plane was the ultimate in luxury travel. It had two decks and we sat on the upper deck to be served a three-course hot meal by a liveried steward. He carved the roast beef from a silver trolley. There was a fully equipped bar on the lower deck where passengers could go for a relaxing drink and a chat.

From New York we flew to Los Angeles, where we played the first game of the tour against the USA before setting off for a month in Australia. We played the Australian national side five times and also played games against State sides and club teams. On the way home, we played in Hong Kong and the whole tour was a fantastic experience. Everywhere we went, people came from miles around just to see Matthews. Even in California, which was hardly a hotbed of football, around 20,000 people turned out, most of whom didn't know the first damn thing about the game, but they cheered and cheered for Matthews, the most famous player in the world. It was the same in Australia, although early on he picked up an ankle injury and sometimes he turned out when he wasn't fully fit. Against New South Wales at Newcastle, Stan played because he knew a large chunk of the crowd had come all the way from the bush just to see him. After about 15 minutes, though, he had to give in and I had the dubious task of replacing him on the right wing. At the time we were 1–0 down and it was anybody's game but I scored the equaliser and collected a second after the interval as we ran out 5–1 winners.

The following day, the New South Wales papers carried banner headlines proclaiming 'Blackpool Have Found The New Matthews'. The report stated that Blackpool had already lined up the next Stanley Matthews, a youngster by the name of Jimmy Armfield. I knew better, even though when we moved on to Melbourne, where we beat Victoria, the man dubbed 'Blackpool's new scoring sensation' hit the target again. Needless to say, as soon as Stan was fit, he regained the number seven shirt and I reverted to right-back – and had to endure non-stop stick from my team-mates for the next few days.

The Matthews adulation reached fever pitch when we arrived in Hong Kong. The fans went absolutely crazy. It must be hard to understand today because it's totally different from something like the David Beckham scenario, where the public have already seen their idol on television or video, and surfed the Internet and bought a replica shirt. In 1958, nobody in Hong Kong had ever set eyes on Matthews. He was just a name and a picture in the newspapers. Two weeks before we played the Hong Kong national side, they had drawn 2–2 with Real Madrid, the best club side in Europe and, perhaps, the world. We beat Hong Kong 10–0! Their players were totally mesmerised by Matthews and Jimmy Hagan, the Sheffield United and England inside-forward who guested for us on the tour. A great player.

In a way, Stan was always a law unto himself and Joe Smith was happy to go along with it. On one occasion, we were due to play Arsenal at Highbury on the Saturday and Matthews had not been seen at the club all week. We assumed he was ill and when the teamsheet went up, his name was missing. We stayed overnight at the Great Northern Hotel in King's Cross and when Ray Charnley and I walked downstairs for breakfast on the Saturday morning, who should be sitting in an armchair reading the morning paper but Stan, looking tanned and wearing a light-weight, cream cotton suit. I was just about to greet him when Joe, who was right behind me, beat me to the punch and asked, 'Hello, Stan, how are you?'

Stan looked a bit bemused and replied, 'I told you last week that I was going to Ghana and I'd meet up with you in the hotel.

I got back last night and here I am.'

It transpired that a tribe in Ghana had crowned him the King of Football, decked him out in ceremonial garb and feasted in his honour all week. Stan insisted that Joe knew all about it and the manager was in no mood to argue.

'Can you play this afternoon, then?'

'Of course.'

He played, turned on a virtuoso performance and we won the match, but you had to feel sorry for the reserve right-winger who missed out at the last minute. Pictures of Stan in a tribal outfit with a wreath around his head appeared in the papers soon afterwards and we pinned one up in the dressing room, making sure we took it down as soon as Stanley approached.

Stan Mortensen used to say that, in some moods, when he was in his prime, Stan was unstoppable, and if all 11 opposing players had lined up against him, he would have found a way round them all. I can believe that. Morty claimed that he and Stan developed a form of telepathy and as Stan approached down the by-line, Morty would know exactly where the cross would go, near post or back. That was how the winning goal was scored in the 1953 Cup final. Stan went to the by-line, Morty came short to the near post but let the ball run and Bill Perry was there to hit the winner.

It wasn't a one-man team, of course, and no one should underestimate the contribution of Ernie Taylor, Mortensen and Harry Johnston to Blackpool's success. Taylor stood 5ft 5in tall and weighed around 9 stone dripping wet. He was a smoker and enjoyed a drink, but he was one of the most naturally gifted footballers I have ever seen. We weren't close off the field but to play behind him was a revelation and a crucial part of my learning process. Ernie was a Geordie who played in FA Cup finals for Newcastle, Blackpool and Manchester United. He supplied the great pass that sent Matthews away to set up the winning goal for Perry in the 1953 final and he always said he did a lot to help Matthews. He was right.

Stan Mortensen helped him, too. And how! Morty was the town idol because of his buoyant personality. He was a one-off. They made him a freeman of the borough in 1990 but they could have given him that award at any time since the war because the whole of Blackpool loved him. Morty was like an electric eel. He wasn't big for a centre-forward but he was lightning fast and would spark off and leave defenders floundering in his wake. He was brave, a good header of the ball and, crucially, in an era that produced great centre-forwards such as Tommy Lawton, Nat Lofthouse and Jackie Milburn, Morty scored 23 goals in 25 appearances for England. Not many people can match that.

Taylor and Morty were the attacking foils for Stan and the fourth member of the quartet that made Blackpool great was Harry Johnston, the skipper and centre-half. Harry was a fine player, good enough to win 10 England caps, but mainly he was the team's driving force. Ten minutes before the kick-off, Harry would take out his front teeth and put them in a dirty old white teacup that he kept on the windowsill. Then he would roll up his sleeves – always from the inside, something I never saw anyone else do – and we knew were in business. He was Blackpool's rock. He was a great tackler, he was good in the air and he could reach the penalty spot with a throw-in, but above all, he was a born leader. I skippered the side for 13 years but I would never claim to be the best captain Blackpool ever had. That accolade could belong only to Harry Johnston.

Throughout my early days at the club, Harry was an inspirational figure. The demands he made of every player were terrific but we accepted that because we knew he made the same demands of himself. I was privileged to be a part of that side, if only for a few years, and extremely fortunate to be in the same line-up as Matthews, whose presence made life so much easier for a young player making his way in the game. I used to look up, pass the ball to Matthews – which could be anything from two yards to 15 yards – and the next day I read that I had never wasted a ball! Did I help Stan in any way? Perhaps. In his last couple of years at Bloomfield Road, I probably did some of his legwork – I saw that as part of my job. With me around, he never had to come back into our final third, but we didn't want him there anyway. We wanted him in the opposition's final third, where he could do serious damage.

Stan was revered by his fellow professionals, as I discovered in the late fifties when the Professional Footballers Association (PFA) was starting to flex its muscles over players' pay. With Jimmy Hill as chairman, there was a growing determination to abolish the maximum wage. Matters came to a head at a meeting at Belle Vue, Manchester, in 1961. A few days before the meeting, Cliff Lloyd, the PFA secretary, rang me, as Blackpool's union delegate, and said, 'You've got to get him there. No matter how you do it, make sure he's there.'

I knew exactly whom Cliff was talking about but nevertheless enquired, 'You mean Stan?'

'Yes, Stan. He has to be there.'

I promised to do my best and spoke to Stan, stressing how important it was for him to be at the meeting. He just said, 'I'm going.' In fact, there was never any doubt about it. He always believed passionately that footballers were underpaid and was very aware of his own market value. He had that professional streak and would never have missed an opportunity like this.

The Blackpool players all sat together, with Stan next to me, and it was fascinating to see how the other players in the hall reacted to Matthews' presence. Some could not take their eyes off him, unashamedly turning round in their seats just to take a look at the Great Man – and that was not only youngsters but also senior professionals, men who were quite simply in awe of him. The press cameramen focused on him, too, and I believe his presence at that meeting marked a significant change in the life of the professional footballer. He was the most famous player in the world but he still wanted to show his colleagues that he was prepared to stand shoulder to shoulder with them in the quest for a better deal.

The debate ebbed and flowed. It may seem strange but there were a lot of players who were guarded, even uncertain, about the abolition of the maximum wage, believing that we were paid quite well enough. A young player from the lower divisions voiced this view when he stood up.

'My dad's a miner, earning £10 a week,' he said. 'I play in the lower divisions and I earn twice as much. I train in the open air and play football on a Saturday – he's down the pit for eight hours at a time, five days a week. That can't be right. We earn quite enough as it is.'

As he sat down, a member of the Bolton Wanderers party rose to his feet. It was Tommy Banks, England's left-back in the 1958 World Cup and a member of what might euphemistically be termed a no-nonsense Bolton defence comprising Hartle, Banks, Hennin, Higgins and Edwards. Banks was reputed to set his stall out by offering the opposition right-winger a choice of hospital casualty units before hostilities commenced but, in truth, Tommy could play a bit, too. He was a very talented left-back and, as we were about to discover, not a man to mince words.

'I'll answer that, Mr Chairman,' said Tommy, before Jimmy Hill could invite a response. 'Now then, son, thee tell thi father from me, I can do his job. In fact, I've done it. And so can any one of these lads in this hall, including thee. But if thi father wants to know why we want more brass, tell him to come and play against Brother Matthews in front of 30,000 fans. That's why we want more money.'

Belle Vue erupted in waves of laughter and cheers. No one laughed louder or cheered more than Brother Matthews and I believe that moment turned the meeting. Jimmy Hill won the day and the professional footballer's lot changed for ever. I had been on £20 a week before the strike and my pay doubled to £40. I thought I was a millionaire – until I heard that my England team-mate Johnny Haynes was getting £100 a week at Fulham. I went straight in to see the manager and was told £40 was all Blackpool could afford, but in the end they relented and gave me an extra fiver a week.

By the time I retired in 1970, I was on £75 plus appearance money and bonuses. I never earned big money and, in the early days, we all earned less in summer than we did during the season, except Stan Matthews. I once tackled Joe Smith about it, saying, 'Why do I get £16 in winter and £14 in summer when Stanley Matthews earns £16 all the year round?'

'Matthews is a better player than you,' he replied.

I agreed but added, 'Not in summer, he isn't.'

That's a tale that has been used and re-used and applied to another generation of sportsmen, but it's exactly what Joe said to me. To be honest, none of us would have minded if Matthews had been paid £100 a week during the season and the rest of us £20. We were under no illusions about the worth of the man who had been persuaded by Joe to move from Stoke in 1947 for £11,500, a relatively small fee even in those days, and a bottle of whisky. The whisky was there to be consumed by the parties involved, in other words Joe and Bob McGrory, the Stoke manager, and Joe never tired of telling people how he signed Stan for £11,500 and a bottle of Scotch. At the time, many people thought Matthews was past his best but he stayed for 14 years before making a sentimental return to the Potteries. Joe always admitted, 'I should have been locked up for getting him at that price.'

Stan and I grew close as the years went by and we spoke regularly on the phone. When we met, I could never resist having a good-natured dig about his dress sense, for even though he remained a quiet, retiring man, he could wear the most audacious clothes. The cream suit in the Great Northern Hotel was an early example but in later years, he excelled himself. I remember him visiting Blackpool at the age of 80, wearing a black bomber jacket, grey slacks, slip-on shoes, light blue shirt, pink tie and a baseball cap. He had a weakness for colourful ties and would always turn up for a dinner wearing something extravagant, perhaps a pink and gold number to offset a sober blue suit. Once he turned up wearing a light grey suit and black shirt teamed with a white silk tie. 'Bloody hell, Stan,' I said. 'You look like Al Capone.' He smiled that knowing smile, glanced down at my footwear and said, 'Wherever did you get those shoes?'

In all the years I knew him, I can honestly say that the only time I felt uneasy in his company was when he was behind the wheel of a car. With the best will in the world, Stan wasn't the greatest driver and would keep taking his eyes off the road to chat to the passengers or admire the scenery. There were times when he frightened me to death. On one occasion the two of us ventured across the Pennines to play in a testimonial for Jimmy

Hagan, the inside-forward who had guested for us on Stanley's world tour. Stan volunteered to drive over to Bramall Lane. During the game it started to snow heavily, but over 30,000 fans had turned out to see Stan and Tom Finney play on the wings in the Invitation XI in honour of Jimmy, so there was no question of calling it off. It was a great night – until we started the return trip, this time with Tom Finney in the back seat. There was no M62 in those days so our intrepid chauffeur headed for home via the old trans-Pennine route, dropping off a relieved Finney in Preston on the way. It was one of the longest journeys of my life.

I remember Stan as a man who never lost his innate humility. He was genuinely embarrassed that the 1953 Cup final went into football folklore as the Matthews final when Stanley Mortensen scored a hat-trick. And he meant every word when, on the town hall steps at the homecoming celebration, he rubbished suggestions that he was the hero. He always knew that it took 11 men to win a football match. He could reach for the stars and still keep his feet firmly on the ground because he was always one of the people. That's why 150,000 stood on the streets of Stoke to pay their respects on the day of his funeral on 3 March 2000. I gave the address at the service and as I drove into the town I simply could not believe that so many people had turned out.

I said in the church that when he died, the game lost a treasure – not just in terms of the game he played but how he played it – and those playing today should honour his heritage. Matthews didn't need an agent or a publicity machine because for over half a century, he was universally accepted as the world's most famous footballer. He was a humble man, adored by the masses, the greatest footballer of them all.

'STAND BACK, HERE COME BLACKPOOL!'

Like Stanley Matthews, Joe Smith was part of Blackpool folklore, the most successful manager in the club's history. He was in charge from 1935 to 1958, a phenomenal length of time when you think how brief a manager's career can be these days. I owed him a lot. I suppose you could even say he saved my life by refusing to let me join Manchester United. After the war, he guided the team to three Cup finals in five years. In many respects, he was a throwback to the 1920s and society doesn't churn out people like him any more. Brought up in the Staffordshire coalfields, he had a difficult early life and football provided a way out. Living in Blackpool was his idea of heaven. He used to stroll down the promenade and pop into the Clifton to have a couple of gills with his mates, or amble into Stanley Park to watch the bowls.

As skipper of the Bolton team in the famous White Horse final in 1923, Joe was the first captain to lift the FA Cup at Wembley. Players from that side would often be there to greet him when we played away from home, just wanting to be reunited with their old captain. Dick Pym, Ted Vizard and one or two more idolised him. I once asked Ted what was so special about Joe and he replied, 'He was everything to us.' Joe was their goalscorer, hard man, leader and captain. The story goes that after that first Wembley final, which Bolton won 2–0, Joe went up to collect the Cup from George V. He'd been told in advance what to say to the King if Bolton won, and after shaking hands and receiving the trophy, Joe said, 'Thank you, Sir,' and then, 'I'm sorry.' Then he held aloft the Cup and led the way back on to the pitch as his team-mates collected their medals before embarking on Wembley's first lap of honour.

Eventually, the press corps gathered around and one of the Bolton players who had overheard the exchange with George V, said to Joe, 'Why did you tell him you were sorry?' Needless to say, the pressmen's ears pricked up at this exchange and Joe replied, 'I just thought the King would have wanted me to score, so I apologised for not doing so.' He really meant it.

Joe had a scar running down the left side of his nose to the top of his lip and I once asked him about its history. He had been playing for Bolton against Birmingham at Burnden Park and when he dived in to head the ball, a Birmingham defender kicked him in the face. Joe's white shirt was covered in blood within seconds and the trainer gave him a sponge to try to staunch the flow. After a while, the referee said, 'You'd better go off, Smith.' There were no subs, of course, so Joe refused to go, insisting he was all right. A few minutes later, the ball was crossed into the Birmingham box and after a bit of a skirmish, the defender who had kicked Joe could be observed flat out on his back in the middle of the penalty area – absolutely spark out. The referee raced up to try to sort out what had happened, whereupon Joe, still clutching the magic sponge to his nose, announced, 'I think I'd better go off now, ref,' and he retreated from the action in search of stitches and other running repairs at the local general hospital. There were no television action replays to discover exactly what had happened but no one, least of all the errant defender, was in any doubt. He was still on the turf, flat out with his toes turned up – like the L.S. Lowry picture, 'Man on a Wall' – and Joe had obviously chinned him.

Joe's team talks were legendary. He would come in to the dressing room and just say, 'Pass the ball around, pass the ball around. We're better than they are. All you have to do is pass the ball around. You'll beat 'em.' Once we were staying overnight at the Grand Hotel in Birmingham before a game at Aston Villa. Joe called us all together. 'Right lads,' he said. 'I want you to get the ball down, pass it around, move it smartly down the flanks. If you see the goals, get a shot in. Keep passing it, you'll beat this lot.' It was the usual thing. I was young, I had just started to play regularly and I suppose I was still a bit impudent, so when Joe asked if anyone had anything to say, 'Yes,' I said. 'What if that plan doesn't work?' It was a joke and the lads were laughing. Joe wasn't laughing. He thought it was a serious question. He fixed me with a steely stare and said, 'If it doesn't work, lad, you can do what you always do. Give it to Matthews.' It became his catch-phrase. As each team talk neared its conclusion, he would say, 'Get the ball forward, give it to Stan.' Needless to say, the plan usually worked.

Before every game, Matthews would go into the bathroom to bring up his wind and we could hear him burping and belching in the background. Without fail, as Matthews closed the door behind him, Joe Smith would say, 'There we are, feeding time at the zoo.' I don't suppose Stanley ever knew.

Sometimes we even managed to win without Stan. In one game, against Newcastle, we came back from 2–0 down at half-time. Before the interval, we were awful and I was dreading what would happen when we returned to the dressing room. My peg was in one of the corners and when things were likely to be a bit heated, I could hide round the corner behind George Farm. So I manoeuvred myself into a position out of Joe's line of vision and waited for the volcano to erupt. It never happened. Joe came in, took off his coat, hung it on a peg behind the door, went over to the basin, gave his hands and face a good wash, collected a towel from Johnny Lynas, dried his hands, took his coat off the peg, put it back on and opened the door. Just before walking out, he turned and said, 'If you think I'm going to watch another forty-five minutes of that rubbish you can bloody well think again.' And out he went.

We won 3–2. Sure enough, as we were celebrating afterwards, Joe came into the dressing room, his face bathed in smiles. 'Well done, lads,' he said, rubbing his hands. 'Mind you, half of you should be collecting half wages this week because you only played forty-five minutes.' I was no longer in my hiding place behind George, of course, and I was smiling away like the rest of the players. When Joe spotted me he said, 'And I don't know what you're laughing at because you're one of them.'

Once, in my early days, we were playing at Cardiff and I travelled down as 12th man. About an hour before the kick-off, Joe said to Harry Johnston, 'Get all the lads in the dressing room. Now!' Harry jumped to it and everyone was summoned forthwith. Blackpool hadn't been doing too well and we all thought he was going to make a stirring speech, or come up with a tactical plan especially designed for the Welshmen, but not a bit of it.

'Right lads,' he said. 'This is important, very important,' and he tapped his fist on the wall for emphasis. 'As soon as the match is over, I want you straight back in here. The train leaves Cardiff Station at five fifteen and there isn't another one until tomorrow night. So if we miss it, we'll be stuck down here all weekend – and I don't want to be in this place all weekend. So you've got fifteen minutes to have a bath, get dressed and be back on the team bus.' And then he walked out. End of team talk. We caught the train home.

On one occasion I was the unwitting victim of a contretemps between Joe and Stan Cullis, his fellow son of Staffordshire who led Wolves to three league championships in the fifties. It was the day of my first game at Molineux and we had stayed overnight at the Victoria Hotel in the town centre. After breakfast Joe and Johnny Lynas asked if I fancied going down to the ground, ostensibly to let me have a look around the place, although what they really needed was someone to help Johnny with the skip.

After depositing the skip in the dressing room, Joe decided to go and see his old sparring partner Cullis but the Wolves manager wasn't in his office under the main stand. So Joe strolled through the door, helped himself to a cigar and told me to sit myself down on a chair in the corridor.

Due to play for Wolves that afternoon was Bill Slater, who had turned out as an amateur for Blackpool before going to Birmingham University, from where Wolves snapped him up.

He subsequently went on to play over 300 league games for the club and won 12 England caps.

However, Slater was probably not in Cullis's thoughts when, a few minutes later, he ambled along the corridor and spotted me sitting outside his door. But I was soon to discover that Joe hadn't forgotten his former player. 'Right son, in you come,' said Cullis as he approached me. Somewhat bemused at this turn of events, I did as I was told.

Joe's greeting to his old sparring partner was less than effusive. 'What do you think you're doing?' he asked.

'Just let me deal with this kid,' replied Stan. 'He's going to play for our juniors and I'm going to give him his expenses.'

'No you aren't,' responded Joe. 'You've already pinched our centre-half, so don't try and pinch the right-back as well.'

He used to love going to Arsenal. On the coach between the team hotel and Highbury, he would regale us with stories of his great games against the Arsenal, insisting, 'I always used to score against this lot.' Mind you, he used to say that at just about every ground we visited! We sometimes asked him if there was a ground where hadn't scored. 'Not if I was playing,' was his reply, but Arsenal occupied a special place in his heart. As the coach rolled slowly down the hill approaching the main entrance, Joe would take down his hatbox from the rack above his seat, put on his grey homburg, don his overcoat and light a large cigar. Then as the door opened, he would say to the assembled throng, 'Stand back, here come Blackpool!' And he would lead us through the main entrance into Highbury's marbled halls. I have to admit, it was impressive stuff. There was always an element of the showman in Joe. He was not sophisticated enough to be the real thing but, in his own way, he had a gift for creating an impression – a working-class showman, perhaps.

Joe used to believe Blackpool were unbeatable and, in the fifties, losing in the FA Cup was a disaster. The year after the Matthews final, York City of the Third Division North caused a sensation by winning at Bloomfield Road in the third round. I wasn't in the side at that stage but I was in 1959 when we lost in the quarter-finals at Luton just as the whole town was starting to feel it could be our year again. We played them off the field for 85 minutes, couldn't score and then lost to a late goal from Allan Brown, a former Blackpool player of all things. Joe took it badly. So did I. When all the players and most of the directors had assembled on the bus, as the youngest in the squad I was nominated to go and find Joe and chairman Harry Evans, a local plumber, who were the only people missing. They were in the boardroom.

I knocked on the door and when it was opened, I was confronted by a solid mass of people enveloped in a blanket of cigarette and cigar smoke and whisky fumes. I asked to speak to Mr Smith and eventually managed to tell him the bus was ready to leave. 'Harry,' he shouted across the crowded room. 'Time for us to get out of this bloody hole.' Harry, who wore a hearing aid, was standing in the opposite corner of the room, still wearing his hat. But he got the message, drank up and the pair of them made their way up the corridor leading to the main entrance and out on to the bus. While he was still within earshot, Joe started grumbling about the quality of the whisky in the Kenilworth Road boardroom. 'Cheap stuff, wasn't it? And another thing, I don't like that lah-di-dah chairman.' Joe didn't like losing in the Cup and always had to have the last word. Later, on the journey home, I ventured to suggest we had been unlucky. I'm still waiting for Joe's answer.

Sometimes he seemed to accept defeat with good grace – but his players and staff knew otherwise and soon learned how he was feeling inside. We once played at Sunderland when they were struggling at the wrong end of the table and we were in the top half. It was a game we should have won but it ended goalless. We didn't play well but we had taken a point. He came into the dressing room afterwards and announced to no one in particular, 'They looked fitter than us.' I had never heard him say anything like that before. Then he turned to Johnny Lynas, his right-hand man who had been with him since the war ended, and said, 'Johnny, this team doesn't look fit. Are you training them properly?'

Johnny, a qualified physio from the Royal Army Medical

Corps, was responsible for our fitness and he was a perfectionist. He was furious, clearly seeing this tirade as a slight on his training regime – it was a regime, after all, that had helped Blackpool reach three Cup finals and retain a position as one of the country's leading sides.

'There's nothing wrong with their fitness,' he retorted, but Joe would not be placated.

'Well I think they want some bloody training,' he replied and marched out of the dressing room. Johnny was livid. He started hurling the boots and kit into the skip from across the other side of the dressing room and when I tried to calm him down, he turned on me.

'You just get in the bath,' he snapped, an indication that I should mind my own business.

Things went downhill from there. On the way back from games in the north east we used to stop off at the King's Head in Barnard Castle for a meal. There was a pecking order about who sat where on the bus with Joe, Johnny, the directors and the senior players at the front and the younger players at the back. I was last to get off and as I reached the front, Johnny was still in his seat, reading the paper.

'Are you coming then, Johnny?' I asked.

'Just close the door,' he replied. So I climbed down the steps, slid the door shut behind me and went into the hotel. Straight away, Joe asked me where Johnny was so I muttered something about him still being outside.

'Well go and tell him to be quick,' said Joe. 'We want to have our meal and get home. What's he eating anyway?' I told Joe that Johnny usually had a steak and went back to the bus. Johnny was still there reading the paper.

'What do you want?' he asked.

'The manager has told me to ask you to come and have your meal.'

'I refuse to eat with that man,' replied Johnny. 'He's rude and uncouth. I know he is, you know he is, all the other players know he is and I'm not eating with him.'

'OK, fair enough.'

Once again, I went back into the King's Head and Joe shouted, 'Where is he, then?'

'He says he's not coming in.'

'All right then, let 'im bloody starve,' was Joe's riposte.

Johnny Lynas resigned on the Monday and he and Joe Smith never exchanged another word. Later, Johnny became a director – but by then, Joe had left.

Joe was a tremendous judge of a player. Virtually all his signings came off. There was George Farm from Hibernian, Eddie Shimwell from Sheffield United, Ernie Taylor from Newcastle, Allan Brown from East Fife and Jimmy Kelly from Watford. All of them did well. He also signed Scots Hughie Kelly and Jackie Mudie, and Bill Perry, a South African. He brought in Tommy Garrett from Horden Colliery in the north east, Jackie Wright from Astley Bridge in Bolton, Harry Johnston from the Manchester area and Ray Charnley from Morecambe for £1,000. What a buy he was! Above all, he brought in Stanley Matthews from Stoke, arguably the greatest signing of all time. Later on, David Durie, Roy Gratrix and myself came through the ranks along with a few more. He seemed to have an instinct for players who would make it.

He was once pushed into going to Barnsley to watch a young-ster who was just making a name for himself at Oakwell. The man who did the pushing was Albert Hindley, a Blackpool director who was also involved with the FA. Albert was a chauffeur by trade and when Joe spotted him wearing an official FA blazer, he asked Albert what was going on.

'I'm a Young England selector,' replied Albert proudly. Joe was not impressed.

'Selector? You're a bloody driver. The only thing you can select is gears. You know nothing about football.'

Even so, and against his better judgement, Joe agreed to travel across to Barnsley with Albert to watch the player in action. At the time, the Barnsley chairman was Joe Richards, who was also president of the Football League. When they climbed up the steps into the directors' box at Oakwell, there was a seat reserved on the front row for Albert, next to Joe Richards – but no seat for

Joe Smith, manager of Blackpool FC. In fact, the rest of the seats were already occupied. So Joe shouted across the directors' box, 'Albert, I thought you'd come with me.'

An embarrassed Albert, safely established in his front-row seat next to the League president, could only motion to Joe to be quiet and find himself a seat. Joe went and sat in the stand. Two minutes later, just as the referee was about to blow his whistle to start the game, there was a tap on Albert's shoulder. It was Joe.

'Right Albert, I'm off.'

'How do you mean? The game hasn't even started.'

'Maybe not, but I've seen enough already. That lad couldn't even score when he was shooting in, with the opposition at the other end of the field. He's no chance.'

And that was it. Albert had to make his excuses and leave early, and he never went to a match with Joe again. Could the lad play? Almost certainly not. Joe knew a player when he saw one. But there was no way Joe was going to allow himself to be demeaned by a director, even in the League president's own backyard – and he never ever felt embarrassed.

Joe wasn't keen on directors and even managed to have the final say on the day he was given three months' notice by the board, 1 February 1958. He learned his fate at the Grand Hotel in Birmingham, where we had stopped for a meal before our game against Aston Villa. Blackpool were tenth in the table and had beaten Wolves, the league leaders and eventual champions, in our previous match. But the board decided Joe's time had come. The era of the tracksuit manager was being ushered in and old stagers such as Joe were regarded as dinosaurs. Directors wanted to see their manager out on the training ground, not sitting behind a desk or wearing a three-piece suit with a pocket watch on a gold chain. So Joe and his ilk – Bill Ridding at Bolton, Andy Beattie at Huddersfield, Harry Storer at Derby and Jimmy Seed at Charlton – were clearly approaching their sell-by date. Joe was one of the last of the breed.

Soon after hearing the news, Joe went to the toilet. By chance, I was already in there and so was Stan Whittaker, the reporter who covered Blackpool for the *Lancashire Evening Post*. It could easily have been a scene from a Whitehall farce as the three of us stood in the stalls, Stan commiserating with Joe over his dismissal.

'They'll learn, they'll bloody well learn,' rasped Joe. 'Just see what happens to them now I've gone. Just you wait and see. Bloody directors! They're all the same. They're only in it for the money, the glory, the fame . . .' – and those words were interspersed with a few expletives.

At that moment, the lavatory door opened and out came Mr Herbert Grime, owner of the *Blackpool Gazette*, a perfect gentleman – and a director of Blackpool Football Club. He could not have failed to hear every word Joe had said. I was looking over my shoulder to see who it was and when I saw Mr Grime, I decided to stick around and faced the wall once again. I didn't want to miss the end of the cabaret. Despite being the unwitting victim of Joe's vitriol, Herbert Grime was far too polite to become involved in a slanging match with his ex-manager, so he quietly washed his hands and prepared to leave. As he reached the door, Joe turned to Stan and, loud enough for Mr Grime to hear, growled, 'See what I mean? They even eavesdrop you when you're having a pee. Bloody directors!'

Joe was succeeded by Ronnie Suart, one of the new breed of tracksuit managers who had played over 100 games for Blackpool in the late forties before moving on to Blackburn. He had done well in his first managerial job at Scunthorpe but his first training session with us was a bit awkward. Some of the senior players, including Matthews and Hughie Kelly, had played alongside him and were calling him Ronnie while the rest of us addressed him as Mr Suart. In the dressing room afterwards, Ronnie decided to sort it out once and for all.

'Look lads,' he said, 'we seem to have a bit of a problem here. At Scunthorpe, everybody called me Boss, so why don't we stick to that here.' We all nodded our agreement. 'Right, any questions?'

'Yes, just one thing, Ronnie . . .' said Stanley, and the whole dressing room smiled. For the rest of us, it was Boss from then on.

Ronnie needed to bring in a few fresh faces. Arthur Kaye, a

right-winger, arrived from Barnsley; Des Horne, who played on the left flank, was signed from Wolves and inside-forward Alan Suddick joined us from Newcastle. Then there were some young players including goalkeepers Tony Waiters and Gordon West, wing-half Emlyn Hughes and a ginger-haired inside-forward by the name of Alan Ball. Alan had been rejected by Bolton before he arrived at Bloomfield Road for a trial. He was still in his teens, a bouncy, aggressive little devil, and he found himself playing alongside Stanley Matthews in a practice match. Everyone on the staff knew that Stan liked the ball played to his feet and woe betide anyone who tried anything different. Ball had not taken that particular message on board and early in the game, he pushed the ball inside the full-back for Stan to run on to. Needless to say, in a practice match Stan didn't bother. He called the young pretender over, pointed to a square yard of turf in front of his feet and said, 'Alan, I like the ball here.' The riposte from 17-year-old Ball left no room for argument.

'Look,' he said, 'when I push the ball inside the full-back, it's your effing job to go after it.'

We were all stunned. No one spoke to the Great Man like that and Stan's expression showed his disgust, but that was young Ball. From day one, it was obvious he was going all the way to the top although I always felt that Blackpool was never going to be big enough for him.

It was a time of change and in 1960, amid much media interest, Blackpool featured in the first Football League game to be televised live, against Bolton at Bloomfield Road. The kick-off was switched to the evening to prevent the new phenomenon from clashing with the afternoon league programme and Billy Wright, the former England captain who was still playing for Wolves, was one of the commentators. There were forecasts that this would be the start of a television revolution but nothing could have been further from the truth. It was a poor game and the experiment was promptly abandoned. The result? We lost 1–0.

Players' wages improved but while Blackpool had been regarded as potentially a top-six side under Joe Smith, Suart was fighting to keep a reshaped team in the top half. Training became even more severe with the arrival of Wilf Dixon from West Brom as Ronnie's coach. He really drove us hard and there was no fitter team in the land. Wilf even made me train after playing a midweek game for England. Irrespective of where we had been playing on a Wednesday, I was under strict instructions to be back at Bloomfield Road by Thursday lunchtime. Wilf would be waiting for me, my training kit would be ready and I would be out on the track in double-quick time. 'This is proper training,' he used to say. 'Get all that England rubbish out of your system. This is what we're really all about.' I'd be on my knees but Wilf insisted it was good for me. I wasn't convinced, although I went on to fulfil his prediction that I would still be playing top-class football at the age of 35. When I bumped into Wilf recently, he said I wouldn't be as fit as I am without all his hard training. Who am I to argue?

When Matthews left in October 1961, we lost our talisman, although I could understand the boss's wish to move him on. Nevertheless, something vital went out of the dressing room and somehow it was never the same place again. Stan was way past his best of course, and we all knew it, but his presence alone was an inspiration to us all. He went to Stoke, put something like 30,000 on their average home gate and, helped by a few more golden oldies such as Jackie Mudie, Jimmy McIlroy and Eddie Clamp, took them back into the top division. It was the start of a golden age for Stoke, but at Bloomfield Road, we were on a downward spiral.

As transfer fees rose, Blackpool found it more and more difficult to keep up. The club concentrated on developing its own talent but always the better players, including Hughes, West and Ball, were sold on. Emlyn went to Liverpool and led them to victory at home and in Europe. He also made 62 appearances for England, many of them as captain. Gordon played over 350 games for Everton and won three England caps while Ball became one of England's most celebrated players. He collected a World Cup winner's medal in 1966, made 72 appearances for his country and played in more than 700 league games for Blackpool, Everton, Arsenal and Southampton.

Nothing summed up the state of Blackpool FC better than Ball's departure to Everton in the summer of 1966. They allowed him to leave just weeks after he had played a leading role in England's World Cup victory. He was a national hero and a cult figure in Blackpool but the club regarded him as expendable and he was sold just before the start of the new season. English football was on a high but as Blackpool travelled to Hillsborough to play Sheffield Wednesday, our mood was sombre. We had lost our World Cup star and we were beaten 3–0. Afterwards, Ronnie and Wilf seemed perplexed.

'I don't know what was up with you lot out there today,' said Ronnie as we sat in the dressing room. It was one of the few times that I spoke out in front of all the lads.

'You don't know what was up with us?' I asked. 'You go and sell our World Cup winner and then you wonder what's wrong. What do you expect?'

Maybe the harsh economics of football were starting to bite, but I have always maintained that years earlier, when Blackpool were the most glamorous club in the land, the directors lacked foresight. Basically, they were small businessmen from the local community and they had small business minds. When times were good, it never occurred to them to develop the ground – that didn't happen until the year 2002. Why couldn't they see 50 years earlier, when Wembley was the club's second home and Matthews was in his pomp, that they needed to move with the times? After all, 'Progress' was the town and club's motto.

Perhaps they assumed Blackpool would always be a Division One side and the money would keep rolling in, but the club was overtaken by teams with more ambition and the directors didn't realise the club's predicament until it was too late. They could and should have held on but when relegation came at the end of the 1966–67 season, it was accompanied by a grim sense of inevitability. We bounced back three years later, but only for one season and Blackpool FC have not been a force since then. It could all have been so different if those directors had possessed any real foresight when times were good.

ENGLAND MY ENGLAND

In June 1962, I was voted the best right-back in the world. Brazil had won the World Cup in Chile, knocking out England in the quarter-finals, and in our four matches, I had encountered some of the finest players on the planet. When the world's press chose their World XI from the players involved in the competition, my name was in there at right-back. It was a huge honour. I was 27, supremely confident, right at the top of my game, and that recognition confirmed my own belief that I had never performed better on the international stage. Chile was the culmination of a six-year journey from my first international call, although strangely enough, I never actually received the commemorative plaque to mark my selection for the World XI. So if anyone out there has it, you know where I am!

I endured my fair share of disappointments on the road to Chile, and the first came on what should have been my England Under-23 debut against Scotland at Hillsborough in February 1956. I was still in the Army and learned about my selection while we were preparing for a game between the Army and East Fife at Bayview Stadium in Methil on the Fife coast, a lovely part of the world. We were staying in a 10-bedroomed hotel in Leven, just outside Methil, with Elie, Pittenweem and Anstruther along the coast road as it winds on to St Andrew's. Colonel Gerry Mitchell, who was our manager and also the Army representative at the FA, called us all together in the hotel and announced, 'I have some very good news, gentlemen. Four of our players have been selected for the England Under-23 team to play Scotland at Hillsborough next week. They are Hodgkinson, Armfield, Smith and Edwards.' There was a polite ripple of applause from the rest of the boys, and soon afterwards we boarded the bus for Methil and a 2–1 win over a decent East Fife side. I was playing left-back against a winger called Matthews, of all things!

I never made it on to the pitch at Hillsborough because I went down with tonsillitis the day before the match and was confined to bed in a Sheffield hotel. I travelled to Sheffield by train, linking up with Duncan Edwards and David Pegg in Manchester. It was the first time I had really met David, although I had played against him once or twice. I hadn't felt too good as I walked across Manchester from Victoria Station to London Road for the Sheffield train but I soon picked up after meeting Big Dunc and David. Manchester United had booked them into the first-class carriage but I had a third-class ticket, so I protested that I couldn't sit with them. Dunc would have none of it, insisting, 'Never mind that. Get yourself sat down here and give me your ticket!' It was a different world from the third-class accommodation I was used to in the Army – we were served with tea and toasted teacakes and when the guard came round to check the tickets, Duncan handed them over and started discussing football. The guard was far more interested in talking to Edwards than checking tickets so he just punched them all and handed them back to Duncan. I retrieved my ticket, put it in my pocket and stayed where I was. Who says fame doesn't pay?

We were staying at the Victoria Hotel, next to Sheffield Midland station, and as soon as I arrived, I told Walter Winterbottom, the England team manager, that I didn't feel so good. He ordered me to get to bed straight away but by midnight I had raging tonsillitis, a high temperature and no chance of playing against the Scots. Don Howe, who was with West Brom at the time, took my place. England won 3–1 and after the match there was a knock on my hotel room door. It was Duncan, asking how I was feeling. To try to cheer me up, he offered me his England shirt as a memento. I turned it down but if I'd known what was going to happen to Duncan two years later, I would have grabbed that shirt and it would now be an exhibit in the Old Trafford Museum. Missing out was a big blow. There were a lot of good full-backs around and no guarantee another chance would come along in a hurry. I was still playing in a very strong British Army side as captain and establishing myself in the Blackpool team, but at international level, Jeff Hall and Roger Byrne were fixtures in the England side and with Howe, Graham Shaw, Jimmy Langley, Bill Foulkes, Mick McNeil, Ray Wilson and George Cohen around, there was a lot of competition behind them.

I learned about my next step on the representative ladder while I was lying on my bed at Bowerham Barracks. We usually had a bit of a rest after lunch and the old Rediffusion radio set in the room would be tuned in to the sports news. I was half-asleep and listening vaguely as the presenter said, 'The Football League team to meet the Irish League in Belfast on 25 April was announced earlier today. It is . . .' The second name was Armfield (Blackpool). I thought I was hearing things. I sat up with a jolt and looked round the room. One of the lads said, 'That was you, Jim. You've been picked for the Football League.' What a way to learn of my selection, but that was Army life.

We travelled by boat from Liverpool to Belfast the day before the match and I knew that as soon as the game was over, I would have to find my way back to the docks to catch the return ferry to make sure I was back in barracks on time. The Irish side included my old schoolmate George Eastham. His father, also called George, had played for Blackpool just after the Second World War and was manager of Ards, the Irish League club. He had already introduced George to senior football with Ards and this was his first step on the international ladder, too. He eventually became a member of England's 1966 World Cup squad and later played for Newcastle, Arsenal and Stoke and was also a central figure in the PFA's campaign to abolish the maximum wage and introduce freedom of contract.

The Irish League were a useful side and had played together a time or two whereas we were a combination of young hopefuls and a few older players who had never quite made the grade as internationals. We weren't so good and lost 5–2. It was another debut disaster for Armfield, following defeat at Portsmouth in my first game for Blackpool and a dose of tonsillitis on what should have been my Young England bow. When I arrived back in camp on Thursday, I bumped into Major Roberts, the officer who had given me a couple of days' leave to travel to Belfast. 'You'd have been better off staying here, by the sound of it!' he joked. He could have been right, too.

I finally made my debut for the Under-23 side against Denmark in Copenhagen five months later and the instructions from Sir Stanley Rous, the FA Secretary, are reproduced on the next two pages. They make interesting reading.

My father couldn't believe that I was going to play football in Denmark. It seemed like another planet to him, even though I had travelled abroad with the Army. My mother still wanted to make me some sandwiches and her parting words were, 'Will you be all right?' The Second World War was still very much on people's minds and it showed when we arrived in Denmark. Britain was popular and the Danes gave us a warm reception wherever we went. The ground was full and wearing the three lions for the first time proved to be an emotional moment, particularly when they played the National Anthem. I received a match fee of £15 from the FA and a bottle opener from the Danes. That was their gift to each England player and it must have been a quality product because I still have it today! Our team was Alan Hodgkinson (Sheffield United), Jimmy Armfield, Graham Shaw (Sheffield United), Ronnie Clayton (Blackburn), Trevor Smith (Birmingham), Dick Neal (Lincoln), Bryan Douglas (Blackburn), Jimmy Bloomfield (Arsenal), Gerry Hitchens (Cardiff), Alick Jeffrey (Doncaster) and Frank Blunstone (Chelsea). We won 3–0.

It was the first time I had seen Alick, who played in the old Second Division. He was only 17 but had all the makings of a great footballer. He was full of life on and off the field, not unlike the young Paul Gascoigne. He broke his leg in the next Under-23

Headquarters:
HOTEL COSMOPOLITE, COPENHAGEN
(Telephone: Copenhagen 80)

ARRANGEMENTS FOR TRAVEL AND ACCOMMODATION

MONDAY, 24th September

Players should make their own travel arrangements to arrive at the Lancaster Court Hotel, 66, Lancaster Gate, London W.2 during the afternoon of Monday, 24th September.

TUESDAY, 25th September

09.30 hrs.   Depart for London Airport (Central).
10.55 hrs.   Depart for Copenhagen (Flight B.E.220A).
13.25 hrs.   Arrive Copenhagen (Kastrup Airport).

A motor coach will meet the party on arrival and convey them to the Hotel Cosmopolite.

WEDNESDAY, 26th September

19.00 hrs.   DENMARK v. ENGLAND at Idraetspark, Copenhagen.

After the match the England party will be the guests of the Danish F.A.

THURSDAY, 27th September

08.55 hrs.   Depart from Headquarters for Kastrup Airport.
10.25 hrs.   Depart Copenhagen (Flight S.K. 501).
13.15 hrs.   Arrive London Airport (Central).

A motor coach will meet the party and return them to the F.A. offices and thence to the London Railway termini.

GENERAL NOTES

1. Each member of the party must have a valid passport.
2. Under the present currency regulations, no individual may take out of the country more than £10 sterling. It is not permissible to spend any of this amount whilst abroad.

3. Currency arrangements have been made to provide members of the party with a limited amount of foreign currency.

4. Officials are advised to take with them a dark lounge suit for evening wear. Members of the party should also take soap and towels for personal use.

5. Members of the party are advised that the free allowance of baggage when travelling by air is 55 lbs. per passenger. It is essential that a minimum of baggage should be taken.

6. Each person will be responsible for his own luggage when passing through the Customs.

SPECIAL NOTES FOR PLAYERS

1. FITNESS TO PLAY. All players are requested to acknowledge receipt of these arrangements and to signify their fitness to play. In the event of a player being subsequently. unfit to play he must telegraph immediately to "Football Association, Padd, London".

2. FEES AND EXPENSES. All players will be allowed travelling expenses to and from London and will be given an allowance of £2 per day during the period spent abroad. Players will receive the following Match Fees: Players £15; Reserves and Trainer £10.

3. EQUIPMENT. Shorts, stockings and numbered shirts will be provided by The Football Association. Players are requested to bring with them athletic slips, gym shoes, shin guards, spikes and football boots which should be properly studded.

4. Players are forbidden to divulge these arrangements to the Press or comment upon the match in television or radio programmes or in Press reports after the game. The Football Association regulations are well known to the players, viz., that players under the jurisdiction of The Football Association must neither write nor allow to be written under their signature articles in which criticism of match officials or players is expressed or the result of any match is forecast.

STANLEY ROUS, *Secretary*

22 LANCASTER GATE
LONDON, W.2
Phone: AMBassador 4542

international against France in Bristol, a game I missed because of injury, and was forced to quit soon afterwards. He made a comeback for Doncaster in 1963 and played for another six years but he was never the same player. It was a shame because he looked as though he had a special talent.

That game in Denmark gave me an inkling about international football but it wasn't until the summer of 1957 that I played for the Under-23 side again, this time against Bulgaria in Sofia at the start of a three-match 'goodwill tour' behind the Iron Curtain. Bill Nicholson of Spurs was the manager and the tour also included matches with Romania and Czechoslovakia. The Cold War was at its height and today's players could have no concept of the conditions we had to face. As soon as we arrived in Bulgaria I was conscious of a strong anti-West feeling. We had an interpreter and whenever we tried to discuss the differences between Communism and our life in the West, he dismissed our arguments. 'Communism is the only way forward,' he would insist. Judging by our hotel in Sofia, they still had a long way to go. It was a dark, decrepit place that reeked of garlic. Trams rumbled by constantly from five o'clock in the morning. Everything in the city seemed grey and dismal.

We were paired off alphabetically to share rooms. I was with Alan A'Court, the Liverpool winger, who is still a good mate. Brian Clough and Bryan Douglas were next door. There was no lift so we trooped upstairs to our allotted rooms. We opened the door to find two iron camp beds, a rug covering the bare floorboards, a small chest of drawers, a lattice window and a washbasin in the corner. Light was provided by a bare bulb in the ceiling. That was all, apart from a giant black beetle sitting on the rug. Alan stamped on it.

Needless to say, Cloughie's language was choice. He was an outspoken character even in those days and made no secret of his views about the accommodation to anyone who was prepared to listen. The four of us found comfort in endless games of cards, mainly Solo or Hearts – anything that took plenty of time. Cloughie was always good company and was forever berating his partner for his choice of card. So, with Bryan's connivance, we decided to set up Cloughie, making sure Bryan played the wrong cards at the wrong time to provoke the inevitable over-the-top reaction. It took a while before Cloughie realised what was happening. In the end, the four of us were able to make our own fun.

At the time, Clough looked every inch a regular England player of the future. He was a natural goalscorer who finished his career with the phenomenal record of 251 goals in 274 league games, mainly in the old Second Division, for Middlesbrough and Sunderland. Yet he played only twice for the full England side before injury cut short his career at 29. Bryan Douglas was another tremendous player, equally at home on the wing or at inside-forward. We became room-mates when we graduated to the senior side and played in the same England team on 23 occasions.

The hotel food was awful, so we came up with the novel idea of providing our own chef in the person of Jimmy Bloomfield. As luck would have it, Jim had spent his National Service in the Army Catering Corps so he volunteered to prepare our meals. Bill Nicholson was happy with the idea and when the hotel raised no objections, Bloomfield was seconded to the kitchen staff where he rustled up some home-made soup, boiled eggs and so on.

Bulgaria beat us 2–1. It was no contest because we were playing 12 men. The referee was awful. They went in front early on but Cloughie equalised and we were denied a blatant penalty before Stan Anderson was sent off. He was kicked by one of the Bulgarian players, had a go back and was dismissed. It wasn't really a sending-off offence – and the Bulgarian stayed on the field. As Stan was running off the pitch, a bottle thrown from well back in the crowd sailed past his head, missing the target by inches. At half-time, the score was 1–1 but I said to Bill Nick, 'You do know that there's no way we are going to win this match, don't you?' I had never experienced refereeing like it. The man was totally biased and, of course, there were no television cameras rolling to provide evidence. Sure enough, Bulgaria scored again late on and that was that.

In those days, we always had to attend an official dinner after the game. It was held in our hotel, although Jimmy Bloomfield had to forego his duties in the kitchen. The first course was beetroot soup. I didn't fancy it but was prepared to give it a try – until the waiter came round and broke a raw egg into it. At the end of the meal, there was the usual round of speeches before an opera singer, an authentic *basso profundo*, provided the cabaret. At the end of his performance, the gathering responded with a round of polite applause.

Leaving Bulgaria certainly wasn't a wrench and after grey days in Sofia, the sun came out for us when we arrived in Romania. Bucharest had a much lighter atmosphere altogether and top of my personal agenda was a get-together with a local medical student, Dan Florescu. Dan and I had been pen friends since our schooldays, exchanging four or five letters a year in French, and when we left school, he went to university while I went into football. This was an opportunity to get together after so many years. He came to see me at the Athena Palace Hotel, where we were based. We had a cup of coffee and a long chat in a combination of French, pidgin English and a fair bit of sign language. When Dan left and walked off into the night, that was the last I saw of him. He seemed a nice chap but we have never exchanged a word or a letter since. Why? I suppose we both felt that was a good time to end it.

Bucharest was also hosting the Women's European Gymnastics Championships at the time and sharing our floor at the hotel were the Danish and Polish gymnasts. Can you imagine that happening today? They commandeered the hotel corridor as a training area and spent hours practising their cartwheels, Arab Turns and so on. They were absolutely terrific. In those days, there was nothing pre-pubescent about female gymnasts. These were 18- and 19-year-olds and very attractive, too, so it will come as no surprise to learn that we started to take more than a passing interest in their progress as the championships progressed. We finished up going along to watch them in what was a world-class competition featuring the top Russian and Romanian gymnasts, too. We also enjoyed a spot of culture, as guests at a performance of 'Carmen' at the Romanian National Opera.

Soon after we arrived in Bucharest we were joined by Walter Winterbottom and three members of the senior England squad, who had just completed their end-of-season programme, Duncan Edwards, David Pegg and Derek Kevan of West Brom. The game was played on a Sunday afternoon and as the team coach made its way to the 80,000-seater stadium, we were baffled to find that there was virtually no one around and absolutely no indication that the Romanian Under-23 side were about to take on England. Little did we know that the fans were already in the stadium, sitting as quiet as lambs in readiness for the kick-off. When we walked out on to the pitch to sample the atmosphere, we were greeted by a round of applause from what was surely the largest crowd to watch an Under-23 match – but it was a different story when the match started. Then it was bedlam. They were by far the most vociferous crowd I had encountered, but we won 1–0 with a goal two minutes from the end from Johnny Haynes. After that, we headed off to Bratislava and the match in which Duncan destroyed the Czechs almost single-handed. They were a good side, featuring several of the players who went on to reach the 1962 World Cup final, but they just couldn't cope with Edwards.

That tour was the start of a good run for the Under-23 side in which we put together straight wins over Romania at Wembley, Poland at Hillsborough and Czechoslovakia at Norwich, a draw with France and a win over Italy. Ron Greenwood had taken over from Bill Nicholson as our manager and he and I were always on the same wavelength. He taught me a lot about competing at this level, about when to play safe and when to be adventurous. He was a great help. The Romania match marked my first appearance at Wembley and my first game alongside Jimmy Greaves. Jim scored twice as we took a three-goal lead. If I close my eyes now, I can still see him closing in on the Romanian goal at the tunnel end with their defence opening up in front of him. They didn't quite know how to handle him – and they weren't alone in that over the years. We won that one 3–2, beat Poland 4–1, the Czechs 3–0 and the France game finished 1–1.

Our summer tour at the end of the 1958–59 season started

with the game against Italy. After playing in Milan, we were due to move on to meet West Germany, a big test for an up-and-coming side. Incredible as it may seem today, the Italians had never beaten England at senior level in seven attempts and the teams had drawn 2–2 in a full international at Wembley the day before our game in the San Siro. It was a sunny afternoon, the stadium was pretty full and the whole of Italy believed this was going to be the day when an Italian team finally put the record straight and put the English in their place. Instead we wiped the floor with them. We won 3–0 and gave easily the best perform-ance of my time as an Under-23 international. It was my fourth game as captain and I was a very proud man.

When we arrived back at the hotel after the match, Walter took Jimmy Greaves and me to one side and said he wanted us to join the senior squad for the four-match tour of Brazil, Peru, Mexico and the USA. Instead of an Under-23 match against the Germans, I would be spending two and a half weeks on the other side of the world with the full England squad. I was absolutely astonished – talk about 'have boots, will travel'! I didn't have long to let the idea sink in either, because we had to catch the overnight train from Milan to Zurich. While our Under-23 team-mates were celebrating a famous victory, Jim and I were in a sleeping car with the England manager en route to Switzerland and an early-morning flight to London. Swissair did us proud. Apart from the crew on the flight deck, the only passengers were Walter, Jim, me, the managing director of Swissair and an air hostess. So we enjoyed a good breakfast with excellent service! As soon as we reached the terminal at London Airport, I rang home to tell them what was happening and then linked up with the rest of the party to climb aboard our flight to Rio. Somehow, I couldn't really believe it was happening to me.

In those days, we didn't see ourselves as superstars. OK, we earned £20 a week and that was more than most people took home after a week's work, but unlike today's players, we weren't so far ahead of the average worker in terms of our earnings or our lifestyle. If a modern Premiership player looks after himself and his money, he will have earned enough by the age of 30 to keep himself and his family secure for the rest of their lives. There was no way the England players on the flight to Rio could feel that kind of security. We knew only too well that football wasn't forever and that those of us who had not taken out insurance might be just one serious injury away from the dole queue. School teachers, bank clerks, mechanics or panel beaters didn't earn as much as we did, nor did they enjoy the perks of life in the public eye, but they had the long-term security professional footballers could never contemplate. It was a good life – but a million miles away from 'Footballers Wives'!

Only Billy Wright, our captain, had played in South America before and Rio was an eye-opening experience for us all. It was very much a beach culture but a different world from Blackpool sands back home. We used to stroll along the promenade alongside the Copacabana beach and watch all the young Brazilians playing football on the sand with a beach ball. They knew all the tricks. Brazil had won the World Cup for the first time a year earlier and we could sense the excitement among their supporters in the build-up to the game. These days, Brazilians believe their team has almost a divine right to win. In 1959, their victory in the World Cup the previous year had propelled them into uncharted territory and the whole country was still on a high. They had a wonderful side that included the talents of Zito, Didi, Vava, Garrincha and Zagalo – as well as Pele, of course – and the fans weren't too interested in the opposition.

After training one day, a few of us walked up the hill to the Corcovado, the monument to Christ that towers over Rio, to discover Zagalo surrounded by fans and press photographers. Through an interpreter, I said, 'I might be playing against you in a couple of days.' He replied that he wasn't in the team. Later on, as we returned to our hotel, we saw another huge crowd gathered around one man. This time it was Didi. The Brazilians were staying out of town and had come in on a shopping trip and every now and then we would come across one of them, surrounded by fans. They were like gods and it was the first time we had witnessed such levels of hero-worship.

I didn't think I had a prayer of playing but after a morning training session in the Maracana Stadium, Walter came over and asked if I'd ever played left-back. I told him just a few times. He said he wanted me or Don Howe to play there. Brazil would have either Julinho or Garrincha on the right wing, both of whom were very quick, and he thought I was the better bet. I said, 'OK, I'll play left-back.' Little did I know I would play there in all four games on that tour.

We had a motorcycle escort all the way from our hotel to the Maracana. By the time we walked through the players' tunnel, which ran under the moat that separated the crowd from the pitch, and out on to the playing surface, there were 160,000 people packed into the place, the biggest crowd I have ever seen. It was absolute bedlam with helicopters circling overhead and fireworks exploding all over the place. There were bands playing, drums pounding, maracas shaking. The noise was incredible. I could feel myself growing more and more tense as the National Anthems were played and the teams were introduced to the official party. Finally, after what seemed an endless build-up, the game got under way – and we found ourselves a goal down after 90 seconds, before I had even kicked the ball. My first touch in international football was to pick the ball out of the net and kick it up to myself two or three times before booting it back to the middle for the kick-off.

I spent the next 10 minutes running around in the wake of Julinho, who had been brought back from Milan to play in the match. He was a very good player – tall and quick with a lovely swaying movement, and he knew all the tricks. Before long, we were two goals down. We contrived to hang on until half-time and returned to the dressing room to find a cylinder of oxygen and a mask, presumably to help players recover from the effects of the heat. We all had a whiff and it must have been good stuff because we played pretty well in the second half. Johnny Haynes hit a post and Bobby Charlton forced a tremendous save out of Gilmar, their goalkeeper. But in the last 10 minutes, they switched on the party tricks and the crowd went wild. They made it look as if we'd been overrun but that wasn't strictly true. We'd acquitted ourselves reasonably well in very testing conditions.

At the reception after the match, all the England players were handed a scroll of paper with an inscription stating that each of us now owned an acre of land somewhere in the rainforests, courtesy of the Brazilian FA. We were also given an aquamarine stone. Anne had it set into a ring that had belonged to her late father. It wouldn't have been very valuable but it meant a lot to us both. Sadly, it was stolen when our home was burgled.

For the record, the side in Rio was Eddie Hopkinson (Bolton), Don Howe (West Brom), Jimmy Armfield, Ronnie Clayton (Blackburn), Billy Wright, Ron Flowers, Norman Deeley and Peter Broadbent (all Wolves), Bobby Charlton (Manchester United), Johnny Haynes (Fulham) and Doug Holden (Bolton).

There were frailties and, as a new player, I was one of them. Nevertheless, I had grown in confidence as the game went on and I had not felt overawed. None of us had experienced anything like the atmosphere at the Maracana on 13 May 1959 but I was certain about one thing – I wanted to sample it again. Change was on the way. Finney and Lofthouse had left the scene and Wright would soon be departing, too. Winterbottom was looking at rebuilding and our next game, against Peru, showed why. We lost 4–1. Peru were good but we were poor. Against Mexico, we kicked off at 12 noon in 103 degrees at 8,000ft and ran out of legs. They were easily the toughest conditions I ever played under, and the heat and the altitude took their toll in the last quarter. We lost 2–1. Three games, three defeats and the simple truth was that we weren't good enough.

We even went a goal down against the United States in Los Angeles, but thankfully, this was not going to be a repeat of England's notorious defeat by the USA at Belo Horizonte in the 1950 World Cup. Warren Bradley of Manchester United equalised just before half-time and we overran them in the second half and won 8–1. It was good to be on the winning side at last – but I had picked up two important lessons on that tour. First, I still had a lot to learn before I could really call myself an international footballer. Second, I was never going to be an international left-back. On the plane home, I told Walter how I felt. I can only believe he felt the same way because I never played there again for my country.

I always liked and respected Walter and I knew I could talk to him with confidence. He was the first full-time England manager and was in charge of the side for four World Cups from 1950. I always suspected his first generation of players, such players as Stanley Matthews, Wilf Mannion and Raich Carter, probably regarded him as a schoolmaster figure rather than a pro's pro. True, he had never played the game at the highest level but he had been good enough to play 27 times for Manchester United before injury ended his career. He was the FA Director of Coaching as well as manager of the England team and he was the man who set up the England youth and Under-23 teams. He founded the FA coaching system, organised courses, which he ran himself, and wrote books on coaching. He was a knowledge-able man, quiet, honest and loyal to his players, who liked and respected him in return. We exchanged Christmas cards until his death in 2002.

Soon after we returned home, I became the first winner of the Young Footballer of the Year award, set up in 1959 to mark Billy Wright's 100th England cap and sponsored by the *News Chronicle*. The trophy was a silver cap and I still have it today, along with the silver football presented to me by Blackpool Corporation in recognition of the award. When I was asked where I would like the presentation to take place, I said Blackpool, of course. Where else? The presentation was held in the Tower Ballroom on a Saturday night and the place was absolutely packed. As well as the hundreds of Saturday night dancers, Anne and all the football gang came along to support me. The trophy was presented by Billy, who drove up from Wolverhampton with his wife Joy, one of the Beverley Sisters. After winning over 100 England caps, many of them as captain, Billy was quite at home standing up and making a speech in front of a big audience. I wasn't. Footballers were used to playing in front of 30,000 fans, we didn't make many speeches. I managed to survive the ordeal, however, which is more than can be said of the award. Jimmy Greaves was the winner in 1960 but it soon lapsed. A young player prize was revived with the inauguration of the PFA awards in 1974.

When the international season began in September, Howe

continued at right-back and Walter brought in Tony Allen of Stoke at left-back. England drew with Wales, lost to Sweden and beat Northern Ireland in the autumn of 1959 but were not convincing. So when the side was named to face Scotland at Hampden Park on 19 April 1960, there was a new full-back pairing – Armfield and Wilson. I played in 37 of the next 38 games at right-back and despite some injury problems, Ray Wilson also became an automatic selection, winning 63 caps over the next eight years. He won almost half of his caps while playing for Huddersfield Town, who were in the old Second Division, before joining Everton in 1964. He never had a problem with the step up from Division Two to international football and was one of those people who seemed to play better for England than he did for his club. He was a fine defender, very quick and extremely difficult to pass. He didn't make many mistakes and his error that presented West Germany with the chance to score the opening goal of the 1966 World Cup final was completely out of character. Little Ray, as we used to call him, and Roger Byrne were the best left-backs of my era.

I always regard that windy spring day in Glasgow, complete with the Hampden Roar and the notorious Hampden swirl, as the first real stride of my international career. The next three games were a period of trial and error for Winterbottom, with a draw against Yugoslavia and defeats in Spain and Hungary, but early in the 1960–61 season, Walter gathered his players together at Lilleshall to announce a change of policy and strategy. He told us we were to be the basis of his squad and would remain so as he planned to establish a settled team in the build-up to the 1962 World Cup. He opted for consistency in selection. We had lost five of my first eight internationals but Walter's change of direction brought us seven wins and a draw in the next eight games as we switched to a 4–2–4 system. We looked full of goals, scoring 44 and conceding only 11. Our results included an 8–0 win over Mexico, a 9–0 victory against Luxembourg and that never-to-be-forgotten 9–3 defeat of the Scots at Wembley. Walter used just 14 players in those eight matches. Wilson was injured and replaced by Mike McNeil of Middlesbrough in a side that read Ron Springett (Sheffield Wednesday), Armfield, McNeil, Bobby Robson (West Brom), Peter Swan (Sheffield Wednesday), Flowers, Douglas (Blackburn), Greaves and Bobby Smith (Spurs), Haynes (Fulham), Charlton (Manchester United). Alan Hodgkinson played one game in goal, Gerry Hitchens appeared twice at centre-forward and Derek Kevan had a run-out in one game instead of Greaves, but Walter stuck to his word about creating a settled side. It proved to be the best England team I played in, a view shared by Haynes, Robson and Greaves. The first blip came in a 3–1 defeat in Austria when Walter made a couple of changes to give fringe players a game but we lost only one of our next seven games, against Scotland of all people, as the countdown to the World Cup in Chile ticked by. In the process, Wilson returned at left-back, John Connelly of Burnley made one or two appearances on the wing and in early 1962, a young wing-half from West Ham by the name of Bobby Moore started to make an impression.

We left for South America in May 1962 with high hopes. It was a journey that never seemed to end. There were no adventure holidays or package tours to Chile in those days and even now, over 40 years later, it involves a 16-hour flight, probably with one change. For the England players, it seemed like a journey to the end of the earth, which is virtually what it was – there isn't much between southern Chile and Antarctica. I set off believing we had a genuine chance of winning the World Cup. As I have said, I always thought that England would have gone very close in Sweden four years earlier but for the Munich air disaster. Duncan Edwards, Roger Byrne and Tommy Taylor were world-class performers and pivotal members of the 1958 side and no team could have withstood their loss just a few months before the start of the competition. By 1962, Walter had put together a side that was, if anything, even stronger.

We played a warm-up match against Peru in Lima in which Moore made his debut as a replacement for the injured Bobby Robson. We avenged our 4–1 defeat three years earlier with a convincing 4–0 victory, Greaves scoring a hat-trick. We ran them off the field. We were allowed out for the night after the match and I went for a meal with Bobby Charlton and a couple of the lads. We opted for a restaurant that had a cabaret and as we were finishing our meal, the compere stood up and announced that some members of the England team were present. We were given a round of applause. 'So come on, then, are you going to give us a song?' said the compere. I looked at Bob, he looked back at me, we nodded, rose to our feet and made our way through the cheering throng on to the stage. After some bi-lingual negotiation with the bandleader, we chose 'Mr Sandman', a popular song at the time. The band struck up and Charlton and Armfield swung into an impromptu 'Mr Sandman, bring me a dream, make her complexion like peaches and cream . . .' Halfway through, the door opened at the back of the room and in walked Walter Winterbottom. I whispered to Bob, 'Don't wave!' We made it through to the end in one piece, milked the standing ovation for all we were worth, declined repeated requests for an encore and informed our manager that it had all been in the interests of team bonding and we all laughed it off. The following morning we set off on the final leg of our journey to Chile.

We were due to play our group matches against Hungary, Argentina and Bulgaria in Rancagua, a small town inland from Santiago, 8,000ft above sea level. Compared with the other group venues, Santiago, Vina del Mar and the northern town of Arica, it was very much out in the sticks. Rancagua was a 90-minute bus ride from Santiago airport and from there we climbed further into the foothills of the Andes on a single-track railway with just one coach. Our destination was a small village called Coya, home of the Braden Copper Company, who owned the village that was to be our home for 10 days of acclimatisation and our base and training camp for those three qualifying games. How Walter had found the place, I will never know.

The only way in and out of Coya was that single-track railway, and while these days Rancagua is a ski resort, 42 years ago it was a one-horse town in the middle of nowhere. It wouldn't have a prayer of being a World Cup venue today. Back in our camp, we were housed in little bungalows and on site there was a café, a cinema and a sort of tenpin bowling alley. The cinema showed

Posing for the camera with my mother
at the age of three

Star of the future? We're all entitled
to dream when we are young

Arnold School Sports Day, with two trophies and the Victor Ludorum shield

above The successful King's Own Royal Lancashire Regiment of 1955. I am on the left in the front row alongside Major Evans ... and, according to this picture, we had only ten men!

left Young hopeful. A right-winger for Blackpool Colts in a game against the Ministry of Pensions to mark the opening of a new ground at Norcross, Blackpool, in 1952

The Blackpool side that finished runners-up to Manchester United in 1955–56. Back row (from the left): Dave Durie, me, George Farm, Roy Gratrix, Tommy Garrett, Jimmy Kelly, Hughie Kelly. Front: Johnny Lynas (trainer), Stanley Matthews, Ernie Taylor, Jackie Mudie, Bill Perry, Joe Smith (manager)

right King of the swingers. I tee off at St Annes Old Links for a round of golf in FA Cup week. Hughie Kelly, Roy Gratrix and Bill Perry don't look too impressed

above In action against Manchester United's Busby Babes at Old Trafford. I support our keeper George Farm as Tommy Taylor challenges. Bobby Charlton looks on

England captain Billy Wright presents the Young Footballer of the Year award at Blackpool Tower, 1959

Back to school. A visit to Arnold School with Stanley Matthews (back left) and George Neal (back right), the man who set me on the football road. Stan Matthews junior is third from left in the front row

Our wedding day in June 1958. My parents, Christopher and Doris, are to my right with Anne's mother, Ann, and her uncle Teddy on her left

Tony Waiters and I get our skates on at Bloomfield Road during the 'Big Freeze' of 1963

A model dad. Helping Duncan (left) and John build their model aeroplanes

A chat with Stan Mortensen during the FA Centenary dinner in 1963

Lucky dip! Alan Ball and I were among the judges at the 1966 Miss UK competition following England's World Cup success

The loneliness of the long-distance runner. Pounding out the miles on Blackpool beach on the way back from the groin injury that disrupted my England career in 1964

Back at the top. Celebrating promotion to the old First Division with Fred Pickering (left) and manager Les Shannon at the end of the 1969-70 season

Ouch! I needed stitches after this clash against Burnley. The fans don't seem too concerned, though!

D.C. THOMSON & CO LTD

HOWARD TALBOT

above Stopping Jimmy Greaves from scoring – not always an easy task! Blackpool goalkeeper Alan Taylor dives at our feet

The last farewell. With Bobby Charlton before my final league game for Blackpool, against Manchester United at Bloomfield Road on Saturday, 1 May 1971

films with Spanish soundtracks – although that didn't really matter when Sophia Loren or Brigitte Bardot was on the screen. Nearby, a nine-hole golf course had been built into the hillside, with stunning views of the Andes. On one occasion, Ray Wilson and I went for a game and a local boy offered to caddy for us. He failed to last the pace, though, and I finished up humping both golf bags while Ray carried our caddy.

By today's standards, the conditions were pretty primitive and the players who assembled for the World Cup in South Korea and Japan 40 years later simply would not have believed the conditions at our camp at Coya. But we lived in a different era and made the best of the situation. The bottom line was that we were about to represent England in the World Cup, and for that privilege we were prepared to put up with a few hardships. We amused ourselves with games of cards and the usual schoolboy pranks. I remember one occasion when Johnny Haynes came running out of his bungalow, yelling about a giant spider that had crawled out from under his bed. It was a convincing performance but we all assumed it was a wind-up. Nevertheless, we followed Johnny back into the chalet and, sure enough, sitting quietly in a corner of the room was an enormous spider, around six inches in diameter and ominously like the kind of thing you could buy in any self-respecting joke shop on Blackpool's Golden Mile. However, this one decided to move just as one of the lads bent down to pick it up – we all beat a hasty retreat and a member of staff was summoned to dispose of the beast.

Eventually, the day of the opening ceremony dawned and we all boarded the single-track railway coach and headed for Rancagua on a grey afternoon. The four squads in the group stood to attention in the town square as the local brass band played each country's National Anthem. They made my local prize band sound like the band of the Grenadier Guards. The Mayor made a speech and then we all climbed back on the train and returned to Coya. The first match was between Argentina and Bulgaria and, once again, we left Coya on our train to watch the action. The stadium held around 10,000 with just one covered stand. These days you would describe it as a decent Conference ground.

Argentina scored after 30 seconds, the quickest goal of the World Cup, then defended for the next 89 minutes and won 1–0.

The weather changed for our opening game against the talented Hungarians. It was wet and the surface was slippery. We were the better side for most of the match but at 1–1 with a few minutes left, Florian Albert scored the winner. It was the worst possible start and the mood on the train back to camp was sombre. We knew we would have to beat Argentina in our next game to have any chance of reaching the quarter-finals. They had plenty of support but we played well and won 3–1. Argentina were one of the favourites but they hadn't convinced me against Bulgaria and we might have won more easily. They had a lot of quality individuals but they weren't a good team, and they were very physical. At one point, one of their players tapped me on the shoulder and when I turned round, he spat in my face. We had to put up with that kind of thing for the full 90 minutes.

The crunch, therefore, came against Bulgaria, always an awkward lot. They had lost both their opening matches but were desperate not to go home without picking up a single point while we needed a point to be sure of qualifying. We pushed forward well to start with but couldn't score and with about 15 minutes left, we actually came within inches of conceding a breakaway goal. Their outstanding player was Ivan Kolev, who was very similar in style to the Italian attacker Gianfranco Zola, and he drove in a cross from the left that beat everyone and whistled just past the far post. It was a warning to the whole team and from then on we were quite happy just to play out time. So were Bulgaria. Both sides sat back and what followed was the worst quarter of an hour of my playing career. We were just passing the ball around among ourselves and they decided not to come and get it. The match finished goalless and the crowd were not slow to let us know what they thought about it, with cries of 'Malo, malo!' as we left the field. As far as we were concerned, we had qualified from the toughest group and the end had justified the means.

We made it into the last eight along with Hungary, Russia, Yugoslavia, Czechoslovakia, West Germany, Brazil and Chile, whose notorious group game against Italy had been dubbed the Battle of Santiago. Chile's Sanchez somehow escaped dismissal after landing a left hook on the nose of the Italian player Maschio that would have graced Madison Square Garden. But two Italians were sent off in what remains one of the most violent matches in World Cup history, a game the England players watched on television back in Coya.

So it was time to climb aboard our railway carriage for the last time. Our quarter-final against Brazil was to be staged at Vina del Mar, on the bay of Valparaiso, 8,000ft below Coya, and so we set off back to sea level, where the weather was hotter and the humidity higher. Our hotel overlooked the bay and from our rooms we could watch the pelicans as they swooped above the blue waters of the Pacific. It was a totally different environment and, significantly, we had only three days to adapt to what were alien conditions while Brazil had been down at sea level from day one.

On the morning of the match, just before our pre-match meal, the tannoy coughed into life: 'Would Mr Armfield please come to reception.' I was told there was a gentleman waiting to see me and there, standing near the desk, was Doc Shepherd, a Blackpool director, the club dentist who had repaired the damage when I received an elbow in the face earlier in my career. I couldn't believe my eyes.

'Doc, what are you doing here?' I said.

'Well, I just thought I'd pop over and see you play.'

All the way from Blackpool to Vina del Mar! There was a slight problem, though – Doc didn't have a ticket for the game. Fortunately, one of the FA officials obliged.

It was a high-tension game. Brazil beat us 3–1 and went on to win the World Cup for the second time in a row. They were a good side, not quite as good as their 1970 team, perhaps, but not far behind. They were without Pele, who was injured in their second group game against Czechoslovakia and played no further part in the tournament. Amarildo proved a more than adequate replacement and, in Pele's absence, Garrincha seized the opportunity to become the star of the tournament. We gave them their toughest match. Garrincha scored in the 31st minute but after Gerry Hitchens equalised seven minutes later, we were in charge for a spell. Bobby Charlton gave Djalma Santos, their right-back, a chasing and we carved out a string of chances. We should have sewn it up but we failed to capitalise when we were on top and gave away two second-half goals to a side inspired by the genius of Garrincha. The scoreline suggests we were well beaten but it was a game we could easily have won. We had more or less matched them in front of a crowd of 17,736, of whom I reckon at least 17,000 were cheering for Brazil. We had gone so close despite having to adapt to conditions at sea level after three weeks up in the mountains, and I firmly believe that if we had beaten Brazil, we would have gone on to win the tournament. The words of an old man talking through his hat? It may seem that way but I genuinely felt it at the time.

After the match, Walter arranged for one or two players to talk to the press. I was one of them and I told the reporters that this was the most disappointing moment of my career, even though I felt I'd had a good tournament. I thought we had the team to win, although losing two key players in the build-up to the competition didn't do us any favours. The first was Bobby Smith, who had established himself at centre-forward but picked up an ankle injury in the game against Scotland and failed to recover. Bob was a much better player than people gave him credit for. He was more than a goalscorer, he was our target man – strong, bulky, with good control and he was aggressive without being dirty. He combined well with Greaves and a front four of Douglas, Greaves, Smith and Charlton would have been as good as anything in the competition. Hitchens and Alan Peacock were class players but Smith had been a key figure throughout our successful run and he and Greaves were a perfect combination. Smith's absence broke our attacking rhythm. Then, soon after we arrived in Chile, our central defender Peter Swan went down with a stomach bug. He was very ill for a while, although we hoped he would recover in time to play some part in the competition. But he didn't – and again, a vital cog in the machine was missing when the action started.

So in the end, it was another England hard-luck story. Four

years earlier, we might easily have won the competition but for the Munich air disaster and the loss of Byrne, Edwards and Taylor. In 1962, we could point to the absence of Smith and Swan and the change of climate and wonder about what might have been. Little did I know that the most successful England team of them all was being moulded out there in Chile. Many of the players who had gone close in 1962 were still going to be around four years later, when the competition would be played in England. They had gained vital experience at the highest level – and the era of England hard-luck stories was drawing to a close as we flew out of Santiago.

Some of the northern-based players travelled home from Chile on their own – international players today would not believe that. The southern contingent flew out on the official team flight, leaving Ray Wilson, Bryan Douglas, Eddie Hopkinson, Roger Hunt, Bobby Charlton and me to make our own way from Santiago to Manchester via New York, where we enjoyed an overnight stop at the Waldorf Astoria. We had a look at Times Square, the Empire State building and one or two more sights before completing our journey. For all the FA knew, we could have been touring the USA for weeks. There were no fanfares and speeches when we arrived home. We went our separate ways and took family holidays. England went on the backburner for a while but when we played our next game against France in September, it was time for me to move onwards and upwards once more.

THE RAMSEY ERA DAWNS

Alf Ramsey was named as Walter Winterbottom's successor in October 1962 and the management of the England team changed forever. I was captain of England for nine of Alf's first 10 matches in charge and but for a serious injury that halted my international career for over two years, I might have been his captain on 30 July 1966, the day England won the World Cup for the first and only time. Who knows? The reality is that I missed matches that were a crucial part of Alf's build-up to the World Cup although, thankfully, I was recalled to the squad in time to win a place in the final 22.

I always felt there was some kind of bond between Alf and me. In fact, he stayed in touch throughout my two-year absence, and on several occasions, even during the World Cup, he took me to one side and asked my opinion. He probably confided in me more than I might have expected and, in return, I always felt reasonably close to him – even though the only things we really had in common were that we both played right-back and both cared passionately about English football. Nevertheless, I always had a tremendous amount of respect for the man and when he died in April 1999, I was the only member of the back-up squad from the 1966 final who attended his funeral in Ipswich.

Alf had real steel. He was a player's man *par excellence*, and believed that players were the only people who really knew about professional football. He never had much time for directors and made no attempt to ingratiate himself with officialdom, the media or people on the periphery of the game. He was unflinchingly loyal to his players and would always defend them in public, taking the criticism himself; nor would he criticise individual players in front of the rest of the squad, instead taking them to one side or having a quiet, private word in his room. In return, the players gave him total loyalty and commitment. He was intensely patriotic. He believed absolutely that English football was the best in the world and English players were a match for anyone. At times, he would resort to near-jingoism in his pre-match talk. He would say, 'This lot don't like the English, you know. So let's go out and show them what real football is all about.' That call to arms was applied to many of our opponents during my time as one of Alf's players, particularly the Scots and the Germans. He wasn't being petty, though. I think he sincerely believed we were the equal of any team in the world.

Yet even though he was the most successful manager in the history of the English game, winning the World Cup in 1966, reaching the last eight four years later and winning 69 and losing just 17 of his 113 matches, I never felt Alf ever searched for personal glory. He wanted to win for England and for his players. The team ethos was everything and he knew exactly what kind of players he was looking for. The secret of his success as a club manager at Ipswich had been organisation and discipline for he was forced to operate on a small budget with little money to spend. That same discipline, organisation and team spirit were the qualities he brought to the England team. He couldn't be doing with 'tanner ball' players, or showboaters as we would call them today. There were individual players around the country who were more talented than some of the 22 Alf chose for his 1966 World Cup squad but Alf was aiming to build a unit, a set of players who would work for one another and play English-style football. He believed that if the team ethic was set in stone, the side would be successful, and so it proved.

Alf understood international football, which is vital in a manager. International football and club football are not alike and international players must be able to step out of their familiar club environment, whether it is Manchester United or Middlesbrough, Arsenal or Aston Villa, and perform with others on a bigger stage. That can take time and Alf understood that. He also expected us to act like international players at all times and assumed we would know how to behave. He never laid down the law or issued a strict code of discipline; we were just expected to do the right thing, and we did. Alf had a compassionate side where his players were concerned but he could give the cold shoulder to any player who got on the wrong side of him.

Until Alf's arrival, the England side had been in the hands of what might be termed well-meaning amateurs at the FA, who selected the squad by committee, with Walter Winterbottom having the final say. Ramsey, who in seven years had transformed Ipswich Town from an average side in the old Third Division South to Football League champions in 1962, was having none of that. He had always been his own man and he took the England job on his terms. He had no intention of being in charge of the coaching department – he wanted to run the team. He was prepared to stand or fall by his own decisions and would not suffer any outside interference.

When he took charge of the team for the first time in February 1963, I was captain of England with 32 previous international caps to my name, although my first game as captain had been a one-off appointment in a World Cup qualifier against Luxembourg at Highbury in September 1961. Johnny Haynes, the first choice, was injured and before the team was announced, Walter told me I would be taking over – but I knew I was a stand-in. We won 4–1, Haynes returned for the following game, against Wales, and skippered the side through to the end of the 1962 World Cup.

Soon after our return from Chile, Johnny was injured in a motor accident on Blackpool promenade of all places and was detained overnight in the town's Victoria Hospital with leg injuries. I went to visit him the following day and while he was in good spirits, it was obvious he was going to be out of action for some time and that England were going to need a new captain. I had been in the England team for three years, led the Under-23 side and been captain of Blackpool for four years so I felt I had a chance. Even so, I was thrilled to bits when Walter turned to me for the match against France at Hillsborough on 3 October 1962.

It was the first round of the European Nations Cup, the forerunner of today's European Championship. To be honest, England didn't put a great deal of store by the competition, which was a straight two-leg knock-out affair as opposed to the qualifying group system in operation today. It was all or nothing over two games. On a cold night at Hillsborough, the game attracted only a small crowd, even though France were very strong with Raymond Kopa and Rene Ferrier in their side. We drew 1–1, Ron Flowers scoring from the penalty spot after my Blackpool team-mate Ray Charnley had been brought down. It was Ray's one and only cap. He and I were room-mates at Blackpool and we have been pals ever since. In fact, he's been our decorator for years. Kopa replied for France. He was a great player, arguably the best French player I have seen, and a member of the all-conquering Real Madrid side of the fifties. Every so often, France produces a soccer genius, such as Michel Platini, Zinedine Zidane and Thierry Henry. Kopa and Just Fontaine, who scored 13 goals in the 1958 World Cup finals in Sweden, were perhaps the founders of the dynasty.

After going out of the World Cup at the quarter-final stage, Walter had decided it was time for a few new faces and in my first three games as captain, he used 19 players. The defence stayed more or less the same but up front, he experimented with Mike Hellawell of Birmingham, Alan Hinton of Wolves, Mike O'Grady of Huddersfield and Bobby Tambling on the wings. Chris Crowe of Wolves and Freddie Hill of Bolton were given an opportunity at inside-forward and Charnley had that single outing against the French. John Connelly, Alan Peacock and Gerry Hitchens were also in the mix and only Jimmy Greaves played in all three games up front. None of the new boys developed into regular choices, although O'Grady must go down as one of the unluckiest players to appear for England. He scored twice on his debut in a 3–1 win against Northern Ireland in Belfast, missed out because of illness in the next game against Wales, which we won 4–0, and was not seen again on the international scene for eight years. By the time he finally reappeared, he had moved to Leeds and he hit the target again in a 5–0 win over France at Wembley. It proved to be his final international appearance and I suppose on goals per game ratio he is one of the most successful players we have ever had!

It was an unsettling time because Walter's experiments took place amid continuous speculation about his future. The papers suggested that he was on his way out as coach after four World Cups and he was reported to be the preferred choice to succeed Sir Stanley Rous as secretary of the FA. However, that job was given to Dennis Follows and Walter eventually moved on to become head of the Central Council for Physical Recreation and later director general of the Sports Council. He was knighted in 1975. The two leading candidates to succeed him were Jimmy Adamson, who was still a player at Burnley but highly regarded as a coach, and Ramsey. When Adamson announced that he didn't want the job, the field was clear for Alf, who had played 32 times for England and made over 300 league appearances for Southampton and Spurs before going into management.

He was named as Walter's successor in October 1962, although the appointment was to be effective from the following May. However, he took charge of the side for a couple of games before he formally assumed control and the first of these was the return Nations Cup tie against France at the old Stade de Colombes in Paris on 27 February 1963. It could hardly be described as an auspicious start to the new era – we lost 5–2. It was snowing, the pitch was icy, the players could hardly stand up and the game should not really have gone ahead. I suspect the authorities took the view that as we were there, we might as well play the match, even though only a small crowd had turned out. Everything about the stadium was sub-standard. The dressing rooms were cramped, the floodlights were poor and our performance matched the ambience. Alf came over to me as I was taking off my boots.

'Do we always play like that?' he asked. I told him we didn't. 'Well, that's the first bit of decent news I've had all night,' he replied. 'We need to have a few words.'

So when we arrived back at the airport, Alf and I got together. Walter Winterbottom would almost certainly have been installed with FA hierarchy after the match but that wasn't Alf's style. His only priority as England's new manager was to build a successful side and he needed to discover what made his players tick. He was not a happy man.

'We don't let Frenchmen beat us at football – at least not like that,' was his opening gambit. We discussed the players, the performance, the reasons why England teams had tended to underachieve in big competitions. We spoke for over an hour and, looking back, that was probably one of the longest conversations Alf ever had with anyone involved in the England set-up. He was genuinely upset about the team's display and his final words as he stood up and headed for the departure gate were, 'We don't want any more performances like that.'

We scarcely covered ourselves in glory in Alf's second match either, losing 2–1 against Scotland at Wembley. The Scots had some class players – Jim Baxter, Dave Mackay, John White, Denis Law, Ian St John and Davie Wilson – and, as ever, they were up for it against the Auld Enemy. Alf changed the England side around a bit, giving Gordon Banks the first of his 73 caps as England's goalkeeper and introducing Gerry Byrne of Liverpool at left-back for the injured Ray Wilson. We were better than we had been against France but not good enough – and I was responsible for their opening goal, scored by Baxter. I was facing my own goal, about 30 yards out, and instead of turning towards the touchline and clearing the ball upfield, I turned inside, lost possession to Baxter and he went on to score. Alf was not best pleased and once again, I found myself on the receiving end in the dressing room.

'You'll never do that again, will you?' he said.

'No,' I replied.

'No, you won't,' retorted Alf meaningfully, and he moved on to the next man. Alf had made his point and I never tried to manoeuvre the ball inside like that ever again in my career. Every time I found myself in that situation for England or Blackpool, I remembered Alf's dictum and cleared the ball down the line.

That defeat was to be Ramsey's lowest point for seven years. Four weeks after losing to Scotland, we took on Brazil at Wembley and played well. Alf made changes again, bringing back Wilson and handing first caps to Gordon Milne and George Eastham in mid-field. We drew 1–1 and set off for a summer tour of Czechoslovakia, East Germany and Switzerland feeling much more confident. I had to miss the game against the Czechs because of a toe injury, providing Chelsea's Ken Shellito with an opportunity he seized with both hands. England were very impressive, won 4–2 and Ken really looked the part. I remember thinking to myself, 'I could struggle to get back here.' But Alf recalled me for the game against the East Germans in Leipzig and we won 2–1, Roger Hunt hitting the winner with a spectacular 25-yard shot.

And so it was on to Basle and the Swiss, an unpredictable side who could beat anybody on their day. This was never going to be their day, though. We won 8–1, Bryan Douglas scored one of the great solo goals and we gave a team performance that confirmed our belief that Alf was moving things in the right direction. Tony Kay of Everton won his one and only cap in front of me at right-half. A good player, Tony, but what looked certain to be a long England career was abruptly cut short soon afterwards when news broke of his involvement in the 1962 betting scandal. Tony, who had been with Sheffield Wednesday at the time of the offences, and two of his Hillsborough team-mates, England defender Peter Swan and David Layne, were jailed, received long-term bans and three careers were ruined.

Over the next 12 months, we defeated Wales, the Rest of the World and Northern Ireland and lost to the Scots again, this time at Hampden. The summer of '64 was going to be a busy time, with games against Uruguay, Portugal, Ireland and the USA before the so-called Little World Cup in Brazil, which would involve matches against the host nation, Argentina and Portugal. It was an exciting prospect and as I led out Blackpool for the last game of the season, against Ipswich at Portman Road on 25 April

1964, I was confident I would be heavily involved over the next two months. Instead, I did not play for my country again for over two years, by which time my dream of leading England in the 1966 World Cup was a distant memory.

On that April afternoon, Alf was sitting in the stand at Portman Road. Down in the dressing room, my suitcase was packed and we were due to travel to London together after the match to link up with the rest of the England party to prepare for the Uruguay game. Midway through the first half, with no other player anywhere near me, I felt a searing pain in my left groin. I pulled up immediately and knew straight away that I would be unable to continue. I hobbled out of the match and out of England's plans for the summer. Instead of driving down to London with Alf, I travelled home on the team bus and spent the night in hospital where the injury was diagnosed as a severely torn groin muscle. It was the most painful injury I ever suffered, worse than the broken left ankle I sustained a few years later, or the injury to my left knee that has caused me problems ever since. The timing could not have been worse.

At first, there were serious doubts that I would play again. If a player suffers a similar injury today, surgeons can tie the torn fibres together and the recuperation process is relatively short. But in 1964, the only cure was a few injections, lots of rest – and plenty of hope. My specialist believed the injury would heal itself eventually and advised me to take plenty of light exercise, gradually building up the strength in the muscle. I went swimming two or three times a week and spent a lot of time on the beach, wading out into the sea and taking the weight of the waves on my injured leg. I called to see Tom Finney, whose career was virtually ended by a similar nagging injury, and he warned me to act with caution. I did so and started with some gentle jogging on the beach, gradually stepping up the speed and distance. I finally returned to full training in the autumn.

Over the years, many people have asked me how I felt in the summer of '64, saying I must have been absolutely heartbroken. It was never as bad as that. It was a severe blow, of course, and the biggest setback of my international career but, to be honest, I came to terms with the England situation fairly quickly. I have always believed in fate and accepted that footballers have to regard injuries as part of the job. I wasn't the first international to suffer a big injury at a bad time and I wasn't going to be the last. I was disappointed – but I could handle that. The possibility of being finished at 29 was a far greater worry.

In my absence, Bobby Moore took over as captain, George Cohen established himself at right-back and Jack Charlton came in to central defence alongside Moore. I stayed in touch. I used to go down to watch England at Wembley and kept a close eye on their progress towards the World Cup, on and off the field. Inevitably, there were a few sympathetic newspaper articles about Armfield, England's forgotten man, but Alf stayed in contact to ask how I was coming along, something I appreciated a lot. It was a side of the man that most people never saw but he really cared for his players.

In March 1966, Alf came to watch me in action for Blackpool and sought me out after the match. He said he'd watched me two or three times and thought I was more or less back to my best. I didn't disagree. In fact, I felt that at 30, I was probably playing the best football of my career. Malcolm Allison, one of the leading English coaches at the time, agreed, saying in a news-paper article that I was playing better than ever before and should be in the England team.

'I want you to be in the World Cup squad,' Alf said. I admit that I was taken aback.

'That's fantastic,' I muttered in reply, absolutely thrilled to bits – I had thought my international career might be over. Alf continued, 'George is established at right-back and he's done well, but I need a good squad of players, experienced people who can come into the side if necessary. I'd like you to be there.'

So I came in from the cold against Yugoslavia at Wembley on 4 May. Alf rang me up a week beforehand and said, 'You'll be playing against Yugoslavia – how do you feel?'

'I'm all right.'

'Good,' he said, and rang off. Alf didn't waste time with small talk.

England's two previous matches had been a 1–0 win over West Germany at Wembley, in which Nobby Stiles scored the only goal of his international career, and a 4–3 victory over the Scots in Glasgow, and Alf made a few changes for the Yugoslavia game. He rested Cohen and Moore and I returned as right-back and captain. Coincidentally, my first game at Wembley had been against Yugoslavia six years earlier – and although I didn't know it at the time, this would be my farewell appearance beneath the Twin Towers. What I did know, however, was that this was a moment of truth for me. After an absence of 23 matches, I was back on the big stage and I had to perform. We won 2–0 and I was happy with my performance. I was marking Dragan Dzajic, at the time a teenage sensation who was attracting the interest of leading Italian clubs. He went on to play for his country 85 times and scored 23 goals – but that night at Wembley was going to be my moment, not his.

Two days later, Alf took the squad to Lilleshall for a final get-together before the summer tour. Everton centre-half Brian Labone had withdrawn from the original party of 28 because of injury, so we knew that five of the 27 players present would not be in his final squad for the World Cup. It was a tense time, although I was confident I would be selected. After all, Alf had already told me on the telephone that he wanted me in his final squad and he was not a man to make that kind of promise lightly. I had performed well against Yugoslavia so he had no reason to change his mind. Even so, I could not be 100 per cent sure.

In the end, the men who failed to make the squad were Peter Thompson, the Liverpool winger, whom I fancied would be included; midfield player Gordon Milne, also of Liverpool; strikers Bobby Tambling of Chelsea and Johnny Byrne of West Ham; and Keith Newton, the Blackburn full-back who must have been wondering if he would be given the nod ahead of me. I really felt for them. While every player in the country dreamed of being a member of the England World Cup squad in England, only a small percentage had a realistic chance of making the final 40 and the group at Lilleshall were an even more select band. To be so close yet so far must have been truly heartbreaking.

Alf's final 22 were goalkeepers Gordon Banks (Leicester), Ron Springett (Sheffield Wednesday), Peter Bonetti (Chelsea); full-backs George Cohen (Fulham), Ray Wilson (Everton), Jimmy Armfield (Blackpool), Gerry Byrne (Liverpool); defenders Bobby Moore (West Ham), Jack Charlton and Norman Hunter (Leeds), Ron Flowers (Wolves); midfield players Nobby Stiles and Bobby Charlton (Manchester United), Alan Ball (Blackpool), Martin Peters (West Ham), George Eastham (Arsenal); attackers Roger Hunt (Liverpool), Geoff Hurst (West Ham), Jimmy Greaves (Spurs), John Connelly (Manchester United), Terry Paine (Southampton) and Ian Callaghan (Liverpool). It was probably the strongest squad England had named for a World Cup.

When Alf announced the side to face Finland in Helsinki in the first game of the summer tour on 26 June, I held my place as right-back and captain. This time we won 3–0 and once again, I played very well. Unfortunately, with about five minutes to go, I was moving forward with the ball at my feet and their cumbersome left-sided midfield player came flying in and caught me on the little toe of my left foot. I made it through the last few minutes and almost scored my first England goal with my last meaningful touch in international football when I connected perfectly with a shot from just outside the box. It was heading inexorably for the top corner when their keeper, who had hardly made a decent save all afternoon, appeared from nowhere and tipped the ball on to the angle of post and bar.

Afterwards, the toe was very sore. I told Harold Shepherdson, our trainer, and although he applied some ice I was unable to get my left shoe on after the match. An x-ray revealed a slight crack in the toe. The next game was in Norway three days later, with matches against Denmark and Poland following on almost immediately. There was no way I could play against the Norwegians and Cohen reclaimed his place. Would I have held on to my place if that Finland midfield player had not clattered into me? Who knows? I never talked about it to Alf, either at the time or later. Maybe he played me in those two games to bring me back up to speed at international level, knowing that Cohen was his first choice; or maybe there was more to it and he was planning to restore me to the starting line-up when the competition began. Either way, the back four of Cohen, Charlton, Moore and Wilson played unchanged right through from the Denmark game to the World Cup final and, in fairness, they were the most consistent part of the team.

Alf's first-choice side had started to take shape on the tour. We had beaten Finland and Norway comfortably and played very impressively indeed in the wins over Denmark and Poland, two strong and talented sides. The starting line-up for the final match against Poland was, in 4–3–3 formation: Banks, Cohen, Charlton, Moore, Wilson; Stiles, Charlton, Peters; Ball, Hunt, Greaves. It looked a strong, settled side and with the exception of Hurst for Greaves, that side would start the final against West Germany just over three weeks later.

CHAPTER 9
ENGLAND'S FINEST HOUR

We returned from tour to find the Swinging Sixties were swinging like never before. In the summer of '66, England was *the* place to be and the English set trends in music and fashion that were followed across the world. The Beatles and the Rolling Stones dominated pop music, Mary Quant was the queen of fashion, Jean Shrimpton the world's most famous model and Carnaby Street and the King's Road were the places to see and be seen. And for the first time, the world's most famous football competition was to be staged in this country. Sixteen teams and 352 of the world's best footballers were preparing to do battle in front of packed stadiums across the length and breadth of the country. England was on red alert for the World Cup and the excitement and expectation were almost tangible. This was going to be the time when all the hard-luck stories and near misses could finally be forgotten.

In the final build-up to the competition, I represented the England squad at a special World Cup service in Westminster Abbey, reading one of the lessons. Stanley Matthews carried the FIFA flag at the head of the procession into the Abbey and among the personalities representing their sports were tennis player Virginia Wade, destined to win the women's singles title at Wimbledon 11 years later, and athlete Menzies Campbell, now a LibDem MP.

Although my injured toe was still troublesome, I was fit enough to play if selected and, like everyone else, excited about what lay ahead. The team spirit at the Hendon Hall Hotel, our headquarters in north London, was sky high and as the count-down to the first game against Uruguay ticked away, Alf Ramsey reminded the country, 'We can win.' The World Cup was Alf's dream and when, soon after his appointment, he had announced that we could win it, which wasn't his style, I wondered whether he was trying to put pressure on his players, to find out who would not crack when the chips were down. Maybe he was hoping to pull the country together behind his team. Only Alf knew, but I was certain of one thing – he had assembled what I still think is the strongest squad of players ever to represent England at a World Cup and to this day, I believe there has never been a better England party in any competition. I remember looking round at the rest of the players as we drove to Hendon Hall after arriving back in England and thinking that there wasn't a single weak link. We had flair, strength, know-how, depth and Alf had covered just about every eventuality by having experienced players in most areas.

All the players who would eventually become the back-up squad were more than good enough to play international foot-ball, and most of them had already collected around 20 or more caps. On top of that, we would be playing at home – and no one should ever underestimate the importance of home advantage in international competition. In 1966, it was a massive plus. We would be on familiar territory at Wembley, which had always been a good ground for England, the crowd would be right behind us and the adrenaline would be flowing. For the first time, I really believed we were going to win the World Cup.

Most of us assumed Alf would start the competition with the side that had finished the tour so strongly against Poland, so I was a little surprised when he tinkered with his selection for the opening game against Uruguay, bringing in John Connelly, an orthodox winger, for Martin Peters. At the time, I couldn't understand his thinking, although now, as a former manager, I can appreciate what he had in mind. A manager doesn't just think about one particular match, he is working on a longer-term strategy and picks particular players for specific situations. While Alf almost certainly knew the basis of his team, there was still some fine tuning to be done.

Barring injury, Banks would be in goal with Cohen, Jack Charlton, Moore and Wilson as his back four. Stiles and Bobby Charlton would be in midfield and none of us seriously doubted that Hunt, and probably Greaves, would play up front. But Alf still wanted to have a look at one or two options and, against Uruguay, he went for Connelly. He was a more progressive player than Peters, a quick, attacking winger who could operate on either flank and roam dangerously during a game. He had plenty of international experience and had won championships with Burnley and Manchester United, but it didn't work out, either for England or for John. He hit the woodwork twice and who knows how things would have turned out if one of those efforts had gone in. Instead, he never played international football again.

Uruguay were always going to be awkward opposition. Traditionally, they have strong players and even though their temperament is suspect, they are a team who must always be treated with the utmost respect. They were content to defend in depth, England never really got started and it finished goalless. To some people, that was almost a national disaster but I thought we'd done OK. We still had Mexico and France to play and the important thing was to avoid defeat in the first game. It was a nervous, twitchy affair – the opening match of a World Cup almost invariably is – and in the first instance, all that matters to the host nation is that they progress beyond the group stages. I have seen host nations literally freeze when the action starts – as Spain did in 1982 – but thankfully it didn't happen to us.

Nevertheless, Alf could not have been overjoyed as he made changes for the Mexico match, calling up Peters and Terry Paine for Alan Ball and Connelly. The Mexicans were not as good as Uruguay and we didn't play particularly well – until Bobby Charlton took centre stage with the goal that really kick-started England's competition. It was a marvellous goal that came from nowhere after a tepid opening half hour. Bob picked up the ball

deep in his own half and as a serious challenge failed to material-
ise, he surged forward before lashing an unstoppable shot into the
top corner from 30 yards. He also played a part in the second goal
15 minutes from time when he passed to Jimmy Greaves, whose
shot was blocked by the keeper and Roger Hunt did the rest. We
were on our way.

For the final group game, against France, Alf introduced
another orthodox winger, Ian Callaghan, who replaced Paine,
suggesting that he still hadn't given up on the idea of playing a
winger. I don't hold with the view that Alf mistrusted wingers. In
fact, I always felt he would have liked a winger in his side. He was
a full-back himself who would have understood the importance of
width in attack and at Ipswich he used flank players, Stephenson
and Leadbeater, in his championship team. Why did he choose
Connelly, Paine and Callaghan in his squad if he wasn't planning
to use them? But somehow the system never worked quite as well
with a winger in the line-up and, like Connelly and Paine,
Callaghan was to feature just once. With hindsight, I still wonder
whether Alf stumbled on his winning formula by chance or
whether it was a process of trial and error. We shall never know –
all that matters is that he found the route to success.

Hunt scored twice in a 2–0 win over a French side that really
offered little threat, but the big issue after the match was a
second-half tackle by Nobby Stiles, who had already been
booked, on the French midfield player Simon, who took no
further part in the match. Nobby's hard-tackling style had
already been fiercely criticised by a hostile international press and
there were calls in the media for FIFA to ban him from the
competition. FA officials suggested to Alf that Stiles might be left
out of the next match. Alf was furious. He established from
Nobby that the tackle, which Stiles admitted was late, was not a
deliberate attempt to hurt Simon, and then rounded on his
critics. He demanded to know whether all players who had been
booked in the group games would now be under scrutiny from
FIFA officials in the stand and insisted that he would not be
intimidated by outside pressures. It was yet another example of
Alf's loyalty to his players and his determination to stand by

Nobby, who went straight into the starting line-up for England's next game, a quarter-final against Argentina.

Reaching the last eight was all that mattered in the opening week of the competition. Maybe we had not been at our best but we had reinforced our reputation as a difficult side to beat and any team with ambitions about winning the Jules Rimet Trophy knew that somewhere along the line, they would have to overcome England. In Bobby Charlton, we had arguably the most influential player in the World Cup. I have always felt that Bob was our key player, the pivotal performer. If he had not been in the side, striking from those deep positions, I don't think we would have carried anything like the same threat. Every other team in the competition was afraid of him from the moment the ball hit the back of the net for his first goal against Mexico. He was one of only two players in the 1966 World Cup – Eusebio was the other – who could score that kind of goal and he proved it again with two in the semi-final against Portugal.

Bob was an explosive player who could glide past defenders as if they didn't exist, and he was much quicker and stronger than people thought. He was perfectly balanced, could play off either foot and when he had operated as an orthodox left-winger in the 1962 World Cup, Djalma Santos, the great Brazilian full-back, said he was the best winger he had ever faced. Even so, I thought he was wasted out on the wing – and, more significantly, so did Alf. Bob was far more dangerous as a central player because of his speed and mobility and, coming from behind, he was difficult for defenders to pick up. There's nothing more deflating for a defence than to see someone bursting through the middle and lashing a spectacular goal from distance. I always sensed an air of expectancy among the Manchester United fans whenever he gained possession in a threatening position. It was as if they knew something extraordinary might be about to happen – and quite often, it did.

The first time I saw Bob play was in a reserve match at Blackpool. I was in the first team by then but went along to watch with one or two of the other players. He was 17 or 18 but he was clearly going to be special. He became a central figure at Old Trafford in the aftermath of the Munich disaster in February 1958, and won his first England cap against Scotland soon afterwards, over a year before I made my international debut. The Scots still speak with awe about the first-time volley from a Tom Finney cross that gave him his first international goal. I always thought he was the ace in the pack for Matt Busby and Manchester United, even though such gifted players as Denis Law and George Best were in the same side.

Bob was a big match player – the bigger the occasion, the better he seemed to perform. That's a view shared by Franz Beckenbauer, for so long Charlton's opponent in midfield for West Germany, as I discovered a while back when I had lunch with Franz at Goodison Park. He and Dieter Hoeness, another former German international, were scouting at a match there and when the conversation turned to English players, Franz was adamant that Bob was the best English player he had faced. I wouldn't argue with that. I rate him as one of the great world footballers, and there have only been a handful in my lifetime – Matthews, Finney, Di Stefano and Pele, and none of those had a shot like Bob had.

In my opinion, he is the best player to appear for Manchester United during my time in football, and I have seen virtually all their great post-war players. So I was surprised, to put it mildly, when a poll among Old Trafford fans put Eric Cantona above him. Obviously, the majority of people who voted had never seen Bobby Charlton play or the way he conducted himself on and off the field. Bob was never sent off in his life and always set an example to his team-mates and, equally important, the people who paid to watch him. We are forever decrying unruly spectators but I am convinced that the players should set the right example, as Bob always did.

Despite all this, football management did not come easy in his two years at Preston in the mid-seventies. For while he's an astute businessman and his summer soccer schools have been a long-running success, he was not so successful at managing footballers. The game came so naturally to him that it was always going to be hard for him to explain what he wanted from others with less natural talents.

Off the field, he could be a little withdrawn and he was certainly not a man to seek publicity. Over the years, he has changed a bit and he is more at ease with life in the spotlight as he has shown in his role as a football and sporting ambassador. But even so, publicity and promotion have sought him out, rather than the other way round. He still prefers the quiet, family life. He's great company, though, and has a good sense of humour that the public rarely sees. I have always looked on Bob and his wife Norma as family friends. Like me, football has been his life and he has now found the perfect niche as a director of Manchester United, his first footballing love.

Bob's contribution to our triumph in the World Cup was immense – and maybe a four-man, after-dinner discussion at the Hendon Hall Hotel between our win over France and the match against Argentina had something to do with England's success as well. I was sitting with Alf, Harold Shepherdson and Bobby Moore, reminiscing about the old days, past World Cups and how football had changed over the years, and I casually remarked, 'You know, I have never yet seen a really successful England team without an old-fashioned centre-forward, a target man.' From there, the conversation turned to past greats Dixie Dean, Tommy Lawton and Nat Lofthouse, and I happened to mention that the only big striker we had in the squad was Geoff Hurst. Moore took up that line, pointing out that West Ham always used Geoff as a target man and how he rated him as just about the best in the business.

Now I'll never know whether Alf led us into that conversation to see how two of his senior players felt about using Geoff as a target man against Argentina – but with Greaves ruled out of the quarter-final because of a gashed shin, Hurst was clearly going to be involved. In the end, Alf changed the system to accommodate Geoff as a target man alongside Hunt.

I believed the Argentina match would prove decisive and I was right. Rattin, Marzolini, Artime, Onega and Mas compared favourably with the world's best and Argentina were a talented side. They were quick, passed the ball well and the defence was very solid. They qualified for the quarter-final by beating Spain and Switzerland and drawing with West Germany, and no one had any doubt that this would be our toughest test so far, the first major hurdle, and so it proved. In one of the most controversial matches in World Cup history, the game was held up for nearly 10 minutes towards the end of the first half when Rattin, the Argentine midfield player and captain, was sent off by German referee Rudolf Kreitlein and refused to go. It was chaos and at one point, there was a serious threat that the match would be abandoned as the entire Argentina team and several members of the coaching staff surrounded Kreitlein. The police eventually intervened and Rattin made the long, slow walk to the tunnel. I didn't think he was going to be sent off. There would be no question about it today but in 1966 it took quite a lot for a player to be given his marching orders. He had collected an earlier booking for a foul and had spent the rest of his time on the field committing minor fouls and arguing with Kreitlein, and I suspect the referee had simply had enough.

Rattin's dismissal was a massive boost for England. He was a terrific player who could control a game because he read it so well and, equally important, he was the leader of the pack. Like so many South American players of that generation, his temperament did not match his skill – as I remembered from the 1962 World Cup in Chile. His departure frustrated Argentina but they hung on until 13 minutes from time when Peters crossed from the left and Hurst rose to head in the only goal of the game. It was a move perfected on the West Ham training ground. I wondered at first if Geoff was offside, but there was no flag and, to this day, I can visualise the tiny figure of Herr Kreitlein running back towards the centre circle with his arm aloft, signalling the goal. He looked almost as relieved that we wouldn't be going into extra time as the 88,000 England fans in the stadium.

Afterwards I said to Alf, 'I think we can do it now.' He looked at me, almost through me, in fact, and never said a word in reply; he just walked on. I suspect he was thinking along the same lines. I never thought for a minute that we would lose to

Portugal in the semi-final. They had some of the great Benfica side's star names – Eusebio, Coluna, Torres, Simoes and Jose Augusto. Eusebio, who in my opinion is the best player Portugal has produced, was capable of anything, as he had proved with four goals in a sensational quarter-final against North Korea. But the fact that the Koreans had run them so close told me that Portugal were not quite the force they had been a few years earlier. Bobby Charlton scored twice and Eusebio replied with a penalty, but it was Bob's night. He performed equally well two years later when Manchester United defeated Benfica on the same ground to win the European Cup for the first time. That was surely his best performance in a United shirt.

Banks was emerging as the best goalkeeper in the world. Cohen, Jack Charlton, Moore and Wilson were a reliable unit who made few mistakes. Stiles was a marker, a prop in the middle of the field, an enthusiast, and Ball, whom I had seen develop into an international player at Blackpool, provided the youthful exuberance that is vital to any team. He would run his heart out for the cause, while Peters, another young player, was cultured and intelligent. Up front, Hunt was strong, totally selfless and a great finisher who had scored three times in the first five matches. Hurst provided the crucial link as the target man. He could play with his back to goal, hold the ball and wait for Bobby Charlton, Ball and Peters to come surging through.

It was a formidable side and we all knew that Alf would not be making changes for the final, even though Greaves was now fit again. The time for experiments had gone. Hurst had come in and done well and Alf was unlikely to gamble on a player who had missed the previous two games. I felt for Jim. At the time, he had played in 54 games for England and scored 43 goals; he had been involved throughout the build-up to the World Cup and appeared in all three group games, without scoring, before picking up that shin injury against France. During the countdown to 30 July, there was speculation that Alf might recall him but I suspect Jim knew that he wouldn't be playing. It hit him hard. In 1991, there was a reunion to commemorate the 25th anniversary of our victory and all the World Cup winners and most of the reserves were there. Jim was one of the absentees.

I accepted that I was unlikely to play a part in the finals unless something went wrong. I had to be content to be a member of the squad and, in a way, I became regarded as the unofficial leader of the Second XI, as I discovered after a friendly against Arsenal at their training ground. It was important to keep the reserve players active and the game against Arsenal enabled us to get some match practice. They had only just started pre-season training so they weren't up to our levels of fitness and we won 3–1. Afterwards, my team-mates hoisted me on to their shoulders and carried me from the pitch in triumph, a gesture that summed up the spirit that ran right through the squad.

We had bonded well off the field as well and once or twice during the tournament we had an opportunity to take a break from the public expectation and the media spotlight. The entire squad went along for a day out at Pinewood Studios, for example, and it was riveting, as far away from the reality of the World Cup as we could possibly get. They were making three films at the time, including *You Only Live Twice*, the fifth James Bond film with Sean Connery, and we were free to stroll around the set and watch the action. Yul Brynner was also working at the studios and a lunch was laid on for the players and some of the leading actors. I sat next to Brynner. He didn't know the first thing about football or, for that matter, the World Cup but instead, he entranced me with stories from his own past, including the time he spent chasing wild horses in Kazakhstan. He barely paused for breath. Lulu joined us for lunch, too, and I'm sure she took a shine to Alan Ball – or maybe it was the other way round. Two little redheads together! As we left, Sean Connery invited us all to a party he was planning to hold at his house later that summer and a few of the players and their wives went along. I decided to give it a miss and Anne hasn't forgiven me to this day.

I watched all the games, desperately wanting England to win and George Cohen to do well. I never once hoped George might make a slip, give away a crucial goal and make Alf wonder if it was time to call me back. I knew I was one injury away from a place in the side, but I did not wish any misfortune on George. It was the

World Cup, it was being staged in England and it was in everyone's interests for the team to do well. I can't know for sure, of course, but I believe the rest of the players who were on the sidelines felt the same way. In a way, we became supporters and, as far as I was aware, there was no feeling of 'us and them' among the back-up players.

But I would be lying if I pretended that every time England played – and especially on Saturday, 30 July 1966 – I wasn't wishing I could be out there on the field instead of sitting in the stand. Over the years, I have been asked many times to describe how the reserves felt and it isn't easy. It was the greatest day in the history of English football and it was impossible not to feel a sense of deep frustration at being so close and yet so far. Generations of football supporters can reel off the 11 names of England's World Cup heroes and those names are there in the record books for all time, but apart from a few pub quiz teams, how many people can remember the 11 who missed out?

We travelled to the stadium on the official coach and all the players went into the dressing room together, but an hour before kick-off, when it was time for the team to start getting changed, we wished them well and walked out into the stadium. It was a time of realisation as we mingled with supporters and made our way into the main stand. In a way we were feeling awkward. Footballers want to play, not watch, and this was the moment of truth. We were in the squad but now we were merely spectators. No more matches, this was it and we weren't on the field. There were no subs, so instead of sitting near the bench, the reserve players were given stand tickets. Alf, typically, wanted everyone to be involved at the end of the match, win or lose, and told me to make sure the Second XI were down at the side of the pitch for the last few minutes. Before the game, he took me to one side and said, 'The FA have arranged with the people at Wembley for you all to come down in the lift to the tunnel near the Royal Box just before the end. There will be some places for you on the bench behind where I will be sitting. Can you make sure everyone is down there?' So, with England leading 2–1, we left our seats and headed for the lift. It took us the best part of five minutes to reach the tunnel and I was the first to emerge – just as Weber scored Germany's equaliser. Some of the players who had made their way down from the stand couldn't have seen that goal but we were all together throughout that extraordinary 30 minutes of extra time.

We witnessed Hurst's controversial second goal that bounced down from the crossbar and, according to the Russian linesman, crossed the line to put England 3–2 ahead. And we saw Hurst hit one of the finest goals of the competition to seal England's victory seconds from the end. I sat immediately behind Alf and when the final whistle blew, I stood up and put my hands on his shoulders and shouted, 'We've done it,' or words to that effect. Everyone around the bench erupted, except Alf, whose expression scarcely changed in his moment of triumph. It made a marvellous picture. In the immediate aftermath, I went through a series of emotions. I was thrilled that my colleagues had triumphed for England and that I had been part of the greatest moment in English football history. At the same time, all the lads who did not play were disappointed that we had not been out there, too – it doesn't get any better than winning a World Cup in your own country. Alf and the players were surrounded by the world's media as they prepared to climb the stairs to the Royal Box to receive the trophy and their medals, and there is a picture that shows me in the middle of the celebrations. I was only trying to reach Alf to ask what the other 11 players should do now, but I couldn't force my way through the melee. So while the players enjoyed their lap of honour, we strolled back to the dressing room and waited for the World Cup winners to arrive. It was an awkward time, even though we were thrilled the lads had won.

The bus journey to the Royal Garden Hotel in Kensington, where the official reception was held, was incredible. I can only compare it with the end of the Second World War and with Blackpool's homecoming after the 1953 FA Cup final. The crowds were six and seven deep on the pavement for the whole journey and the bus struggled to get through Kensington High Street. Alf insisted that the entire squad should go out on to the hotel balcony and we were there for quite some time. Incredibly, that evening at the Royal Garden Hotel proved to be the last time all 22 players and their manager would ever assemble as a squad. The team went into the celebration banquet in an upstairs suite, attended by the football and political hierarchy – but not the players' wives. They had to eat downstairs in the hotel dining room. I can't imagine how Mrs Beckham and the rest would react to that arrangement these days but that's how it was in 1966. We linked up with them afterwards and Bobby Moore and I, plus some of the other lads, took our wives to the Playboy Club on Park Lane. Bob had been invited as a guest of the management and, needless to say, all the drinks were on the house with a bevy of Bunny Girls pouring the champagne like there was no tomorrow. I hadn't played, but I thought, 'What the hell', so Bob and I went to town with the bubbly.

There were a few hangovers the following morning as the players, this time accompanied by our wives, made our way to the ITV studios for a 'lunchtime after the day before' programme. Only Jimmy Greaves was absent. He had already left for a pre-arranged family holiday in Majorca prior to rejoining the Spurs squad on their pre-season tour of Spain a week later. We were sat down in a big square, players and wives in alternate seats, and over lunch the interviewer spoke to all the players in turn. Inevitably, he asked me how it felt to be a former captain sitting on the sidelines. I never quite knew who was responsible for pulling the show together but it was quite a coup and somebody, somewhere – a forerunner of today's agents – must have got a few bob out of it. All I know is that it wasn't the players!

After the programme, Alf led us into a little side room at the studios. It was a bit cramped, to put it mildly, and one or two of the players at the back had to stand on chairs so they could see what was happening. We thought Alf was going to give a farewell speech, saying what a wonderful set of players we were and so on, but he said, 'We need to talk about money. There's £22,000 to be shared among the squad as a bonus for winning the World Cup. How do you want to divide it up?' Incredible as it may seem today, it was the first time anyone had mentioned money since the start of the competition. Now, agents ensure that bonuses and all the other perks are worked out well in advance. All we were given was a suit and tie, a tracksuit that never quite fitted and, of all things, a briefcase. Alf looked vulnerable because he was never at ease talking about money and was waiting for someone else to make the decision. I was just about to say that the money should be shared equally between the whole squad when Bobby Moore beat me to the punch.

'Look Alf, there are twenty-two of us in the squad and £22,000 in the kitty. It looks pretty straightforward to me – £1,000 a man.'

'That's fine by me,' said Alf. 'Are you all agreeable to that?' There was a general hum of approval. 'Good, that's settled then. Thanks for everything. I'll see you all again quite soon.' And he walked out of the room. Just like that!

The bonus arrived shortly afterwards along with a payment of £248 15s, made up of six match fees at £30 a game, daily allowance amounting to £46 and the return train fare (second class) from Blackpool to London. I think the men who actually played in a game received £60 a match.

That gesture summed up Bobby Moore. I'm sure if he had taken a different line, the players who appeared in the final would have been given a larger share of the kitty. But we had decided among ourselves beforehand that we would share any bonuses, although that had not been officially agreed with the FA, and Bob pointed out that there would be plenty of opportunities for the 11 players to earn a bit extra in the aftermath of the victory. I always respected him for that.

As the first English captain to lift the World Cup, Bob became an instant hero, a Boy's Own figure with his blond hair and good looks, and in July 1966, he was approaching world-class. He became a truly great player in the four years after holding aloft the Jules Rimet Trophy, reaching his peak in Mexico in 1970. I didn't think he was really ready in 1962, when he came into the side as a replacement for Bobby Robson and played in all four games. I'm sure people said the same about me in my early days as an England player. But as time went by, he became a superb reader of the game and above all, he was never ruffled. He was

THE FOOTBALL ASSOCIATION

Patron: HER MAJESTY THE QUEEN
President: THE EARL OF HAREWOOD

Secretary:
DENIS FOLLOWS, M B.E., B.A.

Telegraphic Address:
FOOTBALL ASSOCIATION, LONDON, W.2

22 LANCASTER GATE, LONDON, W.2

Ref XNY/YL

The Secretary,
Blackpool F.C.

26th August 1966.

Dear Sir,

    I have pleasure in enclosing a cheque for £ 248.15.-. details of which are shown below.

    I should be pleased if you would pay the player(s) concerned after deducting tax, according to their F.A.Y.E. Coding on the amounts shown in those columns marked 'Subject to Deduction of Tax'.

    Thanking you in advance for your co-operation.

Yours faithfully,

Secretary

.... World Cup 1966 .... Date 8-30th July 1966..

Player(s)	Subject to Deduction of Tax			Currency Advanced	Due to Player
	Match Fees	T.V. Fees	Daily Allowance	Expenses	
			£ s.d.	£ s.d	
J. Armfield	£180		46.-.-.	22.15.-		£248.15.-

Cheque Enclosed:- £248.15.-

My pay slip from the FA after England's World Cup victory

always in control of any situation, never more so than in the dying seconds of the '66 World Cup final when he brought the ball out of defence, looked up and sent Hurst away for his hat-trick goal with that marvellous pass. With England leading 3–2 and the Germans pressing for an equaliser, most players would have been content to hoof the ball into the stand. The legs were tired, the brain was not quite what it had been 119 minutes earlier and it was a real pressure situation. But Bob was composed and skilful enough to play his way out of trouble and set up the decisive goal with a perfect pass.

The one thing that could disturb him was sheer pace and when West Ham came to Blackpool for a third round FA Cup tie in 1971, we pushed Tony Green, our inside-forward, right up front against Moore. Tony was quick, clever and a threat for any defender and we won 4–0 – although it later transpired that Bob and one or two of his team-mates had been out on the town the night before so perhaps they weren't at their brilliant best anyway. Later in his career, Bob was usually able to compensate for his lack of pace with his astute reading of a game.

I played in the same side as Bob for four years but while we got on well, we were never really close. I can honestly say, though, that there was no awkwardness on either side about him succeeding me as England captain. As far as I was concerned, it was just the way the cookie crumbled. I had been unlucky and Bob clearly didn't feel uneasy about the presence of his immediate predecessor in the squad – after all, he invited me to the Playboy Club and greater love hath no man than that! On another occasion during the competition, he asked me to join him for a charity event in east London. He had been asked by a friend who owned a pub to knock over a pile of pennies and wanted to take along another England player. It was a good night.

Towards the end of his life, he worked for a London radio station and we would sometimes bump into one another and talk about old times when he came north. The last time we were together was at Elland Road shortly before his death in 1993 and I could see in his eyes that he was dreadfully ill. We spoke for about half an hour and I felt desperately sad to see him so poorly.

It was a cruel irony that the first member of the World Cup squad to die should be its captain.

One issue that Bob and I felt strongly about was the award of a winner's medal to all 22 members of the squad. Once, when I was manager at Leeds, we had a match in London and were staying at the Royal Garden Hotel, scene of our after-match banquet around 10 years earlier. I arranged for Bob to have a couple of tickets to the game and we had lunch at the hotel beforehand. Halfway through the meal, Bob said, 'There's something I've always meant to ask you, Jim. Did the players who didn't play in the final ever get that medal?' I told him we didn't. Bob said it was something he had mentioned to Alf soon after the competition and he'd been under the impression that medals were going to be awarded. It was a subject I had also raised with Alf. I felt strongly that there should have been some form of recognition for the reserves and a lot of the lads felt the same way.

The squad worked as a unit from day one and Alf would have been faced with real problems if any of the back-up players had caused trouble. But they rallied round from the start and played a crucial part in developing the team spirit that was such big factor in England's success. In more recent World Cups, every member of the winning squad has received a medal but that only applied to the starting 11 in 1966. Maybe one day, while most of us are still alive, someone will give it some consideration, especially for those players who appeared in the early rounds.

Another reflection of the times was that Bobby Moore was the only player to receive any kind of honour when he was awarded the OBE soon after England's victory. One or two more members of the side received honours as the years went by but it wasn't until 1998 that all the players who had featured in English football's finest hour were finally honoured. They deserved it because, in sporting terms, no one before or since has stirred the nation quite like the Boys of '66.

FAREWELL TO THE
TANGERINE SHIRT

English football had never had it so good. World Cup victory raised the game's profile to a new level and when the 1966–67 season began, the fans flocked back to the domestic game in their thousands. But if it was the start of a new era nationally, it was also the beginning of a slide for Blackpool Football Club.

The sale of Alan Ball, our World Cup hero, to Everton for £115,000 had a demoralising effect on everyone connected with the club and defeat in our first game at Hillsborough heralded a disastrous start to the season in which we collected just two points from our first 11 games. We finally recorded a victory by beating Spurs 3–1 at White Hart Lane on 15 October and the following week we hammered Newcastle 6–0 at home. It was a false dawn. We won just two of our next 19 games and finished the season with a paltry 21 points, dropping out of the top division for the first time since 1937.

It may sound egotistical but if I had not played for England, I would have regarded myself as a football failure. I had, after all, given up a university career to play football, so winning 43 England caps and captaining my country gave me the satisfaction of knowing that I had made the right decision. Playing in the First Division had been a determining factor. There has always been a huge gulf in class between the top two divisions and I wanted to play in the top flight, against the top players and at the best grounds. The First Division was the place to be but over the next three years I was going to learn the hard way what life was like below the highest level.

Inevitably, Ronnie Suart paid the price for relegation and was succeeded by Stan Mortensen, Blackpool's Cup final hero of 1953 and one of my boyhood idols. Morty soon pulled off one of the transfer coups of all time by signing Tony Green from Albion Rovers and Tommy Hutchison from Alloa in the space of three days, and then Henry Mowbray from Cowdenbeath soon afterwards, for a combined total of £11,000. Green went on to play six times for Scotland and I believe he would have been a sensational player if his career had not been cut short by injury in his mid-twenties after a big money move to Newcastle in 1971. Tony had everything – speed, control, energy and that magical ability to beat defenders. Hutchison, an old-fashioned left-winger, won 17 Scottish caps and played over 900 games for six different clubs before retiring in 1991 at the age of 43.

They were tremendous signings but by the time we returned to the top division in 1970, Stan had been replaced by Les Shannon. I don't quite know what Morty did wrong. He was popular with the fans, the players liked him and in his only full season, 1967–68, we finished in third place with 58 points, at the time the highest number of points gained by a side who did not win promotion from Division Two. On the final day, we won 3–1 at Huddersfield while QPR won 2–1 at Aston Villa and we lost out to Rangers on goal average by 0.02 of a goal. It was a bitter disappointment but afterwards, we had a meal in the George Hotel in Huddersfield, where the Rugby Football League was founded in August 1895, and I assured everyone we would go up the following season.

In fact, my forecast was premature and we had to wait until the 1969–70 season. We were a pretty good side with Green, Hutchison, Fred Pickering, Bill Bentley and Glyn James. Shannon, a cultured coach who had worked abroad, encouraged us to pass the ball and play with flair and he brought the best out of us. Our penultimate game was a Monday night derby at Preston. We needed a win to go up, North End had to win to have a realistic chance of staying up. It was an unbelievable scenario, the derby of derbies. We spent the weekend at peaceful Grange over Sands – there's no way anyone can get into too much trouble there. Preston had some good players, including Archie Gemmill and Alan Spavin, but nevertheless, I was convinced Preston couldn't beat us. That level of confidence is a wonderful feeling. The gates were closed when we arrived and there were 5,000 Blackpool fans locked out in the park across the road from Deepdale. We won 3–0, with Fred Pickering scoring all three. I was ecstatic. We had done well all season and deserved to be back in the First Division, and on a personal level, I was thrilled to return to the top flight. Promotion took me back there for one last hurrah and my testimonial season.

I had a clause in my final contract to say that I was entitled to a testimonial match and I decided to hold it on my 35th birthday, 21 September 1970, when the town would be busy with the illuminations crowds. I went to see the chairman, Bill Cartmell, and told him my plans. He was wearing a trilby, which he pushed on to the back of his head, and he clearly wasn't thrilled about the idea, muttering something about not wanting to hold matches while the illuminations were on. But I had been at the club for 18 years, I'd played almost 600 matches and I was due a testimonial. So I persisted and he promised to raise the subject with the rest of the directors at that week's board meeting. The day after the meeting, I went to see him again.

'Well,' he said, 'some of them weren't too keen but I've been able to swing it for you.'

I couldn't believe it. How could anyone even think of denying me a testimonial as a reward for the loyalty I had shown Blackpool? The board's attitude taught me that in football, people only live for the moment.

I arranged for Blackpool to play an International XI that included Billy Bremner, Jack Charlton, Colin Bell, Franny Lee, Mike Summerbee and Alan Hodgkinson. I produced the souvenir brochure myself and sold all the advertising space. The club allowed me to use the ground for nothing and helped with the programmes. The game attracted almost 17,000 people on a poor night and raised around £6,000, enough to buy a decent house in those days. So, despite the reluctance of some of the directors to give me the go-ahead, I had every reason to be grateful to the people of Blackpool. The loyal supporters all turned up.

Unfortunately, that night was to be one of the few highlights of a dismal season. We didn't strengthen after promotion and opened with a 3–0 defeat at Huddersfield, who had also been promoted. We won two of our first five games in August but failed to win again until December. Les Shannon departed and after a brief spell with Jimmy Meadows as caretaker-manager, Bob Stokoe came in. We never seriously looked like avoiding the drop and finished with just four wins and 23 points.

It was time for me to think about the future. I was coming up to 36 and I'd had a good run. I'd struggled with a bad knee injury all season, on top of an ankle injury the previous year, and missed six or eight matches. I recovered just before Easter and was due to play a comeback game for the reserves at Blackburn. Bob asked me where I wanted to play and, as I was keen to feel my way back gradually, we decided on central midfield. Though I say it myself, I played very well. It was a position I'd sometimes fancied and straight away one or two people were talking about a first-team return in that role. It was never a serious possibility, not least because there's a world of difference between a run-out in the Central League and a First Division relegation struggle.

It was obvious that Bob wanted to change the club round and bring in fresh faces, and I wasn't going to figure in his long-term plans. Eventually, he called me in and asked what I would like to do.

'Do you fancy a free transfer?' he asked.

'I'm not going to play anywhere else,' I replied. 'Not at my age.'

My last game was on Saturday, 1 May 1971, against Manchester United, a good note to finish on. It was the last time Blackpool attracted 30,000 for a league game and both sides lined up on the pitch to form a guard of honour. Bobby Charlton was United's skipper and after I had walked out between the two sets of players, the press took pictures of Bob and me. We drew 1–1, which was a good result for Blackpool. The club has not played in the top division again to this day – right now I wonder if they will ever return. Oddly, I wasn't too emotional afterwards. I have always been a sensitive person but I have also been a realist and I was wise enough to appreciate that nothing goes on forever. Footballers who play a long time always try to convince themselves that they might go on for another season but time waits for no man, not even Stanley Matthews. I had known this day was on the not-so-distant horizon when I returned to Blackpool after the World Cup.

Nevertheless, retirement was a huge wrench. It was so difficult to come to terms with the knowledge that there was no way back, that I had made an irrevocable decision. At 35, my chosen career was over and I had never known anything else. My time clock had been set around Blackpool Football Club. I got up at eight, had a light breakfast, went to the ground and trained until lunchtime. Two days a week, I would go back to the ground for extra training. On the other days, I would go to the *Gazette*. It was a set routine. Even when Duncan and John were babies, I would do the night feed with the bottle on Sunday, Monday and Tuesday and it would be my turn to do the sleeping for the rest of the week as Saturday approached. 'You're a long time finished' is a popular expression in football and believe me, you are.

So what were the options? Even though I had been working part-time at the *Blackpool Evening Gazette* for a few years, I didn't really think anyone would employ me as a journalist, and I didn't have a business as a sideline. Nowadays, the PFA offers players many different ways to find an alternative career if they decide not to stay in the game, but that wasn't the case in 1971. Above all, I didn't want to leave football and I had already enjoyed a brief taste of what was involved in management as player-manager of the FA tour to Tahiti, New Zealand and the Far East in the summer of 1969.

It was the latest in a series of goodwill tours and Alf Ramsey had put my name forward as manager. We picked the 17-strong squad together and came up with a combination of experienced professionals, up-and-coming youngsters and three players from amateur clubs. My captain was Don Megson, the Sheffield Wednesday defender. Alan Hodgkinson of Sheffield United and

Oxford City's John Shippey were the goalkeepers and the other players were Ken Knighton and Graham Hawkins of Preston, David Payne (Crystal Palace), Keith Eddy (Watford), Ian Morgan (QPR), Keith Weller (Millwall), Tony Hateley (Coventry), George Eastham (Stoke), Colin Dobson (Huddersfield), Bruce Rioch (Luton), Norman Piper (Plymouth), John Charles (Leytonstone), Chris Gedney (Alvechurch) and me.

It was a strong squad. I'd been to New Zealand and the Far East before and I knew what to expect, so I didn't go for 'tanner ball' players. I wanted strong, experienced, reliable performers who would adapt to any conditions. While we were aware of our responsibilities to entertain, we were also determined to win as many games as possible. I like to think we succeeded on both counts, winning all 11 games, scoring 68 goals and conceding only seven. It was a long tour, starting with a 4–1 win in Tahiti on 21 May and ending with a 4–0 win over Thailand on 20 June. We played seven games in New Zealand, three of them against the national side, and we also played Singapore and Hong Kong.

The weather varied from tropical rain in Tahiti to intense heat and humidity in Bangkok and by the time the tour ended, a scratch group of players had become a formidable unit with a strong team ethic. As manager, I wasn't interested in losing. We were there to win because I knew from experience how tough a long tour can be when results are not going well, and I had laid down the disciplinary ground rules at our first get-together at the Bank of England sports ground in Roehampton.

I must admit I was a bit apprehensive about managing an international squad for the first time – or any squad for that matter. I told them to report at 10 o'clock and when I arrived right on the dot, we were one man short, Tony Hateley. In a way, it was a lucky break for me because Tony was one of the big-name players and I took the opportunity to demonstrate to the whole squad that I wasn't prepared to stand any nonsense from anyone, not even the highest-profile player in the party. He arrived five minutes late and I asked him why.

'My shoe lace broke so I had to find another.'

'Right, from now on, when I say I want you in at nine o'clock,

I mean you all have to be here at five to nine – ready to start training when I arrive at nine.' From then on, I never had a single disciplinary problem of any kind and those players were a credit to English football.

I also had to come to terms with the off-the-field pressures a manager may have to face and dealt with two instances of personal tragedy. Keith De Mau, one of the three FA representatives on tour, collapsed and died while we were in New Zealand, and I had to break the news to Colin Dobson that his father had passed away and make arrangements for him to return home. I encountered a hostile media for the first time in Hong Kong, where we beat the national side 6–0 in front of 28,000 fans at Happy Valley. The first question at the opening press conference was, 'How do you think the game between England and Hong Kong will go?' I replied by pointing out that this wasn't the England team, this was a side representing the FA.

'What's the difference?' retorted my interrogator.

'Well, England is the full international side that won the World Cup under Alf Ramsey three years ago and . . .'

'So Hong Kong isn't good enough for the real England team? You don't bring a good side to play against us?'

I tried to placate him by saying that we were only too aware of how strong Hong Kong would be and we had selected a very strong side who had won their first nine games on the tour. One or two of the next day's papers implied that the FA didn't take Hong Kong seriously as a footballing nation but when the action started, we showed them how serious we were with a 6–0 victory.

I came on as a substitute just after half-time and towards the end of the match, I noticed one or two fires were being lit around the stadium and police patrols were moving into position around the pitch. I sensed trouble and said to the players, 'As soon as the final whistle blows, off! No waving to the crowd, just go straight off.' Sure enough, after the game, two cars were set alight and there was a demonstration in the streets around the stadium. It was nothing major but confirmed an undercurrent of hostility, possibly Communist-inspired, that I had sensed from that first press conference. In the end, I was glad when we flew out.

Thailand was a different world. The hospitality was wonderful and featured a traditional dinner with demonstrations of Thai sword fighting and boxing, not to mention dancing and cobra wrestling. Bangkok was also the scene of my first minor altercation with FA authority. It was absolutely sweltering and after our first training session at the stadium, where the dressing rooms were not brilliant, I told the players to go straight back to the hotel on the coach and change and shower there. I decided to do the same thing on match night and told the players to report in the hotel lobby wearing T-shirts and shorts. Ike Robinson and Jack Bowers, two of the FA councillors on the tour and both in their seventies, had other ideas about dress code and Ike appeared in blazer and flannels, wearing a pullover and carrying a raincoat over his arm. He also had a trilby on his head. I politely pointed out that it was going to be far too hot for those clothes.

'The hotel is air conditioned but outside it's 93 degrees and the humidity is incredible,' I said, but he wouldn't be budged.

'We're representing the FA,' he insisted. 'We'll be all right. What are the lads wearing?' I told him they would be in T-shirts and shorts like me and explained that we would be coming straight back to the hotel to shower and change.

'They can't do that. They're FA representatives, too.'

'Maybe so, but they're here to play football. The showers at the stadium are not too good and I want them back here as quickly as possible.'

'But what about us?'

'I've arranged for a car to bring you back as soon as you have finished your official duties.'

I could see they weren't happy but I had all the players ready for the official reception as planned, wearing their blazers. That was the end of the matter as far as I was concerned but a few years later, I happened to see the FA's official report. It was full of praise for the players on what had been one of the most successful tours in FA history but less fulsome in its assessment of the manager, simply stating: 'I'm sure Mr Armfield has learned a lot on this tour.' It was my only mention – and it was absolutely spot on.

That tour had been a wonderful experience on and off the field and had whetted my appetite for club management. When I finished playing, I knew that if I didn't give coaching or management a try, I would probably regret it for the rest of my life. I'd been involved in the game for nearly 20 years and I didn't want to walk away just yet. While I was mulling over my next move, I received a surprise visit at home from Bill Bancroft, the chairman of Blackburn Rovers, and his manager, Johnny Carey. Bill asked if I fancied playing for Rovers. I told him that if I was going to carry on playing, it would be at Blackpool but the knee was dodgy and I'd been advised that it was likely to break down at any time. The three of us chatted for a while before I showed them out. A few minutes later, Bill came back without Johnny. He told me that the long-term plan was for me to go to Rovers as a player but eventually I would succeed Johnny as manager. How did I fancy that? I said I would let him know.

Obviously, the football grapevine was working overtime with rumours that Armfield was considering a move into coaching or management because within a couple of days I had another visit, this time from Bolton Wanderers chairman Jack Banks and Burnden Park legend Nat Lofthouse. Wanderers were in an even worse state than Blackpool and certain to be relegated to the old Third Division for the first time in their history. They asked if I would like to be Bolton's manager.

I've always been reasonable at weighing people up and I liked Jack Banks from the start. I don't know why – call it instinct, if you like. Jack was a big man in every sense. He was a semi-retired builder whose three sons were also in the business. They lived in a big modern house at Blackrod, a village high above Bolton. The villagers used to call it 'The Ponderosa' because with Jack and his sons all living there it was like the Cartwright family in the television series 'Bonanza'. He was a self-made man and was never afraid to remind people about his working-class roots. If anyone started talking about Oxford University, Jack would say, 'The nearest I've been to that place is Oxford United.' He had a nice line in repartee, too. Once, when we were talking about the way things were progressing, I reminded him that Rome wasn't built in a day. Quick as a flash, he responded, 'I wasn't on that bloody building site!'

Throughout my time at the club we used to meet regularly for a chat. He would arrive at the ground and park his Rolls-Royce in front of the main entrance. He usually had a cigarette in his mouth and would be wearing an open-necked shirt and a pair of sandals, whatever the weather. He wore trousers that looked as if they had just been doing service in the garden. In one hand he would be carrying a flask of home-made soup his wife had prepared earlier and in the other hand, a bottle of whisky. The soup was wonderful but I left the hard stuff to him.

In fact, the whisky was conspicuous by its absence at that first meeting at my home with Nat. Jack accepted that I had no experience in the job but was convinced I had the pedigree to make a go of it. He assured me Nat would always be around to give me any help I might need. I promised to think about it and discovered that Bolton reserves were playing their final game of the season at Aston Villa a few days later. I drove down to Villa Park and had a look. There was a good blend of youth and experience, they drew 2–2 and I wondered why the club had being doing so badly with that kind of talent around. The next day, I decided to have a look around Bolton. I don't suppose it's the kind of thing most prospective managers do but even though I had played at Burnden Park several times, I didn't have a feel for the town and its people. So I spent the best part of a day in and around Bolton. It was obviously a football town, even though gates had slumped, and I could sense the massive potential and the fans' genuine feelings for the club. I said to myself, 'Surely I can make something of this.'

Over the years, I had acquired all the coaching certificates and awards and helped Allen Wade, the FA Director of Coaching, on courses at Lilleshall. Coaching wasn't totally accepted in those days but it was something I believed was important and I had discussed it with two England managers, Walter Winterbottom and Alf Ramsey, and also with Bill Nicholson and Ron Greenwood during their time in charge of the Under-23 side. I had watched them and learned. So the coaching side didn't worry me. But did I really want to be a manager? I needed advice so I went straight to the top and rang Matt Busby. United sometimes trained at the Norbreck Hydro in Blackpool and I had met him once or twice when I linked up with Duncan Edwards. Matt was wise – and in many ways, wisdom beats education – and he never lost the common touch or forgot his roots. He was the most famous manager in the game, the man who provided the platform for what Manchester United are today, but he would still find time to chat to the postman or the laundry ladies. I always used to call him Matt while his players referred to him as Boss, so our relationship was on a slightly different footing – and we both smoked a pipe.

I once spent some time with him after playing for England at Wembley and mentioned that I was wondering what I might do when I retired. He told me to give him a call if I ever needed any help. I knew that when I called Matt, he would offer me sound guidance. He invited me to Old Trafford to talk things over. I told him I was unsure whether to start lower down the ladder as a coach or whether to take the job at Bolton. He said, 'Don't go home. Go straight to Bolton and say you'll take the job. Go and find out about yourself.' That was good enough for me. So instead of driving back to Blackpool, I went straight to Burnden Park. It was the close season and the only person around was Teddy Rothwell, the club secretary. I asked him to tell Jack Banks that I was interested in the job. He jumped to his feet and asked me to wait, said he'd get hold of Mr Banks straight away.

A few minutes later, we were joined by Edmund Warburton, the vice-chairman. Edmund lived near me at Lytham St Annes and I always remember that he was wearing a yellow knitted pullover and a brown trilby. Also on the board at the time were Derrick and George Warburton, members of the Warburton bakery family, who were not related to Edmund. They became firm friends of mine and have enjoyed a long involvement with the club. Edmund told me Jack wasn't available but asked if I could come back the next day, which I did – and became Bolton's 18th manager. There were three or four local journalists around and a handful of photographers but, generally speaking, it was a low-key affair. After signing a three-year contract at £8,000 a

169

year, I went out on to the ground and had a walk around. Grass was coming through the concrete on the old railway side terraces, a coat of paint wouldn't have gone amiss and the place seemed down on its luck. But Burnden Park had tradition, a tremendous history and was waiting for someone to come along and bring back the good times. I wondered if I was going to be that man.

I went back into my office to be confronted by an empty desk. I sat down and said to myself, 'Well, what do we do now?' I found some sheets of paper and drafted the pre-season training programme. That was Day One. On the next two days, I called Jimmy Adamson at Burnley and Dave Sexton at Chelsea and arranged pre-season friendlies. I met my coaches – Jim Conway, who had played for Norwich and Celtic and whom I still see occasionally, and Eddie Hopkinson, the former Bolton goalkeeper and an England team-mate from the fifties. Bert Sproston, the old Spurs, Manchester City and England full-back, was the physio. I assured them I wouldn't be bringing in anyone else – not least because I didn't have anyone else in mind. They stayed with me throughout my time at the club. Nat was also involved. He had done a two-year stint as manager, moved upstairs to become general manager and then taken over as caretaker prior to my appointment.

After 18 years as a player with Blackpool, taking over at Bolton was a strange experience. I was no longer one of the boys – the buck stopped with me. I'd always lived within walking distance of the ground, trained in the morning and gone straight home afterwards. Now I was a commuter and there were going to be a million and one things to do when training finished for the day. I knew I would have to start making decisions about players and that it wouldn't be easy. For the first time in 18 years, I felt alone.

I met the players when they reported back for pre-season training at the beginning of July. John Hulme, John Ritson, Arthur Marsh, Gareth Williams, Roy Greaves, Warwick Rimmer, John Byrom and Allan Boswell had been there a while and I had played against most of them. Then there were the young lads – Gary Jones, Paul Jones, Alan Waldron, Stuart Lee and Don McAllister – who had a lot of potential. Behind them in the queue were a bunch of promising kids including Peter Reid, Neil Whatmore, Barry Siddall and Sam Allardyce, who was destined to become Bolton's manager 28 years down the line.

I've always believed in having an experienced goalkeeper and looked down the list of players who were available. One name stood out straight away – Charlie Wright. A Scot in his mid-thirties, he had played nearly 450 league games for Workington, Grimsby and Charlton and he was available on a free transfer. Charlie was my first signing and he wasn't just a good one – he was fantastic. I don't think I made a better signing in the rest of my career. He came straight in and gave the club a lift. His enthusiasm was infectious, he was lively, he'd been around and he was a safe pair of hands in every sense of the word.

The club didn't have its own training ground and so we rented a pitch on nearby Bromwich Street, which involved a 10-minute hike under the bypass. That was no fun in the rain, I can tell you. Sometimes, in dire emergencies, we trained at the greyhound track next to Burnden Park.

We won both the friendlies and made a pretty decent start in the league, too. By the time Manchester City arrived in early September for a League Cup tie, complete with Colin Bell, Mike Summerbee, Franny Lee and the rest, we were near the top of the table and 42,000 supporters came along to see what we were made of. We walloped them 3–0 and all of a sudden, we had moved from has-beens to hopefuls. I couldn't understand it, really, because I knew that the team wasn't as good as that. 'Perhaps, it's down to me,' I thought.

Sure enough, reality soon intruded and by the end of November we were out of the League Cup and two-thirds of the way down the league. We had a spell around Christmas when I wasn't just wondering where the next goal would come from – I was wondering when we might win the next corner. One Monday lunchtime, after yet another tortuous Saturday afternoon, there was a tap on the door and Jack Banks poked his head round.

'Can I come in?'

'Have you come to sack me?' I replied, half-joking.

'No, you won't get away from here as easy as that.'

He collected two glasses from the cupboard, sat down and poured two large whiskies. I said, 'Are those both for you?'

'No. You're going to need one.'

He drank his down while I was still looking at mine. I've never been a drinker, particularly at work, but he insisted that I had one small sip, and then he said, 'I thought you told me you were a football coach when you took this job.'

'Well, perhaps I'm not.'

'Now listen, I haven't come to sack you. If you go, I'll go with you.'

'That's all very commendable and I appreciate the sentiment,' I said. 'But it's not doing a lot for Bolton Wanderers.'

'Perhaps you're a bit of a coward.'

Now I've been called a lot of things in my time but that was a new one. I wasn't happy and I didn't try to hide my feelings. But Jack would not be deterred.

'When you came here, you told me you could develop a team of young players who would be good enough to get Bolton out of the Third Division.'

'Yes, I think they would have a chance.'

'Well, just let me know when you decide to play them because they will be a damn sight better than what we've had out for the last few weeks.'

I told him I didn't want to rush our young hopefuls. I thought it would be better to introduce them gradually into a more successful side.

'Well, I'm not picking the team,' he replied. 'It's up to you.' And he left, taking the whisky bottle with him.

The following Saturday, I gave youth its fling. I had known for a while that it was time but I was reluctant to put them all in together. Jack gave me the nudge I needed. I played Paul Jones and McAllister in the back four, Waldron in midfield and Gary Jones and Lee up front. Wright, John Ritson, Rimmer, Greaves, Byrom and Ronnie Phillips provided the experience. From that moment, we never looked back, and coming up behind that first batch of young players were Reid, Whatmore, Allardyce, Siddall,

Jimmy Redfern and Chris Duffey. Jim Conway and I worked them hard on the training ground with the emphasis on push-and-run play, and after looking down and out around the turn of the year, we put together a terrific run. In the last 10 or 12 matches, I could really see it coming to life. We moved from the bottom six to the top eight and after the last game, I remember thinking that I wouldn't need to sign many new players that summer.

The next year we won the title with something in hand. We didn't start as favourites, although our form at the end of the previous season had made people sit up and take notice. We hit the top of the league in January and from that point, although I never actually said so, I always thought we would go up. When we were still on top at the beginning of April, I was confident we would win the league. Anything else would have been a rank disappointment. In the lower leagues, you must have organisation and a team ethic – and on top of that, our method was different from anyone else's in the division. Jimmy Sirrel's Notts County were one of the favourites for promotion with a side that featured eight basketball players standing about 6ft 10in, and two small, gifted midfield players, Willie Carlin and Don Masson. There were a few more giants around in the division but we were a top-of-the-ground team and won matches by playing through the opposition with our one-touch football.

Seeing those young players in action was one of my greatest pleasures as a manager. Their speed of thought, action and their enthusiasm were a joy. It was simply too much for other teams at that level to handle. I was constantly being asked about selling one or other of them. One day, the chairman came into my office and said he'd heard Manchester City wanted to buy Gary Jones.

'They're good judges,' I replied.

'Yes, but what do you think? Should we see what they are going to offer?'

'You can do what you want but I wouldn't change anything. I'd leave things exactly as they are.'

Jack did and that's why he was such a good chairman. We were never short of enquiries for those young players but he resisted every temptation to sell and it made life a lot easier for me, knowing that the chairman was prepared to back me to the hilt. He was straight, honest and open and he was always prepared to support his manager at board meetings – nor was he afraid to fight my corner against supporters at the annual general meeting.

After promotion, the squad needed tightening up for life in the old Second Division, although I knew that my young players would be able to hold their own. I signed two players, former Scotland striker Hugh Curran from Oxford and Peter Thompson, the former England winger, from Liverpool. Curran was a big strong centre-forward who had played five times for Scotland and had made over 300 league appearances for Millwall, Norwich, Wolves and Oxford. He gave us important experience and know-how up front. And I managed to cajole Anfield manager Bill Shankly into letting me sign Thompson.

Peter, who had started his career at Preston, was 31 and approaching the end of the line at Liverpool after winning 16 England caps and playing in more than 350 games at home and in Europe. I reckoned he would give us the spark we needed to reach another level. I arranged to meet Shanks at Anfield but on the way I learned that Coventry had offered £50,000 for Thompson. My budget was £15,000 but I pressed on regardless. We needed someone of Peter's calibre – and quick. Even though Coventry had offered a lot more money, I suspected that Bill wouldn't want Peter to return to Anfield to play against Liverpool. When we met, he also told me that Peter would prefer to stay in Lancashire rather than uproot to the Midlands. So I said, 'Look Bill, I'll give you £15,000.' I never dreamed he would seriously consider it but he just said, 'All right.' I called Jack Banks.

'How have you got on?' he asked.

'I've just bought Peter Thompson.'

'How much have you paid?'

'I'm not going to tell you.'

'Come on, tell me. Tell me now.'

'He's going to cost us £15,000.'

'Are you sure?'

'Yes.'

'That's terrific.'

The following day, Peter arrived at Burnden Park and by the time all the formalities had been completed, the rest of the players had finished training. So Peter went out and trained on his own. As news spread that he was out there, all the young players came out of the dressing room to watch him. That was the impact he had inside the club – so you can imagine how the fans responded. In his first game we played Sunderland and won 1–0. Peter was the star of the show, even though he hadn't played a first-team game for about four months. We never looked back.

I had a tremendous group of players. Inevitably, the young ones and Thompson received most of the attention but one or two senior players were the real stalwarts of the side – Charlie Wright, my first signing, Rimmer, my captain, and Byrom. Rimmer had been at the club since 1958 and had played over 400 games for the club. He was 32 and had a bad knee but nobody ever outran him. He was 5ft 7in and nobody ever outjumped him. He was amazing. He later became youth development officer at Tranmere, responsible for bringing on the kids, and they couldn't have had a better mentor. We're still in touch today.

Byrom was what I call a cute player and as good a finisher as I have seen outside international football. He proved it in a cup tie against Stoke, who were a First Division side. Unusually for those days, the match was played on a Sunday afternoon because we were in the middle of a power strike, floodlights were banned and matches had to be re-arranged according to the electricity rota. Byrom provided all the sparks and scored a hat-trick. He also scored several crucial goals in our promotion season and convinced Bill Isherwood, one of the directors, that superstition really did play a part in football. I always used to sit in the dug-out during games but on one occasion at Wrexham, I decided to go into the directors' box to look at the shape of the team from up there. When I arrived Bill said, 'What are you doing here?' I explained that I wanted to see things from a different perspective but he wasn't having that. 'You can't come in here,' he insisted. 'They'll be wondering where you are. We won't win if you're not in the dug-out.' I assured him everything would be OK.

Inevitably, perhaps, Wrexham went ahead in the first half. 'I told you so,' said Bill. 'We'll never win with you up here.' I gave it a few minutes, decided to make a change and left the directors' box. As I was walking round the track on my way to the dug-out, Byrom set up the equaliser. I didn't alter a thing and we went on to win 3–1. Afterwards, Bill came over. 'There you are,' he said. 'As soon as you went back to the dug-out, we scored. Don't ever sit in the directors' box again.' I tried to explain that what happened out on the pitch was down to the players, not the whereabouts of the manager, but there was nothing I could say to dissuade him. Dear old Bill, he was a lovely man!

A few weeks later I wished I'd been in the directors' box instead of the Port Vale dug-out when Byrom scored the goal that clinched the old Third Division championship. We needed a point and, late in the game, Byrom met a left-wing cross and headed the equaliser. He didn't score many with his head and as the ball hit the net, I leapt to my feet – and cracked my skull on the concrete roof of the dug-out. As I celebrated, blood was pouring down my face and I needed treatment. I left Vale Park with my head covered in plasters and a splitting headache.

We were due to receive the trophy on the final day of the season when we played Brentford at Burnden. It seemed the whole of Bolton had turned out. Frank Blunstone, an old pal from my Young England days, was the Brentford manager and his team needed a win to avoid the drop. Before the kick-off, Frank joked, 'Come on, Jim, tell 'em to take it easy. We need the points!'

'Sorry Frank,' I said. 'I wouldn't be able to stop them today even if I wanted to. I haven't even bothered with a team talk – they're just going to go out and play and I'm telling you now, you'll lose.' We ran all over them, won 2–0, collected the trophy and it was time to party.

I enjoyed four happy and largely successful years at Bolton. The directors were excellent, I had a great bunch of players and the fans were very loyal. But it hadn't taken me long to discover that all the journalists and ex-players who write in the papers and talk on the radio and television don't really understand the pressures of management. It's a job you can only learn by experience. You can have all the coaching qualifications and know all the theory but you still have to learn as you go along. The manager is the hub at the centre of a big wheel and all the spokes are connected to him. The players, their families, the directors, the supporters, the staff, the media, his own family and friends are all demanding his time. And in my day, the manager didn't have a chief executive handling the money side of things. He was in charge of wages, contracts, transfer fees and so on. I used to sit down with Teddy Rothwell and Jack Banks and decide the club budget. I would ring round hotels to find out how much overnight stops would be and Teddy would make the bookings. Above all, you have to win matches – do that and the rest takes care of itself.

It was a huge burden and sometimes I found it impossible to switch off. I would find myself looking at the television but thinking about training the following day, the injury list, a player I might want to sign or the team for Saturday. I don't think managers ever really switch off, even on holiday. A manager never has a total break. He also has to learn the hard way about taking difficult decisions. That was brought home to me when Nat Lofthouse left the club the year after my appointment. Nat was an institution, the greatest player in Bolton's history, who had been at Burnden Park since 1939. But there wasn't really a job for him. He wanted to be general manager but we were a Third Division side and couldn't afford the luxury of two managers. I offered him the chance to be chief scout but he didn't fancy that. So he left on 8 June 1972, and for a while I was blamed as the man who had forced him out of Burnden Park. It wasn't true. He left because Bolton Wanderers could no longer give him the job he wanted. It wasn't easy for anyone, not least me because I believe Nat is a true football legend. Jack Banks was bitterly upset, too. Happily, Nat returned to the Wanderers eight years later as the front man in the new executive club and quickly immersed himself in raising funds and sponsorship. He was a natural and in 1986, he was made president of the club. Bolton Wanderers wouldn't be the same without him.

Shortly before I left the club, I endured one of the worst experiences of my life when I returned to play a match against Blackpool for the second time as a manager on 24 August 1974. Earlier that year, I'd gone back to Bloomfield Road for the first time and seen my new club come out on top 2–0. I was given a tremendous reception by the fans, even better than when I was a player. When I took my place in the dug-out, I received a standing ovation – and again at the start of the second half – but they were a bit less enthusiastic after the final whistle! Afterwards, the Bolton team and officials went round to our house where we had laid on a few drinks and Anne's mother had prepared a big joint of beef. All the lads dug into roast beef sandwiches and a few beers, one of the directors keeled over after one Scotch too many and a great time was had by all.

It was a very different story when I went back again five months later. A young Blackpool fan was stabbed on the Kop and died that evening and Alan Waldron, one of my most promising players, suffered one of the worst broken legs I have ever seen. It was a nightmare and the 2–1 scoreline in favour of Blackpool an irrelevance. That night, I went to see the family of the boy who had been killed. Anne came with me and we parked in the street a few doors down from their house. I sat outside for a while, wondering whether or not to go in but I knew it had to be faced. I was the only link between Bolton Wanderers and Blackpool. Eventually, I got out of the car and knocked on the door. The boy's father opened it and I said, 'I don't know what I'm going to say to you but I just thought I'd come round.' He recognised me, invited me in and his wife made a cup of tea. I said, 'Everyone at Bolton Wanderers is desperately sorry and we regret what has happened. I don't suppose there's anything I can do, but here I am if you need to talk.'

I stayed for a while and then drove a quarter of a mile to Victoria Hospital to see Alan. He had come round from the operation and was lying in the arms of his girlfriend, Charlie. I was able to raise a smile for the first time since the awful events of the afternoon.

'I thought you'd still be in agony, Alan,' I said, 'but you don't seem to be doing too badly for yourself. Do you think you'll be all right?'

He gave me a brave smile. He eventually recovered from the injury but was never the same player again. I thought he would go right to the top – he was quick, had a good knowledge of the game and good feet. People were just starting to take notice of him. He retired in 1981 at the age of 30 after spells with Blackpool, Bury and York City. It was an awful day and a stark reminder that there are far more important things in life than a game of football, despite what Bill Shankly said.

My first opportunity to move up the managerial ladder came when I was offered the job at Everton after Harry Catterick's retirement in April 1973. Jack Banks walked into my office and told me Sir John Moores, the chairman of Everton, wanted to have a word with me. 'Take my advice, Jim, don't go,' said Jack. But I told him I would at least like the opportunity to meet Moores and see what he had to offer. 'OK, you can do that,' said Jack.

I drove to Sir John's house at Formby. He was a keen artist and showed me into his studio, where he was painting a picture. He asked me if I liked art. I told him I thought it was OK but I preferred music. Then he said, 'I'd like you to be the manager of Everton.' Just like that. I had started at Bolton on about £8,000 a year, which had increased to £11,000 after promotion. Moores offered me £15,000, a lot of money in those days. Everton were a very big club and I admitted that I thought it might be a bit early for me to make the move. He suggested I had a drive round and then let him know. I had already made up my mind when I reached home. I called him the next day and said, 'I've decided I'm not quite ready. I don't want to let you down but I think you need someone with a bit more experience.'

'Fine, that's OK. I'm disappointed because I thought you might have fancied the challenge.'

'Every job in management is a challenge and I'm not frightened of that. But I just think I need another year or eighteen months in the Second Division at Bolton before I'm ready for one of the top jobs.'

When I told Jack Banks, he replied, 'I've already told the board you wouldn't be going.'

The team established itself in the Second Division that season and had made a good start to the 1974–75 campaign when the next offer came along – and this time it was an opportunity to join the league champions and sample the European Cup with Leeds United. Somehow I felt the time had come to go, although leaving Bolton was a wrench. I went to tell the board and suggested they should give the job to Ian Greaves, my number two, who had led Huddersfield into the First Division four years earlier. They did and four years later, Bolton were promoted. No one was more pleased than I was.

CHAPTER 11

WELCOME TO
THE BIG-TIME

Looking back, I suppose I was captivated by the idea of managing a big-city club and especially working with high-profile international players. In 1974, they didn't come any bigger than Leeds United. They were the current league champions, had played European football for the previous 10 years and frequently fielded a team of 11 full internationals – with a few more fighting for the job of substitute. I had spent my entire playing career at Blackpool, a town club, and while we had enjoyed a measure of success, our highest league finish was runners-up in 1956 when I was still learning the ropes.

As manager of Bolton, I had won the old Third Division championship and re-established the club in Division Two. But again, I was operating on a smaller scale and after four years at Burnden Park, it was perhaps time to step on to the big stage. I had turned down Everton a year before so at face value, the chance to take over as manager of Leeds United could not have come at a better time although I suspected the job at Elland Road would come with a considerable amount of baggage – I was right. The club was in a mess following the departure of first Don Revic, the man who had transformed Leeds into one of the most formidable sides in Europe, and then his successor Brian Clough after a turbulent 44 days as manager.

Revie joined Leeds in 1961 and left to take over as England

181

manager on 4 July 1974. He had lifted the club from the depths of the old Second Division to a place among the European élite, winning the league championship twice, the FA Cup and the Inter Cities Fairs Cup twice. Despite this, they were by no means the best-loved team in the land. Many thought they were over-professional although no one doubted their quality. They were probably at the height of their powers when they won their second title in 1974, yet at that moment, Revie chose to leave.

I have never quite understood why he went and I know his players were shocked. He must have known that this set of footballers, the team he had nurtured so diligently for 13 years, had a real chance of winning the European Cup but he chose to walk away. True, he might never have been given another opportunity to manage England – but the European Cup was Leeds United's Holy Grail. He must have known it was within touching distance and because of that his departure surprised most people in the game. Barry Foster, the *Yorkshire Post* journalist who covered Leeds at the time, once told me that everyone connected with the club believed that Revie's ageing side had one big season left. They knew the break-up was coming but time was still on their side – just.

They had been together for a long time and were like a close-knit family. Foster told me that for years, when Revie announced his team to the press, he would say, 'Well, it's the usual lot. B, C and H in the middle [that meant Bremner, Charlton and Hunter would be the half-backs]. Then Paul and Terry at the back in front of Dave [Reaney, Cooper and Harvey] with Peter, Sniffer, Jonesy, Johnny and Eddie up front [Lorimer, Clarke, Mick Jones, Giles, Gray].' Not a surname in sight. One big, happy family – and I often wondered if he left because he simply couldn't bear to break up his family himself.

Revie certainly did not believe Brian Clough was the right man to do that job when he was surprisingly named as his successor on 22 July – he told me so when we met at White's Hotel in London soon after Clough's departure. But to be frank, following in Don's footsteps at Leeds would have been difficult for anyone, let alone Clough who, as manager of Derby County, had severely criticised Revie and his players. Clough was, in my opinion, one of our best managers. He won championships with Derby and Nottingham Forest and two European Cups with Forest, and those teams were as good as any we have seen since the Second World War. Moreover, his players always behaved in an exemplary manner on and off the field. He could have been the right man for any club but this was probably the wrong time for his marriage to Leeds.

Revie had taken his number two, Les Cocker, with him to the FA, so as well as Clough, the players had to come to terms with a new assistant manager, Jimmy Gordon. Clough clearly wanted to make an instant impact. As well as bringing in Gordon, he showed his determination to put his stamp on Leeds' championship-winning side by signing two of his players from Derby, midfield man John McGovern and striker John O'Hare for a combined fee of £125,000. He then paid Nottingham Forest £250,000 for their talented but enigmatic striker Duncan McKenzie.

By all accounts that didn't go down too well with Revie's players and things got worse when Clough, who took a break in Majorca after his appointment, arrived for his first training session. When he held a team meeting a few days later, he proceeded to criticise the players one by one. Peter Lorimer told me later that Eddie Gray, one of the most talented and popular players at the club, who had suffered major injury problems, was told, 'If you were a racehorse, you would have been put down.' Picking on injured players is not the best way to inspire loyalty from a squad already shell-shocked by the departure of their long-term mentor.

To make matters worse, Leeds made a dreadful start. They lost on penalties to Liverpool in the Charity Shield and Billy Bremner and Liverpool's Kevin Keegan were sent off for fighting. They played nine league and cup games during Clough's 44 days in charge and won only once. It was reported that at a team meeting attended by directors, some players said they didn't think Clough was the right man to manage the team. There were also reports that one or two more players went to see the directors privately, demanding Clough's dismissal. If that was true, he had no chance. But while he may have been driven out by player power, I suspect that, in the end, Brian might have had enough, too. So he went and the Leeds directors knew they had a problem. The whole country was following the story day by day. It seemed to be a tangled web and to add to the board's dilemma, two of the senior players, Billy Bremner and Johnny Giles, were both reported to want the job.

That was the scenario I inherited when I moved in on 5 October 1974. The club was in a state of shock, almost as if there had been a family bereavement. The first I knew that I was in the frame to take over was when I picked up a Sunday paper to read that Leeds would be talking to me the following week. Bill Isherwood had replaced Jack Banks as chairman at Bolton by this time and on the Monday morning, he called me.

'What's all this Leeds business about, then?' he asked.

'I haven't a clue,' I replied.

That was the honest truth. All I knew about a move to Leeds United was what I had read in the papers. But even though there had been no approach from Leeds, it was obvious from all the press speculation that I was on the shortlist, and I started to consider the pros and cons should Leeds want me. Eventually, Isherwood told me Bolton had received an official approach and the club would not stand in my way.

So I arranged to meet four Leeds directors, Manny Cussins, the chairman, Bob Roberts, Sydney Simon and Sam Bolton, at the Clifton Arms Hotel in Lytham. They were all getting on in years and didn't look like the hard-nosed, high-powered finan-ciers I had always imagined would run a big-city club such as Leeds. To be honest, they were four men in a flap who needed a manager quick. They didn't really seem to have a handle on what was involved and I learned subsequently that Revie was more or less autonomous in his later years at Elland Road and the board simply went along with him. On one occasion, he even left two directors behind at Tottenham because they weren't on the team coach by the 5.30 p.m. departure time. No one on the board took him to task about it. I dread to think what Jack Banks would have said if I'd done the same thing at Bolton.

It wasn't really an interview. They didn't ask for my thoughts on managing Leeds United. They didn't want to know about my family or whether I was prepared to move house to Leeds. They just offered me the job, simple as that. I wasn't quite convinced about their motives. Did they want me because they thought I was the best manager around? Or was I someone who would come in and fill a hole after Clough's chaotic stay? Was I just a safe pair of hands?

There were plenty of things to weigh up and discuss with Anne. Would we be prepared to move house and uproot our two sons, Duncan and John, from school? Did I want to leave a club where I had been so happy? At the back of my mind, I knew that if I didn't move onwards and upwards now, I could end up becoming entrenched at Bolton for a long time, just as I had at Blackpool in my playing days. I've always believed in putting down roots but the time had come when I no longer wanted to be rooted, even at Bolton. I felt I was better prepared for a top job than I had been 12 months earlier and with Bremner and Giles around, there would be no shortage of experienced support. I realised, of course, that both had been trying to get the job for themselves, which wouldn't make life any easier for me at first.

I asked Leeds for time to think and, while I was mulling it over, I received a call from Don Revie, now the England manager, inviting me down to FA headquarters at Lancaster Gate for a chat. Anne and I travelled down to London but I went alone to meet Revie at White's Hotel, where he was staying. He asked if I would be interested in managing the England Under-23 team and overseeing the youth programme. I said that under normal circumstances I would be very interested, adding, 'But this has come at a strange time. I've just been offered the job at your old club.' He must have known. I cannot believe anything could have happened at Elland Road at that time without someone whispering in Revie's ear. He knew what was going on at that place better than anybody.

'In that case,' said Don. 'Forget all about this. Take the Leeds job.'

To this day, I'm not sure whether the England job was a firm offer or whether Don had been set up to convince me I should move to Elland Road, but I was cute enough to realise it was a distinct possibility. He certainly did a good PR job for Leeds United when he told me, 'All you have to do with those players is send them out on the field. They'll do the rest. You'll be able to sit in the stand and pick up your bonus. They're the best players in the country.'

'That was last season,' I replied, 'and if they're so good, what are they doing at the bottom of the league?'

He said he couldn't understand it either but added, 'They must have fallen out with Cloughie in a big way – perhaps he was the wrong man at the wrong time. You can be the right man. Those players want to be picked up, they want to play, they're ready to go. You'll have no problems.'

He helped to convince me and so I went to Leeds. It was uncharted territory but, as I say, the prospect captivated me.

My first day in charge was Saturday, 5 October 1974, a home game against Arsenal. The team were three places from the bottom of the table with six points from nine matches and they were in a mess. The players were scheduled to have lunch at the Mansion House Hotel in Roundhay Park on the outskirts of Leeds and I arrived just as the players were turning up. I looked around them all and they seemed understandably suspicious and uncertain. I'd played against most of them – Bremner and Giles were only a few years younger than me. In the three weeks between Clough's departure and my arrival, Maurice Lindley, the assistant manager, had been running team affairs. I knew him vaguely and had spoken to him on the telephone the previous day. He had already named the starting line-up and I asked for a look. In 4–4–2 formation, it was Harvey; Reaney, McQueen, Hunter, Cooper; Lorimer, Madeley, Giles, Yorath; Jordan, McKenzie. Bremner and Allan Clarke were injured and Mick Bates was the substitute. I told Maurice, 'Pity about Bremner but that team should be good enough.'

Maurice gave the team talk. He had been Revie's right-hand man, he was experienced, he knew the players and they respected him. I had already been around and shaken everyone's hand and during Maurice's chat, I noticed how the players kept half-looking at me and then looking away as soon as I made eye contact. They seemed edgy. I asked Maurice if I could say a few quick words. I stood in front of the players and said, 'What the hell are you doing near the bottom of the league? I've played against you, I've watched you play many times and I know how good you can be. You won the title only a few months ago. So what the hell's going on?'

I hoped for some feedback and perhaps a fiery reaction. Instead, they were subdued and said nothing. McKenzie made a few comical remarks but the rest remained morose. I wanted a response so, as Bremner, their captain, wasn't there, I singled out Giles. I knew him to be a thinker about the game. I said, 'Right John, what's the matter?' He talked about getting priorities right and a few generalisations, nothing concrete about the state of the team. So I told them, 'For better or worse, it's you and me now. I'm not going to say too much today, I'll form opinions as I go along. But nobody is destined to leave the club and no one is booked to come in. I have a completely clean sheet. I can only believe that we can do better than nineteenth in the table. Beating Arsenal would be a good way to start.'

I was a bit edgy as I drove to Elland Road where the paparazzi were waiting and the fans expectant. I have never had my picture taken as often as I did that day. Earlier there had been television cameras outside my home in Blackpool – something that hadn't happened too often in the past! – and as I arrived at the ground, I was confronted by a mass of press photographers with shutters whirring and bulbs flashing. Keith Archer, the club secretary, escorted me to the far end of the main stand and showed me to my office, where I was introduced to my secretary, Maureen Holdsworth. She had been appointed by Clough so she was uncertain about her future but I assured her I would need all the help I could get and asked if she would consider staying on. She said she would – and we're still in contact today.

Then I was introduced to the other members of the staff – Syd Owen, the first-team trainer; Cyril Partridge, the reserve-team trainer; and Bob English, who looked after the kit and treated injuries. I was flabbergasted to discover that Leeds, a top English club, didn't have a chartered physio and made a mental note to appoint one as soon as possible. My next stop was the dressing room just before the team went out. I didn't stay long and my parting shot was, 'Right, come on, let's get into these . . .' and then I moved upstairs to the directors' box. It was deserted – the board members, the visiting directors and all the guests must have still been in the boardroom and hospitality lounge. So once again it was just me and the press. In those days, I enjoyed the comfort of smoking a pipe, so I lit up, trying to appear cool, calm and collected. Once again, the flashbulbs flared as I put a match to my pipe. It was the same story every time I moved for the next couple of hours or so.

Arsenal lined up with Rimmer; Storey, Matthews, Blockley, Simpson; Armstrong, Ball (my old Blackpool team-mate), Kelly, Brady; Radford, Kidd. It was a strong side but we won 2–0. McKenzie scored before half-time and got another in the second half. It was obvious Leeds shouldn't have been anywhere near the bottom of the table with players like those – not to mention Bremner and Clarke when they were fit again. After the final whistle, I went into the dressing room. Once again, I didn't hang around. 'Well done, lads,' I said. 'If you can beat Arsenal, you can beat anyone. See you on Monday.' The Sunday papers proclaimed Armfield's immediate effect on Leeds whereas I knew I had done nothing. But that's the way it goes with the press.

It was by no means roses all the way from there. We performed excellently to defeat Hungarian champions Ujpest Dozsa home and away in the European Cup second round. It was a straight knock-out tournament in those days, a real cup competition. In Hungary, where we were down to 10 men after McKenzie was sent off, Peter Lorimer scored one of the great European goals, an unstoppable volley, in a 2–1 win over a technically gifted side. He and Terry Yorath were absolutely superb that night and we won the home leg 3–0. But we were up and down in the league, drawing at Ipswich, losing at Birmingham, beating Wolves at home and then going down 1–0 against Liverpool at Anfield. We played really well that day without any luck but even so we were still in 19th place after losing to Derby on 2 November. Things came to a head when we were beaten 3–0 at Chester in the League Cup.

Chester were doing well in the Third Division and they steamrollered us in front of 19,000 people on the old Sealand Road ground. It was hard to stomach a performance like that and we had a sort-out in the dressing room afterwards. On the way home, Sam Bolton said, 'You're going to have to bring some new players in. We won't get any further with this lot.' I didn't agree. I told him I was convinced we would get through the season with the players I had inherited – and we did. What I didn't add was that I knew damn well that changes would have to start the following summer.

The Chester defeat and its immediate aftermath cleared the air and despite losing David Harvey for the rest of the season after he was injured in a road accident in February, we lost only twice in our next 25 games at home and in Europe. David Stewart proved an excellent replacement for Harvey and we reached the sixth round of the FA Cup before losing to Ipswich in a third replay. From January to the end of the season, we played an astonishing 30 matches and finally finished in ninth place.

After all the mayhem at the start of the season, I was content to allow the club to tick over while I tried to get to know all the players. I just wanted to settle everyone down and kept things nice and simple. I resisted making major changes from the Revie era because the last thing we wanted was players growing restless. Indeed, I went out of my way not to upset anyone. I needed to strengthen the bonds between the players and their new manager and came up with the novel idea of staging a pantomime as part of Paul Reaney's testimonial year. I must admit I was a bit dubious about the response I would receive when I first suggested the idea but the lads took to it straight away.

Barney Colehan, who ran the famous City Varieties Music Hall in Leeds, came to matches regularly and one day we were discussing ideas for a Christmas do for the players. I thought fancy dress might go down well – but strictly in-house, of course.

Christmas parties took place behind closed doors in those days. One thing led to another and eventually I suggested writing a panto for the players. 'If you do that,' said Barney, 'I'll stage it at the City Varieties. I'll make a few bob out of it, we'll give some to charity and save the rest for the testimonial fund.'

So for the next few weeks, whenever I had a few spare minutes at home in the evenings, I worked on my script. I chose *Cinderella*, with a liberal helping of gags borrowed from here and there. I went back to Barney after a while to discuss costumes. 'You mean you're serious?' he asked, with a distinct hint of apprehension. I assured him I was and pressed ahead. My first task had been to find a Cinderella and after a little gentle persuasion, Duncan McKenzie agreed to take on the lead role. He was fantastic and whenever we meet today, we have a laugh about it. Billy Bremner was an absolute natural as Buttons, better than any Buttons I have seen before or since. Our Scottish centre-half was persuaded to assume the mantle of the Good Fairy McQueen while Reaney took to the role of Prince Charming like the proverbial duck to water.

All the players entered into it with relish. Everyone was issued with a copy of the script, typed by Maureen, and they were given strict instructions to go home and learn their lines. Twice a week, we held rehearsals in the players' lounge after training. Once the thespians had assembled, I instructed Maureen to lock the door and not allow a soul to cross the portal until rehearsals were over. Eventually, we went public, announcing that the show would run for two nights at the City Varieties in February, giving a date when tickets would go on sale. When the box office opened for business, the place was besieged and a delighted Barney was on the phone, saying, 'I could do with this every week!' The show lasted an hour or so and with tickets priced at around 25p, it was standing room only on both nights. I remember thinking on the evening before the first night, 'I want my head examining for going into this!'

I was Master of Ceremonies, dressed in a red tail-suit and black top hat. I read from the script so whenever any of the cast forgot his lines, I would leave my position at the side of the stage and show him the page – guaranteed to raise a laugh. In true pantomime style, there was no shortage of ad-libbing and totally unscripted was the sight of McKenzie hitching up his skirt to reveal a shapely leg and a packet of cigarettes tucked into the top of his nylon stockings. Cinders lit up and exchanged drags with the faithful Buttons as they debated the slings and arrows of outrageous fortune.

McKenzie was terrific and the kids adored Bremner. The show opened with Cinderella working in the kitchen and I set the scene, introducing Cinders before saying 'And here comes Buttons . . .' No Buttons, so I'd try again. 'Here comes, Buttons . . .' Again, no show. 'Right, children, you know who Billy Buttons is, don't you?' They shrieked, 'Yes, it's Billy Bremner.' I shouted back, 'But where is he?' And a voice from the back of the stalls, replied, 'Here I am . . .' To roars of delight, Billy, dressed in a bright blue Buttons outfit, complete with pillbox hat, came striding down the centre aisle. He was carrying a huge jar of sweets and all the way to the stage he kept dipping into the jar and throwing sweets to the kids. It seemed to take him five minutes to make his way down the aisle and when he reached the front, he spent a couple of minutes with the disabled children. Then he bounced on to the stage, plonked his jar down at the side and told the audience, 'Right, they're our sweets. If anyone comes near them, you tell me.' That was guaranteed to work.

A real showstopper was Terry Yorath singing 'Sonny Boy' with Buttons perched on his knee. The Welsh are supposed to be able to sing but Terry proved there's an exception to every rule. This was his party piece and nothing was going to stop him, even though he was tone deaf. Time after time he would start, 'Climb up on my knee, Sonny Boy . . .' only to be halted in his tracks as the pianist gave him the correct key once more. It absolutely brought the house down.

At the end of each show, the audience was clamouring for more. 'Go through it again,' they shouted as one curtain call followed another and Barney shouted, 'Can I sign this lot up for the panto next year?' In fact, it was such a success that we staged a couple of action replays for Norman Hunter's testimonial 12 months later with Norman taking over the role of Prince Charming. Great stuff! I just wish I'd kept the script. I've never been one to collect mementoes but it would be nice if I could just have a look at my *Cinderella* every now and then and relive some of the memories. It's safe to say that the City Varieties Music Hall has never seen anything like it. Barney, an experienced showman, said it should have been filmed. Little did he know that I had brought along a flask of whisky and before both shows we all had a swig to give ourselves some Dutch courage before we went on stage.

On a more serious note, the pantomime had been a good bonding exercise. I felt closer to the players but I still maintained the softly, softly approach I had adopted from the start. It must have worked – we reached the final of the European Cup. There were some real highs along the way. After defeating Ujpest Dozsa soon after my arrival, our quarter-final opponents were the Belgian champions Anderlecht. We beat them 3–0 at home, then went to Brussels and gave one of the best European displays I have seen. It was pouring with rain, the whole of Belgium seemed to be packed into the ground and the atmosphere was unremittingly hostile. Yet we never gave them a sniff of our goal. Bremner scored the only goal of the game – a real gem, a chip over the keeper from the edge of the box.

That gave us a semi-final against a Barcelona side that featured great players including Johan Cruyff, Johan Neeskens and Carlos Rexach. They were favourites to win the competition and we beat them 2–1 at home in front of more than 50,000 fans in the first leg. Everyone outside the club told me it wouldn't be enough; I believed it could be. I had acquired tremendous faith in those players who, after all, had more European experience than I had. They showed it in the second leg in front of an expectant crowd of 110,000 Catalans at the Nou Camp.

I was never one to mess around with the team or alter a well-tried formation, preferring to leave players in their best positions in a familiar role. But after watching Barcelona play a couple of times, I decided to change things around a bit. Their manager, the experienced Dutchman Rinus Michels, operated a man-for-man marking system with a spare defender. The markers simply followed their opponent everywhere.

I chose my usual front three of Joe Jordan, Peter Lorimer and Allan Clarke. I started with Peter on the left and told him to switch to the right after 10 minutes, which just might expose his marker's weaker side on his left. It's very rare that moves like this come off but on this occasion it did. Peter made the switch, his marker was caught out and Peter ran through to plant a Jordan flick-on into the Barcelona net. That gave us a 3–1 lead overall and we almost got another soon afterwards, which would have killed the game.

Instead, the pace was frantic. Cruyff and Neeskens tried everything they knew – which was a lot – and with about 20 minutes left, Barcelona equalised. Soon afterwards we had a near disaster when McQueen was sent off following a skirmish in the goalmouth. It was something and nothing really, a bit of arm wrestling. Despite the pressure, I still followed him into the dressing room, something I always tried to do if a player was sent off or injured. I was never sent off in my career but I suffered my share of injuries and knew from experience that a dressing room can be one of the loneliest places on earth if you have to leave the game for any reason. It's a low time in a footballer's career. Gordon was in tears. He realised that if we went on to reach the final, he would miss out. I said, 'Look, I can't stay with you for long but will you be OK? I'll send someone down to keep you company as soon as I can.' It was the least I could do for him.

I missed a couple of minutes' play and when I returned to the dug-out it was to witness a magnificent rearguard action from my players as they clung on to that 1–1 scoreline. A man down, they used every ounce of their European experience to deny one of the leading sides in world football. Everything came together for those players that night. It was a magical experience and someone told me later that Don Revie had been in the Nou Camp. He never came to see me so I often wondered how he was feeling. In the dressing room we were ecstatic.

When we eventually climbed aboard the team coach for the trip back to the hotel, I told the players, 'We've had a great night but that's it – nobody's going into Barcelona.' There was a chorus of groans and jeers. I went on, 'We're going back to the hotel. I've ordered some champagne. We're going to sit down together, have a meal and a drink and enjoy the moment. Anyone who isn't prepared to go along with that won't play in the final.' I don't think they thought I was serious at first – but that's what we did. I went to bed at about two o'clock and left the players to get on with their own celebrations. I subsequently received reports that one or two had gone a bit over the top but that didn't worry me. It isn't every night you reach the European Cup final and the Leeds players knew they were heading for the biggest game in the club's history.

I have always said that those players, with a little help from me, were responsible for Leeds United reaching that final. There was no Champions League like today, no second chance, no room for slips, and they never slipped up once. They were terrific and I will always be grateful to every one of them for giving me a European Cup final. They were a superb side and I sometimes wished I could have got my hands on them a couple of years earlier. I had played against them when they were coming to the boil and watched them when they were right at their peak, but until I managed them, I didn't realise quite how good they were.

Our final league match of the season, a 4–2 defeat at Spurs on 28 April, was exactly one month ahead of the final against Bayern Munich at the Parc des Princes in Paris. I needed to maintain momentum and keep the players in shape so I arranged a friendly against Norwegian side Brann Bergen. Then we played a testimonial match for Norman Hunter against Don Revie's XI at Elland Road, took on the Scotland Under-23 team at Hampden Park and finally met Walsall at Fellows Park on 13 May.

With McQueen suspended, I had a bit of a selection problem in central defence. Well, not a problem really because I was able to switch Paul Madeley, one of the finest utility players I have ever seen and a man I christened Rolls-Royce, into central defence in Gordon's place. Maurice Lindley, Tony Collins, the chief scout, and I all felt that Bayern would be very strong down their right-hand side. If McQueen had been available, I would probably have played Madeley on the left of the midfield trio to counter that threat in preference to the more attacking style of Eddie Gray. With Madeley occupied elsewhere, I chose Yorath instead. He was a battler and had done a brilliant job in that role against Ujpest Dozsa and I had no qualms about including him this time. So we lined up in a 4–3-3 formation with Stewart; Reaney, Madeley, Hunter, Frank Gray; Bremner, Giles, Yorath; Lorimer, Jordan, Clarke.

We left for Paris on 27 May. The game should have been one of the highlights of my career but it was one of the biggest disappointments. We were beaten 2–0 and to say 'We wuz robbed' would be one of the understatements of all time. When the match was over, I felt exactly as I did when our home was burgled. Bayern were a class act. They had even more European experience than Barcelona with Franz Beckenbauer, Uli Hoeness, Franz Roth, Gerd Muller and Sepp Maier, the goalkeeper. In all, they had seven German internationals and Germany were the world champions. Yet we overwhelmed them for 70 minutes and might easily have been three or four goals in front.

Unfortunately Monsieur Kitabdijan, the French referee, made so many decisions that went against us. I learned later that he never controlled another big game – I just wish he hadn't been at the Parc des Princes on 28 May 1975. In the first half, Clarke was denied a blatant penalty and when Franz Beckenbauer handled in the box, only Kitabdijan didn't believe that was a penalty, too. In the 66th minute, it looked as though Lorimer had finally put us ahead but the goal was ruled out because Bremner was allegedly offside.

I remember turning to Bob English, who was sitting alongside me in the dug-out, and saying, 'I just hope this finishes 0–0.'

'Why, what are you talking about?'

'Because there's no way we're going to win this match in these circumstances. Our only chance is a replay.'

How true! I was directly in line with Roth when he put them in front soon afterwards – time seemed to stop as the ball trickled agonisingly slowly into the net.

Our supporters had been upset with the referee's performance throughout and when things looked as if they might get out of hand, the police just waded in. The fans responded by breaking up seats and hurling missiles and the situation became really nasty. I could only sit and watch the crowd trouble with a feeling of deepening despair. It was to continue after the final whistle and throughout the night as fans and police waged a running battle across the streets of the French capital. The outcome was a four-year European ban for the club.

After Roth's goal, I sent on Eddie Gray in place of Yorath to give us more attacking options on the left and I was later criticised for not using the unpredictable McKenzie as well. With hindsight, that might have been a worthwhile option, but even when we were behind, I was convinced a goal would come. It didn't. In fact, I don't suppose we would have scored that night if I'd been able to introduce Merlin the Magician. The referee's performance reminded me of the old joke about the player who weaved his way through the entire opposition line-up before slotting the ball past the keeper. On his way back to the halfway line, he turned to the ref and said, 'I'm getting close now, aren't I?' Inevitably, perhaps, Muller scored a late goal for Bayern and the dream was over. It was little consolation to learn later that Beckenbauer admitted his team had been 'very, very lucky'.

I have never felt so deflated. Afterwards the atmosphere in the dressing room was like a wake. Nobody spoke and all the losers' medals were in a ragged pile on the table.

'I just want to say thank you for reaching the final,' I said. 'But I can't begin to explain how low I feel. You have been tremendous, you didn't deserve to lose. The match has been an absolute scandal.'

Eventually, the lads started to change and headed for the team coach, leaving all the medals behind on the table. I felt like leaving mine, too. Instead, I scooped them up and put them into a plastic bag. I handed them all back later on.

We tried to make the most of what should have been a celebration party back in the hotel but it was a low-key affair. I hid my feelings as best I could – so did everyone else – but it was virtually impossible. Nobody seemed to know where to go or what to do. I never went to bed and at one stage found myself walking down the central reservation of the dual carriageway outside the hotel, carrying an empty half-bottle of champagne. I wasn't drunk – I just needed to be away from it all for a while.

There was another reception when we came home and again, it was a subdued affair. Everyone seemed to realise that the Revie era really had come to an end and I recall wondering how Don would have reacted if we had won in Paris. I don't know. Had we beaten Bayern, I would have been the first English manager to lift the European Cup so he might have had mixed feelings. He would have felt like a father who had paid for his children's private education only to discover that their new stepfather had been with them on the day they collected their degrees. But now that was a hypothetical question.

However, one burning issue remained – the four-year ban from European football. I felt very strongly that it was too harsh and urged the board to lodge an appeal with UEFA. They didn't want to know. Bob Roberts, who was normally very supportive, dismissed the idea out of hand, saying, 'You've no chance, Jim. We've seen this before. UEFA won't want to know. Forget it.' I told them I believed the ban was unjust and I was prepared to fight it on my own if necessary. The response was that if I wanted to appeal, that was my business. I was determined to make a stand, so I lodged an appeal.

I asked supporters for evidence about what had exactly happened in Paris and the response was tremendous. There had been problems about tickets and I discovered that no one had been informed that there was an alcohol ban inside the ground. When supporters arrived with their bottles of duty free liquor, they were told it would be confiscated. So what did they do? They drank it before they went in. Now I'm not condoning excessive consumption of alcohol but would they have drunk so much so quickly if they had known there was a ban inside the stadium? I think not. The effects of alcohol no doubt played a part in their response to the many bad decisions by the referee but there was strong evidence that the Parisian police over-reacted when they waded in with batons.

I made two trips to UEFA headquarters in Geneva and paid for my own air ticket and hotel accommodation each time. The first time, I was accompanied by Derek Potter from the *Daily Express* and later by Bill Mallinson from the *Daily Mail*. Apart from those two journalists, I was on my own – an indication, perhaps, that no one rated my chances too highly. These days, a club would be represented by a high-powered team of lawyers and the manager would be little more than an observer. I had to go it alone but I was determined that the club's case should be heard.

The four-man commission gave me a rap over the knuckles on my first visit and told me to go away and prepare a formal case. So I did, and as well as the issues involving supporters, I said that Leeds United felt there had been some very unfortunate refereeing decisions but we had taken them on the chin and not lodged an official complaint that would have reflected badly on UEFA. The commission was very fair. I was given a good hearing and even earned praise for my skills as an advocate.

Waiting outside the chamber, I didn't know whether I had done enough to convince them the ban was unjust but I knew it had been important to state the case. When I was called back before the commission, I was thanked for my efforts on the club's behalf and told the ban would be halved to two years. I was euphoric and assumed the board would be as delighted as me. Maybe they were. I didn't expect the full red carpet treatment when I arrived back at Elland Road but no one ever took the trouble to say a proper thank you. They did reimburse me for the tickets and hotels, though.

Football management can be a lonely business and sometimes you have to face things on your own. This was such a moment. It hadn't been an easy campaign but I had felt a deep sense of injustice about the length of that ban and I could not have looked at myself in the mirror if I had accepted it without a fight. Even so, I was faced with the prospect of two seasons without the chance of European football, a period when I would also have to rebuild the side. I knew there were difficult days ahead and some unpopular decisions would have to be made. The trials and tribulations of the European Cup were over, it was time for Leeds United to move on.

ALL CHANGE AT ELLAND ROAD

So in the summer of 1975, I was faced with the huge task of rebuilding Don Revie's Leeds United, now banned from European football for two years. Welcome to the real world! It was like trying to dismantle a dry stone wall that a master craftsman had spent the best years of his life putting together, knowing there was bad weather on the way. I decided to take it apart stone by stone, discarding some of the cornerstones that had held the wall in place for so long. It was going to be a long, difficult and sometimes painful process that would take time and patience and I believed that if I rushed into it, the entire wall could easily collapse around me.

The team was starting to age and needed freshening up. The fans knew that as well as anyone. In fact, many of them wrote to tell me so. While I could still field a very useful side, I could no longer include all the over thirties. On the other hand, I couldn't move them out all at once although I realised that if they left individually they would almost certainly do well at their new clubs. That was something I would have to live with. In view of their tremendous service to Leeds United, I felt obliged to arrange the best possible deal for them, as well as the club, if they moved. Keeping all those balls in the air at the same time wasn't going to be easy – but that was the plan.

During that first season, I had got to know the players. They were never going to accept me as they had Revie but we went along with one another. We all knew I wasn't going to go down the same road as Brian Clough. Change would have to be like the tide, slow but inexorable. I may not have been the manager the players wanted when Revie left, but we shared the same goals and they knew as well as I did that the club was in the process of change. The Revie era was gone forever. Thankfully, we got on well together and we are still on good terms today. I think that says something about what I achieved on a personal level at Elland Road.

Between February 1975 and May 1978, I transferred 13 players, 10 of them internationals. I retained seven players from Revie's championship-winning squad and brought in six players of my own. When the rebuilding process was complete, the balance sheet showed a profit. Billy Bremner, Johnny Giles, Norman Hunter, Allan Clarke, Paul Reaney, Terry Cooper, Terry Yorath and Mick Bates, long-standing members of Revie's squad, all left the club over that three-year period. So, too, did Clough's signings, John McGovern, John O'Hare and Duncan McKenzie. Joe Jordan and Gordon McQueen were sold for big money because they were unsettled and I also lost Mick Jones, another international, through injury.

Goalkeepers David Harvey and David Stewart stayed at the club throughout my time along with Paul Madeley, Peter Lorimer, Eddie and Frank Gray and Trevor Cherry. I signed Tony Currie, Ray Hankin, Arthur Graham, Paul Hart, Brian Flynn and John Hawley and introduced several young players who were starting to emerge through the reserves and the youth system. I also set up a new backroom team. Despite this ongoing reorganisation of the entire staff, I contrived to keep Leeds in the top half of the table. So it was ironic, to put it mildly, that when I had finally assembled my own squad of players, I lost my job on 28 June 1978. The team I had built went on to qualify for Europe the following season, by which time I had left football management behind. But that's football and possibly one of the reasons I decided to quit team management.

Leeds United was an important part of my life. My four years at Elland Road taught me what a big club is really like, something that didn't take me long to grasp. I had enjoyed success at Blackpool and Bolton but I had not experienced anything the size of Leeds. One example of the difference occurred in June 1976 when we went in for Tony Currie of Sheffield United, who was available at £250,000. I offered £220,000 and Maurice Lindley said, 'What are you playing at? If they want £250,000 give 'em £250,000. Don't mess about for the sake of thirty grand. Get it spent! He'll bring in that much through the gate at his first game.' To Blackpool and Bolton, £30,000 was a hell of a lot of money.

At various times during my stay at Elland Road, I was labelled indecisive, yet I sold a team of internationals and restructured one of the best sides in Europe – not the work of a manager whose indecision was final. I never shied away from difficult decisions. Some people also suggested that I was a soft touch and players took advantage of me. Again, I beg to differ. If I have a weakness – if, indeed, it is a weakness – it is that I really do care about people. I believe the way you treat others is important. Players and their families always mattered to me and if players landed in trouble, I tried to help them rather than turn my back.

Once I had to drag Currie and Hankin, two of my big signings, over the coals when I heard they had been involved in an afternoon drinking session in town. I gave them the biggest rollicking I have ever handed out in my life and finished by saying, 'You have let the club down, you have let me down and you have let yourselves down. And you could have been in serious trouble. If I ever have any problems with either of you again, I'll sell you immediately.' Neither ever gave me another moment's trouble.

I'd had a similar experience at Bolton with Jimmy Redfern, a young midfield player from Liverpool. He missed training for a couple of days so I pulled Nat Lofthouse to one side and asked if he fancied a ride over to Liverpool. We climbed into his car, found Redfern's house, knocked on the door and Jimmy opened it. He saw who it was and turned white. He couldn't speak. He looked as if he'd seen Dracula on the doorstep.

'Hello, Jim,' I said. 'Are you not so good?' He muttered something about a cold. 'Come on then, Jim,' I went on. 'We've driven all this way, aren't you going to invite us in?'

We went inside, suggested that his girlfriend might be better off joining his father in the other room for a few minutes, and had a long, meaningful chat. He was back in training the following day.

Perhaps I made it too personal at times but I believe managers are there to manage and I always tried to treat players as I expected to be treated in my own playing days. I needed to feel that a manager cared for me and respected me and if anyone had ranted or thrown things at me, I would have walked away. I expected managers to understand that I would always be fit and always give it my best shot on the training ground and in matches. Ronnie Suart once called me the ideal professional. I'm not sure how that should be interpreted but I hope he said it because I didn't give him too much trouble on or off the field and always gave the club 100 per cent. It's something I expected from my players when I became a manager, although I soon learned that it takes all sorts to make a football team.

Reshaping the Leeds playing staff was an incredibly tough proposition. Some of those players had been among the best in Europe and were virtually irreplaceable. How could any manager find another pairing like Bremner and Giles? They were unique and finding players remotely good enough to take their places was difficult at any price. But the job had to be done, step by cautious step, retaining some semblance of continuity while introducing players who would be the club's future. The dismantling process started before the European campaign reached its climax when I allowed O'Hare and McGovern to rejoin Clough, who had taken over at Nottingham Forest. I never felt they quite fitted in with the Elland Road family, although I liked them both and asked them individually about any difficulties they might be facing as Clough's additions to the Revie family. They denied there was a problem but I was not so sure. I sensed that the other players perceived them as part of the Clough era, a period the Revie contingent wanted to erase from their memories.

The real break-up began when Terry Cooper moved to Middlesbrough for £50,000, enabling him to link up with his former team-mate Jack Charlton, who had left Leeds to become Middlesbrough's manager two years earlier. Cooper had won 20 England caps as an overlapping full-back but he was 30 and said he wanted a change. Frank Gray and Trevor Cherry were already challenging for his place so I let him go. Middlesbrough was a good move for him.

The first player to depart after the European Cup final was Giles, who left for West Brom as player-manager in July for £45,000. Giles was 35, keen to move into management and led Albion back into the First Division at the end of his first season. That didn't surprise me. I always thought John would make a manager and I was surprised when he opted out after 10 years with West Brom, Ireland and Vancouver Whitecaps. I think he really wanted the Leeds job when Revie left and probably again when Clough was sacked but he never showed any ill feeling towards me. Although I worked with him for just a few months, I will always remember him as a talented and competitive foot-baller. He was by no means quick and he had two stiff hips, which had to be given an Algepan rub before he went out to play. But that never affected his mobility and he had such an astute football brain that he could control a game at his own pace.

He and Bremner were the perfect blend in midfield. They were both excellent passers of the ball and ball winners, too, and if anyone wanted to play rough, they could take care of themselves, even though neither stood much over 5ft. Above all, they under-stood the game. They knew when to pass it long or short, when it was time to slow things down, when to take a quick free-kick or wait for a while. They were master players and had been just about the best midfield pair in Europe.

Giles was the last high-profile departure that year but, sadly, I was also deprived of one of the most important players on the Leeds staff, Mick Jones. Over the years, I had seen a lot of Leeds and I always regarded him as a crucial player, the team's unsung hero. Mick was a genuine lad and when Revie signed him from Sheffield United in 1967, he brought a new dimension to the side. He was an old-fashioned centre-forward who just got on with the job without a word of complaint. He and Clarke were a great combination. They were good pals off the field and developed a telepathic understanding around the penalty area. Jones never played a single first-team game for me because of knee trouble. We did everything to get him fit. He saw the best specialists in the north and when all else failed, we sent him to London to see the top people there. At one point, we thought he might make it and pencilled him into the reserves so he could have a run-out under match conditions. I was cringing, just watching him in that match and eventually he had to give up and limp off the pitch. He retired in October 1975. It was an enormous loss.

On the plus side, I gained Eddie Gray. When I arrived, Eddie was in charge of the youth team after that well-publicised racehorse taunt from Cloughie. He was not expected to play again because of a long-standing thigh problem. As his new manager, I thought the very least I could do was offer him another chance – after all, he was only 26 and had established himself as one of the finest left-sided midfield players of his generation, as I knew from playing against him. Because of his injuries, it was possible he would not reach the same heights but I had a hunch that Eddie Gray 90 per cent fit might still be a pretty useful performer. So I took him to one side one day after training and said, 'I've watched you running round in the five-a-sides, Eddie, and you look all right to me.'

'I'm not too bad,' he replied. Eddie never wasted words.

'OK, there's a reserve match on Wednesday. Why don't you have a run-out?'

'Aye, awright,' he said. And that was that.

I couldn't go because there was a board meeting so I said to Maurice Lindley, 'Eddie's going to play for the reserves tomorrow. Will you go along and have a look?' I gave Maurice time to get home after the match then called him.

'How did we go on?' I asked.

'Oh, we won – and before you ask, Eddie was a division better than anyone else on the field. He had a bit of a limp but he'll be all right.'

So I appointed Brian Doyle, a former manager of Stockport, to look after the kids and brought Eddie in from the cold. He was still playing first-team football eight years later as player-manager.

The next exodus started in the summer of 1976 with the sale of McKenzie to Anderlecht for £200,000. Like McGovern and O'Hare, McKenzie had never seemed to be part of the furniture, although I liked him a lot and he was enormously popular with the fans. They loved his unpredictable style. Nevertheless, I felt some members of the dressing room were less enthusiastic and that was an important factor at the time. He was a likeable lad and life was never dull when he was around. For a party piece at Paul Reaney's testimonial match, he jumped over a Mini in front of around 20,000 fans. I knew he could do it because I'd seen him perform the same trick on the car park – but if he'd injured himself in front of all those people, questions would have been asked about the manager's judgement. Fortunately, all went well.

He could also throw a golf ball over the crossbar from the goalmouth at the other end of the pitch. He once said to me, 'I can throw a golf ball across the pitch as well, you know.'

'I think I might just about be able to manage that, too, Duncan,' I replied.

'What, with your left hand?'

Sure enough, he picked up a ball with his 'wrong' hand and hurled it over the far touchline. He was a remarkable athlete.

I also transferred Mick Bates, a midfield player who had never been able to hold down a regular place during the Bremner–Giles era, to Walsall for £35,000 in July and Yorath moved to Coventry for £140,000 a month later. Yorath was only 26 but felt he needed a change after being on the Leeds books for nine years so I decided not to stand in his way.

The next two departures finally signalled the end of the Revie years. In September 1976, Bremner went to Hull for £35,000. He was coming up to 34 and I asked him to think long and hard before moving. In fact, I begged him not to drop down to the Second Division. I said, 'Look, Bill, you've been one of the all-time greats. Don't go and throw it away in the lower divisions. I understand what you want. You feel your time's up here and you want to carry on playing as long as you can. If you leave, you go with my blessing but if you take my advice, you'll stay where you are and call it a day here.'

One of my pet hates is to see long-time greats struggling in the lower grades. There's real sadness attached to it. I know many people say you should play until you drop but somehow that doesn't apply to the real top-liners. Billy was certainly in that category. Sadly, he went to Hull.

He spent a couple of seasons there before starting a seven-year spell as manager of Doncaster Rovers. In his early days at Belle Vue, I called in to see him a few times and he always made me very welcome. I would give him a few ideas because he had never done any formal coaching courses. He had three years as manager of Leeds in the old Second Division before returning for a second stint at Doncaster. I was desperately sad when he suffered a heart attack and died on 7 December 1997, just two days away from his 55th birthday.

It was only when I went to Leeds that I realised what a tremendous player he was. I'd played against him quite a few times and I knew he was a firebrand who would tackle anything that moved, but he was a hugely talented footballer, too, a man who lived to play football. He had the best reverse pass I had seen since Johnny Haynes, he was quick and tremendous at getting into the box and making chances for himself. Bill's game was about pace and zip, mobility, sharpness and heart. He would have played in any position and given 100 per cent. He would have run through a brick wall for Leeds United, so I felt it was appropriate when they erected a statue of him outside the ground shortly after his death.

He wasn't fit when I took over and at first things didn't go too well on the field. Our old kit man Bob English said, 'Don't worry, it will be different when Billy's back. When Billy's going well, the rest respond. He brings the best out of all of them.' He was dead right. We never looked back once Billy returned. He was a natural leader and his enthusiasm was infectious. You didn't have to ask if Billy was around – you'd hear him yards away.

Like Giles, he had wanted the job before I was appointed and at first I could sense a bit of resentment, but that evaporated and in the end we got on very well, even though we didn't have a great deal in common apart from football. He smoked and liked a drink and we had a few shouting matches, but I could live with that because he was never a problem when playing for Leeds United was involved. I had something of a soft spot for Billy. He and Allan Clarke were always my final port of call when I did a round of the players' rooms on the night before an away game. After a meal, the lads would sit around for a few minutes then quietly wander off to bed as good as gold. A bit later on, I would go upstairs, pop into each room and have a chat. Nothing too serious, just a friendly natter, but I was rarely in with Billy and Allan for less than half an hour. They were an absolute scream, Leeds United's answer to Little and Large. There would always be loads of banter flying in each direction and every week I would try to come up with a new joke. Wonderful times!

Norman Hunter was transferred to Bristol City in October. I'd liked him since our England days and we spent a lot of time together during the 1966 World Cup. He was incredibly superstitious, one of Revie's traits, and I found myself locked into one of his superstitions in that summer of '66. We used to travel together to England's matches and before our first win of the tournament against Mexico on a chilly, rainy evening, Norman was carrying his raincoat over his arm and I was wearing a red pullover. Afterwards, he took me to one side and instructed me to wear that pullover at every game. At first I thought he was joking because I have never been at all superstitious, but Norman was deadly serious and I thought I'd better go along with him. Sure enough, at every match, I wore my red pullover and Norman carried his mac over his arm, right the way through to the final.

I think he missed Don Revie more than anyone else did. He was always talking to me about the man, who had clearly been a huge influence. I suspect that if Revie had told Norman to go and stand on his head in the penalty box, he would have done so without asking why. Norman was a very fine defender, an excellent reader of the game, a good competitor and he gave me everything. People didn't like playing against Norman and not just because of the old 'bites-yer-legs' image. He wasn't just a crunching tackler – he really could play. He certainly didn't make 28 appearances for England because he was a dirty devil, and if Bobby Moore hadn't been around in the same position, Norman would have appeared far more often. He was always well turned-out, clean-living, reliable and very good-natured. He still is. He works for Radio Leeds and I often bump into him at matches. I like Norman a lot. He's the kind of man you would want to have standing next to you in the trenches.

Losing Giles, Bremner and Hunter was an experience that had to be faced, and I was grateful for the support I received from the board. Chairman Manny Cussins, like Jack Banks at Bolton, was completely self-made and a fantastic businessman. He never forgot anything, he was as sharp as a needle, cute and he knew the date on every penny in his pocket. Like Jack, he owned a Rolls-Royce but he didn't waste money and kept an eye on every deal. He was chairman of around 30 companies and used to carry all their accounts around in his pocket. His business career started at the age of 14 when he pushed a handcart around the streets of Hull and he used to tell me that becoming a millionaire was easy. He would say, 'If you took away every business and every penny I possess and turned me out on the streets, I promise you I would be a millionaire again in twelve months. It's a question of knowing the right people and the precise value of things.'

We once went to Glasgow to watch a Scotland v. England international and stayed overnight at the Albany Hotel. At 7 a.m. my telephone rang.

'Where are you?' asked Manny.

'Where am I? I'm in bed. It's seven o'clock.' Manny wasn't having any of that.

'Come on,' he said. 'Get dressed. I'm ready to go.'

That morning he bought two warehouses in Glasgow. In the afternoon, four Leeds players were playing for Scotland but with 20 minutes to go, Manny wanted to be off. I was keen to see the lads but he'd acquired his warehouses and it was time to go. I made him stay and see the players.

In my early days at Leeds, he used to keep on about going out for dinner together. Eventually, I agreed. I put on my best suit and his driver collected me in a green Rolls-Royce before picking up Manny from his home. He had told me about all the fancy restaurants he used to frequent in the West Riding but this time we pulled up outside what looked like an Italian snack bar. Sure enough, the menu was no more than a plastic card with a choice of about six dishes, nothing too exotic and nothing over two quid.

'Have whatever you want,' insisted Manny, so I ordered spaghetti bolognese. He said he would have the usual, which turned out to be macaroni cheese. Manny only toyed with his food and as soon as I'd finished, he said, 'Did you enjoy that?' I told him I had and he said, 'Right then, settle up and we'll be off.' The bill, with drinks and coffee, came to seven or eight pounds only, so I wasn't complaining, and listening to Manny's life story was a fascinating experience. I suspected that trattoria was his regular haunt, especially at that price.

At the end of each of my four seasons at Leeds, I arranged a golfing break in Marbella for the players, and one or two directors also came along, usually Bob Roberts and Sydney Simon. Manny wasn't in the party at first but finally, in response to his constant complaints about not being invited, we asked him to join us. We always stayed at the Andalucia Plaza, one of the best hotels on the Costa del Sol, and on our first morning, we were all sitting around the pool in our swimming trunks. The weather was glorious. Bob and Sydney were lying on their sunbeds, cigars in hand, gin and tonics on the table. The players were diving in and out of the pool before heading off for a round of golf. It was idyllic stuff. Then along came Manny, wearing his everyday clothes.

'My room's awful,' he moaned. 'It's dark and dingy.' As he had been given one of the best rooms in the place, I was puzzled. 'Come and have a look,' he said. So up we went to Manny's room only to discover, as I had half suspected, that he hadn't opened the shutters. I put that straight but he was still muttering about dingy little rooms as we rejoined the rest of the party and soon I heard him say to Bob Roberts, 'I don't like it here.' Bob put down his cigar.

'I told you, Manny,' he said. 'We have to put up with this kind of thing every year. You thought it was going to be a bed of roses, didn't you? But it's always like this. It's no fun, is it?' And so saying, he sipped his gin and tonic, picked up his cigar and assumed a reclining position once more. I suggested a swim but Manny didn't like swimming. So I had to forsake the pool in the afternoon to take Manny for a walk. When we returned to the hotel, he said, 'I want to go home.' And next day he did, recruiting me as his chauffeur to Malaga airport.

Manny was the exception to the rule. Those trips to Malaga were a good team-building exercise. Despite his family ethos, Revie had never taken the players away for an end-of-season break but I saw it as an opportunity to wind down after a long, hard year, a chance to relax and enjoy ourselves away from football. But while the players could savour the prospect of another six weeks off when they returned home, it was always back to business for the manager. Summer is a busy time, with training schedules and a pre-season programme to organise. For me, there was the ongoing task of trying to reshape the team, deciding when to move on some players and, equally important, making sure that others were committed to the club for the foreseeable future.

One man I had to keep was Paul Madeley, even though he had passed the 30 mark when I took over. He could play anywhere, preferring midfield, and Revie always used to say that if he could have played Bremner, Giles and Madeley in the England team, he would have named them *en bloc*. I wouldn't argue with that but unfortunately for Don, John and Billy weren't English. In my four years at the club, Paul played right-back and left-back, both central defensive positions and right across midfield. I once played him at Arsenal as an attacking left-side player and he was brilliant. I always described him as a Rolls-Royce player because he would purr quietly through 90 minutes and could change gear without anyone noticing. He was incredibly quick, something a lot of people didn't appreciate because of his upright running style.

He demonstrated his pace in that game at Arsenal when I

used him in an attacking role. All our strikers were injured so I played Eddie Gray up front with Tony Currie in behind him and Paul out on the left, a role he'd never filled before. Before the kick-off, I took him to one side and said, 'Look, Ed [his second name was Edward and we used to call him Ed] you'll be all right. First time you get the ball, push it past Pat Rice and go . . .' That's exactly what happened. The first time the ball was played out to Madeley, I shouted, 'Go on, Ed!' And he went – he was 10 yards clear before Pat had moved.

Paul was the complete professional in everything he did on and off the field. He rarely complained – if he did, we knew we really had a problem. He once actually signed a new contract on what was virtually a blank piece of paper. I called him in to discuss terms and opened negotiations by saying, 'OK, Paul, we'll give you so much.' He replied that he had no intention of leaving Leeds so he might as well sign the contract and leave me to fill in the details. I said, 'What do you want, then, two years or three?' He answered, 'Either way, I'll leave it to you. I just want to play for Leeds,' and that was that. In those days, you didn't get lumbered with agents and dealing with the Paul Madeleys of this world was a pleasure.

Peter Lorimer stayed, too. Peter was one of the best kickers of a ball I have ever seen and the side's free-kick specialist. I took one or two free-kick routines with me to Leeds but the first time I tried to practise one of them on the training ground, there was a distinct lack of interest among the players. They wouldn't concentrate on what was a simple move involving three players. In the end, I said, 'What's going on? Why won't you concentrate on what you're supposed to be doing?'

A bored Bremner replied, 'We don't need free-kick routines, we've got him,' and he pointed at Lorimer.

'That's ridiculous. However good he is, he'll hit the wall four times out of five. We need something different.'

I never really got through to them and Bremner finally made his point in a game at Wolves. We were leading 1–0 late on but needed a second goal and couldn't afford to take any chances. We won a free-kick just inside the Wolves half on the edge of the

centre circle and I assumed our aim would be to retain possession. Instead, Peter put the ball down and lined up for a shot at
goal. I leapt out of the dug-out and started yelling at Billy that
shooting from that distance was ridiculous, we would be giving
the ball away. He put a hand to his ear and called, 'Can't hear you,
Boss,' or words to that effect. Sure enough, Lorimer took a few
paces and let fly from over 40 yards. I don't think anyone in the
ground really saw the ball until it was on its way back from the
crossbar. It was one of the hardest shots I have seen, and from the
centre of the field Billy, with an impish grin on his face, called
out, 'What's that you were saying, Gaffer?'

Lorimer's volleyed goal against Ujpest Dozsa in the European
Cup in 1974 was technically perfect. I saw him rattle in a few like
that. It wasn't an accident. No one practised harder than Peter.
He would practise, practise, practise his shooting. Every Friday at
the end of training, he would collect six balls and place them on
the penalty spot one by one, driving each ball into an empty net. I
once asked him if he wanted me to fetch one of the junior
goalkeepers or if I should go in goal. He just said no and carried
on drilling the balls into the goal. That was his routine. Like
David Beckham today, Peter practised more than anyone, and
that was the secret of his success.

While Peter will always be remembered for his shooting power,
he was also an extremely gifted footballer. In my last season, I
toyed with the idea of using him as an orthodox midfield player.
He didn't have a lot of pace but he was a fine passer of the ball, an
excellent reader of the game and a good player for me. He was
easy-going and we got on well, but Peter liked a bet and on one
occasion I had to put my foot down when I caught him trying to
cajole Maureen, my secretary, into placing a telephone bet a
couple of hours before a match. I put a stop to that.

Finding new blood had to be a priority and my first major
signing, in June 1976, needed to be a good one. It was. Tony
Currie was a great success and after he had played a handful of
games for me, I called Ron Greenwood, the England manager,
and told him Tony was the best midfield player in the country
and should be in the England team. He was a tremendous talent,

technically gifted, strong and naturally fit. That will come as a surprise to the people who used to knock Tony because he never looked really athletic. On one occasion, he had been out of action for about four weeks and I pushed him straight back into the side as soon as he was off the treatment table. I was told he should have had a run-out with the reserves or a week's full training but I knew he would be OK. He played the full 90 minutes without a problem. He was hugely popular with the crowd and after selling McKenzie, we needed someone with charisma. Currie provided loads of it but I would not have signed him on charisma alone – I was convinced he was the genuine article as a player. I could never understand why he won only 17 England caps.

Three months after signing Currie, I paid Burnley £170,000 for Ray Hankin, a man who brought the best out of Joe Jordan. They were an ideal pairing. Joe would always run his heart out, he was brave and gave everything but I used to wonder why he didn't score more goals. He played alongside Kenny Dalglish for Scotland and Allan Clarke at Leeds – and you don't get many better players than those two – yet he scored relatively few goals. At Leeds, he had always operated right up at the front, at the head of the arrow if you like, because he was so willing and quick. I decided he needed a target player up there alongside him. Hankin was nothing like as mobile or quick as Joe but once Ray had recovered from an injury that kept him out for a long time after signing for us, they quickly became a formidable combination. Hankin had great ball control with chest and feet, was strong and a good finisher, and he took a lot of the weight off Joe.

My next signing, in July 1977, came from north of the border. A few months earlier, I had travelled up to watch Dundee play Aberdeen at Dens Park and the traffic was so bad, I didn't arrive until just before half-time. But the second 45 minutes were more than enough for me to spot the Aberdeen left-winger as a potential Leeds player. His name was Arthur Graham. So I called Davie Wilson, the former Rangers and Scotland left-winger against whom I'd played several times for England, and asked him what he thought about Arthur.

'You mean Bumper?' replied Davie. 'That's what we all call him up here. He's a good lad – used live round the corner from me.'

'How good is he?'

'If you can get him, get him.'

So I got him for £120,000 and what a great buy! He could play right-wing, left-wing or centre-forward and he'd give you 15 or 16 goals a year. He'd play 40 matches a season, was never late, never caused a minute's trouble and always gave total commitment.

I still needed someone to play alongside Currie in midfield so four months after Graham's arrival, I went back to Burnley to sign Brian Flynn. He was only 22 but he'd already played well over 100 games for Burnley and collected getting on for 20 Welsh caps. He wasn't much over 5ft tall but he was very fit, mobile and a good tackler. He could play a bit, too, the ideal foil for Currie. I paid £175,000 and he was worth every penny.

At the end of 1977, the jigsaw was starting to fit into place. From the Revie era, I had retained Harvey and Stewart, along with Reaney, McQueen, Madeley, Cherry, Frank and Eddie Gray, Clarke and Jordan. I had signed Currie, Flynn, Hankin and Graham, and Carl Harris and Peter Hampton had come up through the ranks. In my first three seasons, in what was essentially a transitional phase, we had finished ninth, fifth and tenth. We reached the semi-final of the FA Cup in 1976 and we were on our way to the last four of the League Cup as 1978 began. I felt we were on the brink of real progress.

Then in January, I had a massive jolt when Jordan and McQueen decided they wanted to leave. Joe and I had got on well – in fact, Anne and I had attended his wedding – so it was a blow when he told me he fancied playing abroad. I actually fixed up for him to have an interview with Ajax of Amsterdam but he turned them down. I wasn't surprised and hoped he might stay. Instead, Manchester United came in for him and on 15 January, he moved to Old Trafford for £350,000, a lot of money in those days. Losing Joe made McQueen restless. They were big mates and a few weeks later, Gordon said via the press that he felt Leeds were going nowhere. That upset me because there's nothing worse for a manager than a leading player claiming the club lacks ambition. I was very disappointed in him and said so. I also knew what the fans would think when they read his outburst. But there's no point in trying to keep a dissatisfied player and, in the end, I decided that if Gordon felt like that, he could go. It was no secret that Manchester United were keen to reunite Gordon and Joe and, incredibly, I got £495,000 for him.

So, out of the blue, I needed a new striker and a centre-half to replace two established internationals who were a big part of my plans for the future. Ideally, I would have liked to sign Paul Jones from Bolton to replace McQueen. I had seen him grow up at Burnden Park and by early 1978, he was one of the best defenders in the country. Not surprisingly, Ian Greaves wouldn't let him go. My next target was Paul Hart at Blackpool. They were reluctant to release him at first but I persisted and he signed for Leeds in March 1978 – and scored an own goal in his first game at Elland Road. He was crestfallen afterwards but I tapped him on the shoulder and said, 'Don't worry, lad, things can only get better.' And they did.

My last signing was John Hawley, a striker from Hull City who had made a bit of a name for himself early in his career by playing Second Division football as an amateur. The family had an antiques business in Beverley and John used to train with Hull in the mornings and revert to the antiques trade in the afternoons. He was dubbed the 'Last of the Corinthians'. He had played the best part of 100 league games before he finally signed professional forms in 1977 and a year later he was a Leeds United player.

You have to be careful with players from the lower divisions but I watched John four times and the more I saw him, the more I liked him. I fancied he would be all right alongside Hankin. He was mobile, he had two good feet, he was eager and as soon as the 1977–78 season ended, I paid Hull £80,000 for him. John, who is still in the antiques trade, dines out on the story of how Jimmy Armfield signed him, went back to Elland Road to inform the directors and was promptly sacked – not strictly accurate but a

215

good tale. Leeds later sold him to Sunderland for £200,000. I had no idea when I signed him that my days as Leeds manager were drawing to a close.

The last two high-profile players to leave the club were Paul Reaney, who moved to Bradford City in May, and Allan Clarke, who took over as manager of Barnsley at the same time. Reaney was 33 and Clarke a couple of months away from his 32nd birthday, and it was time for them to move on. I kept Clarkey as long as I could. He was a natural finisher and, like Bremner and Giles, he knew the game inside out. He was kicked around a lot but he could look after himself. He missed Mick Jones, though. Jordan was a fine player but he wasn't the same kind of animal as Mick, and he and Allan never quite established the same rapport on the pitch. Losing Jones and Revie at the same time was a blow for Allan but he did well for me. I never had any complaints about Clarke, and contrary to the dour image he acquired during his managerial career at Barnsley, Leeds and Scunthorpe, he was one of the funniest men I have ever known. He was naturally humorous and Anne often recalls the way Clarkey could make her laugh.

My revolution was completed with a clear-out among the reserves and a new backroom team. I brought in Geoff Ladley, a qualified physiotherapist at Pinderfields Hospital in Wakefield, and he proved to be one of my best signings, a top man. Brian Green and Stan Ternent joined the coaching staff and Don Howe arrived as my assistant in November 1975. He came to Leeds from a job in Turkey, which I felt was a waste for English football, and stayed for almost two years before he joined Arsenal. I felt the players needed someone who was a complete contrast to me, more verbal, more outgoing, and we were a good combination. I've never been frightened of bringing in top people and certainly didn't regard Don as a threat to my own position. I was disappointed when he decided to leave – although I knew Arsenal was his true love.

I always knew that the long-term future of Leeds United depended on developing a successful youth policy. I used to keep an eye on the juniors in training and always watched their games whenever I could. Their home matches took place on the training ground behind the main stand on a Saturday morning so I didn't miss many. I liked what I saw. A few of them had a realistic chance of going all the way and I introduced Gwyn Thomas and Billy McGhie to first-team football. My last youth signing was goalkeeper John Lukic, who went on to enjoy a successful career with Leeds and Arsenal. There were also high hopes for a young Scot, George Boyd, who had been labelled the new Billy Bremner. Like Billy, he was a ginger-haired midfield player with a tigerish temperament, and he had earned rave reviews for his performance for Scotland Schoolboys against England at Wembley. Maybe the bright lights turned his head but he got into a spot of bother. I decided enough was enough and sent him home, but I didn't sleep a wink that night.

It wasn't the first time I'd suffered a sleepless night after telling a young player he was being released. Back at Bolton, two young lads arrived from Liverpool schools football, Peter Reid and Tommy Evans. They were good pals but while it soon became obvious that Peter had real potential, we could see that Tommy wouldn't make it. When I told him he was being released, he broke down in tears. It was awful and I really felt for him. In my eight years as a manager, I must have told around 40 young kids that they were being released and it never got any easier.

On Saturday, 29 April 1978, I turned out my last team – not only for Leeds but also as a club manager. In 4–3–3 formation, it was Harvey; Madeley, Hart, Cherry, Frank Gray; Currie, Flynn, Eddie Gray; Hankin, Clarke, Graham. It was a decent side and we drew 0–0 with QPR. I believed I had the basis of a really good team for the future. We went on a tour of Switzerland at the end of the season, beating Etoile Carouge 4–1 and Young Boys of Berne 5–2. Then we all headed off for our annual break in Marbella. We had a week's golf, plenty of sunshine and a lot of fun and as May drew to a close, I felt secure as Leeds manager and optimistic about the future. A month later, I was out of work and all those difficult decisions I had made were about to come to nothing.

On my first day back in the office after we returned from

Spain, Maureen told me that Tom Holley of the *Sunday People* had asked if he could pop in. Tom was a former Leeds player who covered Yorkshire football and I always enjoyed a chat. This proved to be one of our less enjoyable conversations. He came straight to the point.

'Look, Jim,' he said, 'we've always had a good relationship and I didn't want to go behind your back. We're running a story this weekend that you're on your way out. I wanted to tell you straight to your face.' I thanked him for that.

'But where does this come from?' I had to ask.

'I can't reveal my source but believe me, it's genuine.'

The May board meeting was held the following Monday. In my four years, I'd changed the team round, turned a £400,000 deficit into a £250,000 profit and built a new stand at the Elland Road end of the ground. I was in the process of signing two more players. I didn't doubt Tom Holley's source but somehow I didn't think his story stood up, although I appreciated that three new directors had recently joined the board, Brian Woodward, Brian Roberts and Rayner Barker, and they might want their own man.

Manny Cussins wasn't at the meeting so Bob Roberts was in the chair and when it was time for the manager's report, I told them about the trip to Switzerland and one or two more things. Then Bob said, 'Are there any more questions for the manager?' Silence. 'Right, off you go, Jim,' said Bob. So I picked up my bags and walked out. When I reached the main reception, I was confronted by the local press corps.

'What's happened, Jim? Are you still the manager?' I don't remember who asked the question.

'How do you mean?' I replied. 'No one's discussed my future – ask Bob Roberts.'

They did and Bob told them, 'You've just been talking to the manager of Leeds United. You can see for yourselves that nothing's happening. You've all jumped the gun.'

Over the next few days, I tried to work out exactly where the rumours had been coming from, and took a detached look at my record and position. I knew we needed a couple of players and was working to bring them in. I realised that finishing 10th was

The England Under-23 line-up against Czechoslovakia in Bratislava, May 1957: (left to right) Ronnie Clayton, Trevor Smith, Derek Kevan, Eddie Hopkinson, me, Bryan Douglas, Dennis Stevens, Duncan Edwards, Alan A'Court, Johnny Haynes, Maurice Norman

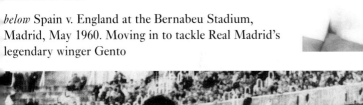

right The cap fits. A studio picture taken after winning my first England cap on the summer tour of South America in 1959

below Spain v. England at the Bernabeu Stadium, Madrid, May 1960. Moving in to tackle Real Madrid's legendary winger Gento

ZARCO GRÁFICO, MADRID

above Carry your bag, sir? The England team as they used to travel, arriving in Glasgow to play Scotland in April 1964. Left to right: Gordon Milne, Gordon Banks, me, Maurice Norman, Terry Paine, George Eastham (behind), John Byrne and Bobby Moore

right Los tres amigos ... Sharing a joke with Gerry Hitchens (left) and goalkeeper Ron Springett during a break in training for the 1962 World Cup in Chile

Enjoying the banter
in the dressing room
after an England
training session with
(from the left)
Bryan Douglas,
Bobby Smith,
Jimmy Greaves
and coach
Ron Greenwood

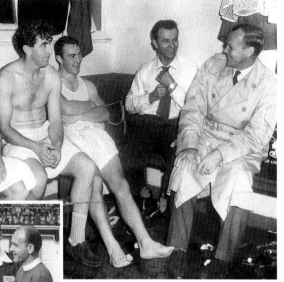

left Shaking hands with Alfredo Di Stefano before the FA Centenary match between England and the Rest of the World in October 1963

below World Cup quarter-final, 10 June 1962: Brazil 3 England 1. Although surrounded by England players, Brazilian striker Didi manages to take a shot at goal

POPPERFOTO

The best England team I played in … wearing Bolton kit for a practice match at Burnden Park in 1960. Back row (left to right): me, Bobby Robson, Ron Springett, Peter Swan, Ron Flowers, Mike McNeil. Front: Bryan Douglas, Jimmy Greaves, Bobby Smith, Johnny Haynes, Bobby Charlton

The World Cup winners of 1966. Back row (left to right): Jimmy Greaves, Roger Hunt, Martin Peters, Gordon Banks, Jack Charlton, Norman Hunter, Ron Flowers, Peter Bonetti, Ron Springett, George Cohen. Centre: Ray Wilson, Geoff Hurst, me, Dr Alan Bass, Harold Shepherdson, Alf Ramsey, Les Cocker, Bobby Moore, Gerry Byrne, Bobby Charlton. Front: Alan Ball, Ian Callaghan, Nobby Stiles, John Connelly, George Eastham, Terry Paine

ERIC THOMPSON

above Welcome to Singapore … as manager of the FA tour to New Zealand and the Far East in 1969. FA official Jack Bowers greets his Singapore counterpart watched by 'Doc' Stephens, chairman of the FA

Management man. In the Burnden Park dug-out with Nat Lofthouse after taking over as manager of Bolton in 1971

BLACKPOOL EVENING GAZETTE

above The 1975 European Cup final in Paris. A dejected bench as Leeds lose 2-0 to Bayern Munich. The expressions tell the story

On stage at the City Varieties, Leeds, with Prince Charming (otherwise known as Norman 'Bites-yer-legs' Hunter) during one of our sell-out performances of *Cinderella*

Man of letters. Working on my column at the *Blackpool Evening Gazette*

The three wise men. With Mike Ingham (left) and Alan Green at the 1994 World Cup final in the Pasadena Rose Bowl

With former England coach Terry Venables, who had been my strong recommendation for the job when the FA asked me to find a replacement for Graham Taylor

A proud moment. Anne and me at Buckingham Palace after I'd received the OBE from Prince Charles in 2000

below Receiving the freedom of the borough from Blackpool's mayor, Ivan Taylor, in 2003

not acceptable to some people but felt that the team I had put together was capable of doing significantly better – and they did. The following season Leeds qualified for Europe. I wondered about Manny Cussins, too. Why hadn't he been at the meeting? Were reports true that he had been seen chatting to Jock Stein, the former Celtic manager, at a race meeting? Rumours, rumours . . .

I spent the next month preparing the pre-season training programme and arranging a few friendly matches. I appointed Jim McAnearney as Don Howe's successor and signed one of the two players I was seeking, John Hawley. I booked a two-week holiday to start on 30 June, two days after the June board meeting. I never made it through that meeting. From the start, the atmosphere was very tense and after giving my report, I decided to bring things to a head once and for all. Anne and I had come to like Leeds and we had been to look at houses in the area. In fact, at the time, Manny was building some houses at Harewood and we were going to see them when we returned from holiday. I was happy in the job and thought I had done the hard part; we were ready to move to another level.

'Manny,' I said, 'my contract runs out at the end of October and I'm thinking about coming to live in Leeds. I'd like a new contract.'

'What's the matter, have you no confidence in yourself? Wait until November and we're top of the league – we'll be falling over ourselves to give you another contract.'

'Maybe so, but I'm thinking of moving my family over here and I'm not going to do that without getting a new contract first.'

It was a catch-22 situation, as Manny explained outside the boardroom when we adjourned.

'They won't give you another contract, they want you to prove yourself in the early part of next season,' he said. Clearly the writing was starting to appear on the wall.

If I'd said OK, who knows what might have happened, but I sensed there was more to it. So when we resumed the meeting, once again I took the initiative, saying, 'The chairman tells me you won't give me a contract unless I move – but you know

RIGHT BACK TO THE BEGINNING

perfectly well that I'm not going to uproot my family without the security of a contract. The current one has only three months to go, so it looks as if that's it.'

'Come on, aren't you going to fight for your job then?' Barker responded.

'Do you mean am I going to beg for it? No, I'm not. I'm not begging you for anything. After four years, you either know me or you don't, and if you don't want me, I'll have to live with it.'

I really needed to know if they wanted me or not. No one spoke. They all looked down at the table or at the floor. Nobody wanted to meet my eye. There was a long silence and I realised what that silence meant. It was me who said, 'OK, I understand.' I made the decision for them. I knew I could have had another job within a month because my contract was about to expire and there had been approaches, but I never wanted to leave Leeds.

Before I left, Bob Roberts came to see me. I thought he was going to give me reasons, or at least offer sympathy but he just said, 'You'll be fully paid up, you know.' Wow, I thought, three months' money! They also put £5,000 into a pension – for which I have been very grateful. I had one request.

'I'm going on holiday in two days' time so can you delay the announcement until I'm out of the country?' Bob agreed and the press never found me. And that was that. After almost four years, my Leeds career had just petered out. I said nothing but I was gutted.

The day after the board meeting, I went back to clear everything out. Anne was very upset about what had happened and when I arrived at the ground, Maureen was upset, too. So were all my staff. I had to go and say goodbye to them individually and it was an emotional day.

Leeds appointed Stein on 21 August and, like Clough, he lasted just 44 days before taking over as Scotland's manager. He was succeeded by Jimmy Adamson. I had no contact with the club until, completely out of the blue, the phone rang on Christmas Day morning, six months later. It was Manny Cussins. He said, 'I'm disappointed in you. You haven't sent me a Christmas card.'

The ironic thing is that I had probably become a good manager by the time I left. I had served an eight-year apprenticeship in three divisions and in Europe and none of my teams finished in the bottom half of the table. I had gone through two crucial learning periods, the first year at Bolton and the first 18 months at Leeds and by the time I finished I had really learned about controlling a football club. I was terribly disappointed because I genuinely liked Leeds.

Despite being unemployed, my credibility was good. As time went by, I was asked if I was interested in jobs at Leicester, Blackburn Rovers, Newcastle, Chelsea and Hearts – I even received an approach from Athletic Bilbao. I thought seriously about all of them but leaving Leeds had upset me more than I allowed people to see. It was time to move on.

THE BLACK
LUBIANKA

I've been told I have the perfect face for radio and, not long ago, I discovered how true that old gag can be. Anne and I were attending a function in Blackpool and, before the official proceedings began, we were making small talk among a group of eight or 10 people. I soon became aware that one of the women in our midst kept staring at me. It was a bit unnerving, to say the least, and after a while she said, 'I definitely know you from somewhere. I just can't place you. I can't quite remember where we met but I'm sure I know you.' For the next 15 minutes or so, my past flashed before me. Who was she? Where had I encountered her? How could she be so sure she knew me? I was baffled but she refused to let it drop, constantly asking, 'Why do I know you?' It was starting to become embarrassing when suddenly she interrupted the general flow of conversation and cried, 'That's it, you're the chap on the radio! My sons listen to you every week.'

People tell me I have a distinctive voice but that's something only others can judge. Very few people know quite how their own voice sounds but it seems a lot of people recognise mine – the power of radio! Recently, I did an interview with the editor of a newspaper for the blind, based in Staffordshire, and as he approached I was in conversation with someone else. He walked towards me unerringly and said, 'That's Jimmy Armfield, isn't it? Hello, nice to meet you.' He went on to explain how many blind people are regular listeners to football on Radio Five Live. When I set out with the BBC 25 years ago, I never appreciated what a service radio provides for blind people.

I'm also told I have a distinctive radio manner. Apparently, when I am on air I always sound at ease and never flustered. Again, that isn't something I have worked on deliberately. When I first started on radio in 1979, I was offered all sorts of advice about how to pitch my approach but, from day one, I have just tried to be myself. I can honestly say that I have enjoyed every minute of my time, first on Radio 2 and, more recently, on Radio Five Live. It is a genuine pleasure for me to go to a match and do a commentary.

What do I give the programme? It's not easy for me to say but I suppose I can call on 50 years' experience in the game and a comprehensive knowledge of past players and matches. I have been a commentator at five World Cups, three European Championships, 17 FA Cup finals and numerous European games. I lost count long ago of the number of domestic matches I have covered but at around 60 a season, it must be about 1,500 by now. Yet I still get that tinge of excitement every time I sit down behind the microphone, although I never become twitchy or nervous as some people clearly do. Sometimes, at very big matches, I can sense the tension affecting some broadcasters but, quite honestly, I never feel stressed. The knowledge that there may be millions of people about to listen to the broadcast should, if anything, be a stimulus.

Of course, I appreciate that a whole generation of the listening public has grown up knowing me only as a radio man. On air, I am sometimes asked for my views as a former player or manager and people remember that a few years back I played a role in the appointment of two England managers. There are also those who recall my days as a newspaper reporter on the *Daily Express* but I'm sure a lot of listeners regard me only as a radio journalist and I have no problem with that. After all, today and tomorrow are what count.

When I lost my job at Leeds United in the summer of 1978, a career in radio hardly seemed a possibility, however. Indeed, I found myself out of work for a while, even though from my early days as a player I had considered a career outside football. As a young first teamer at Blackpool I had seen players come to the end of their careers and leave the club with no real prospect of regular work. It wasn't a problem for people such as Stanley Matthews or Stan Mortensen, but I watched many of the men I grew up alongside leave the club with a question mark over their future. I was determined it wouldn't happen to me and relatively early in my time at Blackpool, I embarked on two potential careers: coaching and journalism.

I had come from a totally different background from most of the Blackpool players. The usual route to the club was through junior football or leaving school early to become a professional. I had stayed on at school to do my A levels and been accepted at university before opting for football. From day one, I realised that the time would come when I would have to find another career, but sport had always played a huge part in my life and I used to wonder how I could retain my involvement when I finished playing.

The first option was to take my football coaching badges under Allen Wade at Lilleshall. Tony Waiters, the Blackpool goalkeeper of the sixties who won five England caps, was also keen on coaching and we went along together. That earned us our fair share of stick from the rest of the Blackpool players, who greeted us with cries of, 'Here come the boys from the FA!' when we returned to the club. We could take that. We believed we were doing the right thing, even though coaching wasn't in vogue in those days. Until fairly recently, the general opinion was that a player could step straight into coaching and management without any serious preparation and obviously that has worked in the past, but not any more. The *laissez-faire* days of trial and error have gone. By attending all the coaching courses, I believe a player shows how dedicated he is to his intended profession and a future in the game. It didn't surprise me when, with the rest of Europe leading the way, the Premiership decided to make coaching qualifications mandatory.

My tutors at Lilleshall were Les Shannon, later to become my manager at Blackpool, and Jimmy Adamson, the man who pulled out of the contest to succeed Walter Winterbottom as England coach in 1962 but later went on to have a long managerial career with Burnley, Sunderland and Leeds United. They were both excellent teachers. They had been around a long time, knew the professional game inside out and taught me a tremendous amount, not least the art of handling players without screaming and shouting. In the end, coaching and management became my first choice when I retired as a player in 1971. Tony Waiters used the coaching badge well. He emigrated to Canada 30 years ago and has coached throughout North America, including the national team.

Journalism was another string to my bow. Between 1959 and 1971 I had learned the rudiments of newspaper journalism. It all began with a chat on the team bus with Don Creedy, assistant sports editor at the *Evening Gazette* in Blackpool, who used to cover our away games. Cliff Greenwood, the sports editor, reported home matches. After telling Don I was interested in journalism as a possible career when my playing days were over, I received a phone call from Cliff. He'd had a word with the editor and owner, Sir Harold Grime, who was keen to have me on board on a part-time basis, writing a regular column and possibly covering a football match on a weekly basis. I had to point out that I would be struggling to report matches as I tended to be otherwise involved at weekends and they suggested it might be an idea for me to cover a Blackpool Wednesday League game instead. The players were all local amateurs so it was a humble beginning.

The league's teams included Victorians, the Police, Foxhall, Layton Institute and the Fire Brigade, and Cliff was adamant that it would be a good starting point. 'It's a good way to get a few words down,' was how he put it. My first assignment, as a trial run, was a match between Foxhall, the area of Blackpool in which I grew up, and the Fire Brigade on a local park pitch. When I arrived, complete with notebook and pencil, it suddenly dawned on me that I didn't have a clue who the players were, and there was no match programme or teamsheet. So Blackpool's first choice right-back and future captain of England had to knock on the dressing-room doors and ask who would be playing.

Inevitably, my appearance created something of a stir. 'Hello, Jim, have you come to play for a decent team for a change!' was the gist of the players' comments and I remember one young lad saying, 'You'll probably learn a few things down here, Jim!' I replied, 'Yes, I will. In fact, that's what I'm here for.' I told them I was training to be a journalist and, quick as a flash, came the retort, 'Good idea – I saw you playing last week!' I managed to retain a semblance of dignity between then and the kick-off and, after the match, I went back to the office, wrote my report and proudly presented the fruits of my labours to Cliff. He slowly read my 20 paragraphs of purple prose.

'That's good, Jim, very good,' he said. 'But it won't be going in the paper. Next week, cover the match in ten paragraphs instead of twenty.'

'How will I do that?'

'I'll show you,' and he proceeded to give me my first lesson in sub-editing, skilfully taking out all the unnecessary words and phrases before presenting me with a new, improved and much shorter version of Foxhall v. the Fire Brigade by Jimmy Armfield. 'And next time,' he added, 'start the report so that people will read the first paragraph and instantly want to read on. In your case, the name Jimmy Armfield will probably be enough because readers will want to have a look out of curiosity. But that first paragraph is vital.'

I took him at his word and a week later submitted 10 paragraphs, complete with punchy introduction. He must have been impressed because the following day's paper carried a taster on the lines of 'Next week, Jimmy Armfield will be covering the Wednesday League match between Victorians and the Police. Don't miss his exclusive report here in the *Gazette*!' I was on my way . . .

The match was played at a pitch in Crosland Road – it's not there any more – and I stood on the touchline in pouring rain under an umbrella, trying to make notes as the game progressed. I went home straight afterwards and typed out my report, which had to be on Cliff's desk at eight the next morning. I was paid the princely sum of 10 shillings, or 50p in today's money. The feature became known as Armfield's Match and, as the weeks went by, the games started to attract considerable interest among the public. I would find myself standing on the touchline, surrounded by a sizeable gathering of inquisitive football fans, most of whom had no interest whatsoever in the affairs of Foxhall, the Fire Brigade, Victorians or any of the other clubs. I was subjected to a fair bit of barracking, too, along the lines of, 'I read your report last week, Armfield – you can't have been at the same match as me.' It was good fun and worked wonders for the profile of the Wednesday League. It even gave the circulation a bit of a lift.

The weekly column gave me a chance to comment on a topical issue and, like all columns, it was relatively easy at first but as time went by I found it more and more difficult to find something totally original to say. I soon realised I was never going to threaten the job security of writers such as J.L. Manning of the *Daily Mail* or the *Express*'s Desmond Hackett but my column proved popular among readers in Blackpool and I enjoyed my years on the paper immensely. I was given an opportunity to express myself through one of my favourite mediums – words. I like art and appreciate the skills of the artist but not even the finest paintings can move me in the same way as a piece of music or a great work of literature. I have always admired people who have control of the language, either the spoken or written word, people who are well read. I rarely saw Peter Jones, my former BBC Radio colleague and a marvellous wordsmith, Ken Hardacre, my English teacher at Arnold School, or Cliff Greenwood without a book – and it is no coincidence that all three had a comprehensive vocabulary.

Cliff was a delightful man, a true gentleman. Tall and slim, he was a Yorkshireman without an ounce of malice. He was a naturally gifted writer, who once won a competition in the *Sunday People* for a sports feature that he wrote on the train between St Annes and Blackpool, a journey of less than 10 minutes. As well as covering football for the *Gazette*, he reported on the affairs of Blackpool Cricket Club in first the Ribblesdale League and, from 1952, the Northern League as they developed into one of the leading club sides in the north west. Once, when we were having lunch at a little café in West Street, Blackpool, just across the road from the *Gazette* offices in those days, he recounted the story of his first big break on the paper, back in April 1928.

Cliff lived in Lytham and, every evening, he used to walk his dog in a field near his home. The regular occupant of the field was a horse, which befriended Cliff and his dog, not least because Cliff regularly fed it with apples from his garden. One morning, Cliff went into the office and was told by the editor that somewhere in Lytham was a horse that would be taking part in the Grand National the following Saturday. Nobody seemed to know the identity or whereabouts of the animal and Cliff was despatched to locate horse and owner and discover all the necessary background. Incredibly, it turned out to be the same horse that Cliff had been feeding for the past two weeks. He knew it as Tim. The owner was a lady who lived nearby and had recently inherited the horse from her father. She had no particular interest in racing but her father's lifetime ambition had been to run a horse in the National. He had bought Tim, a decent jumper but hardly a pedigree racehorse, especially for Aintree, so she had decided to run the horse in his memory.

The editor was impressed and asked Cliff, 'Is the owner going to the Grand National on Saturday?'

'Yes.'

'Good. Has she got a jockey?'

'No, not yet.'

'Well you'd better get in a bit of practice because you might be riding Tim yourself if you're not careful. I want you to go to Aintree on Saturday, never let the horse out of your sight and report on everything that happens. And if they can't find a jockey – tell them you'll do it!'

Saturday morning dawned to find Cliff, now established in his editor's eyes as the *Gazette*'s racing correspondent, en route to Aintree in the cabin of a horsebox occupied by Lytham's great white hope for the National. It was the first horse race he had ever seen and, to his considerable relief, the owner succeeded in recruiting a jockey. Cliff was in attendance in the parade ring as the rider was given his instructions: 'Under no circumstances are you to take any risks. I want Tim back in Lytham in one piece tonight. He's fit – he's been running round in a field for the last fortnight – and a good jumper so he'll have no trouble with the fences. But I don't want him to get hurt. Just let him run round on the outside and try to make sure he completes the course.'

The bemused jockey protested in vain that these instructions gave him absolutely no chance of winning the race but the owner was adamant. So when the starting tapes went up, he steered Tim to the outside of the pack and kept him there in splendid isolation. True to form, Tim negotiated the fences without undue difficulty – which is more than could be said for the rest of the field, who almost all came to grief in a massive pile-up at the Canal Turn second time around. Only Tim and one other straggler were left standing and in contention for steeplechasing's greatest prize. With the winning post just a few fences away, the jockey felt obliged to disregard the owner's instructions and went for glory, urging Tipperary Tim, to give the horse his full name, home at 100–1. Cliff Greenwood's exclusive inside stories behind one of the greatest Grand National upsets of all time were a major coup for the *Gazette* and featured in the paper every night for a week. For months, visitors descended on Lytham for a glimpse of Tim in his field, Cliff's future on the sports desk was secured and, in time, he moved up the ladder to become sports editor. He always said he owed everything to Tipperary Tim!

In the office, I used to sit between Don Creedy and Eric Littler, the man who was responsible for a daily column known as Seasider's Diary. Eric was an old-fashioned hack who knew everybody who was anybody in the town. What he didn't know about the council and councillors wasn't worth knowing and influential people were forever ringing him up with confidential inside information. These two and Cliff were wonderful characters and I was perfectly content to be the cub reporter, learning the trade. In the office, I was Armfield, trainee journalist, not

Armfield, international footballer – and that suited me down to the ground. I was always proud of what I achieved as a footballer but I didn't expect any favours because of it.

I was keen to continue my association with the *Gazette* after my appointment as manager of Bolton in the summer of 1971 and discussed the situation at some length with Don Creedy, who had by that time succeeded Cliff as sports editor. Obviously, I wouldn't be able to go into the office three or four afternoons a week any more but there was some suggestion that I might carry on writing a column. In the end, we decided it wouldn't work as I would have more than enough on my plate at Burnden Park. That proved to be the case and it applied even more when I moved to Leeds in 1974, so journalism went on to the back burner for the foreseeable future.

So after leaving Leeds, I was in no-man's land for a while. I was actually advised to sign on but I couldn't face that. As well as the offers from clubs in the UK and Athletic Bilbao, I was contacted by someone representing the Iranian FA about becoming their national coach. But the situation in Iran was pretty volatile, to put it mildly, and it was not long afterwards that the Shah was deposed and the US Embassy stormed by militants. So I can safely say I made the correct decision in rejecting a trip to the Middle East. In the end, I agreed to help out at Blackburn when they were without a manager and soon afterwards they asked if I could recommend anyone to take over. I did have someone in mind and drove down to Stoke on behalf of Rovers to talk to a young man who was making a reputation for himself as a coach. He impressed me and soon afterwards he was given the job at Blackburn. His name was Howard Kendall, a man I had earmarked as a possible number two if I ever did return to management.

Shortly after he was appointed, I went into his office and said, 'Look, Howard, I know you want to be your own man and the last thing you want is me hanging around in the background. So as soon as you think the time is right, I'll go. Don't worry about me.' Howard replied, 'OK then, off you go.' I never felt any resentment. Howard had a job to do and wanted to do it his way. I would have done exactly the same thing in his position. So I left, confident that I had found the right man. Howard led Rovers to promotion from the old Third Division and, two years later, he moved on to Everton, where he won two championships, the FA Cup and European Cup-Winners' Cup and became a legend. He should really have been a contender for the England job.

As far as I was concerned, football management was becoming more of a non-starter. I wasn't keen on uprooting the family to wander around the country but I needed work from somewhere. It was just that I wasn't sure what I wanted to do. At one stage, I seriously considered a career swerve into the teaching profession and enrolling on a teacher training course at what is now Loughborough University. Funnily enough, that's the route my younger son, John, took when he left school and went to Carnegie College in Leeds, but somehow I was never quite convinced about myself as a teacher, let alone a mature student.

Then one day I had a call from Paul Doherty at Granada Television, asking if I would be interested in doing a bit for 'Kick Off', their weekly football programme. I knew Paul quite well – he was the son of Peter Doherty, the great Northern Ireland inside-forward of the forties and fifties – and the 'Kick Off' team were a very professional outfit.

I agreed to work on a few programmes and returned to the studios for the first time since the early sixties, when I won the Granada TV Sports Personality of the Year award, but I never really felt at ease. The camera either likes you or it doesn't and I didn't look at myself on screen and immediately think 'Hollywood, here I come!' I'm probably better on television now than I was back in the seventies because after years on the radio and speaking at various events, I feel a lot more relaxed. In those early days, I was unsure about where my future lay and I was still smarting from losing the Leeds job, wondering what to do for the best for my family. I went into television at a bit of a loose end, not totally committed. If I do something, I like to do it properly and at Granada, I found myself turning up on a Friday, churning out a few scripts, picking up the cheque and going home. I was in the squad but felt like a sub – and I'd never been a substitute in my life.

Fate took a hand, however, when I was covering a match with

the 'Kick Off' team and was introduced to Mike Dempsey, northern sports editor of the *Daily Express*. A couple of days later, he gave me a call, asking if I would like to meet for lunch; he had one or two ideas to discuss. We went to a café Mike used to frequent in Oldham Street, just across the road from the *Express* building in the Ancoats area of Manchester. He asked if I would be interested in working part-time for the *Express* and doing a match at weekends. I was very interested. The *Express* still commanded a circulation of around two million in those days and, once I had established that Granada were happy for me to double up, I rang Mike and said yes.

For me, it was a chance to pick up the pieces from my early days as a cub reporter on the *Evening Gazette* and I was happy to start at the bottom of the ladder. In fact, I would not have had it any other way – I had no intention of acting the Big-time Charlie. For the first couple of weeks, I arrived at the Black Lubianka, as the old *Express* HQ was known to inmates, every morning and was handed a mountain of copy from correspondents in the north-east, Yorkshire, Merseyside and north-west, the paper's main edition areas. It was my job to knock it into some semblance of order. Stories from major clubs were, in general, handled by staffmen based in the four regions so I was putting together round-ups of around 10 paragraphs from the lower divisions, sometimes having to call club managers to double check the facts or follow up a particular line. Mike or another member of the backbench team would check my copy and suggest possible alterations before it was passed on to the night desk and sub-editors.

After two weeks, Mike decided it was time to turn me loose on the outside world and I started to cover matches. In those days, Stockport County and Tranmere, both in the old Fourth Division, played on alternate Friday nights, usually without much coverage in the national press, who were more concerned with the following day's action. Mike decided they deserved a better show and despatched me to sample the press facilities at Edgeley Park and Prenton Park on a regular basis. My brief was to file a six-paragraph match report on the final whistle, although, disconcertingly, I would sometimes pick up my paper the following morning to discover that not a line had been used. It took several Saturday morning phone calls to Mike before I came to appreciate that on occasions my match had to give way to weightier matters involving clubs at the top end of the Football League.

I soon became a regular at Bury, Rochdale, Wigan and Crewe, occasionally crossing the Pennines to Scunthorpe, York or Halifax. Carlisle and Wrexham also featured on my travels and, as time went by, I started to move up in the world to Preston, Blackburn, Burnley, Huddersfield and Barnsley. But I rarely visited Blackpool as Mike appreciated it might be a bit sensitive for everyone concerned. Those early days at Ancoats gave me an insight into sports journalism and how a reporter has to think on his feet and adapt to whatever situation may arise. In that short time, Mike taught me more about the profession than anyone before or since. Cliff Greenwood at Blackpool taught me the basics at regional level; Mike Dempsey did the same on national newspapers.

Eventually, I moved up another notch to become the stand-in for our staffmen on Merseyside or in Manchester. John Keith covered Liverpool and Everton and if, on his day off, there was a press conference or a major story broke, I was sent out into the field as his replacement. The same applied at Manchester United and Manchester City if either of the regular writers, Derek Potter or John Bean, was off duty. Those jobs meant I had to go in and hack it with staffmen from the other national papers and from the start I was determined to become accepted as a journalist, not as a football manager biding his time before another job cropped up. I think they were guarded about me to start with but once I demonstrated I was willing to mix in with the rest of them, they warmed to me. I adopted exactly the same approach with the sports desk staff in the office. I am sure some of them were uncertain about how to approach me and not convinced about my pedigree, but I kept my head down and concentrated on being one of the team.

I worked closely with Peter Thomas, the paper's sports columnist and a man who was never afraid to stick his neck out;

the bigger the issue, the better. Peter was a lifelong follower of Yorkshire cricket and a vociferous supporter of Geoffrey Boycott throughout the tempestuous days of the early eighties when Yorkshire appeared to be in a state of constant turmoil and Boycott's name was rarely out of the headlines. Peter and I covered a host of meetings where I wrote the news angle and Peter supplied the hard-hitting comment. I actually managed to land the front-page lead for two days running when Geoffrey finally left the club.

It was well known among the Yorkshire press fraternity that Peter was close to Geoffrey, so whenever Thomas and Armfield arrived at a Yorkshire match as a duo, the local boys sprung to action stations. They never let Peter out of their sight in case he was working on another exclusive. Peter milked the situation for all it was worth. I recall one occasion at Park Avenue, Bradford, when Peter and I arrived at the ground together and immediately went into a prearranged huddle in a corner of the press box, muttering quietly to one another. After a while, Peter said in a conspiratorial stage whisper, 'Right, Jim, you keep an eye on things in here – and you know where I'll be if you need me.' Then he slipped quietly but not wholly unobtrusively out of the box.

Sure enough, after allowing an acceptable time to elapse, one of the Yorkshire boys casually stood up, announced, 'I think I'll get a bit of air, gentlemen,' and out he went in pursuit of his quarry. Once Peter had established that he was being tailed, he embarked on a royal progress around Park Avenue. First, he sat down among the members to watch the cricket for a few minutes before nipping into the toilet to answer a call of nature. On emerging, he established that his 'tail' was still *in situ* and went in search of an old pal to have another natter about cricket. He rounded off his grand tour with a lap of the ground before calling at the refreshment bar and buying two cups of tea, one of which he handed to me on his return to the box. Then, an innocent smile on his face, he sat back to await the return of his pursuer. Meanwhile, back in Ancoats, the *Express* staff would be working on the Boycott exclusive Peter had dropped into Mike's in-tray before setting off across the Pennines for what he used to describe as 'having a bit of fun with those Yorkies'.

The Boycott saga ran and ran and, in time, I became a regular in the press boxes at Yorkshire, Lancashire and Derbyshire, savouring the White Rose passion for the game, appreciating the professionalism of the Yorkshire press corps and lapping up the one-day glory days with the Red Rose. I became friendly with Jack Bond, the Lancashire captain, and wrote features with big-name players such as Clive Lloyd, who appeared on the Old Trafford stage.

I moved up the pecking order in the football reporting team, too, and finally attained the dizzy heights of the Manchester United press box in the early eighties. United were having an average season and manager Dave Sexton was under fire for his style of play. Peter Thomas, who was one of his arch critics and had caused a stir among the Old Trafford hierarchy with a stinging criticism – Mike headlined it 'Cold Trafford' – was also at Old Trafford for a game that ended in a soulless, goalless draw. Mike had asked me to put plenty of background colour into my report and I began with: 'I never believed 50,000 people could be so quiet for so long.' I mentioned the supporter sitting in front of me who preferred reading the paper to watching United and stressed the lack of atmosphere in the ground and shortage of passion among the fans. I was pleased with the piece – and so was Mike. Yet when I picked up the paper on Monday morning, Armfield's match report was given second billing to another Thomas attack, which finished with the words: 'I never believed 50,000 people could be so quiet for so long . . .' My line!

I was a bit narked, to put it mildly, and rang Mike immediately. He explained that the paper couldn't have two people saying the same thing about the same match, adding, 'And at the end of the day, Peter is the senior writer.' There was no answer to that and over the years I came to realise I wasn't the first person to have my best lines poached by the main columnist, nor would I be the last.

However, I did hit the feature pages with an exclusive interview with Jack Walker, the steel millionaire who ploughed a small fortune into Blackburn Rovers, his home-town club. I had interviewed Jack at Ewood Park some years earlier when he started to back the club, then in the old Second Division, asking him, 'So what is your ambition, Jack?' He replied, 'To win the championship.' Few believed him at the time but the appointment of Kenny Dalglish as manager soon afterwards convinced the world he was serious. His dream came true in 1995.

Jack lived in Jersey and was allegedly out of bounds to journalists – but the *Express* would not take no for an answer and I was despatched to the Channel Islands. I located Jack's mansion, knocked on the door and was greeted by the man himself.

'Hello, Jack, I'm Jim Armfield from the *Daily Express*. . . '

'I know who you are. What do you want?'

'I've come to talk to you about the championship.'

'You're a cheeky bugger. Right, come in. You've got ten minutes and you're not taking notes.'

In the end, I hung in there for 20 minutes before Jack announced, 'Time's up.'

'Thanks, Jack,' I said, as he escorted me to the front door. 'I won't forget this, you know. Anyway, I've enjoyed talking to you . . .'

'I won't forget, either, and it had better be good.'

I rushed back to the car and furiously scribbled down every last detail of the interview and we ran the story as an exclusive the next day. Soon after 10 a.m., the editor had a call from Jack Walker, saying thank you for an excellent article. It was a rewarding moment – and there were many, many more in my 15 years on the paper. I was lucky in my formative years on the *Express* to be surrounded by a very strong, knowledgeable and experienced team. Mike Dempsey, who became a close friend, was an excellent sports editor and his senior staff included Len Gould, Cammie Stewart, Andy Collomosse, Graham Fisher and David Mankelow, who all knew the job backwards. The same applied to the sub-editors.

Mike was intensely proud of the paper's northern roots and would not entertain interference from London. On one occasion, the London sports editor, supposedly Mike's superior, telephoned to say he was leading the back page on a story about Spurs and suggested Manchester should do the same. Mike explained that we were a northern paper and would be leading on Liverpool. When London persisted with the Spurs story, he responded, 'This is my paper and I lead on what I want,' and put down the phone. It was a sad day for Mike and the rest of the team when, in 1989, the *Express* closed down the Manchester office as a northern production centre and moved the entire operation to London. There was no way I was going to follow and I spent the next few years in a small office in Manchester, working alongside two more sports reporters, three news reporters and a couple of photographers. The great days of the Black Lubianka were over.

I will never forget working in a national newspaper office before the advent of computers. It was full of people, buzzing around, talking on phones, hammering away at typewriters, spiking stories that would not make tomorrow's pages – human movement, thought and involvement, and real excitement when the presses began to roll.

CHAPTER 14

FROM THE COMMENTARY BOX

I always regarded myself as a footballer who went into journalism rather than a journalist who was once a footballer although at times I have had to tread a tightrope between the two. At first, both sides were wary but in time I gained their trust and I have never been one to break a confidence. I have spent a fair amount of time on both sides of the fence and I have come to realise that journalists don't always understand football people and vice versa. Both sides lack insight into the ethos of the other profession because they exist for different reasons. The journalist is usually looking for a story the football man doesn't want him to have, and both guard their secrets jealously – and why not?

The world of players, former players and managers can be a bit of a clique, based on what they see as an exclusive, intimate working knowledge of their game. Outsiders, however close to football they may be, don't share that intimacy and are not always allowed into the inner circle. I sometimes wonder how I would respond to today's media if I had stayed in the game. In my time as a manager, I always gave all the arms of the press as much access as I thought was reasonable and there was plenty of give and take on both sides. Today, I might not be so tolerant in the face of the after-match media avalanche. I sometimes sit and watch managers as they make their way through the crush, first dealing with television interviews, then moving on to the radio boys and finally into the interview room for interrogation by the written press, with the Sunday and daily papers wanting separate interviews. It isn't easy but I think managers should lighten their load and allow players to speak more freely to the media after matches. After all, they are the people in whom the public are really interested and the media have far greater access in other countries.

In many ways, players get off lightly these days. In my time, reporters were far more critical of individual players and some, such as Henry Rose of the *Express*, were renowned for their strident opinions. I remember one occasion in the mid-fifties when Henry had a real go at Tommy Taylor, the Manchester United and England centre-forward who was killed at Munich in 1958. One Saturday morning, Henry wrote, 'If Taylor is England's best centre-forward, then I'm Father Christmas,' and announced that he would be at Old Trafford that afternoon to gather further evidence for his argument. He was roundly booed when he took his seat in the press box and Taylor duly answered his critic with a hat-trick. Henry ate a large helping of humble pie on the Monday morning when he was pictured in a Santa Claus outfit. Reportedly, sales of the *Express* doubled in the Manchester area. He was by no means the only outspoken reporter on the circuit but today I feel reporters seem to be more generous, especially to the players, and their editors seem keen to fill their columns with quotes from managers or other players.

Television has prompted a major re-think of the role of the football journalist. By the time a reader picks up his paper on a Monday morning, he has had an opportunity to see all the Premiership action on television and has read a match report in the Sunday papers. He has been bombarded with expert TV analysis and has had time to form his own opinions without actually being at the match. There isn't a lot more for the reporter to say. Agents, too, can play a role in deciding what appears in the sports pages. If a journalist wanted to interview a Blackpool player during my time at the club, he simply turned up at the ground after a training session or waited for the player to appear after a match. There was no middle man deciding who could interview a player, no manager to ask if it was all right or what kind of fee would be involved. It isn't always easy for today's hacks.

I believe that even in these days of blanket television and newspaper coverage, radio still has an important role to play. Radio is a more outspoken medium than it used to be but integrity is still perceived as an important part of BBC Radio sports journalism. For the most part, sportsmen and women don't mind being associated with us and I have never had any trouble persuading anyone to take part in the programme. Players don't always know my face but when I tell them I'm Jimmy Armfield from Radio Five Live, the penny drops. In my playing days, I always knew about players from the past and I think the same largely applies today.

In a way, Leeds United gave me my 'open sesame' into radio because during my time as manager at Elland Road I became friendly with John Helm, now a respected television commentator, who worked for BBC Radio Leeds and came down to Elland Road just about every day. He was a lively, experienced broadcaster. We always got on well and I think he worked behind the scenes to arrange for me to do a series of interviews with Yorkshire person-alities. Among others, I spoke to cricketer Ray Illingworth, miners' leader Arthur Scargill, author Stan Barstow, actor James Fox and the Archbishop of York. The series gave me my first insight into what life was like on the other side of the microphone.

Shortly after that, I left the club and while I was still trying to find my feet at Granada and with the *Express*, I bumped into John at a Manchester United match. It proved to be a defining moment in my life. He had moved on from Leeds and was working as Network Producer on BBC Radio 2. He told me he was looking for one or two people to strengthen the reporting team in the north-west and was keen to add another former player to the line-up. He already had Larry Canning, the former Aston Villa defender. John said, 'Why don't you come and do a match with us? We're covering the game at Manchester City next week so I'll put you down to be the expert summariser.' Without a second thought, I just said yes and I have never regretted it.

I knew a bit about what was involved on radio. My first appearance on the airwaves had been way back in the late fifties when Eamonn Andrews used to present 'Sports Report' on the old BBC Light Programme. Blackpool were playing Arsenal at Highbury and I was asked if I would talk live to Eamonn after the game. As soon as the match finished, I showered, rushed out of the players' entrance into a waiting taxi and raced across London to Broadcasting House. I had just enough time to think what a musty old place it was before I was taken into a small studio with a table in the middle. Empty boxes were piled in a corner, there were a couple of old chairs on either side of the table and behind one of them stood Angus McKay, the doyen of BBC Radio sports producers. On the table was an old-fashioned stand-up microphone. I had expected to be confronted with some state-of-the-art broadcasting equipment but all I got was a microphone and a table. I sat at one side and Eamonn, dressed in a suit, collar and tie, came in and sat at the other side. We chatted for a few minutes and then I was ushered out of the studio, down the stairs and into a taxi to Euston for the 6.15 back to Blackpool.

Needless to say, things had changed by the time I arrived on the scene in the late seventies but I can honestly say that from the moment I sat down in the commentary box at Maine Road and picked up the microphone, I felt at home. Before the advent of Radio Five Live, football commentaries were on Radio 2 Sport, with Brian Tremble as our producer. Jim Rosenthal, who now fronts the ITV coverage of Formula One, was our main presenter and the commentary team featured Bryon Butler, the BBC Football Correspondent, Peter Jones and Alan Parry. Denis Law and I shared most of the summaries.

It was a much smaller proposition than today's Radio Five Live, which presents daily in-depth coverage of events around the world. I've spent just one Saturday afternoon in the studio with the Sport on Five team because I'm usually involved at a match but I was hugely impressed with the professionalism and expertise of everyone involved. The high-tech equipment was mind-boggling – and so was the team's ability to keep so many balls in the air at one time. I have always been captivated by their professionalism. A lot of people come up to me and say they like the programme and I take that as a big compliment – for not only does it mean they like my contribution, it also means that I play a part in such a professional outfit.

Radio has, in many ways, been more exacting than newspaper journalism. A writer has sub-editors, a sports editor and, if necessary, a team of lawyers behind him to make sure he doesn't say the wrong thing at the wrong time too often. In broadcasting, a split second is all it takes to do a lot of damage and you have to be very careful and, above all, well prepared. That doesn't mean a summariser cannot say what he genuinely believes – one of the great things about telling the truth is that you never need to try to remember what you said. But a summariser needs knowledge and experience and, fortunately, my 50 years in football means I have something to fall back on. At the 2003 FA Cup final, for instance, I was able to describe from personal experience how it felt to be involved in the Matthews final 50 years earlier. Most of the lads I work with never even saw Stanley, let alone played with him or knew what made him tick. Caj Sohal, the Head of Football at Radio Five Live and a Nottingham Forest fan, made the point afterwards when he said, 'You are our football historian.'

I follow the same routine for each match. As soon as I know which game I will be covering, I read all the background about injuries and so on and try to work out what the teams and formations will be. I check recent results and league positions, transfer speculation and news about the clubs, and put everything down on one page in a notebook, amending the teams as necessary when they are announced an hour or so before kick-off. Like a lot of journalists, I have plenty of information in my head because I follow a season through from first kick to last. I stay in touch with events at all the Premiership clubs and if, for example, someone were to ask me at any given time in the season what a particular team's last starting line-up was, I would probably be able to name most of them. That kind of thing is just part and parcel of the press routine and my days of hacking at the *Express* have certainly paid off.

I can only speak highly of all the people I have worked with.

When I first joined the BBC I was told, 'Remember, you are there to paint a picture for people at home. They want you to transport them out of their front rooms and into the football ground.' Radio is the only medium where that happens and, while my fellow commentators are all very different in style and personality, each one of them has, in his own way, been an artist as well as a journalist, painting a picture for the listener.

Alan Green has developed a style all of his own. Greenie, as I have always called him on and off air, is a natural commentator. His voice is electric, he is argumentative, opinionated and not frightened of criticising anyone, whatever his standing in the game. We have always got on well and I'm told we are a good team, even though we are a total contrast. I am forever being asked, 'How do you manage to get on with that chap Green?' and I'll make some light-hearted response about being the only person who can calm him down when he gets worked up. I have been with him at World Cup finals, European Championships and all sorts of major games and, of course, he has frenetic moments. There are times when I feel like strangling him, but we gel perfectly and we've been together for a few years now.

Like all good journalists, he has a habit of making things happen. Our trip back to the airport after a 1994 World Cup match in San Francisco is an example. We had hired a Buick and by the time the game finished we had less than an hour to get from the ground to the airport, a distance of around 10 miles. Over 70,000 people were making their way out of the stadium, many roads were closed to control the flow of traffic and it seemed an impossible task, but not with Greenie at the wheel.

How we made it on to the plane I will never know – and I don't suppose Greenie will either. It was like Steve McQueen's car chase sequence in *Bullitt*. If Greenie saw a barrier, he took to the footpath; if there was a corner to cut, he cut it; if there was a speed limit to break, he broke it. We arrived in the airport car park 10 minutes before the flight was due to leave, left the car, dropped off the keys, raced through the departure gate and clambered up the gangway. As Greenie made it across the threshold, the stewardess closed the door, the pilot started the engines and we were off.

'How did you manage that?' I gasped, as I regained the power of speech.

'Oh, nothing to it,' he smiled. Only Greenie would have even attempted it.

The two of us have broadcast from some weird and wonderful commentary positions – a bus in Moscow, for example, when Manchester United were playing a European match in the Russian capital. It was bitterly cold and when the media corps arrived at the stadium, the written press boys were directed to the press box at the rear of the main stand. Greenie and I made to follow, only to be halted in our tracks. Instead, we were directed towards a single-decker bus parked alongside the pitch. We entered the vehicle with some trepidation to discover our engineer, who didn't speak English, pointing at his radio equipment saying, 'London, London.' We picked up our microphones and, sure enough, London was on the other end of the line.

I said to Greenie, 'You know what, I think we're going to have to do our commentary from this bus.'

'You know what, I'm *sure* we are,' he replied.

So we slid open the windows, exposing ourselves to 90 minutes of sub-zero temperatures and biting winds, and got on with the job.

A ground in Austria provided a different experience when our commentary box was situated immediately above a hot-dog stand. Throughout the game we were assailed by the smell of sausages and fried onions with the effects microphone picking up the vendor's frequent cries of 'Hot dogs, hot dogs!' or whatever they shout in Austrian.

Once, at the Nou Camp, our position was way up on the fourth tier in a far-flung corner of the stadium. The players looked like ants and it was virtually impossible to identify them with any degree of certainty. On air, we were praising the wonderful stadium and saying what a fantastic sight it was, but off microphone we were moaning like hell because we couldn't make out who the players were.

Mike Ingham is a contrast to Greenie. He is the same sort of person as his predecessor as BBC Football Correspondent, Bryon

Butler. Like BB, as we called Bryon, Mike is a wordsmith and excels at considered pieces. He is also a very professional broadcaster and was top-class in his spell in the chair on 'Sport on Five', soon after he arrived from local radio. He was always in control and had an extensive supply of background information at his fingertips for use in any given situation. As a journalist and broadcaster, he is totally reliable although he is one of the members of the team who feels the tension on big occasions.

Mike has a tough job. As the BBC Football Correspondent, he has to be available any time, anywhere for all the sports and news programmes. There's no summer break for the football man when David Beckham is on the brink of joining Real Madrid. Fortunately, we rarely have to read his handwriting. If we did, there would be plenty of pregnant pauses on air because the Ingham script is virtually illegible to anyone except the man himself. He is something of a football nut and an avid collector of football programmes with a collection dating back many years. In fact, I have provided him with quite a number of additions to the collection. He's married to Lorna Dickinson, the TV producer who was made a Member of the Royal Victorian Order in the Queen's Special Golden Jubilee Honours List for her work as executive producer of the Party at the Palace. The Inghams are a talented lot.

The team of Mike, Greenie and I has been together now for quite a few years and Alan once suggested that the secret of our success, if that's the right word, is that we are total contrasts. Mike is the football buff and wordsmith, Greenie sparks with opinion and passion, and I'm the one who adds the football expertise, I hope. To illustrate the essential difference between us, both Greenie and Mike tell the story of our journey back to the hotel from the 1994 World Cup final between Italy and Brazil at the Rose Bowl Stadium in Pasadena. It wasn't much of a game, ended goalless and eventually Brazil won on penalties. Mike and Alan were sitting in the front seats for the trip back. They were quiet and a bit subdued, perhaps because neither had been given the opportunity to describe a goal, the staple diet of the radio football commentator. When, in years to come, the commentary of the 1994 World Cup final is dug out of the BBC archives, the main event will be Italy's Roberto Baggio missing a penalty, not Mike or Greenie describing an historic goal. Their chance to be part of a classic final had, for the time being, gone.

In contrast, my adrenaline was still running high. They describe how, throughout the journey, I was bouncing about in the back seat, analysing the technical points of the game. I enthused about how Brazil had managed to play with two markers and a spare player at the back. I wondered why the Italians had stuck rigidly to their time-honoured system instead of trying something different, and marvelled at the way the half-fit Franco Baresi had stepped off the treatment table to produce an exceptional performance at the heart of Italy's defence. Above all, I couldn't understand how a marvellous player such as Baggio could miss the decisive penalty. In fact, even today I still wonder why so many teams save the last penalty for their main goalscorer instead of giving him the chance to notch the first goal – but that's another story. According to Greenie and Mike, I didn't return to terra firma in downtown Los Angeles for a considerable time and therein, I suppose, lies one difference between the two commentators and their summariser. But it's a chemistry that has served us well down the years.

Mike had the unenviable task of following in the footsteps of Bryon Butler, a BBC legend. I was privileged to give the address at Bryon's funeral in April 2001 and began by saying, 'I bet old BB is having a laugh now at the thought of me standing here today.' He had a lovely sense of humour. A man of Somerset, who was equally at home writing in a press box or talking behind a microphone, he trained as a journalist on the *Leicester Mercury* and worked his way up the ladder to the *Daily Telegraph* before moving into radio. He was a football historian, a man with vast knowledge of the game and its traditions and, like Greenie, his voice was instantly recognisable to listeners.

Who will ever forget his measured tones as he greeted listeners to the FA Cup draw in the days when it was held on a Monday lunchtime and BBC Radio was the sole broadcaster? He would welcome his audience from the ante-room outside the FA chamber and, on receiving a signal that the draw was about to be made, he would inform the waiting nation that he was about to walk through the door and into the holy of holies. I'm sure we all had our own image of the wise men of the FA, gathered around a mahogany table, as they prepared to make the draw. Bryon would describe how the balls were being taken out of the box and put into the black velvet bag, which would then be shaken for the listeners' benefit. He would announce the dramatis personae, starting with, 'And the first voice you will hear will be the Chairman of the FA Challenge Cup committee . . .' and the draw would commence. Dreams would come true and millions of listeners around the country would absorb every word before Bryon returned to the ante-chamber to repeat the line-up. No fancy gimmicks, just radio theatre of the highest quality.

I've never been totally convinced that BB wasn't in the chamber all the time and that someone closed a door in the background to indicate his alleged arrival from the ante-room. But if that was the case, he never let on, and surely the joy of radio and great broadcasters is that each listener can paint a different portrait in his mind's eye of the events being described.

Bryon's contemporary, Peter Jones, remains one of the best broadcasters in radio history. Strangely, he didn't know a lot about football but that didn't matter because he was such an astute observer and so professional as a commentator. He was equally at home at the Cup final or the boat race, a royal wedding or funeral, the Maundy Service or the State Opening of Parliament. He was originally a schoolmaster who hailed from Swansea before going on to Cambridge University and, in common with many Welsh people, he had an excellent speaking voice. He combined his Cambridge English with a slight Welsh lilt and sounded his consonants meticulously. So did Richard Burton and so does Sir Anthony Hopkins – it's a trait that gives the speaker an air of authority. That certainly applied to Peter, one of those people who was habitually unpunctual. When he was on a trip, the two most popular questions were 'Where's Jonesy?' and 'How much longer have we got?'

Peter provided Bryon Butler and me with a novel experience at the friendly match between England and West Germany at Wembley in October 1982, Bobby Robson's first home match in charge of the England team. Prior to the match, Peter had been working flat out at the World Swimming Championships in Australia and had flown into London earlier that day. He was suffering from the effects of hard work, lack of sleep and jetlag and, quite frankly, he was not really in a fit state to do the broadcast – but like all professionals, Jonesy didn't want to miss out on the big occasion. I was sitting between Bryon and Peter in our little box at Wembley, with Mike Ingham, the presenter, on Peter's left. Peter took the first stint at the mike and I soon noticed that his speech was gradually getting slower and slower. I looked to my left and sure enough, his eyes were starting to close. I nudged BB and said, 'Quick, pick up the mike!' Bryon began to describe the scene before the kick-off while I did my best to rouse Jonesy, but to no avail. In no time at all, Peter was virtually asleep and more or less oblivious to the events unfolding down below on the pitch over the next 90 minutes. So BB and I did the whole commentary in tandem.

Ian Brown and Ron Jones also hail from South Wales, and share Peter's perfect intonation with just a hint of their native Welsh lilt. Ron trained to be a teacher, too, and played football at a decent level. He has been involved in coaching and acquired a knowledge of the game that comes across in his commentaries. Ian has a wonderful vocabulary and an innate ability to find exactly the right words at the right time, a remarkable quality. Over the last few years, Ingham and Green have been the two main commentators but I can think of a lot of radio stations who would be delighted to have either Ron or Ian on their staff – and preferably both.

Of course, over the years there have been a few hitches. I once covered an England match in Bulgaria with Peter Jones and Alan Parry and, on the morning of the match, John Helm, our producer, went down to the ground to set up the equipment in the commentary box. We linked up for lunch at 12.30 p.m. before setting off for the stadium. On the way, John admitted there was a slight problem, telling us, 'We don't have the best view of the pitch, but you'll see why when we get there.' Too right! From our commentary position we were unable to see the penalty area at one end. In fact, a quarter of the pitch was out of our line of vision. The only way we could see everything was to open the window and lean out above the crowd – and that's how we did the broadcast.

A few days later, the four of us travelled to Sweden and the pre-match reconnaissance revealed that the box, which was supposed to house three commentators, a producer and all the recording equipment, was about 6ft square. There was absolutely no room for manoeuvre so for the whole match, the three commentators had to stand in a line abreast, with me in the middle, while John hovered outside in the corridor with the equipment.

One way or another it was quite a trip for Parry, who was obliged to share a double bed with me. These days, all the members of the party are allocated single rooms but 20 years ago we often had to double up and, on this occasion, Alan and I were paired off. I didn't see it as a problem and went straight to sleep as soon as my head hit the pillow but Alan didn't manage anything more than a fitful doze. To this day, he is apt to announce, 'I once slept with that man – but there again, he is a former England captain!'

Quite what Stuart Hall would have made of that situation, I dread to think. Stuart is a delight, a man for whom life is always fun. In my view, he is a great broadcaster, a complete one-off. A lot of people take the mickey out of Stuart because of his unconventional approach but he has stood the test of time and, above all, he is a complete professional. But that sense of fun is never out of sight for long, as I discovered one wintry afternoon at Burnden Park when Bolton were playing Everton on a snowbound pitch. Lots of games had been called off so the BBC decided to send us both along to give a different angle on one of the few matches that remained. Sadly, Peter Reid broke his leg early in the game and soon afterwards referee Trelford Mills decided it was too dangerous to continue. Apart from the Reid injury, there had been few incidents of note and we realised we would be struggling to find anything to talk about on air afterwards. Before the kick-off, however, Stuart had somehow discovered that it was the referee's birthday and he sensed a prank might be in the offing.

'Right, Jim,' he said. 'They asked for something different – so we'll give 'em something different. You go and find the referee and leave the rest to me.'

I had no idea what he was planning but I went down to the dressing rooms, located Mills and asked if he was prepared to come up and talk on radio. No problem. We returned to the box to find Stuart, microphone in hand and surrounded by a group of fans who had earlier asked for our autographs.

'Ah welcome to the BBC, Trelford,' cried Stuart on air as the bemused official climbed into the box. 'I believe it's your birthday.' Mills confirmed that it was. 'Right,' said Stuart. 'One, two three . . .' And right on cue, the six supporters launched into a rousing rendition of 'Happy Birthday To You'.

These days, Greenie, Mike, Ron, Ian and Stuart are the senior contributors to the programme but they are kept on their toes by a talented group of young commentators including John Murray, Simon Brotherton, Dave Woods, Ian Dennis, Steve Wilson, Jonathan Pearce, David Oates and Connor McNamara. I have no doubt they are destined to follow in the great traditions of BBC football commentary, established all those years ago by Raymond Glendenning, Alan Clarke and Maurice Edelston.

I have worked in commentary boxes all over the world and I would nominate the Rose Bowl Stadium in Pasadena and Roker Park, the old home of Sunderland, as the ultimate extremes in working conditions. That 1994 World Cup final in Pasadena gave me the most uncomfortable three and a half hours of my working life. The temperature was over 100 degrees and the press box was out in the open under the boiling sun. There was virtually no cover anywhere in the stadium and Messrs Ingham, Green and Armfield just had to sit and bear it. I wore a white hat and stuffed a handkerchief down the back of my neck as protection against the blazing sun. It was so hot that every so often I dipped another handkerchief into the ice buckets that were provided and put it on the top of my head to try to cool down.

All the commentators were equipped with a monitor screen for action replays but we couldn't see a thing because of the intense glare of the sun. To make matters worse, the match went to extra time and a penalty shoot-out. One interesting sideline, though, was the identity of the match summariser for our neighbours, a commentary team from Swedish television – Sven Goran Eriksson. At the time, he was the coach of Sampdoria in Italy's *Serie A*. None of us could have foreseen that eight years later he would be in charge of the England team in South Korea and Japan.

Sunderland v. Bristol Rovers in the late seventies was a total contrast. It was deep winter, there was a lot of snow around and when I woke up on Saturday morning I was surprised to discover my match was one of the few games not postponed overnight. I checked with the BBC desk in London early on to be told that, as far as they were aware, the match was still on. So I left home at 10 a.m., planning to drive up the M6 to Carlisle and then across to Sunderland. It was single file all the way because the two outside lanes were closed, and as I headed north, I kept thinking to myself, 'This is crazy. Sunderland is bound to be off in this weather.'

I made it as far as the motorway service station near Carlisle and rang the office – no mobiles then – to be told that yes, the game was still on. 'Tune in to Radio 2 and as soon as we hear it's off, we'll announce it especially for you!' There was no announcement and as I neared my destination, the weather improved dramatically, so much so that when I arrived at Roker, the sun was shimmering on a calm North Sea and I even toyed with the idea of a bracing walk along the seafront.

I sat down in my corner of the press box, which was situated at the front of the main stand and open to anything the elements might decide to throw at it, and set up my equipment. It was absolutely freezing and, soon after the kick-off, it began to snow. I was sitting on the front row of the box and was soon seeking shelter under a blanket. As I was waiting for the call to do my half-time piece, one of the stewards took pity on me.

'Why don't you come in for a cup of tea?' he asked.

'I can't, I've got to go on air in a minute.'

'Right, well, have a drink of this then – and there's a cup of tea waiting for you when you've finished.'

He handed me a glass of brandy and returned to the warmth inside the Roker Park stand. I gulped it down in one and felt marginally better. When the match ended, a full-scale blizzard was gathering momentum and I was huddled in my corner, still wrapped in the blanket, still trying to keep the equipment dry – writing notes had been impossible since midway through the first half so I had been forced to ad-lib all my reports. All the written press boys had made a rapid exit, leaving me alone to wait for the call for my 5.15 report.

'Have a safe journey home, Jim,' said the producer as I signed off – and it suddenly dawned on me that I would have to find my way back to Blackpool, 160 miles away across the frozen wastes of northern England. The first priority was a cup of tea and a sandwich and then I enlisted the help of the car park attendant to dig my car out of the snow. I slid sideways down Roker promenade, somehow managed to negotiate the bridge over the Wear and completed the 10-mile journey to the A1 motorway in around two hours. There I was accosted by an AA man, who asked, 'Where the hell are you going?'

'Blackpool.'

'Where?'

'Blackpool.'

He clearly thought I had lost the plot completely and said, 'Well, you don't want to be going down the A1. It's blocked near Wetherby. Go to Scotch Corner and then over the top to Penrith.'

Now it was my turn to wonder about people losing the plot, but I took him at his word, made my way to Scotch Corner and headed over the A66 towards Penrith. I was the only car on the road and incredibly, as I approached the summit, the snow stopped. I decided to have a break and climbed out of the car. What a wonderful sight! The hills were covered in a thick blanket of pure white and dotted around the landscape were farmhouses, their lights shining brightly on the snow. It was a scene from a

Christmas card and I stood alone for five minutes just taking in the sheer beauty of it all. It's something I'll never forget and it made the whole arduous day worthwhile. I finally staggered through the front door at 11 p.m.

I suppose the most unconventional radio position I have used is my bedroom at home in Blackpool. I was unable to cover the 2002 World Cup in Japan and South Korea because I was recovering from a knee operation. However, I was determined to play some part in the BBC's coverage and was given the opportunity of a daily slot on the 'Five Live Drive' programme with Peter Allen and Jane Garvey. I set up a mini-studio in the bedroom, watched all the games on television and each evening shared a 15-minute chat about the progress of the competition with the presenters. My venue may have been a bit low on atmosphere compared with the real thing but it offered a far better line in creature comforts than the Rose Bowl in Pasadena, not to mention the dungeon, as my hotel room in Bilbao for the first fortnight of the 1982 World Cup, was christened. I certainly drew the short straw when the rooms were allocated on that trip.

I was really looking forward to the competition, not least because I thought England had a good chance of doing well, and I walked into my room eager with anticipation about what the next few weeks would hold. It was a bit dark, something I attributed to the closed shutters, but when I opened them, I was confronted by the outside wall of the adjacent building, just touching distance away. There were no other rooms available so I was confined to the 'dungeon' for the rest of our two-week stay. Things improved when we moved on to Madrid for the second phase, though, because we were sharing a hotel with the German squad who made it through to the final before losing 3–1 to Italy. Access to the players and coaching staff couldn't have been easier and we had everything first hand all the way to the final.

Radio has been a very big item in my life over the last 25 years and people who were once colleagues and workmates have become firm friends. So much so that when I was presented with the OBE for Services to Association Football in 2000, BBC Radio

Sport laid on a magnificent celebration lunch in a top-class London restaurant for Anne and me after the Buckingham Palace ceremony. It was the perfect end to a wonderful occasion. BBC Radio has always been good to me and I am grateful.

TALKING WITH
L E G E N D S

Was Matthews better than Finney? It's an impossible question to answer and I always respond by saying it depends on whether you lived in Blackpool or Preston. It's something I have been asked countless times, just as I have been quizzed about how Stan, Tom and all the other great players of yesterday would fare in the modern game. I have absolutely no doubt that they would be just as effective because the skills they possessed were timeless. They would have adapted to the demands of any age simply because they were truly great performers.

Yet I have always been intrigued to know what made those players tick, to find out about their background. That is why, in the mid-1990s, I approached the BBC with an idea for a series called 'Football Legends'. I believed it was important to build up a library of live interviews with some of the big names from the past, men who were not getting any younger and, let's face it, might not be with us for much longer. First, I took the idea along to Audrey Adams, a personal friend and one of the most experienced producers at the BBC. Her response was, 'Shall we start with you then, Jim?' She was joking, of course, but she liked the idea and agreed to put it in front of her bosses.

They were keen as well and agreed to a pilot series of six programmes. So far, so good – but who would be the first six names on the list? Audrey and I met in the coffee bar at Euston

Station to discuss the project in more detail and whittle down the list of candidates to half a dozen. Ideally, I wanted to focus on players from a generation ahead of my own and, in the end, we opted for Stanley Matthews, Tom Finney, Nat Lofthouse and Wilf Mannion – all undisputed England greats of the early post-war years. John Charles of Leeds United and Wales, who also played in Italy for Juventus, and Bert Trautmann, the German-born Manchester City goalkeeper who played for 17 minutes of the 1956 Cup final with a broken neck, made up the first half dozen.

In the hope of a second series, we drew up another list that featured three Englishmen – centre-forward Tommy Lawton, defender George Hardwick and inside-forward Johnny Haynes, the UK's first £100 a week footballer. We added Northern Ireland inside-forward Jimmy McIlroy, Welsh winger Cliff Jones and Scottish centre-forward Lawrie Reilly. Those two collections proved very popular and we later recorded two more series. In the third, I spoke to six members of England's World Cup-winning squad of 1966 – Gordon Banks, Ray Wilson, Jack and Bobby Charlton, Geoff Hurst and Jimmy Greaves. The fourth series featured three Irishmen – Johnny Giles, George Best and Pat Jennings – and three Scots – Denis Law, Dave Mackay and Billy McNeill. All 24 were true legends in the eyes of football people, football supporters – and me.

It was an adventure. One of the beauties of radio is that the reporter doesn't need an army of technicians around him so all I had to do each week was set out with my microphone, recording equipment and a 60-minute cassette tape. I would record the one-to-one interview and then return the tape for Audrey to edit down to a 25-minute programme. That was the real skill. Some of the programmes were devoted exclusively to the player's own memories and opinions and sometimes we introduced the views and comments of others.

I preferred to speak to the interviewees at their homes, although it wasn't always possible. Hurst, for instance, was involved with a successful insurance company so I met him at the office. I interviewed Greaves in the old FA headquarters in

Lancaster Gate and Best in a pub in Chelsea. I travelled north of the border to talk to Reilly, McNeill and Haynes, who now lives in Edinburgh where his wife has a dry-cleaning business, just off Princes Street. Think of it, the captain of the England team that beat Scotland 9–3 at Wembley in 1961 living in the Scottish capital! I drove down to Hertfordshire to link up with Jennings and Jones, talked to Matthews at home in the Potteries, Finney in the lounge of his bungalow in Preston and Charles in a little conservatory at his modest home in West Yorkshire. Wilson was perhaps the hardest to track down. My former England full-back partner lives in a remote farmhouse in the Pennines and enjoys nothing more than a trek in the hills, away from it all. He rarely watches football, even on television.

Over a cup of tea, I outlined what the programme was about. Then I switched on the recorder and away we would go. I can't think of a single interview in which I didn't feel relaxed and I like to think the 24 legends felt the same. That certainly comes over in the interviews. I think it was important that they knew me and trusted me, and without being boastful, I believe I got more out of them because I am a football person, too. They knew I wasn't interested in sensational angles or distorting the facts.

Of course, I knew most of the players, having played with or against them, and some, Bobby and Big Jack for instance, were close friends. I discovered as the series went on that they were prepared to reveal parts of their lives that had been kept out of the public eye before. For example, Banks talked in some detail about the road accident that cost him the sight of one eye, something he had never really spoken about. I respected their confidences entirely. Once or twice, a player would say something, think again and ask me to leave that section out. I always did so.

Once I started, I couldn't put the programme down. I was hooked, and so were a lot of other people, judging by the number of requests the BBC have received for recordings. The programme went on air at seven o'clock on a Monday evening, just before the live match, although at first I would have preferred a Saturday lunchtime slot to catch people on their way to the match. But the BBC marketing people decided otherwise and they probably knew what was best.

What I enjoyed most was spending time with these great players. It isn't often that even a former professional can sit down and talk football at length with people who are part of the game's fabric. On one occasion, when I interviewed Tommy Lawton, it proved to be an extremely sad and moving occasion. Lawton, arguably the finest centre-forward of them all, scored 22 goals in 23 games for England. He also scored 24 in 23 wartime internationals, yet when I met him he was living in a single room in a residential home in Nottingham. There was a bed in one corner, a sink and a stove and only two mementoes from his career with Burnley, Everton, Chelsea, Notts County, Brentford and Arsenal – a framed picture and an old cartoon. He was one of my boyhood heroes. I had once stood in the rain behind the goal at Bloomfield Road watching him in action for Everton in a wartime game against Blackpool. Blackpool won 7–1 but my most abiding memory of that match is of Lawton scoring Everton's only goal. No less an authority than Stan Mortensen described Lawton as the finest header of a ball he had ever seen.

In his later years, Tommy walked with the aid of a stick but the centre parting in his hair and Bolton accent were still evident – and so was his pride, of course. Many people in Nottingham didn't even know who he was and I was told by the matron that he had been looking forward to my visit for weeks. I stayed with him longer than I should have, more than four hours, because I felt he craved my company and was eager to hear about players of this generation such as David Beckham and Michael Owen. 'Pity they didn't see Matthews!' was his only comment. He was simply content to talk football and even though we had met briefly two or three times before, he treated me like a long lost son. He was desperate for me to stay and insisted on walking to the car with me. He would not let go of my hand and the tears were rolling down his face. As I drove away I glanced in my mirror and there he was, waving his stick above his head in farewell. I still have the image in my mind today and I don't mind admitting there was a lump in my throat, too. Tom died two weeks later.

Sadly, there were others who died before I had an opportunity to talk to them. Ivor Allchurch, the Welsh inside-forward of the fifties, was, in my view, one of the outstanding players of his era. I contacted Ivor after talking to John Charles but he had not been well and we agreed to postpone the interview until the second series. When I called for the second time, his health had deteriorated further and we never got together. I once played against Ivor when he was at Newcastle. We beat them 5–1 at Bloomfield Road but after the match, the Blackpool players could not stop talking about Ivor's individual performance. Billy Bremner would have been on the list, too. So, of course, would Bobby Moore and Danny Blanchflower and I would have loved a chance to talk to Peter Doherty – but time beat them and me.

Doherty was one of the names that always cropped up when I chatted to the older legends about their contemporaries. Matthews and Finney were usually the first to be mentioned but Doherty was never far behind. George Hardwick described him as the first all-purpose footballer and the prototype of today's midfield player. Lawton said that apart from Matthews and Finney, Doherty was the greatest player he had seen, one of the first really deep thinkers about the game. Once, when he was manager of Bristol City, Blackpool played a cup tie at Ashton Gate and the night before the game, Peter came to see us in our hotel. Can you imagine that today? Blackpool had been his first club when he arrived from Northern Ireland before the war. I was impressed with his knowledge of the game. Like most Irishmen, he was a good talker and beguiled us with some fascinating stories, but I suspect he was nervous about the cup tie and talking was a good way of covering up his anxieties.

I'm sorry I missed Raich Carter, too. When Billy Wright was the subject of 'This Is Your Life' back in the late fifties, the BBC invited a group of his former team-mates, young and old, to appear on the programme. I represented the young brigade. We travelled to the studios in a bus and I sat alongside Carter. I hardly got a word in on the way there or on the way back. I was intrigued by his analysis of old players and his theories about the game. He was also a great thinker and both he and Doherty had played for the Derby side that reached the FA Cup final in 1946. I remember wondering who would have been in charge in the dressing room – probably not the manager!

I reached George Best via his agent, Phil Hughes, and, after a brief chat on the phone, George gave me an address in Chelsea and we fixed a time in the morning. When I arrived, I discovered it was a pub. I can't remember the name. It was deserted but as soon as I walked in, the barman said, 'George has just called – he'll be here in five minutes.' I'd never set eyes on the barman in my life but he must have recognised me – and that doesn't happen too often in London. George arrived right on cue and, as he walked in, the barman put a drink on the bar and George collected it on his way to my table. I've no idea what it was and I never asked, although it didn't appear to be alcoholic. I outlined what the interview would be about and told him there would be no fancy fee. 'That's fine,' he said. 'No problem at all.' So we chatted for an hour or so.

I'd never been particularly close to George. I had played against him a few times and he was aware that I was a good friend of Bobby Charlton and that I knew Denis Law quite well, but any contact between George and myself had been fairly brief. It was an excellent interview that I enjoyed very much and when I stood up to say goodbye, George grabbed hold of me and hugged me. There was a tear in his eye. 'I've really enjoyed that,' he said. It was a time in his life when things had not been going well and being able to talk about football and the good times must have been a release for him. Perhaps I had touched the real George Best.

It was a pity he didn't last longer as a player and he must regret that now. He is one of the finest raw talents ever produced in these islands. Speed, control, bravery – he had them all. Nobody taught Best; it was just an inborn talent. But he was also a product of the Swinging Sixties, dubbed the fifth Beatle in some quarters, and the first player to assume the status of a pop idol and feel the full force of the media machine. It can't have been easy for him to come to terms with all the adulation and there must have been many times when he wished he was simply

George Best, footballer, rather than George Best, cult figure.

Jimmy Greaves left the game before his time, too. God put Jim on this earth to put the ball in the back of the net. He was quite simply the best finisher I have seen, and I have seen the really top-class players who would usually stick the ball away if they got a sniff of the goal. Denis Law, the quicksilver Scot who was a bit useful himself when he saw the whites of the keeper's eyes, agrees with me. As a defender, you knew you really were in big trouble if Jim worked his way into the danger zone and got behind you. When he returned to England and signed for Spurs after his brief stay with AC Milan in the early sixties, Blackpool had the dubious distinction of providing the opposition in his first game at White Hart Lane on 16 December 1961.

There had been a huge amount of publicity all week about the man who was returning from Italy with a price tag of £99,999 around his neck. Jim hadn't actually been playing for Milan while he was in dispute with the club and on the morning of the match, the Blackpool players sat down to discuss how we would approach the match and how we would handle Greaves. I remember Ronnie Suart, our manager, saying, 'Look, Greaves hasn't played for weeks and weeks so he can't really be fit, can he? Surely he won't be too much of a problem if he isn't match fit.' I knew better.

'Greaves doesn't need training,' I said. 'I know Jim and I know what coming back to London will mean to him. He has a point to prove and he has a natural gift for scoring goals, fit or unfit.' Almost inevitably, he scored a hat-trick – one with his right foot, one with his left foot and one with his head. One of the goals was a spectacular scissors kick that effectively turned the match because we were just getting back into it at 2–1 down. The final score was 5–2.

Jim had two great feet, he was very fast – people didn't appreciate that – and he had a marvellous temperament. He loved scoring goals. On the training ground he would always be working around the goal, and if he wasn't practising his finishing, he would be between the posts with the gloves on making saves. He used to love that. He didn't really bother about what went on in the middle of the pitch; he was a penalty-area animal. I suspect that when he went in goal, it was a deliberate ploy to try to find out how opposing keepers might react in a given situation.

I've described before how defences seemed to open up in front of him and it was something I could never really understand. Playing right-back for England with Jim at inside-right, I had a perfect view and I used to ask myself why international defenders didn't close in on him. Instead, they seemed to veer away in the wrong direction, leaving Jim free to home in on goal. I came to realise it was Jim's skill, pace and positional sense that created this impression. When he reached the danger zone, he was so cool. Even in the tightest situations he had the ability to slip past defenders, go round the keeper and plant the ball in the net. There would be no histrionics. He would calmly walk away and accept the congratulations of his team-mates.

It was difficult for him when he finished playing and I think he always regretted retiring at the age of 31. He could have gone on for a lot longer because he was naturally fit and loved his football. We always had an affinity after our England call-up in 1962 but over the years there had been one or two downs for him. Thankfully, he was back to his old self when I went to see him for 'Legends'.

Nat Lofthouse was equally devastating in the penalty box and you can't leave him out of any list of the great players from the last 50 years of the old millennium. The Lion of Vienna was not what you would call a technically gifted footballer, but he was a terrific centre-forward and I used to hate playing against him. At around 5ft 11in, he wasn't much bigger than I was, but he was really quick, totally aggressive, unbelievably powerful and truly great in the air. It was impossible to hurt Nat because he didn't seem to feel pain. He would knock you all over the place but if you whacked him back, he would just get up, walk away and come back for more. In Nat's time, Bolton had a right-winger called Dougie Holden, whose crosses seemed to hang in the air and as the ball was floating down, defenders would be waiting for Nat to arrive. He always did. Whenever the ball came into the box, in the air or on the ground, Nat was there. He was a physical and a mental threat and no defender could relax when he was around. If the ball was out on the flanks, you had to look to see where Nat was and where he would be coming from. If you couldn't see him, you were in serious trouble. Come to think of it, you were in trouble even if you could see him. If you allowed the ball to drop in the box, he'd get you. I once used the expression that Nat would run all over you if you let him.

Nat scored 30 goals in 33 games for England, including two in that famous 3–2 win over Austria in Vienna in 1952 where he earned his nickname, and he played on the losing side just four times. Like Finney, he never left his home-town club, scoring 255 goals in 452 league games for Bolton. Also like Finney, he never forgot his humble roots. There has never been a more aggressive centre-forward and he would be absolutely sensational in today's game.

So, needless to say, would John Charles, at one time arguably the best centre-half and the best centre-forward in Europe. That's hard to believe today but it's true. He left Leeds United for Juventus in 1957 and was twice voted Italy's Footballer of the Year. No other British player has generated that kind of adulation among supporters of another nationality and while Juve's side included Giampiero Boniperti, the idol of Italian football, King John, as he was and is still known in Turin, was always the fans' favourite. He is the most successful British player to go abroad and, over 40 years on, he still goes back every year and is treated like royalty. He was a towering presence as a man and as a player, and like Matthews, Finney and Lofthouse, he had no edge. They all preferred to let their football do the talking.

When he was just a youngster at Swansea, his home-town club, and was informed that Leeds had come to sign him, John asked, 'Where's Leeds?' He had never been out of Swansea in his life, something else that people will find difficult to comprehend nowadays. He went to the station to catch the train north and he didn't even possess a coat. After he had played one or two games in the reserves at centre-half, the manager, Major Buckley, summoned him and said, 'Now then, John, you're strong, you're good in the air and we've no one to play centre-forward in the first team this weekend. Have you played there before?' John hadn't but he said yes and a couple of games later, he went out and scored a hat-trick.

The following Monday morning, he arrived at the ground to discover the Leeds chairman waiting for him, surrounded by a cluster of pressmen. The chairman put his arm around John's shoulder, or at least he did his best – at 6ft 3in and 14 stone, John was a big lad – and told the press corps, 'This is our new sensation, boys!' Then he turned to John and said, 'Now, John, I want you to take your car down to my garage and put in a gallon of petrol for each one of those goals you scored on Saturday.'

'There's a bit of a problem there, Mr Chairman,' big John replied. 'I haven't got a bloody car!'

John played centre-forward in Italy but back home he switched between centre-half and centre-forward to suit the needs of his team. Think about it – a man who could perform equally well at the highest level in either position. That's fantastic! What would he be worth today? I once played for England against Wales at Ninian Park and picked up a hamstring injury in the first half. I spent the rest of the game limping on the right wing and had the perfect opportunity to see just how good a centre-half John was. Quite simply, he kept them in the game against Greaves, Bobby Charlton and Bryan Douglas, and when the Welsh manager pushed him up front with 10 minutes left, he terrorised the England defence. The game ended 1–1 but we would have won it comfortably if King John had not been around.

I first came across him in a league game against Leeds at Elland Road in the mid-fifties. The main stand had recently burned down and the players had to change in the car park in what were the forerunners of the modern Portakabin. It was midwinter and there must have been a foot of snow on the pitch when we arrived. We thought it was unplayable but Leeds were expecting a sell-out crowd, they needed the money, and were determined that the game should go ahead. They had a right-winger called George Meek who supplied the ammunition for Charles and, sure enough, the game had not been going for long when Meek got away down the right and floated in the cross. I was under no illusions about what was about to happen as I moved in to head clear. On cue, a steamroller by the name of Charles came hurtling into view, towering high above me as he leaped to plant a rocket-like header into the Blackpool net. There was absolutely nothing I could have done to prevent that goal.

I talked to Lawrie Reilly, the former Scotland centre-forward and member of Hibernian's 'Famous Five' forward line of the early fifties, at his home in Edinburgh. His passion for Scotland and the game of football was undimmed from the days when he was a thorn in the side of England's defenders. Memories of his first call-up to the Scottish side in 1949 still brought a tear to his eye. He learned of his selection while he was standing at the bus stop on his way to a training session. A passer-by said: 'Hey, Lawrie, you've been picked for Scotland' and the young centre-forward had stood transfixed on hearing the news. Almost 50 years later, his voice choking with emotion, he recalled the moment with real pride. 'I will never forget it,' he said. 'I was going to wear the blue shirt of Scotland. It meant everything . . . and in those days, you couldn't go out and buy a Scotland shirt in a sports shop; you had to *earn* it.' How true.

The best foreign footballer I ever encountered was Alfredo Di Stefano of Real Madrid and Spain. I played against Pele three times but, to me, Di Stefano was the complete player, the key figure in one of the greatest club sides the game has ever seen. He could dribble, he could shoot, he could run forever even though he was a heavy smoker. He had fantastic skill and an ability to bring others into the game, making Puskas, Gento and Del Sol even more effective performers than they were already. He did things with a football that I had never seen before, such as swerving it and bending it. He had fantastic control and balance and he showed me how important a player's first touch can be. He was like poetry in motion and the ball was always right there where he wanted it. Di Stefano was captain of the Rest of the World side that played against England at Wembley in 1963 as part of the FA Centenary celebrations. I was the England captain and the photograph of our handshake in the centre circle before the kick-off remains one of my most prized possessions.

The European Cup final between Real Madrid and Eintracht

Frankfurt that took place at Hampden Park three years earlier is rightly remembered as one of the finest exhibitions of football in the post-war era. I will never forget Di Stefano's reaction after Eintracht had pulled back Madrid's 3–0 lead to 3–2. Straight from the kick-off, he ran through the middle of the Germans' defence and cracked in Real's fourth goal. I remember saying to a pal, 'Oh dear, they're really in trouble now – they've got him annoyed!'

Pele could get annoyed, too, and he was a hard player. Not many people know that but he could mix it with the best of them. I once saw him play against Argentina and he was lucky not to be sent off after one particular challenge. There's nothing wrong with being physical, though. It's something you have to expect in competitive football and I always admired Pele's physical input as well as his skill. You could probably count on one hand the number of truly great players who did not also have a physical side. I certainly didn't encounter many. He was very strong and hard to knock off the ball; he had good arms, good legs and could play with his back to goal.

I first saw him on a television screen as a young player in the Brazil squad that won the World Cup in Sweden in 1958. A year later, we were on opposite sides in my international debut in Rio. Like Bobby Moore, he was at his peak in the 1970 World Cup in Mexico. In the four years since 1966, he had developed into a true footballers' footballer and he possessed all the skills and know-how. He had weighed up the whole package over the previous 12 years and matured into a great all-round footballer. The 1970 side was arguably the best Brazilian line-up of all and Pele was pulling all the strings. He did it at the right time, too, as colour TV had arrived and the Mexico World Cup was its first big football extravaganza.

Di Stefano and Pele were supreme attacking players and it's fair to say that back players rarely come into consideration when people talk about the great teams and outstanding individuals. How many people can name the defenders in the Real Madrid side of the sixties or the Brazil line-up of 1970? The forward players take the eye, but without good defenders you don't have a prayer. Franz Beckenbauer was arguably the greatest all-round back player of them all, a football genius, but when he played his first game for West Germany in the mid-sixties he wasn't a sweeper, he was an old-fashioned wing-half. He was a bit one-paced but always seemed to be in control and, like all great footballers, he had time on the ball. That was because his first touch was excellent and he knew exactly what he was going to do next.

When the Germans talked about moving him to the back, I thought it might be a bit of a waste. But for Germany, the sweeper is often the key player and when they have an experienced, world-class performer, they are inclined to push him to the back and let him control proceedings from there. They did the same thing with Matthias Sammer at Euro '96 and again with Lothar Matthaus in the 1998 World Cup. Beckenbauer introduced a new dimension to the role of sweeper because, as he had been an attacking wing-half, he was totally at ease surging out of defence and into attacking positions. It was something we had never seen a sweeper do before.

I once watched him in action for Bayern Munich against Schalke in the German *Bundesliga*, and for 90 minutes, he made it look as if the Schalke players were passing the ball straight to him instead of trying to open up the Bayern defence. He never looked as though he was moving at more than a gentle trot and his distribution was excellent. When Leeds were preparing to play Bayern in the 1975 European Cup final, I repeatedly stressed that we needed to play a high-pressure, high-tempo game specifically to try to disturb Beckenbauer. I knew that if he stayed calm and in control, we had a problem. For a time the plan worked and we had him rattled, but the longer the game went on, the cooler and calmer he became and the Bayern performance improved accordingly.

His career with Bayern, where he is now club president, and the German national side must be one of the greatest in the history of the game. He is one of only two men (the other being Brazil's Mario Zagalo) to win the World Cup as a player and manager and he also led Germany to the European Championship. He lifted the *Bundesliga* title as captain and manager of

Bayern, captained Bayern to three successive European Cup victories in the seventies and was named European Footballer of the Year in 1972 and 1976. He is probably the best player Germany has produced – and, make no mistake, there have been some truly outstanding Germans over the last 50 years. Even when they had a relatively ordinary side in 1990, they won the World Cup.

In South Korea and Japan in 2002, they were again labelled average and not rated serious contenders by many people, particularly after England had beaten them 5–1 in their own backyard in a qualifying match. But what happened when it mattered? Germany finished runners-up to Brazil and England were eliminated in the quarter-finals. No serious thinker about football would ever underestimate a German side. They will always have a method, they will always be organised and they will always believe in themselves, and Beckenbauer was the man who laid down the game plan and helped to establish that unquenchable belief.

The only English defender to compare with Beckenbauer has been Bobby Moore, a man from the same era. Like Beckenbauer, Bob read the game brilliantly, he was a good passer of the ball, improved as the years went by and never had to gallop all over the field to make his mark. He was confident, even a touch arrogant, and we haven't produced anyone of his class since he played his last game for England in 1974.

It was an enormous privilege to play against some of the true greats of the post-war era, and perhaps none more so than Tom Finney. If anyone asked Bill Shankly, Tommy Docherty, Tommy Thompson or any of Finney's Preston team-mates about Tom, they would wax lyrical about his skills as a player and his qualities as a man. They idolised him as we idolised Matthews at Blackpool. He had a lot of Matthews' attributes but he also had versatility. I saw Tom play outside-right, outside-left and centre-forward and, to be honest, he could have played any-where. He had wonderful balance, he was two-footed, a great finisher, good in the air and as brave as a lion. In fact, when you played against him – and I did several times – you had to get on with it right from the start because Tom could be pretty aggressive. That wasn't obvious from the stands or from his body language, but you knew you'd been in a game after marking Tom.

Like Matthews, he could stand opponents still and then beat them, and if you were back on your heels against Tom you were in big trouble. He would drop his right shoulder and from there he could go either left or right. If you guessed wrongly, you'd had it because he would be away. His first touch was terrific. He won 76 England caps and scored 30 goals, and, time after time, he tore the opposition apart. Yet the greatest display I ever saw him give was for an injury-hit Preston against Arsenal at Highbury a couple of days before I was due to play for Young England down in London. We all went along to the game, which ended in a 1–1 draw. Tom played centre-forward and he played Arsenal virtually on his own. Everybody in the stand was talking about his performance but it was by no means a one-off.

My father thought he was absolutely wonderful and in the days when Blackpool and Preston alternated home games, he would sometimes go to Deepdale on a Saturday just to see Tom play. He would stand in the paddock to be as close as he could to Finney for 45 minutes. I went with him once or twice. A few years later, I was invited to a function and asked my dad if he'd like to come along. He wasn't bothered until I mentioned that Tom Finney was going. 'Right, I'll be there,' he said. He met Tom and never forgot it.

I have become close to Tom in recent years and, like Matthews, he is a humble man who never courted fame. It followed him. When I went to Hong Kong as player-manager of the FA team in the early seventies, the hotel reception clerk said, 'Ah, Mr Armfield, you play for Blackpool?' I said I did and he replied, 'Yes, Stanley Matthews! But where *is* Blackpool?' I asked him if knew Lancashire. No, he didn't. Did he know Preston? 'Yes, Tom Finney!' Even now, if you ask anyone in the country what they understand by the word Finney, I'm pretty sure 90 per cent would say Tom Finney, the footballer. That says it all.

I suppose that when we reminisce about players of the calibre of Finney and the rest of the legends, we may tend to exaggerate a bit. I discussed it with Matthews in his later years. He reminded me that every player had good days and bad days and it's far easier for people to remember the good ones, which is a fair point. I recall one occasion at home when some old football footage appeared on the television screen featuring a certain Jimmy Armfield in an England shirt. Inevitably, my sons, Duncan and John, were not going to miss an opportunity to have a joke at their father's expense along the lines of, 'You always said you were a good player, Dad. You could have fooled us!' But they have subsequently asked if I wished there were more videos of me in action so they and the grandkids could see me playing – not to mention Matthews, Finney, Di Stefano, Lofthouse, Charles and the others. After giving it some thought, the old head came into place and I replied, 'No. It's probably better to let people think I was a good player!'

C H A P T E R   1 6

'THERE'S A MR KELLY ON THE LINE . . .'

Graham Taylor resigned as England manager on 23 November 1993 after the failure to qualify for the 1994 World Cup finals in the USA. Two days later, I was invited to dine in the Grill Room at Old Trafford, an invitation that was to change my life's direction. I was working in the Manchester office of the *Daily Express* when one of the sports desk telephones rang and I was told there was a Mr Kelly on the line. It was Graham Kelly, chief executive of the Football Association.

I had known Graham for a long time. He grew up in the Blackpool area, in Cleveleys, just north of the town, and as a kid he was a fanatical Blackpool fan and a useful goalkeeper. He still recalls how I sometimes used to coach the Anchorsholme Under-14 team and I once refereed a junior six-a-side competition in which Graham played for Anchorsholme – he has a picture of the team at the tournament, lining up with their celebrity referee! He was a good enough keeper to play for the town's Under-15 side, signed junior forms with Accrington Stanley and had trials with Blackpool.

His first involvement with the professional game came when he was appointed assistant secretary of the Football League, which was based in Lytham St Annes in those days. His boss was the redoubtable Alan Hardaker, and that gave Graham a terrific schooling in the world of football administration. He succeeded

Alan in 1980 before becoming FA secretary in 1989 after the retirement of Ted Croker. He resigned as chief executive in 1998 and later became a director of Luton Town.

He is a likeable chap with a terrific sense of humour, which doesn't always come across in public, and he loves football. I'm sure he always wanted to be a professional, so a job in football administration was a dream come true for him. When he was with the FA, Graham would travel miles to watch a match – and I'm not just talking about Wembley, Old Trafford or St James' Park. Far from it! Graham could always relate to the grassroots of the game and was just as likely to be found on the terraces at a non-league club such as Horwich RMI or Halesowen, Guiseley or Gravesend, wearing his wellies and chatting with the locals. He was content to travel incognito and would slip away before the final whistle to make sure no one made a fuss. Graham never had an ego to feed and now he is back in the Blackpool area, we often find time for a natter to put the world to rights.

Back in November 1993, more serious matters were on the agenda. After we had exchanged the usual telephone pleasantries, Graham said, 'Where are you going to be tomorrow night?' I told him I would be doing the BBC Radio commentary at the Manchester United game against Ipswich.

'I thought you might be,' he said. 'I'm going there, too. Would you like to have tea somewhere?'

'Who's paying?'

'You, of course! But on reflection, I think the FA will be able to afford a bite of tea – as long as you only have two courses.' That's the sort of banter we often exchange.

We met at Old Trafford, where the fans were already starting to gather. It didn't take Graham long to come to the point and when he did it was quite a shock.

'How would you like to work for the FA?' he asked.

'Doing what?'

I assumed he would be thinking about something on the communications side.

'Well, you can go and find us an England manager for starters.'

I must admit I was taken aback.

'Why me?' I asked.

'You've been on the international scene and you know the game backwards. You're still involved through your work at the *Express* and the BBC and you're at ease with the media. I'm sure you can be useful.'

'I'm not going to live in London.'

'You won't have to.'

We talked a bit more and he asked how much I was earning at the *Express*. It would probably have been around £18,000 a year but I don't remember exactly. He said they could do better than that. The call had come completely out of the blue. I was happy at the *Daily Express* and enjoyed my work for the BBC but as I drove home to Blackpool that night, I knew what my answer was going to be. I was being asked to find the man who could lead England to victory in the 1996 European Championship to be held in this country. In some ways, the future of English football would be in my hands. It was a fantastic opportunity.

I went down to London to talk things over with Graham and FA chairman Bert Millichip. Graham was worried that the FA committee that was to appoint a new manager did not include a football professional with inside knowledge of the game. It comprised Millichip, Noel White of Liverpool, Ian Stott of Oldham and Graham himself and while no one could question their experience as administrators, Graham feared they would be seen in many quarters as unqualified amateurs. He wanted to bring in someone to act as a conduit between the FA and people within the game whose opinions the FA were seeking. I was that man. 'Right, off you go then. Go and find us a new manager,' said Graham as we shook hands at the end of the meeting. I walked out into the night, and that's how it all started.

I began with a blank sheet of paper and, in some ways, a blank mind. First, what was the job description? What kind of person were we looking for? International management is a job that requires experience as well as tactical know-how and technical knowledge. Ideally, the manager should have had some European or foreign experience, either as a player or coach. He has to be able to handle big-time players and that's not easy, particularly if he has never been involved at the top level. He must be able to talk with agents and club chairmen, to handle the media and feel at home in the limelight. He has to be assured, confident and have communication skills that will engage the players and the public. Those skills are not acquired overnight. But above all, he must be able to cope with the pressures of the job – and they are considerable. Looking back, I was probably searching for Clark Kent, alias Superman.

In this country, we tend to treat the national team as we do the family silver. Every now and then, when there is an international match or a major competition, we take it out of the cupboard and give it a polish. We scrutinise it from every angle and in minute detail and have a bit of argument about how much it's worth. Then we put it away again until the next time. But while the team is out of the cupboard, the glare of the media spotlight is intense and the manager has to live life under the microscope. There is no hiding place. Not too many people can cope with that kind of pressure.

I drew up a list of all the managers in the Premiership and one or two other possible candidates who were either out of work or involved elsewhere. In those days, there was absolutely no suggestion of appointing an outsider so that ruled out Alex Ferguson, George Graham, Kenny Dalglish, Graeme Souness and Joe Kinnear, all of whom were in charge at top clubs and fulfilled many of the criteria we were looking for. Bert Millichip simply wouldn't entertain the idea of Ron Atkinson so he was also discounted before the runners came under starter's orders. So after a minor pruning operation, I was left with eight league managers on the list – Gerry Francis, Howard Kendall, Howard Wilkinson, Joe Royle, Peter Reid, Trevor Francis, Glenn Hoddle and Billy Bonds. Ray Wilkins and Bryan Robson were not managers at that time but, as experienced England internationals, were regarded in some quarters as realistic candidates. After all, Franz Beckenbauer had no managerial experience when he was appointed West Germany's coach in 1984 and he guided them to the World Cup final in Argentina two years later before winning the competition in Italy in 1990. So the appointment of a young coach was a route favoured by one or two people within the FA, including Millichip – not by me, though. I didn't think either Robson or Wilkins was ready.

And then there was Terry Venables. He had won the Spanish championship at Barcelona in 1985 and reached the final of the European Cup the following year. He was out of work following an acrimonious parting of the ways at Tottenham a few months earlier after winning the FA Cup in 1991.

I needed to delve behind those names, to find out what made them tick and why one of them would be the ideal candidate. I wanted to talk to people and canvass a few opinions, and I was determined to meet the fans and discover what they were thinking, too. And so, I embarked on my journey of discovery.

As soon as my involvement became public knowledge, I was labelled the FA headhunter in the national press. In some ways, I received more publicity over the next few weeks than at any time in my career as a player or manager, with the possible exception of my arrival at Leeds in 1974. But I was smart enough to appreciate that all the publicity I received then was because I was succeeding Brian Clough, not because I was Jimmy Armfield. Now I had become a public figure again with the media building up an image of me leaving my Blackpool home in the early hours and travelling the length and breadth of the country in pursuit of my quarry. One tabloid even put a tail on me, although I wasn't aware of it at the time and I 'lost' them anyway.

I didn't travel quite as far and wide as some elements of the media suggested because there is such a thing as the telephone and I was able to garner some information that way without stepping outside my front door. I canvassed the views of a lot of people, including Ferguson, Graham and Wilkinson. I spoke to Gordon Taylor at the PFA, Dave Sexton, a former manager and member of the England coaching hierarchy, and Johnny Giles, one of my players at Leeds United, a manager at club and international level and a respected pundit. I also talked to Graham Taylor and his assistant Lawrie McMenemy, and to Bobby Robson, who had taken England to the last eight in 1986 and the semi-finals four years later.

Of course the publicity surrounding my quest didn't make the job any easier. Football people are difficult to pin down for meetings at the best of times but trying to find somewhere away from the media spotlight was almost impossible. As soon as I was spotted talking to anyone, people put two and two together and, almost inevitably, came up with the answer five. But I never had a problem with the press or the image they built up. As Graham Kelly appreciated when he offered me the job, I knew most of the journalists from my time on the *Express* and with the BBC and we got on well. As a pressman myself, I knew what to expect and accepted the daily bombardment of calls. They wanted a name and I was the only person who could provide it. So I was open and up front with them and the relationship worked well although, of course, I told them only what I wanted them to know.

Then there were the candidates. Gerry Francis was one of the early front runners. I saw him twice, the second time at a hotel near Haydock Park racecourse. QPR were playing Liverpool at Anfield that night and I was doing the commentary for the BBC. So we agreed to meet at the team hotel after lunch. We went to his room. Gerry sat on the bed, I sat in the chair and he talked for an hour about the England job. The more he talked, the further he slipped down the pecking order. I liked Gerry a lot, and I agreed with his attitude to football. He had a lot of international experience and had done well at QPR but he kept repeating how he could live without all the pressure of the England job and how he didn't fancy the hassle. Pressure and hassle come with the territory, of course, so eventually, I said I had to be off and I'd see him at the match later. I didn't interview him again.

I saw Bryan Robson at his home. He was still a Manchester United player and I didn't feel he had the experience we were looking for. His first managerial job at Middlesbrough was six months away. Wilkins came into the same category. He was still a player and while he was possibly destined to become a coach, was he really ready to take on the England job and everything it entailed? Hoddle had more experience but even though he had done exceptionally well to guide Swindon into the top division and made a good start at Chelsea, he was gaining experience and I noted him down as one for the future. There were similar reservations about Trevor Francis at Sheffield Wednesday although, like Hoddle, he had played in Europe and experienced a different footballing culture. Reid was still cutting his teeth as a player-manager at Manchester City and the same could be said of Bonds at West Ham.

Royle had done an incredible job in taking Oldham into the top flight and, more to the point, keeping them there, but did that qualify him for international management? Not really. After talking to Kendall at Everton, I wasn't convinced he really fancied it, even though he had won trophies here and success-fully coached abroad. While I had a lot of admiration for Howard Wilkinson and everything he had achieved with Leeds, I always saw him as a potential technical director rather than team manager or coach. So gradually, the contenders fell by the wayside. Just one name stayed in the frame throughout – Terry Venables. I suppose I knew all along that he was the man to take us into Euro '96.

As I travelled around the country watching games and talking to the ordinary fans as well as the professionals, I sensed a growing groundswell of opinion in favour of Venables. That was important because we needed someone to whom the people could relate. I particularly remember a cup tie at Grimsby early in 1994. I was doing the commentary and spent a few minutes in the BBC radio van before the match. A couple of people wandered across the little car park as I clambered down from the van, and said, 'I hope you're going to appoint Venables.' We started chatting and within five minutes, there were 20 or 30 people there, all putting their oar into the water about the England team, telling me why I should talk to the fans and why Venables should have the job. The public wanted him. Grimsby, of all places, was where it really struck home.

On a train journey from Blackpool to Birmingham, I was amazed at the number of total strangers who came up and spoke to me about the England job – and again, Venables emerged as the people's choice. I was inundated with letters from all over the country, a lot of them addressed simply to Jimmy Armfield, The FA, London. As I expected, most of the letters from the south were strongly in favour of Venables; less predictable was the strong support he received in the north.

On the other hand, there was no shortage of opposition to Venables, either. I received letters from people inside and outside the game urging me not to appoint him. One club chairman who, incidentally, was a Scot, said to me, 'I hope we're not going to have that barrow boy in charge of our national team.' I replied that the last person I would ask about the job of England manager was a Scot. That silenced him. There were concerns within the FA, too, where doubts were expressed about the suitability of having an England manager whose business interests were under scrutiny in the media and elsewhere. His situation at Spurs was also an ongoing worry. Venables, who had taken over as co-owner of the club alongside Alan Sugar, had been ousted earlier in the year and dirty linen was still being washed in public amid threats of litigation.

Terry had wanted the job when Bobby Robson quit in 1990. Instead, Graham Taylor was appointed and Terry's name was not even on the shortlist, which had featured Kendall and Royle. Venables was devastated and took a sideswipe at the FA hierarchy. Needless to say, that had ruffled one or two feathers at Lancaster Gate. However, I preferred to look at the plus side of the equation. Terry was out of work after leaving Spurs, so he was instantly available. He had been involved with the England set-up in 1978, when Ron Greenwood appointed him coach to the Under-21 side, working alongside Dave Sexton. He had proved himself an innovative coach during managerial spells with Crystal Palace and QPR. He had done outstandingly well at Barcelona and at Spurs. He had a good rapport with coaches in this country, he was outgoing and he was a Londoner. I think that's important, even though it may seem daft to some people. But I believed it was easier for a Londoner to do the job because the manager spends so much time at the FA and there are fewer problems if he and his family are familiar with life in the capital. I'm not so sure if it's quite so relevant now – times have changed.

His detractors derided him as little more than an East End wide boy but I didn't think that was fair. People insinuated all sorts of things about him and his business dealings but I was looking for someone to run a football team, someone the players could relate to and someone who would light a spark among the fans. I believed he might be the man to help us win Euro '96 and, at that stage, I didn't consider the long-term at all. So I mentioned Terry's name at the first meeting of the appointments committee, pointing out that he had all the necessary football credentials for the job and reminding them that we were looking for a man to run an international football team not a Sunday school outing. We needed someone to lift the players after the disappointment of failing to qualify for the World Cup finals. If the players were right, everything else would fit into place, and there was always a chance it would be short-term anyway.

The response was mixed, to say the least. Noel White didn't want him at any price, Bert Millichip was almost as strongly against him, and Ian Stott said let's see how it works out between now and the next meeting, a sentiment shared by Graham Kelly, who already knew which way I was leaning. There was no dispute about his coaching qualifications, he had an excellent reputation for handling big-name players and he had proved he could hold his own with the media both here and in Barcelona. But some people within the FA were concerned about what they called the 'baggage' that came with him in the shape of his business interests and his problems at Spurs. I was prepared to give him the benefit of the doubt.

I arranged to meet Terry and he picked me up outside Euston Station in his Mercedes. He hadn't shaved and the car absolutely reeked of garlic. I don't know where he'd been the night before but I got the distinct impression that if I'd been with him I might have enjoyed myself. I asked him if he always ate garlic. 'Always,' he laughed. I hate the stuff. I offered him a stick of chewing gum to douse down the fumes a bit but he wasn't interested. We drove to the Royal Lancaster Hotel, where the manager was one of his mates, and were ushered into a private room. We sat down and chatted for a couple of hours. He was good company but, above all, I was impressed with his football knowledge and his ideas about the England job. I went to see him at his apartment in Hammersmith, near the bridge, where I met his wife, Yvette. We talked again and I made another trip to the apartment soon afterwards. The fourth time, we met at his club, Scribes – I needed to see that, too – completing a three-week round trip from a garlic-ridden Mercedes at Euston Station to a West End nightclub via a Hammersmith apartment. By the end of that circuitous journey, two facts had emerged – Terry could do the job and he wanted the job. I decided to put his name forward.

So it was time for another meeting with the FA. The press had discovered by this stage that Terry was number one on my list. I don't know whether Terry told them or whether it was his agent, Eric Hall, or his wife, or someone at the Royal Lancaster Hotel, but they were on to it. So I didn't bother with the cloak and dagger stuff because the key decisions would be made when Terry and I sat around the table with the other four members of the committee. Even so, we tried to head off the media pack by meeting at the Football League offices on Marylebone Road, rather than FA headquarters in Lancaster Gate. That gave us a bit of peace and privacy.

The committee grilled Terry about his business interests and about the circumstances surrounding his departure from Spurs, which had involved a lot of mud-slinging between Venables and Alan Sugar. All sorts of rumours were still doing the rounds. Terry seemed to satisfy them on both counts and he was impressing them with his ideas for the job and his footballing philosophy in general when Graham glanced out of the window and spotted a woman sitting on a ledge not much more than a couple of yards away. As she was 200 feet above the street and seemed poised to jump, everything stopped. We checked that someone in the building had called 999 and that the rescue services were on their way and eventually, she was persuaded to climb back into the building. Was that an omen? It had been a bizarre interlude but when normal service was resumed, Terry continued to create a favourable impression.

I had already briefed Graham and told him that Terry was

my choice. He accepted that decision. Bert Millichip was beginning to soften, wanting to know about his virtues rather than his vices, and Ian Stott was coming round, too. Noel White was still against Terry and I admired his steadfast attitude. Even so, I believed the committee were starting to see things my way and my next stop was Manchester and Peter Swales, chairman of the FA International Committee and a friend of Noel White's. He was due to stand down soon afterwards and had agreed not to be part of the appointments committee but he was still an influential figure. He had recently quit as chairman of Manchester City after a long-running feud with the Maine Road fans.

Peter had a television shop in Altrincham with his own private office at the back and I went to see him there.

'I know what you've come for,' he said. 'You're here for my blessing on Venables, aren't you?'

'No, I've come to see if you have any thoughts on the subject.'

'Yes, I have. I wouldn't have him at any price and you'll never, ever change my mind. He's not the right man for the England job.'

We discussed the situation for a long time and I tried to persuade him that Terry was the only serious candidate and, what's more, the choice of the ordinary supporters. Peter had taken enormous stick from the Manchester City fans over the last few years so he, more than anyone, knew how important it was to have the supporters on your side. But no, he was adamant. Like so many other people, he kept raising doubts about Terry's business interests and his situation at Spurs.

'Look, Peter,' I said. 'What has he done? I've spent the last few weeks talking to people in football at all levels and nobody has given me any solid factual evidence that Terry has done anything wrong. It seems to be all rumours and innuendo, second-hand information. There's nothing definite, not even pinching a knife and fork from a hotel dining room. If someone gives me proof that Terry has been dishonest, OK, I'll hold up my hands. But my brief is to find the best coach for the England football team, and right now, Terry is that man.'

Swales would not be moved and I continued my search for proof that Venables should be ruled out of contention for non-football reasons – and believe me, I tried. Whenever anyone hinted that there were skeletons in the cupboard, I challenged them to come forward, but the nearest I got was unsigned letters. No one provided anything substantial, and Venables continued to be favoured by the football lobby. After meeting Swales, I talked to Alex Ferguson at Old Trafford. He thought Terry would be OK. Alex knows better than most what is involved in managing a top club, and he felt that if Terry could handle the pressure at Barcelona, he would cope with the England job. I also talked to Gordon Taylor at the PFA, who assured me that if we appointed Venables, the players would be behind him all the way. That was important. The players like Gordon and for him to back Terry so strongly sent a clear message to those who, in little more than two years, would be wearing the England shirt at Euro '96.

The appointments committee met for the final time at the County Court Hotel in Solihull and, once again, I emphasised my belief that Terry was the only realistic candidate for the job. The die was cast. Graham and I met Terry the following day to sort out the contractual details and Terry agreed to try to sort out his affairs with Spurs and his business interests over the next six months. He agreed to be appointed coach, in the continental manner, rather than manager, and asked for Don Howe as his number two and Bryan Robson as assistant coach. He was formally unveiled as England's new coach at a Wembley press conference on Friday, 28 January 1994.

His first match in charge was against Denmark, the European champions, at Wembley on 9 March. I never really suffered from nerves as a player for Blackpool or England, or as a manager, but I was certainly nervous as I took my place in the FA seats in front of the Royal Box. Since Terry's appointment, a lot of people had suggested that without my support, he would never have had a look-in, and I think Terry appreciated that, too. So I desperately wanted him to make a winning start. The performance didn't really matter; a win was everything. I watched in silence as he made the long walk from the Wembley tunnel to the dug-out, even though I was surrounded by a capacity crowd of 72,000 people, all of whom seemed to be on their feet, cheering and applauding him. I must have been the only person sitting down. But when David Platt cut in from the left and beat Peter Schmeichel with a low shot to score the only goal of the game, I was suddenly a fan all over again. I leapt to my feet and cheered with the best of them. I almost threw my flat cap into the air!

Afterwards, I had a bite to eat and waited for Terry. I don't normally fuss around but I wanted to shake his hand and say well done. I wanted him to see us through Euro '96 and then build from there towards the 1998 World Cup. It should have been the start of something special, but sadly, it was not to be. Terry's record speaks for itself – 23 games, 11 wins, 11 draws and just a single defeat, by Brazil. It's true that because England, as hosts, were not required to qualify for Euro '96, 18 of his matches in charge were friendlies, and of the five European Championship matches, two went to penalty shoot-outs. But nevertheless, Terry scarcely put a foot wrong in the build-up to the competition. This was his record:

1994: 9 March, Denmark (h) 1–0; 17 May, Greece (h) 5–0; 22 May, Norway (h) 0–0; 7 September, USA (h) 2–0; 12 October, Romania (h) 1–1; 16 November, Nigeria (h) 1–0
    1995: 15 February, Ireland (a) abandoned after 27 minutes because of crowd trouble; 29 March, Uruguay (h) 0–0; 3 June, Japan (h) 2–1; 8 June, Sweden (h) 3–3; 11 June, Brazil (h) 1–3; 6 September, Colombia (h) 0–0; 11 October, Norway (a) 0–0; 15 November, Switzerland (h) 3–1; 12 December, Portugal (h) 1–1
    1996: 27 March, Bulgaria (h) 1–0; 24 April, Croatia (h) 0–0; 18 May, Hungary (h) 3–0; 23 May, China (a) 3–0; 8 June, Switzerland (h) 1–1*; 15 June, Scotland (h) 2–0*; 18 June, Holland (h) 4–1*; 22 June, Spain (h) 0–0 (4–2 pens)*; 26 June, Germany (h) 1–1 (5–6 pens)* (* European Championship)

Venables came in and lifted the players and the fans and although there were people at the FA who doubted him all the way through, I think he did well – so well that when we reached the semi-finals of the European Championship and lost on penalties, I was bitterly disappointed. Then Terry walked away. He had informed Graham Kelly at the draw for Euro '96, which took place in Birmingham in December 1995, that he would not be seeking a new contract, and he repeated his determination to leave at a hastily convened meeting in a Birmingham hotel shortly afterwards. Graham, Bert Millichip and Noel White were there. Millichip had already stated publicly that he wanted Terry to continue until after the 1998 World Cup in France while White had countered by saying that the FA needed to consider one or two other matters before handing Terry a new contract. Those 'other matters' remained his business interests, still a subject of newspaper speculation, and the legal wrangling with Alan Sugar over his departure from Spurs.

Terry was not convinced that he had 100 per cent backing from within the FA, saying it was bad enough taking on the snipers outside Lancaster Gate without having to fight insiders as well. I really wanted him to delay his resignation until after the European Championship, arguing that if England did well, the whole country would demand that he be given a new contract. But Terry would not be dissuaded, even though he had the players on his side. Graham had several meetings with him in the hope of persuading him to stay but he was adamant. And so the search for a replacement began.

RETURN OF THE HEADHUNTER

I had never even heard of Eileen Drewery when Glenn Hoddle was appointed England coach in May 1996. I have not met her and it still seems scarcely credible that she could figure in the downfall of the man I recommended to the FA as Terry Venables' successor. Yet Mrs Drewery, a faith healer, Glenn's ill-advised book about the 1998 World Cup and a hostile media were the factors contributing to his demise in February 1999, rather than his record as a coach. That was a pity. I believe Hoddle did a decent job for England, far better than many people give him credit for, and he's a proud man. Losing the England job would have hit him hard.

He didn't come to the job at an easy time. England were about to embark on their campaign to win the European Championship on home soil, Terry Venables had already announced he would not be staying when his contract expired at the end of the competition, and we needed to find a replacement urgently. Once again, I was charged with the task of finding the right man for the job, someone who could pick up the reins from Terry and go straight into the qualifying competition for the 1998 World Cup, which was due to start two and a half months after Euro '96.

The media circus moved into overdrive as soon as it was announced that Terry would be leaving, as we all knew it would. The press had their own ideas about who should get the job and were demanding a quick decision, but as I had discovered before the appointment of Venables, it isn't as easy as that. As the country's football authority, the FA has to play it strictly by the book and everything has to be above board. The press were right about one thing, though – we needed someone who was available more or less immediately.

Fortunately, I had done a lot of the spadework when we appointed Venables, little more than a couple of years earlier. Most of the current candidates had also been in the frame at the end of 1993. A sub-committee was formed, this time made up of Graham Kelly, Bert Millichip, Keith Wiseman, FA vice chairman Chris Willcox, Noel White and me. Before our first meeting, on 15 January 1996, Bryan Robson, Kevin Keegan and Gerry Francis had ruled themselves out of the reckoning. We met again at the end of the month, by which time Bobby Robson and Howard Kendall had also been discounted. There was press speculation at this stage that Kenny Dalglish and Ruud Gullit were interested in the job but no approaches were made on either side.

One man I did see, however, was Alex Ferguson. During my days as a reporter at the *Daily Express*, I was a regular visitor to United's training ground at the Cliff, either attending press conferences or having a chat with Alex and members of his backroom staff, including Archie Knox. We would sit in his office and exchange old football tales over a cup of tea. I had always enjoyed a good relationship with Alex and, of course, I had discussed the ins and outs of the England position with him three years earlier. As a former Scotland manager, he was able to tell me all about the differences between management at club and international level and what sort of person we were looking for. I remember asking him in 1993 if he thought he might ever return to international management one day but it was no more than an idle talking point. He was totally involved at United where he had a tremendous group of emerging young players, including Beckham, Scholes, Giggs, Butt and the two Nevilles. That was a priceless situation for him. They were bound to be successful. He was in the same position as Matt Busby at Old

Trafford in the fifties and Don Revie at Leeds a decade later. Any manager would be loath to give up a crop of players like that and, in 1993, the name of Ferguson was never mentioned.

But we stayed in touch and when Venables resigned, I returned to The Cliff for another chat. Like me, Alex studies people and he is a shrewd judge of character. I wanted to throw a few names at him and hear his reaction, and he knew I would never betray his confidence. It wasn't a cloak and dagger meeting by any means. Neither of us tried to disguise the purpose of my visit and while people in the media knew I had been to see Alex, they never really regarded him as a candidate for the England job. He was very helpful and towards the end of our chat, I said, 'And what about you, then?' It was a bit of a hunch, really. I knew Alex was approaching the end of his contract and wondered if he might be looking for a new challenge – or, for that matter, if the Old Trafford board might be considering a change. He had not had a particularly happy time as stand-in manager of Scotland after Jock Stein died in 1985 but no one could argue with his record at Manchester United. It was the first time the possibility of having a non-Englishman in the job had been contemplated and after talking to Alex, I had the distinct impression that he might be interested. It was no more than an impression but, nevertheless, I told Graham Kelly, even though I was unsure about having a non-English manager in charge of the national team.

Whatever, it was enough for Kelly to have a word with Martin Edwards, United's chief executive, asking for permission to interview their manager. Edwards said he would put our request before the Old Trafford board but doubted that they would release him, and so it transpired. Edwards came back to say Alex still had a year left on his contract and they were not prepared to let him go. I didn't know that Graham had spoken to Martin and if I had been consulted, I would have advised more of a soft-shoe approach. Instead, Alex was given a new deal and that was the end of the matter. He was never offered the job but when Graham met him at a dinner soon afterwards, Alex admitted that he would have liked a chance to talk a bit more. But it was not to be.

One person who was available, though, was Hoddle, whom I had noted down as a man for the future during my earlier search. He was popular in London at the time – as Venables had been in 1993 – and had already made it clear that he was going to leave Chelsea when his contract expired in the summer. So I gave him a call and he agreed to meet me. He arranged to pick me up outside the Royal Lancaster Hotel in London, ironically the venue for his final press conference three years later, and I was waiting on the kerb as he approached in his BMW. We drove into Hyde Park and sat facing the Serpentine. That was the first time I had had a really long talk with him. He was interested and his credentials were good. After guiding Swindon to promotion to the top division in 1993, he had put a spark into Chelsea, reaching the FA Cup final in 1995 and the Cup-Winners' Cup semi-final the following year. An international player with over 50 caps to his credit, he had played abroad, in Monaco, worked for a few different managers and technically he was a very gifted footballer.

Despite all the pluses, though, I had been warned that he could be a bit stand-offish, perhaps a touch arrogant, and that he couldn't be told – he knew everything. However, after our first meeting, I decided he was a confident person and I was impressed with his football and personal qualifications. Our second get-together took place at his home in Ascot, not far from the racecourse. It was the first time I had ever been to Ascot. He had a beautiful home and seemed the perfect family man with a wife and three children, another thing I warmed to. In fact, if you'd told me he would no longer be with that family in four years' time, I simply would not have believed you.

Our third and final meeting took place in a disused car park somewhere near Ascot. It was a hot day and we ambled around and chatted, and then talked a bit more while we sat on the bonnet of my car. Obviously, in all our conversations, football was the main priority. I wanted to learn about his thoughts on the game, players, England's chances, how he would do the job and his relations with the media. How would he react on the plane home after a defeat in some far-flung corner of Europe? How would he spend his time between matches? Would his wife and family be able to cope if he was struggling? Things like that are important. We talked about other non-football issues, too. That was an aspect of all my interviews in 1993 and 1996. I wanted to find out about the man, not just the football coach. I would try to throw in difficult questions to see how each one reacted. I remember saying to Glenn, 'You say you're religious but you don't go to church. Why not?' He gave me a plausible answer about his faith and what he believed. I soon learned that he was a deep thinker.

There appeared to be no skeletons in the cupboard and he agreed to meet the chairman and Graham Kelly. I went back home to Blackpool and I must admit I wrestled with the decision for a while. With Venables, I was convinced we had found the right man at the right time. With Glenn, I wondered if he would stay for four or five years, which is what we were looking for. But I warmed to him, and frankly, I didn't have a long list of candidates. He was strong and it was not necessarily a bad thing that he was a bit opinionated – that meant he was probably pretty thick-skinned, too. So I recommended him for an interview and after meeting the committee, he was given the nod.

One of his first requests was to meet the England squad. Terry was still in charge as the build-up to Euro '96 gathered momentum but Glenn wanted to join in at the training camp, to start working with the players and get to know them on a personal level. It was a peculiar request in some ways and I could understand why Terry wasn't keen. However, after we had talked it over, he agreed to allow Glenn to go to Burnham Beeches, the team hotel, for one visit to say hello to the men who would be playing a World Cup qualifier for him against Moldova in three months' time. That's as far as it went. It was a strange period, the only time England have had two managers. I think Venables was a bit miffed about Glenn being appointed before he had left – but what else could we have done? Nobody wanted England to win Euro '96 more than I did because I had been the driving force behind Terry's appointment. If he had won, it would have reflected on me and, of course, as an Englishman and former England captain, I wanted the team to win a major tournament for the first time since 1966. But Terry was leaving and we had to move on.

After the championship, there was a huge sense of anti-climax. The whole country knew how close we had been and the players must have been very disappointed, too. Yet Glenn had to come in and prepare them straightaway for World Cup qualifying. He changed a few things around with the backroom staff – out went Ted Buxton and Don Howe and in came John Gorman and Ray Clemence, and Peter Taylor to run the Under-21s – but basically he stuck with the same players. He inherited a decent team, organised them in his own way and they did well for him. It was an awkward qualifying group that included Georgia, Moldova, Poland and Italy and a lot of people thought we might not make it. I certainly wasn't the only one who was anxious before the first match in Moldova.

We didn't know much about them but Glenn had used his contacts to obtain videos from UEFA, England won 3–0 at a canter and the disappointments of Euro '96 were forgotten. Terry had raised expectations and gone close but in one match, Glenn had moved the same players on. The expectancy was high but he handled it well. We beat Poland 2–1 at Wembley, won 2–0 in Georgia but lost at home to Italy to a goal by Gianfranco Zola.

That game certainly sticks in my memory, not least because it took me eight and a half hours to reach Wembley from Blackpool, a journey that normally takes about half that time. The motorways were gridlocked and I was stuck in a traffic jam five miles from Wembley for 90 minutes. When I finally made it to my seat, the teams were being announced and I couldn't believe what I was hearing. Glenn had changed the set-up, bringing in Matthew Le Tissier on the right flank, which altered the pattern that had proved so successful in the previous three games. I didn't ask why he had changed things but whatever his reason, it didn't work and defeat left us with a lot to do. But that was Hoddle, he'd made up his own mind.

Nevertheless, he bounced back. We beat Georgia again, 2–0 at Wembley, won 2–0 in Poland and, during the summer of 1997, won Le Tournoi in France, a competition that also featured

Brazil, Italy and France. After beating Moldova 4–0 at Wembley in the penultimate qualifier, we went to Rome for the last game in good heart, needing a draw to reach France and the World Cup finals. The *Azzurri* were on a high at the time. They had enjoyed a good World Cup in the USA three years earlier, losing to Brazil on penalties in the final, and Juventus and AC Milan formed the power base of European football. Although the game finished 0–0, it was probably Hoddle's finest hour. In the very last minute, Christian Vieri missed a straightforward chance and I remember thinking to myself, 'Glenn has that extra bit of luck that could be vital.' There's an old football saying, better to be a lucky manager than a good one. When we arrived home, I had a quiet word with him.

'The 1998 World Cup is going to be played on our doorstep and I reckon we might do well.'

'I'm sure we'll do well,' he replied. The confidence factor was coming through and the players were buoyant.

In France, we made it through the group stage comfortably enough, even though we lost to Romania. We defeated Tunisia and Colombia to earn a tie with Argentina in St Etienne in the last 16. I was working for the BBC at the Argentina match, doing half-time and full-time radio reports, and it was the first time I had been to St Etienne since a pre-season game with Leeds back in the mid-seventies. I had lunch with Alan Green before heading for the media centre where it was the usual scrummage, caused mainly by people who have no real right to be there, a growing frustration at World Cup matches.

The game should have been one of the high spots of Glenn's career but it proved to be one of the lowest. After Gabriele Batistuta had given Argentina an early lead, we hit back through Alan Shearer. Michael Owen scored a wonderful goal to put us in front but Javier Zanetti equalised on the stroke of half-time. Then, early in the second half, David Beckham was sent off for nothing more than petulance in a tangle with Diego Simeone. I still can't understand the red-card decision. It made no football sense. Beckham didn't really do anything worse than flick out with his foot, catching the Argentine player's leg. It wasn't a deliberate kick at an opponent. It was immature and he deserved a yellow card – nothing more. So did Simeone for diving and bringing the game into disrepute. Instead, the referee, Kim Milton Nielsen, chose to play it strictly by the book and, in doing so, illustrated how refereeing to the letter of the law has become part of the modern professional game. So with 10 men, we had a late goal by Sol Campbell disallowed and missed out in the penalty shoot-out. On reflection, Beckham's dismissal was vital.

At the end, I felt total disappointment and made a point of seeking out Glenn. Until then, I had kept a low profile. When England beat Holland 4–1 at Wembley in Euro '96, it never entered my head to go down to the interview zone to give my views as the man behind the appointment of the triumphant Venables; nor would I have hung around if things had gone badly. Right from the start, I made it a policy to stay away from the interviews and the dressing room. But in St Etienne, I decided to break my own rule and drifted down to the interview zone, primarily to offer a few words of consolation to Glenn. As the players walked through, he spotted me, came over and shook my hand. I told him not to worry. I said he would be OK. It never occurred to me that this was the beginning of the end. On the media coach back to Paris, one or two pressmen were discussing whether Glenn would stay on but I didn't believe it would be an issue. I accepted that the honeymoon was over but thought he was safe in the job because, for the most part, the players and the country were behind him.

But the tide was turning. One or two people in the media began to raise doubts about Glenn and soon the spotlight fell on Eileen Drewery, the faith healer he had recruited to help his players' mental preparations. The press wouldn't let it go. I don't profess to know what Glenn had in mind when he appointed her but we can be a bit insular in this country and until recently we have not really recognised that there is a psychological side to professional sport. There always has been – particularly when a player reaches the international arena. Just as there is a world of difference between county cricket and Test cricket, so there is a big step-up between the Premiership and international football, and part of that gap is psychological.

Putting on an England shirt can create pressure on some players and they have to be able to handle it on and off the field. From my own experience, particularly as an England captain, I know how difficult it can be. For example, when I played away from home in league matches, the fans were waiting to pounce on any individual errors I made. Johnny Haynes and Bobby Moore endured the same level of criticism, especially when they played up north. Nothing has changed today. Beckham experienced it when he was at Manchester United, particularly in Yorkshire, on Merseyside or in the north-east.

Players must learn to live with national and international criticism as opposed to the local criticism to which they are usually subjected. They have to conquer the fear of failure. Glenn knew these elements existed when he took the job and though they didn't worry him, he was concerned they might affect his players. Presumably that's why he engaged Eileen Drewery. But her involvement aroused a lot of media interest, conjecture and, after England's elimination, hostility. People started to question her role and Glenn's suitability for the job. He never involved me at all and I didn't raise the subject with him.

It was his decision, as was the *World Cup Diary* he had been writing during the competition with David Davies, the FA's director of public affairs. Before it was published, I had a chat with Graham Kelly and suggested the book might raise a few questions but Graham couldn't understand what I was fussing about. He reminded me that England managers had written during their time in the job before, citing Bobby Robson as an example. Of course, he was right. There had been no witchhunt on that occasion but somehow I suspected that this time it might just be different. Times had changed and some in the media claimed Glenn was out of order as soon as they learned about the book. They alleged that by keeping a diary during the competition, he was betraying dressing-room secrets and breaking precious confidences between a coach and his players. I sensed a problem as one story followed another.

The book came out two months after England's elimination

and, in truth, it wasn't particularly controversial. Even so, it contained more than enough for Hoddle's critics in the press, a few of whom had not been best pleased with some of his briefings during France '98. Publication on 1 September cranked up the anti-Hoddle lobby another notch or two. All Glenn needed was for performances to suffer and there would be enough ammunition to knock the manager off his perch.

The FA had seconded me to the PFA in Manchester soon after the World Cup to head up their coaching department so I had to observe Glenn's downfall from a distance of 200 miles. Clearly, support for him was dwindling and, on top of his problems with the media, he didn't seem to enjoy the happiest of relationships with Howard Wilkinson, the FA technical director. I had been behind the appointment of Wilkinson in January 1997, seeing him as a man who could take the national coaching scheme forward following the retirement of his predecessor, Charles Hughes. Charles was a brilliant administrator but I believed Wilkinson, a former player and manager, a qualified teacher and chairman of the League Managers' Association, would be a more acceptable face for the professional game.

Howard was keen to expand the role of technical director to include the running of England's junior sides and felt the Under-21 squad should have been his responsibility. Glenn, however, was determined to have Peter Taylor in charge. It reached the point where Hoddle didn't always attend technical meetings and Howard sometimes missed England matches. It was clearly an unsatisfactory situation and after the World Cup, Graham Kelly told me he had spoken to Glenn and Howard, urging them to work more closely together. Things improved but it was never an easy peace.

To make matters worse for Glenn, we lost in Sweden in the first qualifying game for Euro 2000 and drew with Bulgaria at Wembley. People, including me, started to question whether or not we would reach the finals, and it was evident Glenn was under pressure for the first time. One of the final nails went into the coffin at the end of January 1999. Matt Dickinson, the man who had replaced me at the *Daily Express* before moving on to *The Times*, wrote a feature in which Hoddle suggested that disabled people might be paying for misdemeanours in a previous life. His remarks sparked furious protests. People openly suggested that he had lost the plot and even Prime Minister Tony Blair came out in strong condemnation. Glenn immediately apologised for giving offence to the disabled but the damage had been done. I sat and watched it all unfurl right up to the final, fateful press conference at the Royal Lancaster Hotel on 2 February when Glenn announced his resignation. I felt sorry it had ended this way. He could have done well and, in the end, it was all a bit of a waste.

When I had first interviewed Glenn, I wondered whether he would be resilient enough. He was a bit of a loner but the quality that some people called arrogance was, in fact, a deep-seated conviction and he was prepared to stand by that conviction at all costs. He had an ego but he wasn't afraid of getting it scarred. We had a good professional relationship, never particularly close, but I wasn't necessarily looking for friendship. All I was interested in was finding a manager who would do a good job for England. From the start, he worked hard, got the team organised, lifted players who had suffered disappointment at Euro '96 and qualified well for the 1998 World Cup in France, where we went out in the last 16 in controversial circumstances on a penalty shoot-out. After losing the England job, Glenn had a spell at Southampton before returning to his roots at Tottenham, but he left after a bad start to the 2003–04 season.

Hardly had the dust settled on his departure from the England post than I was asked by a journalist in the north-east if it was true that Bert Millichip, David Davies and Howard Wilkinson were on their way north to offer the job to Kevin Keegan, at the time manager of Newcastle United. The reporter asked if I would be going to Newcastle, too, but I told him I was working at the PFA in Manchester and knew nothing about it. I was not consulted about offering the job to Kevin and if I had been, I might have counselled against rushing in. Don't get me wrong. I like Kevin and he has done a lot of good things for the English game as a player and manager, but I wondered about him for the

England job, mainly because I wasn't totally convinced that he would really want it. He seemed settled at Newcastle. I hoped some of his infectious enthusiasm and bouncy personality would rub off on his players and, in some ways, it did. But he came under fire in the media and his record of seven wins and four defeats in 18 matches did little to deter his critics. In the end, after less than 18 months in the job, I think he decided he had just had enough and could live without the hassle. History shows that when Kevin feels like that, he walks away.

Kevin's final game in charge, the last match to be played at the old Wembley Stadium, was a day I'll never forget. To lose to the Germans of all people in a World Cup qualifier was no way to say farewell to a venue that held so many happy memories for so many people. Afterwards, I went for a meal in the stadium restaurant to find all my FA colleagues and indeed everyone connected with the England set-up totally subdued. I felt a bit like jumping off one of the twin towers, too, but I did my best to cheer people up. All was not lost. We'd bounced back from worse situations and if Germany could win at Wembley, we could go over there and do the same to them. But nothing could lighten the gloom and I sensed that something momentous had happened, a feeling confirmed by Adam Crozier, the FA chief executive. Adam could usually be relied on to see the bright side of life, but not this time.

'Kevin's resigned,' he told me.

'Resigned to what?' I asked, thinking he meant Keegan was accepting our fate.

'No,' said Adam. 'He's resigned as England manager.' I could hardly believe what I was hearing.

'Look, I'll go downstairs and see him, try to talk him out of it,' I offered.

'It's no good, he's already told the players.'

Under those circumstances, I would clearly have been wasting my time if I had tried to persuade Keegan to think again.

So between January 1994 and October 2000, England had appointed and lost three managers, none of whom had been a total disaster. Venables had reached the semi-final of the European Championship and lost on penalties, Hoddle had taken his team to the last 16 of the World Cup and when Keegan departed, England still had a chance of qualifying for the 2002 World Cup finals, as his successor proved. For one reason or another, however, all three had left and it was time to start all over again. Adam believed we should look outside England but I disagreed. 'Fans in this country will never accept an outsider as the England manager,' I told him. I was wrong. Sven Goran Eriksson was named as the new England coach less than a month later, although he did not officially take charge until January 2001, and there was very little opposition to the FA's decision, particularly among younger supporters.

On his first day at the new FA headquarters in Soho Square, I happened to be having a meeting with Adam, who said he had arranged for me to talk to Sven. So I went up to his office, we shook hands and I said something along the lines of what a pleasure it was to meet him.

'So you don't remember me, then?' Sven replied. I had to admit I didn't. 'When I was a player in Sweden, wanting to become a coach, I wrote to several big clubs in England asking if I could come over and watch their training methods. You were the manager of Leeds United at the time and you said yes. I spent two days at Elland Road and it's something I have always been grateful for. I have never forgotten.'

In common with many leading European coaches, Sven was not a top player but I respected his work as a coach, with Swedish club Gothenburg, Benfica in Portugal and four *Serie A* clubs in Italy – Roma, Fiorentina, Sampdoria and Lazio. He was success-ful in his first mission, which was to qualify for the World Cup finals – and any lingering doubts that any England supporters may have been harbouring about the appointment of a foreign coach evaporated after that 5–1 victory over Germany in Munich in September 2001. That must be one of the most incredible results in English football history. I thought Sven did a reasonable job in Japan and South Korea, qualifying well from an awkward group involving Argentina, Nigeria and Denmark, but, yet again, England could not sustain their early promise.

One of the problems facing the England manager these days is that he is short of options where players are concerned. There simply aren't as many quality English players to choose from as there were in the past – and it's the same in Scotland. In one way, that can be a good thing because it can bolster team spirit. But England players will invariably be chosen from Premiership clubs and if a large percentage of players at those clubs are from overseas, the number at the manager's disposal will inevitably be seriously restricted. Many Premiership matches feature just a handful of English players and there was a time when supporters would not have been happy about that. It doesn't seem to matter any more, though.

I believe that an English club side should be required to have a minimum number of English players in the starting line-up and the same should apply in all countries. I think it's something FIFA and UEFA may well address over the next few years, although there's no sign of it at the moment. They have a responsibility to the future of football and it is important that a country such as England should continue to produce its own players and not rely too heavily on foreign imports. I hope that the academy system will eventually bear fruit but at the moment there are not enough players coming through at some of our biggest clubs – and obviously the increasing reliance on foreigners has a lot to do with this. If there is a gap on the playing staff, a manager tends to go out and sign a ready-made foreign star instead of promoting a youngster from the reserves or signing a young player from the lower divisions. There's no waiting time in the Premiership. Success has to be instantaneous and not many home-grown players come through the system and establish themselves in the first team. That can't be good for the long-term prospects of the English game and the England team.

Having said that, I don't dispute that playing with and against some of the best performers in the world has had a beneficial effect on established players. Thierry Henry, Gianfranco Zola, Ruud van Nistelrooy and Patrick Vieira, for instance, have been outstanding footballers who have raised the standards on the field, in training and in the way players conduct themselves. Players of that calibre take other players along with them in the way that Matthews and Mortensen used to do at Blackpool when

I was a youngster. The same applies to leading foreign coaches. But there has to be a balance.

People from my generation would also be happier if we had a home-grown England coach. I accept that patriotism is an old-fashioned concept for some people but in my opinion everyone involved with the England football team should be English – from the manager to the man who carries the kit. Isn't that the whole point of international football? This is not a personal criticism of Eriksson, the first foreigner to be appointed. I like him. But I do believe that we should be able to provide our own team manager. There are English managers out there who need to prove themselves at the top level and one of them should be in charge of the national side, although in the end it's having good players that really matters.

CHAPTER 18

THE WAY WE ARE

On my occasional ventures into the world of after-dinner speaking, I usually say somewhere along the line: 'I suppose most of you will be thinking that I'm a bit envious because the likes of David Beckham earned more in the close season than I did in the whole of my career, and that I wished I was playing now. You can bet your damned life I do!'

I mean it, too. There has never been a better time to be a top-class footballer in this country. Players today are well paid, facilities at the top clubs especially are excellent and the pitches bear no comparison to the surfaces on which I was sometimes required to perform. Training and coaching methods are more advanced, the treatment of injuries is better and the players are encouraged to look after themselves properly. The big clubs have a far higher profile than ever before. No longer just a part of the community, they are famous throughout the world. The stadiums are first-class and the presentation of the game at the highest level has improved out of all recognition. In fact, the whole package is unrecognisable even from my time as a manager.

The lifestyle and earning power of today's stars are things that many players of my generation, brought up in an era of post-war austerity and the maximum wage, find hard to come to terms with. When I talk to them about it, they almost always react with a bemused shake of the head. But I don't have a problem with it.

Working with the FA, the PFA and the BBC has made me move with the game and the times.

I am still involved with the FA and the PFA, albeit on a part-time basis, and as well as helping the FA to appoint two England managers, I have sat on the Technical Control Board, the Technical Liaison Committee and the International Committee. I have also been a consultant to the chief executive, worked on the coaching side and supported the former National School of Excellence at Lilleshall. I also used to visit the French national school at Clairefontaine. French football was very strong and we felt it would be beneficial to see how their development programme worked. Gerard Houllier, a former French national coach later to become manager of Liverpool, was in charge of the centre at the time. I worked closely with Adam Crozier when he succeeded Graham Kelly as the FA chief executive in 1999. I liked Adam a lot. He was very go-ahead, a younger man who genuinely liked football and was prepared to make changes to the way the FA was run. Together with Howard Wilkinson, the FA technical director, he put forward the proposal to set up a national football centre near Burton upon Trent in Staffordshire.

In the early 1990s, the PFA started its own coaching development programme headed by Paul Power, the former Manchester City and Everton player. When he decided to move on in the late nineties, Gordon Taylor, the chief executive of the PFA, approached the FA to see if I would be available to take over on a secondment, based in Manchester. I've been there ever since and while my colleagues Joe Joyce and Julian Hayes have taken over the day-to-day running of the scheme, I am still very much involved. Our courses enable professional footballers to gain full coaching qualifications, something I have always felt strongly about. I attend some of the courses, help with the admin and run the department's website. I like to think that as coaching methods have changed, I have changed with them – and I certainly don't see myself as purely an elder statesman in either organisation.

So I feel almost as involved as I did 50 years ago, albeit in a very different role, and I say good luck to all the players who are making big money today. I don't envy their wage packets and lifestyles one little bit. Times change but football doesn't and they all know that they could suffer a career-threatening injury or, as the demands for success increase, find themselves without a contract. There has always been a risk factor from the day the first ball was kicked.

Football plays a giant role in English society these days and almost everyone has at least a passing interest. Fifty years ago it was a game played mainly by the working class for the amusement of the working and middle classes, and in my early days there were very few women spectators. My teachers at Arnold School actually did their best to dissuade me from a career in football because it wasn't seen as a suitable way for a grammar school boy to make a living. How times have changed. Football is now big business and everyone seems to want a slice of the action. In fact, peers of the realm, cabinet ministers, actors, film stars, pop stars and all the other so-called celebrities are falling over themselves to be associated with a Premiership football club because it's fashionable to be linked with the game, however tenuous that link may be. How long it will last, I don't know. We live in a world of supply and demand and fashions do change.

In my day, we never had more than a handful of celebrity supporters following Blackpool even though we were one of the most glamorous clubs in the land. The comedian Al Read lived in St Annes and he was a regular at Bloomfield Road. On one trip to London, the team went to his show at the Adelphi Theatre on the Friday night and Al picked us out in the audience, saying, 'There they are, Blackpool FC. They're down here to beat Chelsea tomorrow!' Norman Evans, the famous pantomime dame, was another of our fans and Cheerful Charlie Chester was a big pal of Stanley Matthews. Charlie stayed with Stan whenever he was doing a season at one of the Pier shows and came along to our matches.

I can't remember many more well-known fans whereas today a football match, with the television cameras present, offers a heaven-sent opportunity for celebs to see and be seen. To be fair, some of the celebrity fans have always been passionate about the game. Rod Stewart, for example, is a fully paid-up member of

Scotland's Tartan Army. He was sitting in the seat immediately behind me at England's Euro '96 game against Scotland and, believe me, he's a true fan – he was absolutely gutted when England scored. When the Scots missed a penalty he buried his head in his hands and I couldn't resist turning round to ask, 'You're not really enjoying this, are you?' I expect he would have liked to respond with a few well-chosen expletives but he could not even speak. Football is in the blood of the nation and Rod was demonstrating how much it means to so many people.

When I was a boy, cricket had a claim to being our national sport – it may have been once but it hasn't attracted the same number of people as football. Numbers alone mean that title can only belong to football. It's incredible how many people watch, play, coach, referee, run a local club, mark out the pitches or clean the kit every weekend. We have boys' teams, girls' teams, men's teams, women's teams, professionals, part-timers and amateurs, and a sizeable percentage of the population is involved in football in some capacity in any one week. The game used to take a breather between the Cup final in early May and the start of the new season in late August, World Cup years excepted. The nation put football on the back-burner, concentrating on five Test matches, Wimbledon tennis, the Open Championship, the British Grand Prix, the Derby and all the other great events of the summer sporting calendar – not any more. In 2003, Tim Henman reached the last eight of the men's singles at Wimbledon for the seventh time in eight years, an incredible achievement for a player from a nation that seems to think tennis exists for two weeks a year. Yet even the annual outbreak of Henmania was shunted aside by the news that Chelsea had been taken over by a Russian billionaire. The game has a hold on the nation's sporting pulse that no other sport has ever attained.

Television companies fight one another for the right to broadcast big games that will be watched by millions in homes, pubs, clubs, even on giant screens in city centres. Some fans have become almost professional supporters, arranging their work and leisure time around a football club, hating to miss a match all season – even though games are played every day of the week and there's no way of knowing how matches might be re-arranged from the original fixture list. I've no idea how they manage it. We are a great spectator nation. No other country in Europe can match the English attendances in so many major sports. We love our sport and when the big event comes along we are out in force. It's a slight change from my day when we didn't have as much money – and we preferred to play rather than watch.

Football club directors can be paid now and are more than happy to bask in their share of the limelight. Their role has changed. In my day, they were mainly background men you heard about occasionally or local businessmen who came to watch the match on a Saturday and met once a week to discuss team affairs with the manager and the business side of the club with the secretary. They were rarely high-profile people. A typical example was England selector Harold Shentall, a greengrocer, director of Chesterfield and a member of the FA International Committee. Dear old Harold came on England trips wearing a three-piece suit and his bowler hat. A gold pocket watch and chain adorned the waistcoat he always wore, whatever the weather. The archetypal director of his day.

In my playing days, the only things you could buy at a match, apart from a ticket, were a programme, a pie and a cup of tea. Now the marketing of the game has been transformed to the point where representatives from several leading Spanish and Italian clubs have visited these shores to see how our top clubs run their superstores. Clearly we have beaten them to the drop. Everything in football is now spoken about in millions of pounds, from transfer fees to gate receipts, and with that comes the downside – debts. To the ordinary man in the street, it must seem as though the money, the high profile and TV exposure have taken the game into a fantasy world, but I don't see football as fantasy. Because one thing can never change – it will always be 11 against 11 as played by the likes of Billy Meredith, Hughie Gallacher and Alex James, men who made their names before I was even born.

Whether the standard of the game out there on the pitch is better than it has ever been is another matter. It's quicker and teams are better organised but there is a shortage of players who can dribble and leave defenders trailing. The change of rules has meant there is less tackling but there is more top-of-the-ground passing and retaining possession than there was in my time. But I can still see men like Greaves, Law, Best, Douglas and Charlton from my era being stars in today's game. Yet while we are constantly being told that English football is the strongest in the world and the Premiership the best league of them all, we haven't won the World Cup since 1966. In 1990, when Bobby Robson's team reached the semi-finals of the World Cup and lost on penalties, I thought we were the strongest side in the competition but we still didn't win it. Six years later, we suffered the same fate in the European Championship when we should have been favourites because we were the host nation. We have not seriously threatened to go any further since then, and just scraped into the finals of the 2002 World Cup with a draw against Greece thanks to a last-minute Beckham free-kick in a match we didn't deserve to win. By the highest standards, England have been pretty ordinary and, of our top clubs, only Liverpool and Manchester United have made a consistent impact in Europe since 1966, while Celtic have flown the flag for Scotland. Yet that doesn't seem to affect the fans, who roll up at Premiership grounds week after week and sit glued to their television screens for hours. Everybody, it seems, has an opinion on football. So have I and here are some of them.

Today's players: Some, especially the imports, appear to be little more than mercenaries, happy to join a club, play for a couple of years, make their money and then move on and start all over again, in another country if necessary. That's up to them. It's a short career and players should make what they can while they can. These days, the top players tend to gravitate to the élite clubs who win the trophies whereas in my time many top internationals played for smaller clubs and never received a winner's medal of any kind. That applied to my predecessors as England captain, Ronnie Clayton and Johnny Haynes, not to mention Bryan Douglas, Ron Springett, Bobby Robson and Tom Finney. Nat Lofthouse, Tom Finney and I, among many others, only ever played for one club, but life was different then. There was no freedom of contract and the clubs had total control. When Finney was approached by Italian club Palermo in the fifties, he asked Preston if he could talk to them. Preston said no and that was the end of it. Since I retired, I have often asked myself whether I would have remained with one club if I had been free to move on at the end of my contract. The answer is probably not.

However, I wonder if today's top players think about what will happen when they finish playing and are faced with the question, 'Where do I go from here?' My generation had a similar problem but most knew what was coming. If they decided not to stay in the game, they had to go out and get a job or start a business. Of my colleagues at Blackpool, Ray Charnley became a decorator, Glyn James ran a launderette and Johnny McPhee had a hotel. My England team-mates were the same. Douglas had a job with a firm of stationers, Roger Hunt ran a haulage company, Clayton bought a newsagent's, John Connelly opened a fish and chip shop and Ian Callaghan took a pub, a popular choice for many players of my era. Even England's World Cup winners didn't retire to a life of luxury, far from it. They had to work for a living when they quit the game. Geoff Hurst, Wembley hat-trick hero, worked for an insurance company. The Leeds United players who reached the European Cup final in 1975 all had to go out and find work.

That won't necessarily apply to today's top players, provided they look after their money, but I believe they could face a potentially bigger problem than their predecessors did. The adulation is massive and the big names live in the constant glare of publicity and enjoy celebrity status. They are superstars. One morning, though, they will wake up to discover they are *former* superstars, no longer in demand, and handling that won't be easy. Having a few million pounds in the bank will help but money never has been everything, it never will be, and there will still be a huge void in their live. Unless they manage to stay in the game, they may find it hard to adapt. It's an issue I have discussed with Gordon Taylor at the PFA and I feel it is important that modern players should have some idea of what may be in store for them.

Finishing playing wasn't easy for me so I know what lies ahead for them. When it comes it is a jolt to the system.

The Premier League: For the players, the Premier League arrived at the perfect time. Its birth more or less coincided with the start of Sky Television and also with the breaking down of transfer boundaries because of the Bosman ruling. The door opened for players to trip backwards and forwards across Europe and to be seen on countless television channels. Instead of the BBC and ITV squabbling between themselves over rights, there was a serious competitor in Sky and, consequently, the money available rocketed. The Premier League saw what was on offer, said thank you very much and the Football League clubs had no option but to accept the new regime. It's been particularly good for the Premiership clubs, especially the élite few who monopolise the silverware. Whether it's been a good thing for all 92 clubs is another matter.

Back at the start of the 1970–71 season, my last as a player, it was virtually impossible to predict the First Division champions with any degree of certainty. You could make out a reasonable case for any one of a dozen clubs. It's not the same today when, because of the money involved, success for many teams simply amounts to Premiership survival. Nevertheless, fans still flock to the grounds week in and week out to support a team they know hasn't the slightest chance of winning the title. There was a time when supporters would start to drift away if it became obvious that their team was not going to be challenging for honours, but not now. At the start of each season, I am usually asked on the radio to suggest which club will win the title, and it has become one of the easier questions to answer. The statistics show that since the Premier League began in 1992–93, Manchester United have been the dominant force, winning the title eight times in the first 11 seasons. We used to laugh about the way a few clubs monopolised the championship in Italy, Spain and Portugal but now it's happening here. The big-city clubs, those with most money, hold sway and with reasonable management should continue to do so. Every so often a club from outside the élite group may break the monopoly, as Blackburn did in 1995. But could they do it again? Not unless they find another Jack Walker. To make it even more galling for the rest, home success means the big clubs monopolise entry to the Champions League, where even bigger rewards await them. Incredibly, if they are knocked out at the first attempt, they are currently given another chance with free entry into the UEFA Cup. I can't understand the thinking behind that and, to me, it has totally devalued the UEFA Cup.

Nevertheless, it has to be said the Premier League has been a massive success and it has become the centrepiece in football in this country. It dominates the TV money because the Premiership is home to the top players. That's why many people in the game regard it as a thoroughbred – but I know that many others lower down the ladder regard it as more of a runaway horse.

Referees: In my playing days, it was a major event when a player was booked. These days they could employ croupiers as referees, given the number of cards they flourish over 90 minutes. A booking doesn't seem to mean anything any more. I collected one booking in 17 years, in a cup tie against Norwich, and the following day's headlines were along the lines of 'England skipper booked as Blackpool crash out'. Football was much tougher then and you had to learn to take care of yourself. There were no television cameras to expose what was going on off the ball. Early in my career, I came up against Jimmy Scoular, captain of Newcastle, in a game at St James' Park. Scoular was a wonderful personality who did a lot of work for charity. We once bumped into him on a family holiday in Camp de Mar in Majorca when Duncan and John were small. Jim and his family were marvellous company – Anne and I can still recall our sore heads after a night on the champagne cocktails with Scoular. But he didn't take any prisoners on the pitch, as I discovered when I skipped past him at the Gallowgate end, crossed from the right, saw their goalkeeper Ronnie Simpson tip the cross over the bar and then felt the impact of Scoular's challenge. Everybody else, including the referee, was watching the ball. We wrestled around on the floor for a few seconds before I staggered to my feet and limped away.

'Have I hurt you?' called Scoular.

'No.'

'Then why are you limping?'

As I did my best to hobble away, I had the temerity to answer, 'Don't worry, I'll soon run that off.'

You never let anyone know he had hurt you – not even Jimmy Scoular – and one of the standing jokes of the time was to refer to a player as the late Charlie Smith. 'Has he died?' was the next line, which elicited the response, 'No, that's just the way he tackles!'

It was accepted that football was a tough game and there was no point moaning about the kind of challenges that would mean an instant red card these days. What's more, the referee's decision was final. Few players dived and no one ever asked the referee to book an opponent. I hate that.

Yet even though the game is less physical, I still think that today's referee has a far more difficult job than his counterpart of 40 years ago when there were no television action replays for the pundits to analyse and no assessor in the stand watching his every move. I recall in one game, at Bolton, one of their players took a piece out of me early on. I waited a while and then had a go back and we niggled on for a few minutes before the referee, that wily old Yorkshireman Arthur Ellis, stepped in.

'Come here you two,' he said. 'Right, I've seen what's going on. You had the first go and [pointing at me] you had a go back – next time it will be my turn. Now beggar off!'

We took it in good faith and got on with the game. Quite what today's assessor in the stand would have made of Arthur's handling of the incident is a moot point but it worked. Arthur was free to adopt a common-sense approach and we both accepted it.

These days, referees do not have the same freedom because there are so many guidelines laid down. I believe we have reached the stage where referees should at least be allowed to take advantage of goal-line technology. Constant television replays of an incident can only serve to undermine the authority of the officials. If the TV analysts can have the benefit of an action replay, so should the referee. Equally, the speed of the game is such that the time is approaching when we should perhaps consider having a referee in each half.

While I sympathise with referees in many ways, however, I'm not convinced that having an élite group of officials controlling Premiership matches has been a step in the right direction. It's the élite looking after the élite. Call it human nature if you like, but I suspect a few have been affected by constant exposure on television. Some even employ an agent. Then there is the issue of neutrality. An arbiter in any sport should be strictly neutral but I have heard Football League people moaning about Premiership officials when the FA Cup and League Cup come around – and vice versa. Why have an élite group in the first place?

The England captaincy: It used to be the greatest honour in the game but nowadays we sometimes have three or four captains in a single friendly match. I hate to see the skipper's armband being tossed about – sometimes it even lands on the pitch. Being chosen to captain your country is something to be earned and to be proud of. It was certainly a tremendous honour for me. Billy Wright and Bobby Moore were chosen because of their performances at club and international level, and also because of their standing in the game and their powers of leadership. It's up to players like David Beckham and his successors to follow their example.

Of course at one time, it would have been inconceivable for the captain of England to play for a foreign club …but football has changed and Beckham is one of the people who have changed it. His career is something of a football phenomenon, and that has nothing to do with whether or not he's a better player than Stanley Matthews, George Best, Bobby Charlton or, to give a more recent example, Gary Lineker. More than anyone else, he has changed the role of the professional footballer, giving it a much higher profile on the world stage. He must have one of the most instantly recognisable faces on the planet. He has a celebrity wife, he's a fashion icon and when he changes his hairstyle, millions copy him. Despite all the adulation, he has managed to retain his modesty, he is a good family man and he dotes on his children – qualities that have endeared him to millions of people.

He has also played for arguably the two most famous clubs in the world so it is important to recognise that it is not just a question of profile; he is a good footballer. If I had to analyse his game, I would say he is as accurate a crosser of a ball as I have ever seen. He bends the ball in, judges distances perfectly and has an uncanny ability to land crosses in the most difficult areas for defenders. His free-kicks are equally exceptional. I have seen some of the great free-kick artists in the last 50 years – Garrincha, Puskas and Rivelino to name three – and in my opinion Beckham is better than any of them. I have never seen a player hit the target more often in crucial situations from either side of the penalty area.

These qualities have not arrived by chance. Beckham is a true professional who has worked tirelessly to improve his game. He doesn't beat defenders with the ball and he isn't pacy, but he has compensated by practising what he is good at. In my early days at the FA, I sometimes used to go down to The Cliff to watch Manchester United train. Beckham was just a young lad working with youth coach Eric Harrison and I remember watching him practise those free-kicks. He would spend hours on the training ground and all that hard work has paid off for him. When he joined Real Madrid, he was given the chance to do something that few English players have achieved: become a real success in a foreign country.

Whatever, no player has achieved Beckham's profile in my lifetime. I suppose only George Best has come close to the level of publicity Beckham receives but the difference between the two is that Beckham has been sustained by his image as a loving husband and doting father. Best had more raw talent and it was that exciting natural ability plus his good looks that took him to where he was, but George on his own could never match the Beckhams.

Agents: They are everywhere these days, not just in football, and it appears to be almost impossible to speak face to face to anyone in sport or showbusiness without going through his or her agent first. I've never had any dealings with an agent in my life. The closest I came was at a dinner to raise money for the victims of the Valley Parade fire that claimed the lives of 56 Bradford City fans in 1985. I was one of the guest speakers and afterwards a chap came up and asked if he could be my agent. He said he could help me earn £500 a dinner, which was a lot of money in those days. I said no. I am often told by managers that dealing with agents can be a waking nightmare and I have no reason to doubt that claim. I have always preferred to stand on my own two feet and sort out my own life rather than rely on someone else to do it for me. But that's my belief – self-motivation is necessary if you want to make progress.

However, agents are here to stay and, as a result, they will affect the flow of money and of course it is in their interests to have their players moving around simply because they take a slice of the transfer fees. Nevertheless there are still quite a number of players who will remain loyal to their clubs although as soon as a pile of money appears, as it did at Chelsea in the summer of 2003, there will always be some who will volunteer to move ... it's just human nature.

European league: Over the last few years, there has been speculation about a European league, but I can't see the point. We currently have the Champions League, which involves the cream of European club football, and English spectators will roll up to watch Manchester United play AC Milan, Liverpool take on Real Madrid or Arsenal face Bayern Munich. But with the greatest of respect, the prospect of Manchester United playing Sturm Graz of Austria or Liverpool against Lille of France would not have the same appeal. When AC Milan, Real Madrid or any of the other big hitters are in town, it is a different story, but not all countries have a Milan or a Real. But if you have a European league, Austrian, Polish, Turkish and Slovakian clubs will feel they have just as much right to be there as anyone else – and so will UEFA.

All-seater stadiums: Those of us who witnessed the events at the Heysel Stadium in 1985 and Hillsborough four years later could never advocate the return of standing at a major football match. I had a clear view of the Hillsborough tragedy as it developed and it remains one of the worst things I have ever experienced. Investigators talked to me afterwards and I remember saying I thought the time had come for each person attending a football match to have his or her own space. I know fans still stand up but at least they have their own area and do not face the threat of being crushed by a pushing, swaying, out-of-control crowd.

I used to stand on the terraces as a lad and, like many people, I can recall with a hint of nostalgia how small boys were passed over the heads of the crowd so that they could see the match from the front. Yet there is a danger of looking at the past through rose-tinted spectacles, because I can also remember that it wasn't much fun down there at the front of a packed terrace when the crowd started to push and shove and sway. I know what supporters of the terraces mean about atmosphere – as would anyone who once stood on an upturned biscuit tin to catch a glimpse of the 1948 FA Cup semi-final at Villa Park – but safety must always be a priority.

The play-offs: They have been a success, especially with the fans, but as a football man I don't easily come to terms with the idea that a team finishing as low as seventh in Division Three, perhaps 12 points adrift of the fourth-placed club, can actually win promotion. Is it really a measure of success to finish sixth or seventh in the table – or are we just admitting that financial considerations are paramount? Why don't we have the top team winning automatic promotion with the next two playing off against the bottom two sides from the division above? But if the authorities insist that the play-offs should include teams from further down the table, why not go the whole hog and let the top half play off for the last promotion spot? That idea seems to have worked for the rugby league championship play-offs.

One popular argument in favour of the play-offs is that they prevent a string of meaningless matches for middle-of-the-table clubs at the end of the season. Meaningless matches? The end of the season used to be the time when managers of mid-table clubs gave young players a chance to show their capabilities. But now middle-of-the-table teams are fighting for a bit of extra prize money because the Football League ladder provides pounds for league positions. If the difference between finishing 13th and 11th is a few thousand pounds, directors are not going to be too impressed with a manager who wants to give the young hopefuls a chance. So they remain on the sidelines and, in the summer, managers end up signing ready-made players from abroad because they haven't given their own young players an opportunity. There should be far more young players coming through and fewer short-term measures.

While we're on the subject, to my mind, three up and three down was not a particularly progressive step. Many will disagree but I feel two up and two down brought more stability and I believe fewer clubs would have suffered financial problems if we had stuck with that system. There would be less temptation for clubs on the fringes to hit trouble by spending money they could not really afford, although, in saying that, football clubs do always seem to be able to find a route out of their problems. I've lost count of the times a club has been on the brink of extinction only for a rescue package to be put together at the 11th hour. That's why the retention of 92 professional clubs has been one of the real success stories of English football – it hasn't happened anywhere else and we should be proud of it and protect it. I don't see any need for Divisions Two and Three to go part-time.

Emerging nations: I expect Asian countries to start making a footballing impact soon and to perform strongly at the next two or three World Cups. The traditional power bases of Europe and South America could come under threat for the first time from Japan, South Korea, Malaysia, Thailand and China – not to mention Australia, South Africa and other African nations. There are a lot of European coaches working in developing countries and their influence is beginning to produce results.

Nearer to home, in Europe the competition is also getting tougher. Countries such as Malta, Cyprus and Luxembourg can't be rolled over any more. Even the smallest nation can usually find 11 players who are performing at a decent level somewhere in Europe. Bring them together, stir up a bit of national pride and that team can soon become an awkward hurdle.

I also expect FIFA to once again press for artificial pitches, probably in the next two or three years. Fortunately, the new version of these surfaces will bear little resemblance to the ones laid at Oldham, Luton, QPR and Preston in the eighties. The modern pitches are much closer to the real thing and FIFA may be swayed by the argument that their introduction will mean uniform surfaces around the world. Thus countries that face climate problems at various times of the year will not be penalised because they cannot grow grass to the required standard. I will need to be convinced.

Ticket prices: When wall-to-wall televised football was introduced in the early nineties, I was one of the people who expressed fears about overkill. I was genuinely worried that the people who rushed out to buy their Sky dishes and tuned in to every match and all the different football programmes would soon tire of the new phenomenon and eventually turn their backs on the game, both as viewers and spectators. I was wrong; professional football has never been so popular. Premiership gates rose in the first 10 years, even though prices have increased dramatically. In the early nineties, I recall covering a European game between Genoa and Liverpool as part of the BBC commentary team. At half-time, I started talking to an Italian fan in the stand nearby and asked him how much he had paid for his ticket. The answer was £40. I was stunned and said I could never envisage the day when tickets would cost anything like that in England, but it has happened now.

The FA Cup: The competition used to be all about romance and glory along the road to Wembley, the most famous stadium in the land, and I wonder if some of those elements will return to the competition when the new Wembley Stadium is completed. I hope so. I have no complaints about the Millennium Stadium in Cardiff. It's an excellent venue and far better than the old Wembley in its later days. But the move to Cardiff broke the FA Cup habit for a lot of people and the long-term appeal of the competition could depend on how the public responds to the new national stadium.

The third round of the FA Cup used to be one of the great events of the sporting calendar. If the draw resulted in a match between, for example, Bolton and Manchester United, the build-up would hog the headlines for several days. Now clubs like United are more interested in the Champions League and winning the Premiership, and Bolton's priority is staying in the Premiership because that's where the money is. Until the FA Cup reaches the quarter-final stage and a place in the final becomes a serious possibility, those priorities do not change. So the media concentrates on potential giant-killers and the FA Cup offers an opportunity for Football League clubs to move on to centre stage while the Premiership takes a breather.

Yet the FA Cup continues to demonstrate that, on the day, David can still beat Goliath and it remains one of football's most enduring and endearing traits. I have gone to games where the commentators have announced that the result is almost a foregone conclusion but I learned a long time ago that there is no such thing in football, and there never will be. Perhaps it's the size of the target area. Unlike the try-line in rugby or the boundary in cricket, the goal in football measures just 8 yards by 8ft and there is a man between the posts whose sole job is to prevent the other team from scoring. The stronger side may have 95 per cent of the possession, may camp in the opposition half and create dozens of chances, hit the woodwork and see the goalkeeper pull off a dozen outstanding saves. Then the underdog breaks away, wins a corner, the marking is slack, the ball ends up in the net and one player has grabbed the opportunity to write his name into football folklore.

At a much more exalted level, Geoff Hurst did that in the final of the World Cup. Geoff will forever be known as 'the man who scored a hat-trick in the World Cup final' and he has told me that hardly a day passes without someone reminding him of that magic moment. Even now, nearly 40 years after his goals won the World Cup for England, complete strangers approach him in the street and say, 'They think it's all over – it is now!' Nothing he does will change that. I've never possessed such a lavish claim to fame. I've been called the first overlapping full-back, the footballer who played the church organ, that chap from the radio, but I never seized the moment like Hurst did.

ALWAYS SOMETHING THERE TO REMIND ME

When I was young and not totally thrilled about the prospect of an hour's piano practice when I could have been outside playing football, my father used to say that, one day, I would be eternally grateful that I had learned to play a musical instrument. How right he was! Music has become an integral part of my life and I still find that one of the best ways to relax these days is to tinker on the piano for a little while, although the fingers aren't quite as supple as they used to be. I was sent for piano lessons when I was nine. My father's grocer's shop in Bairstow Street was more or less opposite the home of Mr Jones, a retired piano teacher. I don't recall ever knowing his first name. His son, Ivor, was my age and played the drums although not, I hasten to add, during my piano lessons. I still see Ivor occasionally. Mr Jones was well into his sixties when my father asked him if he would be interested in taking me on as a pupil and he agreed. I didn't have any say in the matter.

Mr Jones was from the old-fashioned school of piano teachers who believed in a complete musical education and a firm grounding in the theory of music, so much so that it was several weeks before I actually laid my hands on the keyboard. I had to learn how to write the treble and bass clefs, learn the notes, find out about sharps and flats and what all the musical terms such as andante and allegro meant. He taught me the names of all the instruments in each section of the orchestra. 'Right,' he would say, 'name me the strings section,' and I would have to list first violin, second violin, viola, cello, double bass and go on until I had named them all. At the next lesson he would ask for the brass section, then the woodwind and the percussion, and so on, until I knew every single instrument and its function. A lesson rarely passed without me having to recite at least one of the sections of the orchestra. He also introduced me to the history of music and the great composers, and he was always a stickler for theory.

'What was Chopin famous for?' he would ask.

'Piano music.'

'And what is Beethoven's Ninth Symphony also known as?'

'The Choral Symphony.'

'Very good. What is the key of G Major?'

'One sharp.'

'And the key of F Major?'

'One flat.'

'And what key has three flats?'

'E Major.'

I was learning parrot fashion, I suppose, but it worked. I've never forgotten what he taught me all those years ago.

Like most nine- and 10-year-olds, I was never too keen on practice when I got home from school but my father made sure I didn't skip it. He had been a musician all his life, which was no doubt why he was so keen for me to learn the piano, and played the violin to a reasonable standard. He used to select a simple piece from my book of music and stand behind me with his violin at the ready.

'Let's get the timing right first,' he would say. 'This piece is dah-dee-dah-dah-dee ...dah-dee-dah-dah-dee,' and away we would go, me on the piano, my father on the violin.

I wasn't a brilliant pianist by any means. I had probably reached around Grade Five by the age of 12 or 13, by which time Mr Jones, whom I liked, had become a bit exasperated. He had seen me forever kicking a ball against the wall and I can remember him saying to me after one lesson, 'Maybe your talents don't lie in your fingers after all, perhaps they lie in your feet.'

The first airing of my musical talents in public came in rather bizarre circumstances at St Peter's Church Sunday school. As a young teenager, Sunday school and the local youth club were the focal points of my social life – as they were for most lads of my age. That's where the girls were, after all. Bert Ellis, a lawyer, and his wife Mary ran the Sunday school. They were a friendly, caring couple who didn't have children of their own and the Sunday school was always a happy place to be. One day, Bert took me to one side and said, 'You play the piano, don't you?' I replied that I did, without quite appreciating what might come next. 'Good,' he said. 'We need someone to play one or two hymns. I'll give you the numbers of the hymns, you go away and practise them and then come along and play for us next Sunday.'

I must admit I was a bit uneasy about the arrangement – not least because I was unsure about how playing hymns on the piano would fit in with my image among my peers, male and female, at the Sunday school and youth club. But I was in no position to turn down his request and duly arrived the following week armed with my copy of *Hymns Ancient and Modern*. At the given moment, I took a deep breath and embarked on my solo career with hymn number 334, 'Loving Shepherd Of Thy Sheep' (in two sharps). The rest of the kids were aghast at the sight of Armfield sitting at the piano but they joined in and, oddly, nobody gave me any stick about it afterwards. So I continued to play at Sunday school until I was about 16. Then came the fateful day when the vicar, Ernest Roulson, approached me.

'We don't have an organist,' he said. 'Will you come and have a try?'

I decided this was a step too far. I'd never sat at the keyboard of an organ in my life.

'No,' I said. 'I'm sorry, I can't. I've never played the organ. I just don't know how.'

He clearly wasn't going to take no for an answer, though.

'Come on, of course you can,' he insisted. Vicars are obviously instructed to be persuasive.

So the following Sunday, up I went into the loft to be con-fronted by the St Peter's Church organ. It looked massive, with two keyboards, several rows of stops and, down at ground level, a set of foot pedals. It seemed like something from another planet at first but it didn't take me long to work out that the keys were the same as the piano and that if I ignored the second keyboard, the stops and foot pedals, I could probably get by. I struck my first note at 10 o'clock and, off I went, playing matins. With due deference to my inexperience, the vicar decided that the 'Te Deum' and 'Jubilate' should be spoken not sung and I somehow contrived to get through the hymns, playing quietly and with more than a little help from the choir. It was quite an ordeal and, to my great relief, it proved to be a one-off appearance for the time being.

Nevertheless, I was quite taken with the power and versatility of the organ and the Reverend Roulson said I would be welcome to pop into church at any time to practise. Over the next few years, I did exactly that, gradually acquiring a reasonable level of efficiency. To borrow an old Peter Sellers line, 'I had never had a lesson in my life!' Eventually, in the seventies we were once again without an organist and I said I was prepared to stand in on a temporary basis. I'm still standing in over 30 years later, and I take choir practice, too. The size of the choir has fallen over the years – although I don't think I can be entirely blamed for that – and we practise only when we are preparing for a special occasion or if there is going to be a change to the order of service.

It has been a rewarding experience and these days I can use both keyboards, I know all the stops and I can play with my feet, the feature that makes the organ different from other keyboard instruments. It takes a lot of getting used to at first and in the early days I was forever looking down at my feet and losing my place in the music. It's a bit like driving a car. A learner driver soon acquires a feel for the positions of the pedals and, thankfully, doesn't need to look down at the clutch pedal every time he changes gear. It's the same with the foot pedals of the organ, although some hymns such as 'Oh Praise Ye The Lord' and 'For All The Saints' do involve a bit of a route march.

Over the years, I've played at weddings and funerals as well as church services. I don't pretend to be anything more than an enthusiastic amateur, an accompanist rather than an organist, and I often say that the secret of my success is that I am cheap – in fact, nobody comes cheaper. I stay strictly within my own limitations and the limitations of the choir – we are never going to make a go of 'The Hallelujah Chorus' but if we keep it nice and simple things usually go according to plan.

Sometimes I am asked to play the organ at another church and that means I need to go on a reconnaissance mission in advance. No two organs are the same and sitting in front of an unfamiliar instrument can be a daunting experience. For example, I would find it hard to play the organ at Blackburn Cathedral without a considerable amount of instruction first.

I once took the choir to Liverpool Parish Church to sing Evensong and during the week before the service, I nipped over to Liverpool for a trial run. I did the same when I was asked to play at a friend's daughter's wedding in Sedbergh and it's a good job I did because the organ had definitely seen better days and it helped to know all about its foibles. One organ that I have always fancied playing is the Mighty Wurlitzer in the Blackpool Tower Ballroom although I would draw the line at being raised up on to the stage from below to the strains of 'I Do Like To Be Beside The Seaside'! I have been offered the chance to have a go once or twice and I suppose one day I'll take up the invitation, provided there is no one in the ballroom at the time.

Playing the organ at St Peter's has become part of my life as a grassroots Christian. I am a regular church-goer. Even when Anne and I are staying at our caravan in the Lake District we make a point of attending the service at Cartmel Priory, sometimes receiving a few odd looks when we set off from the caravan site first thing in the morning wearing our Sunday best. I suppose my appointment as a lay canon at Blackburn Cathedral in 2001 was in recognition of the work I have done at St Peter's, and I am now a member of the Blackburn Cathedral Council. It is a role that enables me to attend services and hear how an organ really should be played and how marvellous a high-class choir can sound. I believe the Blackburn choir, currently conducted by Richard Tanner, is as good as any in the north of England.

I love liturgical music, particularly the great requiems and oratorios but then I enjoy all kinds of music. I sometimes look at the lads on 'Top of the Pops' with their rap music and while it doesn't totally grab me, I think some of it is quite clever. I don't just reject it because it isn't to my particular taste. I thought the Beatles' music was terrific, some of the best popular music that has ever been written, although I never really thought they were outstanding singers. In my later years I've turned more towards the classics, particularly the great Russian composers Tchaikovsky, Prokofiev, Borodin, Rimsky-Korsakov and Rachmaninov, and appreciate Mozart, Beethoven and Schubert. I also enjoy more modern work. Elgar, for example, is wonderful. In a lighter vein, I love Gershwin – to me, his music represents the soul of America – and I marvel at the work of Irving Berlin and Richard Rodgers. How could anyone write so many wonderful songs for so many musicals?

Having interests is important and it has meant that life shows no sign of slowing down as the years go by. The church and music are just a part of it and, in fact, I am probably busier now than I have ever been, even though I am now an old age pensioner. If, when I left the *Daily Express* in the early nineties, I had been asked what I would be doing in 2004, I would never have imagined I would still be so actively involved in so many things. I was 58 at the time and I suppose I could have settled for the easy life on the rundown to retirement. Instead, the opportunity came along to join the FA and I jumped at the chance.

Away from the game, I have been a director of a National Health Service Trust board since 1992 when I had a call out of the blue from E. Johnston Young, chairman of the Blackpool, Fylde and Wyre Community Health Trust. I had never been involved with the NHS before, although Anne had been a nurse for 35 years, and when I told her I had been invited to become a director she shook her head in disbelief. I suppose I react in the same way when football clubs appoint non-professionals as directors. She seemed to be convinced that this was the beginning of the end for the NHS.

Nevertheless, I joined the board as a non-executive director and immediately became absorbed in a world that was totally different from anything I had ever done in my life. I had to undergo a year's training and it was at least another year before I felt I had come to terms with the role. I stayed with the Community Trust until it was abolished three years ago and then I was asked if I would stay on as a director of the new Blackpool Fylde and Wyre Hospital Trust. This Trust is responsible for the running of nine hospitals. I am now the vice-chairman, which is supposed to involve three half days a month but I put in considerably more time than that, and I also keep my hand in as a journalist by editing the Trust's in-house magazine.

When I was 65, I was invited to become president of the local branch of Age Concern, and I have been vice-president of Lancashire Outward Bound for many years. It's something in which I have always been interested. I have also been a governor at Arnold School since the late seventies and vice chairman for the last 12 years. I went to the school as an 11-plus entrant but things have changed now and Arnold has become one of the leading independent schools in the north-west with an excellent scholastic record. We have a board meeting every month and I try to attend all the major functions including speech days, school plays and carol services. I've been a member of the Old Arnoldians committee for more than 30 years.

I do get involved in community life and receive invitations to speak at functions of one kind or another or to take part in charity events. Last year, for example, the Macmillan Cancer Relief charity put on 'The Biggest Coffee Morning in the World' to raise money, and many organisations in Blackpool took part. I was invited to open the Civic Trust coffee morning in the town hall. As a freeman of the borough, I was also asked to be a member of the official party for the switch-on of the Blackpool illuminations.

It's a busy life and I'm fortunate that apart from a few creaking joints, the legacy of nearly 700 professional appearances, I have stayed pretty fit. We do have some spare time and there's nothing Anne and I like more than spending a few days at our caravan in the Lake District. We bought it about 12 years ago and it's a safe bet that if we are not in residence, Duncan or

John will be there with their families. Both boys followed in my footsteps to Arnold School and afterwards Duncan moved on to Manchester Polytechnic to study food technology. At the time, it was one of only three centres in the UK that ran the course and after qualifying, he worked for Warburton's, the Lancashire firm of bakers, who sent him on a one-year course to Winnipeg University in Canada. He married Deborah, a girl from just around the corner, in 1985 and they have two children, James and Nicholas. They live on the Wirral where Duncan is the development manager for the food giant Bakemark UK.

After leaving Arnold, John went to Carnegie College in Leeds to train as a PE teacher. He and Julie were married in 1989 and have two children, Thomas and Hannah. They live at Poulton near Blackpool and John is head of his faculty at St Aidan's School. When he was at Carnegie he was a useful goalkeeper and played for Manchester United's youth team. He was tempted to try his hand at the professional game but I advised him to obtain his teaching qualifications first and then make a decision. It was the same dilemma I had faced many years earlier but I was older and a regular member of the Blackpool side so the circumstances were different. He went on to play in the GM Conference for Runcorn and also had spells with Barrow and Workington but teaching came first.

Anne and I have been lovers of Lakeland for a long time. We must have been walking the Fells for over 40 years and there aren't many places that we haven't visited – on foot, of course. There's no point going to the Lakes and driving around in a car. The only way to appreciate the place is to put on walking boots. If you transported the Lake District to Italy or Austria, it would be a sensation, and luckily for us, it's just up the road. Our particular favourites are Buttermere and Crummock Water – awkward to reach but well worth the effort. If you are looking for something on the grand scale, there are few better places than Wastwater. We like Windermere, too, and that's where our boat is moored. The boys always wanted a boat and, eventually, Anne gave in and bought a Four Winns 170. In return, it was named after her.

It's a pretty powerful machine but I leave the high-speed stuff to Duncan and John and operate at a more leisurely pace. What could be better than taking out the boat for a gentle cruise, stopping off at a lakeside pub or hotel for lunch and then tootling back to port? One of the joys of Lakeland is that we have our own base and can keep ourselves to ourselves. Few people know my face these days – I can walk down a street in Blackpool without being recognised – but my name is still known through football mainly because of the radio.

I suppose, when I look back, being named captain of England was my greatest honour. But since then I have been fortunate enough to receive the OBE for services to football in 2000 and, three years later, the freedom of Blackpool. On top of that I am an honorary Fellow of the University of Central Lancashire. I believe you appreciate things like that more as you grow older and while I suspect the OBE might not mean an awful lot to a 20-year-old, to be recognised in the millennium awards was a tremendous honour for me. The award came completely out of the blue. A letter arrived with the morning post, I opened it and said to Anne, 'Good God, I've got the OBE!' Over the years, one or two people had suggested I might be in line for an honour of some kind but, quite honestly, the possibility had never really entered my mind. Suddenly there it was in front of me, on a sheet of royal notepaper. I was the only person from the football world in the Queen's birthday honours and, appropriately perhaps, the official announcement was made while I was on duty as a radio commentator for the BBC at the European Championship in Belgium and Holland.

The investiture at Buckingham Palace was a memorable occasion. The invitation specified that I could be accompanied by Anne and two guests, so Duncan and John came along, too. I decided we would stay overnight at the Royal Garden Hotel in Kensington, where we had celebrated England's World Cup victory 34 years earlier. I told the hotel staff about the award when I made the reservations and when we checked in, we discovered that Anne and I had been given a suite for the price of a standard double room. The hotel manager told us the Royal Garden would like to provide a chauffeur, so we were driven to the Palace in a brand new Jaguar.

The presentations took place in the main ballroom, where all the guests had assembled, and I waited in an ante room until called – Mr James Armfield, the OBE for services to association football. The band of the Blues and Royals were playing as I walked across the red carpet to meet the Prince of Wales, who shook me by the hand and said, 'I'm sorry it's taken so long to get you here.' All I could do in response was shrug my shoulders and smile. He continued, 'Now what are we going to do about this England football team? Football is an important part in the life of this country and I think it's important that the England team does well. You tell your people at the FA that's how I feel.' I must admit I was completely taken aback and none of the answers I had prepared in advance seemed quite appropriate.

I had no reason to suppose any more honours would be heading my way but three years later, the telephone rang at home and a voice said, 'Mr Armfield, the Mayor would like to have a word.'

'Right, fine.'

'Hello Jim. It's Ivan Taylor.'

'Hello Ivan, how are you?'

'I'm all right, thanks. I'm ringing to say we'd like you to be a freeman of Blackpool.'

All I could say in reply was 'OK!' I was more or less speechless – you don't receive many telephone calls with news like that.

'We'll have to put your name forward to a full meeting of the town council but I can't see any problems.'

'OK.'

'We haven't had any new freemen since 1978, that's twenty-five years, and the last one was Stan Mortensen. So we thought the time had come to reward two more people. You've always lived here, you've done a lot of community work for the people of Blackpool and brought a lot of credit to the town, and not just through football.'

I had regained my powers of speech by this stage so I thanked him profusely and said what an honour it would be. I received a formal letter shortly afterwards.

The other person to be honoured was Doris Thompson, one of the founders of the Blackpool Pleasure Beach who had reached the age of 100. There had been some speculation in the *Blackpool Evening Gazette* that Mrs Thompson was going to receive the freedom of the borough but, as far as I was aware, there was no suggestion that anyone else would receive the award at the same time. As well as Stan Mortensen, our predecessors included Winston Churchill, Field Marshal Montgomery and Lloyd George so Doris and I were in pretty good company.

The ceremony took place in the council chamber at the town hall on 9 April 2003 and it was quite a moving occasion. Doris said a few words before I stood up to thank the people of Blackpool for the honour. Then we all moved on to the Imperial Hotel for a civic lunch. All our friends and families were there to share the experience whereas at Buckingham Palace, it was just the four of us. They were different occasions but in a way, to be honoured by my own people was indeed very special. To receive both awards in the autumn of my life has been doubly memorable.

The Armfield Stand at Bloomfield Road is due to be completed soon and the club have asked me to perform the opening ceremony. It will be a proud moment – particularly as the first two new stands in the redevelopment programme were named after Stanley Matthews and Stan Mortensen, the two icons of Blackpool Football Club. Inevitably, honours such as these tend to come late in life and it is such a pity that my mother and father are no longer alive to share some of the pride that I feel. Without them, none of this would have happened.

It is over 60 years since a little boy wearing a school cap, carrying a small leather suitcase and clutching his mother's hand, arrived at Blackpool station on a cold, dark winter's night. Thankfully, the ravages of war have long departed but the house on Tyldesley Road, where my mother and I shared a single room for three years, still stands as a reminder. Like me, it's not in such good condition these days but no doubt it has its own store of memories, too.

JAMES CHRISTOPHER
A R M F I E L D

Born Denton 21 September 1935. League debut for Blackpool 27 December 1954 v Portsmouth. England debut 13 May 1959 v Brazil. Young Player of the Year 1959. Bolton Wanderers manager May 1971. Leeds United manager September 1974. Awarded OBE 2000. Freeman of Blackpool 2003.

ENGLAND UNDER–23
1956 v Denmark; 1957 v Bulgaria, Romania, Czechoslovakia, Romania; 1958 v Poland, Czechoslovakia; 1959 v France, Italy

FOOTBALL LEAGUE
1956 v Irish League; 1957 v League of Ireland; 1959 v League of Ireland; 1960 v Scottish League, Irish League, Italian League; 1961 v League of Ireland, Italian League; 1962 v Scottish League, Irish League, Italian League; 1963 v League of Ireland

ENGLAND INTERNATIONALS
1959 v Brazil, Peru, Mexico, USA; 1960 v Scotland, Yugoslavia, Spain, Hungary, Northern Ireland, Luxembourg, Spain, Wales; 1961 v Scotland, Mexico, Portugal, Italy, Austria, Luxembourg*, Wales, Portugal, Northern Ireland; 1962 v Austria, Scotland, Switzerland, Peru, Hungary, Argentina, Bulgaria, Brazil, France*, Northern Ireland*, Wales*; 1963 v France*, Scotland*, Brazil*, East Germany*, Switzerland*, Wales*, Rest of the World*, Northern Ireland*; 1964 v Scotland*; 1966 v Yugoslavia*, Finland*
    *Captain

| Season | League | | FA Cup | | League Cup | | Under–23 | | Foot Lge | | Internationals | |
Apps Goals	Apps	Goals	Apps	Goals	Apps	Goals	Apps	Goals	Apps	Goals	Apps	Goals
BLACKPOOL												
1954–55	2	–	–	–	–	–	–	–	–	–	–	–
1955–56	30	–	1	–	–	–	–	–	1	–	–	–
1956–57	38	–	4	–	–	–	4	–	–	–	–	–
1957–58	28	–	1	–	–	–	1	–	1	–	–	–
1958–59	32	–	6	–	–	–	4	–	–	–	4	–
1959–60	41	1	3	–	–	–	–	–	2	–	4	–
1960–61	40	–	1	–	1	–	–	–	2	–	9	–
1961–62	37	–	2	–	6	–	–	–	3	–	12	–
1962–63	39	–	2	–	2	–	–	–	2	–	8	–
1963–64	35	–	2	–	2	–	–	–	1	–	4	–
1964–65	40	2	1	–	1	–	–	–	–	–	–	–
1965–66	35	1	2	–	2	–	–	–	–	–	2	–
1966–67	29	–	–	–	2	–	–	–	–	–	–	–
1967–68	41	1	2	–	2	–	–	–	–	–	–	–
1968–69	34	–	1	–	4	–	–	–	–	–	–	–
1969–70	40	1	3	–	2	–	–	–	–	–	–	–
1970–71	27	–	2	–	1	–	–	–	–	–	–	–
Totals	568	6	33	0	25	0	9	0	12	0	43	0

I N D E X

Note: Abbreviations used in the index are BW for Bolton Wanderers FC; Eng. for England team; JA for Jimmy Armfield; LU for Leeds United FC; WC for World Cup

Aberdeen 213
AC Milan 262, 315
Accrington Stanley 3, 273
A'Court, Alan 111
Adams, Audrey 257–8
Adamson, Jimmy 133, 170, 220, 226
adidas boots 64–5
Age Concern 4, 327
agents 314–15
Ajax 214
Albert, Florian 124
alcohol 197
Aldershot 47–8
Allardyce, Sam 171, 172
Allchurch, Ivor 261
Allen, John (grandfather of JA) 7, 8–10, 11
Allen, Peter (broadcaster) 254
Allen, Sally (grandmother of JA) 9, 11, 12, 13
Allen, Tony 120
Allison, Malcolm 137
Alloa 160
Amarildo 125
Anchorsholme 273
Anderlecht 192, 205
Anderson, Stan 52, 112
Andrews, Eamonn 242
Angel, The, pub, Denton 10
Archer, Keith 176
Ards 107
Argentina 268; *1962* 122, 123, 124; *1964* 135;

1966 v. Eng. 145, 147–8; *1998* World Cup 293–4
Armfield, Anne (wife of JA): meets JA 20; courtship 41; wedding 66; childbirths 67; as JA's wife 14, 67, 118, 119, 150, 178, 185, 214, 216, 219, 220, 223, 255, 311, 326, 327, 328
Armfield, Christopher (father of JA) 8, 12, 13, 21, 25, 26, 28, 29, 35, 36, 37, 41, 56–7, 108, 271, 321, 322, 331; early life 10–11; marriage 13; in WWII 14, 15, 19
Armfield, Doris (mother of JA) 8–9, 12–13, 15–16, 17, 18, 19, 23, 27, 108, 331; early life 11–12; marriage 13
Armfield, Duncan (son of JA) 67, 185, 272, 327–8, 329; career and family 328
Armfield, James (Jimmy): birth 1, 333; childhood 1–2, 4, 9–10, 13–24, 25–9; schools 14–15, 17, 25–6, 28–34, 37, 39, 40, 42, 305; tried for Blackpool 33–4; plays for Blackpool 7–9, 34–7, 39–40, 42–57, 59–73, 75–89, 91–103, 105–6, 137, 159–62, 333–4; National Service 39–52, 54–6; enters world of professional sport 57, 59, 225; marriage 66; with Eng. Under-23s 68, 105–6, 108–15, 334; injuries 69, 136–7, 139, 162; with Football League 107–8, 334; with Eng. 105, 115–27, 129–36, 138–40, 141–57, 334; captain of Eng. 129, 131–6, 138–9, 334; testimonial match 161–2; manages

1969 FA tour 163–7; retires from playing 162–3; offers made to 167–9, 179, 184–6, 231; manager at BW 169–80, 181; manager at LU 157, 181, 184–98, 199–221, 333; journalism 68, 163, 225, 226–31, 233–8, 239; voice 223–4; broadcasting 223–4, 232–3, 241–55, 257–60; coaching 225–6, 304; OBE 254–5, 329–30, 333; works for FA 273–86, 287–97, 304; works for PFA 296, 304; piano playing 321–3; later years 2–4, 5, 324–31; freedom of Blackpool 329, 330–1; playing record 7, 59; career statistics 332–3

Armfield, John (son of JA) 67, 185, 232, 272, 329; career and family 328

Armfield, Joseph (grandfather of JA) 10

Armstrong, George 188

Army, British 39, 50, 55–6, 105, 106, 107, 108; *see also* British Army team; King's Own Royal Regiment; Western Command team 42, 50, 54

Army School of Physical Training 33, 46

Arnold School, Blackpool 25–6, 28–34, 37, 39, 305; Cadet Force 33, 40, 42, 327, 328; Feathers rugby team 30–1

Arsenal 83, 95, 150, 216; v. LU 186, 187–8, 210–11; v. Preston 271

Artime, Luis 147

Ashurst, Ann (mother of Anne) 178

Ashurst, Anne *see* Armfield, Anne

Aston Villa 99, 160, 168

Athletic Bilbao 221, 231

Atkinson, Ron 276

Augusto, Jose 149

Australia 82–3

Austria 245, 315; *1952* 265; *1961* v. Eng. 121

Baggio, Roberto 247

Ball, Alan 101, 102, 139, 140, 143, 149, 150, 188; sold to Everton 103, 159

Bancroft, Bill 167

Bangkok 164, 166

Banks, Gordon 134, 139, 140, 143, 149, 258, 259

Banks, Jack 167–8, 169, 171–2, 173–4, 177, 179–80, 184, 208

Banks, Tommy 87

Barcelona 192–4, 284

Baresi, Franco 247

Barker, Rayner 218, 220

Barnard, Michael 44

Barnsley 98–9, 216

Barrow 3

Barstow, Stan 241

Bates, Mick 200, 205

Batistuta, Gabriele 293

Baxter, Jim 134

Bayern Munich: *1975* v. LU 194–7, 269; Beckenbauer with 269–70

BBC 2, 223–4, 228, 241–4, 245–7, 250–1, 252, 254–5, 257–61, 274, 275, 279, 293, 310, 329

Bean, John 234

Beattie, Andy 99

Beckenbauer, Franz 146, 195, 196, 269–70, 276

Beckham, David 83, 212, 246, 260, 288, 293–4, 295, 313–14

Belgium 192

Bell, Colin 161, 171

Benfica 149

Bentley, Bill 160

Berlin 53

Best, George 146, 258, 259, 262–3, 314

Beverley, Joy 119

Bilbao 254

Birmingham: Grand Hotel 99–100

Birmingham City 188; v. BW 92

Bispham Education ground 34

Blackburn Cathedral 4, 325, 329

Blackburn Rovers 138, 162, 231–2, 237, 310; makes offer to JA 167

Blackpool 1, 12, 15, 26–8, 91, 223; in WWII 15–24; 'The Bowery' 26–7; Central Pier 27; Coliseum Bus Station 20; Foxhall 226–7, 228; freedom of 329, 330–1; Rosedale Avenue 66; St Peter's Church 28, 323–5; South Shore 65–6, 79; Stanley Park 20; Talbot Square 2; Tyldesley Road 15–17, 22–4, 26–9, 331; *see also* Arnold School

Blackpool Corporation 119

Blackpool Cricket Club 229

Blackpool Evening Gazette 59, 68, 100, 163, 226–9, 230–1, 233, 331

Blackpool FC 1, 7, 29, 201, 215, 225, 261, 273, 305, 331, 333–4; Stanley Matthews 1–2, 75–6, 78–9, 81–5, 87–8; pay 60, 87–8; in WWII 20–1; JA tried for 33–4; Colts 34; *1953* 34–7; *1954* 37, 38, 39–40, 42–5, (v. Portsmouth 42–5); *1955* (v. Newcastle 7, 8–9), 45–6, (v. Manchester United 45), 48–52; *1956* 59; *1957* 75; *1959–60* 59–67; v. Wolves 72–3; v. Chelsea 77; v. Leicester 80–1; *1961* v. Spurs 263; *1966* 103; relegated 103, 159; *1967* 67, 68–74, 77–8, 80–1, 83–6, 87–9, 145–6, (v. Preston 160–1); *1971* 156–7, (JA's testimonial match 161–2), (v. Manchester United 162–3); JA leaves 163; *1974* v. BW 178; fan killed 178; v. Everton 260; talent money 70; *see also* Bloomfield Road

Blackpool Fylde and Wyre Hospital 327

Blackpool Grammar School 31, 32

Blackpool Services team 21
Blackpool Tower Ballroom 119, 325
Blackpool Wednesday League 226–8
Blair, Danny 34
Blair, Tony 297
Blanchflower, Danny 261
Bliard, Rene 52
Blockley, Jeff 188
Bloomfield, Jimmy 108, 113
Bloomfield Road, Blackpool FC ground 7–8,
    9, 20–1, 33, 34–5, 62–5, 77; Armfield
    Stand 331
Blunstone, Frank 108, 176
Boardman, Stan 46
Bocking, Mrs (of Gorton) 11
Boeing Stratocruiser 82
Bolton, Sam 184, 189
Bolton Wanderers 2, 35, 87, 91–2, 99, 101,
    181, 184, 201, 264, 265, 312, 318–19; JA
    offered managership 167–70; JA as
    manager 170–80, 181, 185, 201–2, 217;
    1974 v. Blackpool 178
Bond, Jack 236
Bond, John 68
Bonds, Billy 276, 279
Bonetti, Peter 139
Boniperti, Giampiero 265
Booth family 15, 23
Booth, Kenny 20, 23
boots 64–5
Boswell, Allan 170
Bowerham Barracks, Lancaster 39, 40–2, 45,
    46, 47, 50, 107, 108
Bowers, Dave 47
Bowers, Jack 166
boxing 32, 76
Boycott, Geoffrey 235, 236
Boyd, George 217
Bradford City 216, 315
Bradley, Warren 118, 188
Brady, Liam 188
Brann Bergen 194
Bratislava 114
Brazil: 1958 WC 115, 268; 1959 v. Eng. 44,
    116–18; 1962 WC 105, 124, 125–6; 1963 v.
    Eng. 135; 1994 WC 246, 247; 1998 WC
    285
Bremner, Billy 161, 217; with LU 182, 183,
    184, 185, 186–7, 188, 192, 195, 200, 202,
    203, 206–7, 211–12; in pantomime 190,
    191; transfers to Hull 205–6; to Doncaster
    206; death 206, 261
Brentford 176
Brice, Joe 29
Bristol City 20, 261
Bristol Rovers 252
British Army team 42, 50, 54, 105, 107

British Restaurant 14
Broadbent, Peter 118
Brotherton, Simon 251
Brown, Allan 96, 98
Brown, Ian 249, 251
Brynner, Yul 150
Bucharest 113–14
Buckingham Palace 329–30
Buckley, Major 265
Bulgaria 249–50, 296; 1957 111–13; 1962
    v. Eng. 122, 123, 124
Burbanks, Eddie 21
Burnden Park 167, 168, 169–70, 171, 175,
    176, 177, 215; 2000 250
Burnley 133, 143, 170, 213, 214
Burtonwood 21
Bury 35
Busby, Matt 55, 146, 169, 288–9
Busby Babes, Manchester United 52, 55
Butler, Bryon 242, 245–6, 247–9
Buxton, Ted 292
Byrne, Gerry 134, 139
Byrne, Johnny 138
Byrne, Roger 53, 107, 120, 121, 126
Byrom, John 170, 172, 175, 176

California 82
Callaghan, Ian 139, 144, 309
Cambridge 31
Campbell, Menzies 141
Campbell, Sol 294
Canning, Larry 241
Cantona, Eric 32, 146
Cardiff 94; Millennium Stadium 318
Carey, Johnny 167
Carlin, Willie 173
Carter, Raich 119, 261–2
Cartmel Priory 325
Cartmell, Bill 161
Cathcart, Corporal 39, 41
Catterick, Harry 179
Celtic 308
Champions League 194, 311, 315, 319
Charles, John 164, 258, 259, 261, 265–7
Charles, Prince of Wales 330
Charlton, Bobby 82, 146–7, 258, 259, 262;
    playing for Eng. 117, 118, 121, 122, 126,
    127, 139, 140, 143–4, 145–6, 147, 149, 266;
    at Manchester United 145–6, 147, 149,
    162; Preston 146–7
Charlton, Jack 137, 139, 140, 143, 149, 161,
    203, 258, 259
Charlton, Norma 147
Charlton Athletic 99; 1957 v. Blackpool 75
Charnley, Ray 83, 98, 132, 309
Chelsea 170, 262, 290, 306, 315; v. Blackpool
    77

Cherry, Trevor 200, 203, 214, 217
Chester, Charlie 305
Chester City: *1974* v. LU 189
Chile 121–2; *1962* WC 105, (v. Italy 124–5, 126–7)
Cinderella performed in Leeds 190–2
cinemas and films 4, 13–14, 23
Clairefontaine, French Football Academy 32, 304
Clamp, Eddie 102
Clarke, Alan 251
Clarke, Allan ('Sniffer') 182, 186, 188, 193, 195, 200, 204, 206, 213, 214, 216, 217
Clayton, Ronnie 108, 118, 308, 309
Clemence, Ray 292
Clough, Brian 111–12, 181, 182–4, 185, 186, 187, 200, 202, 220, 277
coaching 168, 225–6, 304
Cocker, Les 183
Cohen, George 107, 137, 138, 139–40, 143, 149, 150
Colehan, Barney 189–90, 191
Collins, Tony 194
Collomosse, Andy 237
Colman, Eddie 52, 53
Coluna, Mario 149
Connelly, John 121, 132, 139, 142, 143, 144, 309
Connery, Sean 150
Conway, Jim 170, 173
Cooper, Terry 182, 186, 200, 203
Copenhagen 76, 108, 109
Costa del Sol 67–8, 209–10
Coventry City 174, 205
Cowdenbeath 160
Crag Bank, Morecambe Bay 41
Creedy, Don 226, 230–1
cricket 25–6, 76, 235, 306; Blackpool Cricket Club 229
Croker, Ted 274
Crowe, Chris 132
Crozier, Adam 298, 299, 304
Cruyff, Johan 192, 193
Cullis, Stan 94–5
Cummings, Harry 63–4
Curran, Hugh 174
Currie, Tony 200, 201, 202, 211, 212–13, 214, 217
Cussins, Manny 184, 208–10, 218, 219, 220
Cyprus 317
Czechoslovakia: *1957* v. Young England 54; *1958* (v. Young England 111), 114; *1962* WC 124, 125; *1963* 135

Daily Express 52, 198, 228, 240, 296–7; JA works for 2, 224, 233–8, 243, 273, 275, 278, 288, 326

Daily Mail 198, 228
Daily Telegraph 247
Dale, Gordon 44–5
Dalglish, Kenny 213, 237, 276, 288
Davies, David 295, 297
De Mau, Keith 165
Dean, Dixie 147
Deeley, Norman 118
Dempsey, Mike 233–4, 236, 237–8
Denmark: *1956* v. Eng. Under-23s 108–11; *1957* WC 76; *1966* 139, 140; *1994* 284–5
Dennis, Ian 251
Denton, near Manchester 10, 14–15, 19, 25; Marina Avenue 13, 17
Denton Council School 14–15
Derby County 99, 182–3, 189, 262
Di Stefano, Alfredo 146, 267–8
Dickinson, Lorna 246
Dickinson, Matt 296–7
Didi 116
Dix, Ronnie 21
Dixon, Wilf 102, 103
Dobson, Colin 164, 165
Docherty, Tommy 270
Dodd, Ken 27
Dodds, Jock 20–1
Doherty, Paul 232
Doherty, Peter 21, 232, 261–2
Doncaster Rovers 108, 206
Douglas, Bryan 108, 111–12, 121, 126, 127, 135, 266, 308, 309
Doyle, Brian 205
Drewery, Eileen 287, 294–5
Duffey, Chris 173
Dundee 213
Dunmore, Dave 52
Durie, David 42, 69, 98
Dzajic, Dragan 138

East Fife 52, 105–6
East Germany: *1963* v. Eng. 135
Eastham, George (father) 107
Eastham, George (son) 31, 107, 135, 139, 164
Eddy, Keith 164
Edelston, Maurice 251
Edwards, Duncan 52, 53–5, 87, 106–7, 114, 121, 126, 169
Edwards, Louis 55
Edwards, Martin 289
Eintracht Frankfurt 52, 267–8
Elgar, Edward 326
Ellis, Arthur 312
Ellis, Bert and Mary 323
emerging nations 317
England 7, 31, 67, 102, 112, 113–14, 267; appointment of managers/coaches 274–85, 287–91, 297–8; captaincy 313; captains

308; Jimmy Greaves 264; medals 157; reserve team 150–2; Young England *see* Under-23s: *1959* 115–20 (v. Brazil 44, 115–18), (v. Scotland 120); *1960–1* 120–1; *1961–2* 121–7, 129–30; under Winterbottom 131–3; under Ramsey 129, 131, 133–40, 142–4, 147–54, 157, 163; JA as captain 129, 131–6, 138–9, 334; *1963* 131–5, (v. France 132, 133–4), (v. Scotland 134–5); *1964* 135–6, 137; *1966* 130, 137–40, (v. Finland 139, 140), 141–5, (v. Mexico 143–4), (v. France 144), 147–57, (v. Germany 152), 159; *1991* World Cup reunion 149–50; *1994* v. Denmark 284–5; under Venables 284–6; under Hoddle 287–97

English, Bob 188, 195, 206
Eriksson, Sven Goran 252, 299, 301
Etoile Carouge 217
European Championship: *1996* 275, 279, 281, 284–6, (Denmark v. Eng. 284–5), 291–2, 294, 297, 306, 308; *2000* 296
European Cup 70, 183, 270; *1960* 267–8; *1966* 149; *1974–5* 180, 182, 188, 192–4, 195–8, 269
European league 315
European Nations Cup 132, 133
Eusebio 145, 149
Evans, Harry 96
Evans, Major 50
Evans, Norman 305
Evans, Tommy 217
Everton 52, 102, 120, 138, 232, 250, 260, 279; Alan Ball sold to 103, 159; JA offered management 179–80, 181

FA Cup 3, 29, 49, 84, 313, 318–19, 333–4; *1923* 91–2; *1946* 262; *1948* 316; *1953* 1–2, 7, 34–5, 36–7, 84, 89; *1954* 95; *1956* 258; *1959* 95; *1969* tour 163–7; *1971* 156; *1975* 189; *1976* 214; *1991* 277; *2003* 243
fans 59, 83, 116, 306–7, 308, 310, 316; in Romania 118; killed 178; in Paris, *1975* 196; celebrities 305–6
Far East 163, 164
Farm, George 7, 43, 44, 61, 68, 69, 71, 93, 94, 98
Farrow, George 21
Ferguson, Alex 276, 277, 284, 288–9
Ferrier, Rene 132
FIFA 141, 144, 317
Fife 105–6
Finan, Bob 21
Finland: *1966* v. Eng. 139, 140
Finney, Tom 69, 79, 80, 82, 89, 118, 136, 146, 257, 258, 259, 261, 265, 270–2, 308–9
Fisher, Graham 237

'Five Live Drive' 254
flick soccer 20, 23
Florescu, Dan 113
Flowers, Ron 118, 121, 132, 139
Flynn, Brian 200, 214, 217
Follows, Dennis 133
Fontaine, Just 52, 132
Football Association (FA) 2, 98, 119, 127, 131, 133, 134, 144, 154, 155, 166, 248, 273, 304; centenary celebrations 267; appointment of Eng. managers 274–85, 287–91, 297–8, 299; *see also* FA Cup
football club directors 307
Football League 3, 52, 98–9, 131, 273, 282, 310, 313, 316–17, 319, 333–4; *1956* Irish League 107–8; *1960* Blackpool v. BW 101; *see also* League Cup
'Football Legends' 257–60
Foster, Barry 182
Foulkes, Bill 52, 107
Fox, James 241
France: *1955* 52; *1956* 108; *1958* 114, 127; *1962* v. Eng. 132; *1963* v. Eng. 133–4; *1966* 144, 147; *1998* 293; Le Tournoi 292–3
Francis, Gerry 276, 278, 288
Francis, Trevor 276, 279
Fulham 29, 87
Fylde League 34

Garrett, Tommy 69, 98
Garrincha 116, 117, 125, 126, 314
Garstang, near Preston 56
Garvey, Jane 254
Gascoigne, Paul 108
Gateshead 3
Gedney, Chris 164
Gemmill, Archie 161
Georgia 292
Germany 269, 270; *1990* 270, 276; *1996* 269; *1998* 269; *2000* v. Eng. 298; *2001* v. Eng. 299; *2002* 270; *see also* East Germany; West Germany; *and teams' names*
Gershwin, Ira 326
Ghana 83–4
Giles, Johnny 182, 184, 185, 186–7, 195, 200, 202, 203, 206, 258, 277
Gilmar 117
Glasgow 208
Glasgow Rangers 52; *1968* v. Blackpool 160
Glendenning, Raymond 251
goalkeeping 69, 319
Gordon, Jimmy 183
Gordon, John 44
Gorman, John 292
Gould, Len 237
Graham, Arthur 200, 213–14, 217
Graham, George 276, 277

Granada Television 232–3
Grand National 229–30
Gratrix, Roy 44, 64, 69, 70, 98
Gray, Eddie 182, 183, 195, 196, 200, 204–5, 211, 214, 217
Gray, Frank 195, 200, 203, 214, 217
Greaves, Ian 180, 215
Greaves, Jimmy 115, 119, 121, 126, 132, 139, 140, 143, 144, 147, 149–50, 153, 258–9, 263–4, 266; playing v. Romania 114
Greaves, Roy 170, 172
Greece 308
Green, Alan 244–5, 246–7, 249, 251, 293
Green, Brian 216
Green, Tony 156, 160
Greenwood, Cliff 68, 226, 227, 228–30, 231, 234
Greenwood, Ron 114, 168, 212, 280
Grime, Sir Harold 226
Grime, Herbert 100
Grimsby 279
Gullit, Ruud 288
gymnastics 113

Hackett, Desmond 228
Hagan, Jimmy 83, 88–9
Hall, Eric 282
Hall, Jeff 107
Hall, Stuart 250–1
Halliwell, Sid 46
Hampton, Peter 214
Hankin, Ray 200, 202, 213, 214, 215, 217
Hanover 52
Hardacre, Ken 228
Hardaker, Alan 273–4
Hardwick, George 258, 261
Hargreaves, Corporal 39, 41
Harper, Brian (Brian London) 32
Harris, Carl 214
Harris, Peter 44
Harris, Sandy 70–1
Harrison, Eric 314
Hart, Paul 200, 215, 217
Hartle, Roy 87
Harvey, David 182, 186, 189, 200, 214, 217
Hateley, Tony 164
Hawkins, Graham 164
Hawley, John 200, 215–16, 219
Hayes, Julian 304
Haynes, Johnny 87, 114, 117, 118, 121, 123, 206, 258, 259, 295, 308; injured 131–2
Haythornwaite, Bill 30
Hayward, Eric 21, 81
Heath, Joe 50
Hellawell, Mike 132
Helm, John 241, 249–50
Henderson, Jackie 44

Henman, Tim 306
Hennin, Derek 87
Henry, Thierry 132, 300
Heysel Stadium 315
Higgins, John 87
Hill, Captain 50
Hill, Freddie 132
Hill, Jimmy 86
Hillsborough 315–16
Hindley, Albert 98–9
Hinton, Alan 132
Hitchens, Gerry 108, 121, 126, 132
hockey 34
Hoddle, Glenn 276, 278–9, 287, 290–7, 298–9; World Cup Diary 295–6; in Daily Express 297
Hodgkinson, Alan 52, 106, 108, 121, 161, 163–4
Hoeness, Dieter 146
Hoeness, Uli 195
Holden, Doug 118, 264
Holdgate, Frank 28, 29–30
Holdsworth, Maureen 187, 190, 212, 218, 220
Holland 294
Holley, Tom 218
Hong Kong 42, 271; 1958 82, 83; 1969 164, 165
honours 157
Hopkinson, Eddie 118, 127, 170
Horne, Des 101
Houlkar, Alan 11, 13, 49
Houllier, Gerard 304
Howarth, Bill 31, 34
Howe, Don 106, 107, 117, 118, 119, 216, 219, 284, 292
Huddersfield Town 99, 120, 180; 1968 v. Blackpool 160; 1970 v. Blackpool 162
Hughes, Charles 296
Hughes, Emlyn 101, 102
Hughes, Phil 262
Hull City 205–6, 215
Hulme, John 170
Hungary: 1960 v. Eng. 120; 1962 122, 124; 1974 188
Hunt, Roger 127, 135, 139, 140, 143, 144, 149, 309
Hunter, Norman 139, 182, 186, 191–2, 194, 195, 200, 207–8
Hurst, Geoff 139, 140, 147, 148, 149, 152, 156, 258, 309, 319
Hutchison, Tommy 160

Illingworth, Ray 241
Ingham, Mike 245–7, 249, 251
injuries 136–7, 193
international football 130–1, 142, 300–1
international management 275–6, 288

Ipswich: Ramsey's funeral 129
Ipswich Town 130, 131, 135, 144, 188, 189, 274
Iran 231
Ireland: *1964* 135
Irish League: *1956* 107, 108
Isherwood, Bill 175–6, 184
Italy 263, 265; *Serie A* 252; *1958* 115; *1962* v. Chile 124–5; *1982* 254; *1994* v. Brazil 246–7; *1998* 292

Jackson, Teddy 66
Jaglinski, Frank 16
James, Glyn 160, 309
Jeffrey, Alick 108, 111
Jennings, Pat 258, 259
Jersey 237
Johnston, Harry 1, 37, 42, 43, 44, 69, 84, 85, 94, 98
Jones, Mr (piano teacher) 321–2
Jones, Cliff 258, 259
Jones, Gary 170, 172, 173
Jones, Ivor 321
Jones, Mick 182, 200, 203–4, 216
Jones, Paul 170, 172, 215
Jones, Peter 228, 242, 248–9
Jones, Ron 249, 251
Jones, Sam 35
Jordan, Joe 186, 193, 195, 200, 213, 214, 215, 216
journalism 68, 226–38, 239–40, 241
Joyce, Joe 304
Jules Rimet Trophy 145, 154
Julinho 117
Juventus 265, 293

Kay, Tony 135
Kaye, Arthur 100
Keeble, Vic 7, 71
Keegan, Kevin 183, 288; Eng. manager 297–9
Keith, John 234
Kelly, Eddie 188
Kelly, Graham 273–5, 278, 281, 282–3, 284, 286, 288, 289, 291, 295, 296, 304
Kelly, Hughie 43, 44, 61, 69, 98, 100
Kelly, Jim 44, 69, 98
Kendall, Howard 231–2, 276, 279, 280, 288
Kentish Cup 52
Kevan, Derek 114, 121
'Kick Off' (tv programme) 232–3
Kidd, Brian 188
King's Head, Barnard Castle 97–8
King's Own Royal Regiment 39, 40–3, 46–8, 49–51, 56, 107, 108
Kinnear, Joe 276
Kinsell, Harry 21

Kirkham 21
Kitabdijan, M. (referee) 195–6
Knighton, Ken 164
Kolev, Ivan 124
Kopa, Raymond 132
Korean War 46
Kreitlein, Rudolf 148

Labone, Brian 138
Ladley, Geoff 216
Lake District 325, 327, 328–9
Lancashire Evening Post 100
Lancashire League 34
Lancashire Outward Bound 4, 327
Langley, Jimmy 107
Law, Denis 134, 146, 242, 258, 262, 263
Lawton, Tommy 85, 147, 258, 261; last years 260
Layne, David 135
Le Tissier, Matthew 292
Leadbeater, Jimmy 144
League Cup 313, 333–4; *1971* 171; *1974* 189; *1978* 214
Lee, Franny 161, 171
Lee, Stuart 170, 174
Leeds: City Varieties Music Hall 189–92
Leeds United 32, 35; under Revie 181–3; under Clough 182–4; JA offered managership 180, 184–6; JA as manager 37, 49, 157, 181, 186–221, 299; *1974* v. Chester 189; perform pantomime 189–92; *1975* v. Bayern Munich 195–6; banned from Europe 196–8, 199; JA sacked 220–1, 224; John Charles with 265–7
Leicester City 80–1
Leicester Mercury 247
Lill, Micky 46
Lilleshall National School of Excellence 120, 138, 168, 225, 226, 304
Lindley, Maurice 186–7, 194, 201, 204
Lineker, Gary 313
Littler, Eric 230
Liverpool FC 68, 102, 174, 183, 188–9, 308
Liverpool Parish Church 325
Liverpool University 37, 38, 56
Lloyd, Cliff 86
Lloyd, Clive 236
Lockwood, Jimmy 50
Lofthouse, Nat 79, 85, 118, 147, 167, 168, 170, 177, 201, 258, 264–5, 308
London, Brian (Brian Harper) 32
London Underground 48
Lorimer, Peter 182, 183, 186, 188, 193, 195, 200, 211–12
Los Angeles 82, 118, 247
Loughborough College of Physical Education 37, 38, 56

Loughborough University 232
Lukic, John 217
Luton Town 95–6, 274
Luxembourg 317; *1960* v. Eng. 120; *1961* v.
  Eng. 131
Lynas, Johnny 51, 63, 93, 94, 96–8

McAllister, Don 170, 172
McAnearney, Jim 219
McFarlane, Ian 77
McGhee, Tom 44
McGhie, Billy 217
McGovern, John 183, 200, 202, 205
McGrory, Bob 88
McIlroy, Jimmy 102, 258
McKay, Angus 242
Mackay, Dave 134, 258
McKenna, Johnny 44, 70, 71
McKenna, Vince 33–4, 35
McKenzie, Duncan 183, 186–7, 188, 196, 200,
  205, 213; in pantomime 190, 191
McKnight, George 70
McMenemy, Lawrie 68, 277
Macmillan Cancer Relief 327
McNamara, Connor 251
McNeil, Mike 107, 121
McNeill, Billy 258, 259
McPhee, Johnny 309
McQueen, Gordon 186, 193, 194, 200, 214–15
Madeley, Paul 186, 194–5, 200, 210–11, 214,
  217
Maier, Sepp 195
Majorca 67, 153, 183, 311
Mallinson, Bill 198
Malta 317
management, football 142–3, 163, 177, 198,
  201–2, 231–2; international 275–6, 288
Manchester 1, 7, 9, 26, 106; blitz 14; cinemas
  13; Gorton 11–12
Manchester City 21, 173, 283; *1955* 48–9;
  1971 171
Manchester United 119, 169, 214–15, 236,
  245, 274, 308, 310, 318–19; *1948* 36; *1954*
  45; *1956* 70, 106; *1957* 55; Busby Babes 52,
  55; Bobby Charlton 145–6, 147, 149, 162;
  Munich air disaster 53, 55, 146; v.
  Blackpool 162–3; press box 236; Tommy
  Taylor 240; Alex Ferguson 288–9; youth
  team 328
Mankelow, David 237
Manning, J.L. 228
Mannion, Wilf 119, 258
Mansell, Jack 44
Marbella 209, 217
Marriott, US Army sergeant 48
Marsh, Arthur 170
Marzolini, Silvio 147

Mas, Oscar 147
Maschio, Humberto 125
Masson, Don 173
Matthaus, Lothar 269
Matthews, John 188
Matthews, Sir Stanley 119, 141, 146, 163,
  257, 258, 259, 260, 261, 271, 272, 305;
  with Stoke 78, 102; at Blackpool 7, 20, 21,
  36–7, 43, 44, 60, 61, 64–5, 69, 70, 71, 72,
  76–8, 79, 80–1, 91, 93, 98, 100, 101, 102,
  103; *1953* FA Cup 1–2, 36–7; with Eng.
  70, 76; 42nd birthday 75; leaves Blackpool
  102; playing record 76; Round the World
  Tour 82–4; dress sense 88; driving 88–9;
  funeral 89
Meadows, Jimmy 162
Meek, George 266
Megson, Don 163
Mersey Tunnel 47
Mexico: *1959* 115, 118; *1961* v. Eng. 120; *1966*
  v. Eng. 143–4, 145, 207; *1970* 154, 268
Michels, Rinus 192
Middlesbrough 203
Milburn, Jackie 7, 85
Millichip, Bert 275, 276, 277, 281, 283, 286,
  288, 297
Mills, Trelford 250–1
Milne, Gordon 135, 138
Mitchell, Bobby 7
Mitchell, Gerry 105–6
Moldova 291, 292, 293
Molineux, Wolverhampton 94
Moore, Bobby 82, 121, 137, 138, 139, 140,
  143, 147, 149, 153, 154–7, 208, 261, 268,
  270, 295, 313; honours 157; death 156
Moores, Sir John 179
Morgan, Ian 164
Morrison, Ken 12–13
Mortensen, Stan 1–2, 36, 42, 43, 64, 67, 69,
  84–5, 89, 160, 260; honours 330, 331
Moscow 245
Mowbray, Henry 160
Mudie, Jack 7, 43, 44, 60, 69, 98, 102
Mullen, Jimmy 72
Muller, Gerd 195, 196
Munich air disaster 53, 55
Munster 52
Murray, John 251
music 5, 321–6

National Health Service Trust 4, 326–7
National Service *see* Army, British
Neal, Dick 108
Neal, George 33
Neeskens, Johan 192, 193
Nesscliffe, near Shrewsbury 54
New South Wales 82–3

New York 127
New Zealand 163, 164, 165
Newcastle United 7, 8, 36, 70, 93, 159, 160, 261, 297–8, 311–12
News Chronicle 46, 119
Newton, Keith 138
Nicholson, Bill 111, 112, 114, 168
Nielsen, Kim Milton 294
North Korea 149
Northern Ireland: v. British Army 52; *1960* v. Eng. 120; *1961* v. Eng. 132–3; *1964* v. Eng. 135
Norway: *1964* 139, 140
Norwich City 7, 311
Nottingham Forest 183, 202
Notts County 173
Nou Camp 245

Oates, David 251
O'Grady, Mike 132–3
O'Hare, John 183, 200, 202, 205
Oldham Athletic 279
Olympics: *1912* 4
Onega, Ermindo 147
organ, church 323–5
Ormskirk, hospital in 20
Oswestry, Shropshire 46–7
overseas players 300–1, 308
Owen, Michael 260, 293
Owen, Syd 187
Oxford University 31

Paine, Terry 139, 143, 144
Palermo 309
Paris 195–7
Parry, Alan 242, 249, 250
Partridge, Cyril 187–8
payment 60, 87–8, 115–16, 303
Payne, David 164
Peacock, Alan 126, 132
Pearce, Jonathan 251
Pegg, David 106, 114
Pele 116, 125, 146, 267, 268
Perry, Bill 7, 43, 44, 60, 69, 70, 84, 98
Peru: *1959* 115, 118; *1962* 121–2
Peters, Martin 139, 140, 142, 143, 148, 149
Phillips, Len 44
Phillips, Malcolm 31
Phillips, Ronnie 172
piano playing 321–3
Pickering, Fred 160, 161
Pickett, Reg 44
Pinewood Studios 150
Piper, Norman 164
pitches, artificial 317–18
Platini, Michel 132

Platt, David 285
Playboy Club 153, 156
players: bonuses and perks 153–4, 155; overseas 300–1, 308; payment 60, 87–8, 115–16, 303; after playing career 309–10
play-offs 316
Poland: *1957* 114; *1964* 139, 140, 142; *1998* 292
Polish dancing 19–20
Polish services 19–20, 21, 22–3
Pontin, Sir Fred 67–8
Pontin's holiday camps 67
Pope, Alf 21
Port Vale 176
Portsmouth: *1954* v. Blackpool 42–5
Portugal: *1961* 145; *1964* v. Eng. 135, 149
Potter, Derek 198, 234
Powell, Ivor 21
Power, Paul 304
Premier League 3, 70, 115, 225, 308, 310–11, 313, 319; overseas players 300–1
Preston 48, 51, 52, 89
Preston North End: v. Blackpool 68, 80, 160–1; Bobby Charlton 146–7; Tom Finney 270–1, 309
Princess, pub, Blackpool 26–7
Professional Footballers Association (PFA) 2, 86, 107, 119, 163, 284, 296, 297, 304, 309
Puskas, Ferenc 314
Pym, Dick 91

Queens Park Rangers (QPR) 160, 217, 278, 280

Radford, John 188
radio 223–4, 228, 239–40, 241–4, 245–55, 274, 279, 310, 329; 'Football Legends' 257–60; 'Sports Report' 242
Radio Five Live 224, 241, 242
Ramsey, Alf 79, 129–31, 133–5, 136, 137–40, 142–5, 147, 148, 149, 150–4, 157, 163, 168; funeral 129
Rancagua, Chile 122–5
Rattin, Antonio 147, 148
Read, Al 305
Real Madrid 83, 132, 267–8, 314, 315
Reaney, Paul 182, 186, 189, 190, 195, 200, 205, 214, 216
Redfern, Jimmy 172, 201–2
referees 311–13
Reid, Doug 44
Reid, Peter 171, 172, 217, 250, 276, 279
Reilly, Lawrie 258, 259, 267
Rest of the World: *1963* 135, 267
Revie, Don 49, 181–3, 184, 185–6, 193, 197, 200, 203, 207, 210, 289

Revoe Primary School, Blackpool 17, 18–19
Rexach, Carlos 192
Rice, Pat 211
Richards, Joe 98
Ridding, Bill 99
Rimmer, Jimmy 188
Rimmer, Warwick 170, 172, 175
Rio: *1959* 44, 115–18
Rioch, Bruce 164
Ritson, John 170, 172
Rivelino 314
Roberts, Bob 184, 197, 209–10
Roberts, Brian 218, 220
Roberts, Frank 40
Roberts, Major 50, 108
Robinson, Ike 166
Robson, Bobby 121, 154, 249, 277, 280, 288,
    295, 308
Robson, Bryan 276, 277, 278, 284, 288
Roker Park, Sunderland 251, 252–3
Romania 111, 113–14, 293
Roulson, Ernest 323–4
Rose, Henry 52, 240
Rose Bowl Stadium, Pasadena 246, 251–2, 254
Rosenthal, Jim 242
Roth, Franz 195, 196
Rothwell, Teddy 169, 177
Rous, Sir Stanley 108, 133
Roxburgh, Alex 34
Royal Army Ordnance Corps 54
Royal Garden Hotel, Kensington 152–3, 157,
    329
Royle, Joe 276, 279, 280
Rugby Football League 160, 316
rugby union 25, 30–2, 34
running 4–5
Russia 124

St John, Ian 134
Sammer, Matthias 269
San Francisco 244
Sanchez, Lionel 125
Santos, Djalma 126, 145
Savage, Reg 21
Scargill, Arthur 241
Schalke 269
Schmeichel, Peter 285
Scotland 160, 208; *1949* 267; *1956* 105, 106;
    1958 146; *1960* v. Eng. 120; *1961* v. Eng.
    120, 121; *1962* 126; *1963* v. Eng. 134–5;
    1966 138; *1975* Under-23s 194; *1996* 306
Scotland Schoolboys 217
Scottish League 334; *1955* 52
Scoular, Jimmy 7, 311–12
Scribes club 282
Scunthorpe 100
Sedbergh 325

Seed, Jimmy 99
Setters, Maurice 52
Sexton, Dave 170, 236, 277, 280
Shankly, Bill 174, 179, 270
Shannon, Les 160, 162, 225
Shaw, Graham 52, 107, 108
Shearer, Alan 293
Sheffield 106
Sheffield United 52, 163, 201, 203; Bramall
    Lane 89
Sheffield Wednesday 103, 135, 163
Shellito, Ken 135
Shentall, Harold 307
Shepherd, Doc 125
Shepherdson, Harold 139, 147
Shimwell, Eddie 48, 64, 69, 72, 98
Shippey, John 164
Siddall, Barry 171, 172
Simeone, Diego 293–4
Simoes, Antonio 149
Simon, Sydney 144, 184, 209
Simpson, Peter 188
Simpson, Ronnie 311
Singapore 164
Sirrel, Jimmy 173
Sky Television 310, 318
Slater, Bill 94–5
Smith, Bobby 121, 126, 127
Smith, Jack 17
Smith, Joe 8, 34, 43, 45–6, 48, 49, 51–2, 55,
    60, 63, 65, 70–3, 78, 81, 83–4, 87–8,
    93–100, 101; plays for BW 91–2; collects
    FA Cup 91–2; injured 92
Smith, Trevor 52, 106, 108
Sofia 111–13
Sohal, Caj 243
Souness, Graeme 276
Southampton 133, 297
Spain: *1960* v. Eng. 120; *1966* 148, 153; *1982*
    143
Spavin, Alan 161
'Sport on Five' 246
'Sports Report' 242
Springett, Ron 121, 139, 308
Sproston, Bert 170
stadiums, all-seater 315–16
Steele, Freddie 78
Stein, Jock 219, 220, 289
Stephenson, Len 44, 144
Stewart, Cammie 237
Stewart, David 189, 195, 200, 214
Stewart, Rod 305–6
Stiles, Nobby 138, 139, 140, 143, 144–5, 149
Stoke City 76, 78, 88, 102, 119, 175, 231
Stokoe, Bob 162
Storer, Harry 99
Storey, Peter 188

Stott, Ian 275, 281, 283
Sturm Graz 315
Suart, Ronnie 100, 101–2, 103, 160, 202, 263
Suddick, Alan 101
Suez Canal 55–6
Sugar, Alan 280, 282, 286
Summerbee, Mike 161, 171
Sunday People 218, 228
Sunday school 2, 28, 323
Sunderland 96, 216; *1972* v. BW 175; Roker
    Park 251, 252–3; v. Bristol Rovers 252–3
Swales, Peter 283–4
Swan, Peter 121, 126, 127, 135
Sweden 119, 121, 250, 299
Swindon 290
Swissair 115
Switzerland: *1962* v. Eng. 135; *1966* 148; *1978*
    217, 218

Tadek, Mr (Polish army officer) 19
Tahiti 163, 164
Tambling, Bobby 132, 138
Tanner, Richard 325
Taylor, Ernie 7, 43, 44, 69, 84, 98
Taylor, Gordon 277, 284, 304, 309
Taylor, Graham 273, 277, 280
Taylor, Ivan 330
Taylor, Peter 292, 296
Taylor, Tommy 53, 121, 127, 240
television 101, 232–3, 239, 240–1, 268, 306,
    310, 312–13
tennis 306
Ternent, Stan 216
Thailand 164, 166
Thomas, Gwyn 217
Thomas, Peter 234–6
Thomas, Stephen 30
Thompson, Doris 331
Thompson, Peter 138, 174–5
Thompson, Tommy 270
Thornton, ICI football ground 20
Thorpe, Jim 4
ticket prices 318
Torres, Jose 149
Tottenham Hotspur 133, 153, 238; *1953* v.
    Blackpool 34, 35; *1958* 82; *1966* v.
    Blackpool 159; *1975* 194; *2003* 297; Jimmy
    Greaves 263; Terry Venables 280, 281, 282
Tranmere Rovers 175
Trautmann, Bert 258
Tremble, Brian 242
Tyldesley Youth Club 32

UEFA 292, 315; *1975* JA appeals to 197–8;
    Cup 311
Ujpest Dozsa 188, 192, 195, 212

University of Central Lancashire 329
Uprichard, Norman 44
Uruguay: *1964* 135, 136; *1966* 142, 143
US National Soccer team: *1950* 118; *1958* 82;
    1959 v. Eng. 115, 118; *1964* 135

van Nistelrooy, Ruud 300
Venables, Terry 277, 279–86, 287–8, 291–2,
    298; Eng. record 285
Vieira, Patrick 300
Vieri, Christian 293
Vina del Mar 125
Vizard, Ted 91

Wade, Allen 168, 225
Wade, Virginia 141
Waiters, Tony 101, 225, 226
Waldron, Alan 170, 172; injured 178–9
Wales 135, 266; *1934* 76; *1960* v. Eng. 131;
    1962 v. Eng. 133, 135, 266
Walker, Jack 236, 310
Walsall 194, 205
Warburton, Derrick 169
Warburton, Edmund 169
Warburton, George 169
Wartime Cup 21
Weber, Wolfgang 152
Weller, Keith 164
Wembley Stadium 36, 48, 91–2, 114, 115, 120,
    133, 134, 138, 142, 284–5; press box 249;
    last match played at 298; new 318
Werder Bremen 52
West, Gordon 101, 102
West Bromwich Albion 67, 203
West Germany 269–70, 276; *1955* 52; *1956* 53;
    1958 114; *1962* 124; *1966* v. Eng. 156, 120,
    138, 140, 148, 269; *1986* 276; *see also*
    Germany *and teams' names*
West Ham United 71, 121, 147, 148, 156
Western Command team 42, 50, 54
Westminster Abbey 141
Whatmore, Neil 171, 172
White, John 134
White, Noel 275, 281, 283, 286, 288
Whittaker, Stan 99–100
Wilkins, Ray 276, 277, 278
Wilkinson, Howard 276, 277, 279, 296, 297,
    304
Willcox, Chris 288
Williams, Mr (headmaster) 18–19
Williams, Bert 72
Williams, Brian 46
Williams, Gareth 170
Wilson, Davie 134, 213–14
Wilson, Ray 107, 120, 121, 123, 127, 134, 139,
    140, 143, 149, 258, 259

Wilson, Steve 251
Winterbottom, Sir Walter 106, 114, 115, 116, 118–19, 120–1, 122, 126, 129, 131–4, 168, 226
Wiseman, Keith 288
Wolverhampton Wanderers (Wolves) 72, 94, 101, 188, 211–12
Women's European Gymnastics Championships 113
Woods, Dave 251
Woodward, Brian 218
Woolwich Barracks 52
Workington 3
World Cups 2–3, 54, 76, 119, 269, 308; *1950* 118; *1958* 52, 53, 116, 121, 132, 268; *1962* 105, 120, 121–7, 131, 145, 148; *1966* 102, 103, 107, 120, 127, 129, 130, 137–40, 141–5, (Abbey Service 141), 147–52, (celebrations 152–3, 329), (bonus pay 153–4), 155–6, (medals 156–7), 159, 207, 319; *1970* 268; *1982* 254; *1986* 276; *1990* 270, 276, 308; *1994* 244, 246–7, 251–2, 273; *1998* 269, 287, 291, 292–6, 297; *2002* 3, 123, 254, 270, 298–9, 308
World War II 14–17, 19–24, 25–6
Wrexham 175, 176
Wright, Billy 79, 101, 116, 118, 119, 313; 'This Is Your Life' 261

Wright, Charlie 171, 172, 175
Wright, Jackie 98

Yorath, Terry 186, 188, 191, 195, 196, 200, 205
York City 95, 179
Yorkshire cricket 235, 236
Yorkshire Post 182
Young, E. Johnston 326
Young Boys of Berne 217
Young England (Under-23s) 7, 52–3, 56, 98; *1956* (v. Scotland 105, 106–7), (v. Ireland 107–8), (v. Denmark 108–11); *1957* 111–15, (v. Bulgaria 111–13), (v. Romania 113–14), (v. Czechoslovakia 54); *1958* (v. Poland 114), (v. Czechoslovakia 111, 114); *1958–9* tour 114–15; *1959* (v. France 114), (v. Italy 114–15); JA offered management 185–6
Young Player of the Year award 119
Yugoslavia: *1960* v. Eng. 120; *1962* 124; *1966* WC 137–8

Zagalo, Mario 116, 269
Zanetti, Javier 293
Zidane, Zinedine 132
Zola, Gianfranco 124, 292, 300